To Drive the Enemy from Southern Soil

Col. Francis Marion Parker
30th Regt. N.C.T.

To Drive the Enemy from Southern Soil

The Letters of Col. Francis Marion Parker and the History of the 30th Regiment North Carolina Troops

By
Michael W. Taylor

Morningside
1998

ISBN: 0-89029-332-5

Morningside House, Inc.
260 Oak Street
Dayton, Ohio 45410
1-800-648-9710
Fax: 937-461-4260
E-mail: msbooks@erinet.com
http://www.morningsidebooks.com

Dedication

Dedicated to the memory of Judge Frank M. Parker (1912-1995), Colonel Parker's grandson, who turned a law school graduate into a lawyer.

"[T]here is a very strong feeling in our Regt. to drive the enemy from Southern soil."

—Letter from Francis Marion Parker, then serving as 2nd lieutenant of the "Enfield Blues," Company I of the Bethel Regiment, from Yorktown, Virginia, written home to his wife in Halifax County, North Carolina, June 2, 1861.

Table of Contents

Photographs

Maps
(by John Heiser)

Acknowledgements

The writing of this book has required the help of many people, and I thank the ones I speak of here and those whom I inadvertently fail to mention. Frank M. Parker, Jr., my high school and college classmate, has given me permission to publish his great-grandfather's letters (which reside at the North Carolina Division of Archives and History in Raleigh) and served as an essential resource for the history of the Parker and Philips families and the life of Colonel Francis Marion Parker. Frank's father, Judge Frank M. Parker, provided me with much information about his grandfather, Col. F. M. Parker, while I worked for him at the North Carolina Court of Appeals, 1978-79. My publishers, Bob and Mary Younger, have been tremendously supportive of me and my efforts in writing this book. The editor of this book at Morningside, Andrew McMillan, has also been very helpful.

The advice and counsel of Robert K. Krick, Chief Historian, Fredericksburg and Spotsylvania National Military Park, has been of great help. Without Bob's tireless enthusiasm for tracking down original sources for the Army of Northern Virginia and the ready access he and his staff gave me to the vast collection of such material at Fredericksburg, this book would have had a much thinner basis in eyewitness accounts. Frank O'Reilly at Fredericksburg spent a day with me on the May 3, 1863, battlefield of Chancellorsville and at the Bloody Angle of Spotsylvania. My good friend John Bass of Spring Hope has always willingly shared with me his encyclopedic knowledge of Confederate imprints and of North Carolina Confederate sources in general.

Walt Hilderman and other members of the Charlotte-based Mecklenburg Beauregards helped me get access to original sources and photographs. Jack Betts of the Raleigh bureau of the *Charlotte Observer* sent me a copy of the published diary of his ancestor, Chaplain A. D. Betts. Martha Brown of Winston-Salem gave me permission to publish excerpts of the papers of her great-grandfather, Sgt. Aaron Leonidas DeArmond. Paul Lader of New Jersey helped me understand the actions of the 7th New Jersey on the morning of May 3 at Chancellorsville. Greg Mast of Roxboro has been of great assistance, both with respect to photographs of members of the 30th, and also on the subject of the 30th's casualties in comparison to those of other North Carolina units. George Stephenson of the North Carolina Division of Archives and Records in Raleigh has always answered my every request for copies of documents with alacrity and has helped me decipher several key papers including Capt. James I. Harris' letter about the Gettysburg Campaign and the very interesting letter of October, 1864, from Bryan Grimes to F. M. Parker.

Robert Mabry and David Deese of Stanly County have been very helpful in helping me understand the movements of the 30th's fellow regiment, the 14th North Carolina, and in locating sources relating to this unit. Linda Evans and LeAnna Hill of my office have rendered cheerful service in producing this book.

I am grateful to Peggy B. Tousignant, Barbara B. Biggs, and Shirley B. Beal for granting me permission to publish Capt. James I. Harris' account of the battle of Gettysburg. Many thanks are due to my neighbor, Kevin G. Carle, for the expertise he has shared with me about the Army of the Potomac, particularly concerning New York and Pennsylvania units. I also want to thank Lu Koontz of the Stanly County Library for her many efforts to assist me.

Finally, I could not have written this book without the constant support and encouragement of my wife, Susan, and our three sons, William, Samuel and John.

— Michael W. Taylor
February 23, 1998

"F. M. Parker, the courteous and refined Colonel of the Thirtieth
Regiment, was a brave, cool, and excellent officer. . ."
— William Ruffin Cox

INTRODUCTION

What manner of men were these? This is the question that
motivates many students of the Confederate army in the war
between the states. Who were these butternut soldiers, as fierce
in battle as patient on the march? And who were their bold and
dashing officers, gazing at us out of their photographs in their
ill-fitting uniforms like participants in a masked ball, yet brave
as lions? Something of the enduring fascination of the war
arises out of this enduring question. A study of the life and
letters of Col. Francis Marion Parker, one of Lee's dauntless
colonels, and of the history of the regiment he trained and led
provides some answers and gives us a deeper understanding of
the woof and warp of the fabric of one of the great armies of
American history, the Army of Northern Virginia.

"F. M. Parker, the courteous and refined Colonel of the
Thirtieth Regiment, was a brave, cool, and excellent officer and
ever observant of his duties to the cause and to his command."
This was the assessment of one of his fellow colonels, William
Ruffin Cox, who later commanded the brigade containing his
regiment. Colonel Parker and his command repeatedly proved
their mettle on the field of battle. Francis Marion Parker and his
30th Regiment North Carolina Troops were at the forefront of
nearly every important engagement of the Army of Northern
Virginia. Moreover, Parker and his men (along with the other
regiments of their famous brigade, that of George Burgwyn
Anderson, Stephen Dodson Ramseur, and William Ruffin Cox)
literally saved the day for the army on several critical occasions. Among these was on September 17, 1862, at Sharpsburg,
Maryland, where they held Bloody Lane long enough to deter
McClellan from breaking Lee's Army in two until Parker fell
with his skull creased by a bullet; on May 3, 1863 at Chancellorsville where, detached from Ramseur's brigade the 30th
succeeded where so many other Confederates that morning had

failed in driving the enemy from their breastworks south of the Plank Road and carrying the Fairview Heights; on the First Day at Gettysburg when, coming up after the massacre of Iverson's brigade, they succeeded in routing the Union First Corps troops along the Mummasburg Road northeast of the town where Colonel Parker fell severely wounded, shot through the face; and on the morning of May 12, 1864, where Parker and the 30th, along with their comrades of Ramseur's brigade, were the first Confederates to charge in counterattack upon the Union troops pouring through the breach in the Confederate line at the toe of the Mule Shoe, holding their position for some 22 hours in what was probably the fiercest hand-to-hand fighting of the whole war in the works forever after known as the Bloody Angle.

Although Colonel Parker fell a week later at Harris Farm northeast of Spotsylvania Court House with a shot through the abdomen that would disable him for the balance of the war, his few remaining men continued to fight, taking the war to the gates of Washington, fighting to the last at Third Winchester and Cedar Creek, enduring the siege of Petersburg and keeping their organization and fighting spirit intact. At Sailor's Creek during the retreat, these men provided Lee with one of the few organized bodies of troops available to him, causing Lee to exclaim, "God bless gallant old North Carolina!" As the final act of the drama, they fired some of the last (if not *the* last) shots at Appomattox on the morning of April 9, 1865, and caused Maj. Gen. John B. Gordon to remark as they withdrew from the last charge, "Grandly and gloriously done!"

The dark clouds of Confederate winter hung over Raleigh as the Administration's party in the North Carolina General Assembly, 63 (out of 120) members of the House of Commons and 20 (out of 50) members of the Senate, caucused to deliberate on December 1, 1864. Defeat was in the air, its sting sharpened for these leaders of the Old North State by the lack of preferment given to North Carolina officers in the Army under Lee in Virginia. So many brave North Carolinians had fallen, most recently Lincolnton's Stephen Dodson Ramseur at Cedar Creek, Virginia, the previous October. Where was the State to turn for leadership? Where was the hard-earned recognition of North Carolina valor?

14

It was the peculiar lot of North Carolina's soldiers in the war to resist the Yankee invaders stubbornly first, foremost, and last, to stand and fight valiantly, to charge gallantly in the forefront of battle, and to suffer appalling losses stoically, all while being labeled as inferior by their comrades from Virginia and South Carolina. Shining examples of virtue and valor remained unnoticed. Looming defeat was hard enough. Lack of recognition of their sacrifice, vain though it might be, made the situation unbearably bitter.

As these legislators gathered that day, one name came to the fore, one soldier whose valiant deeds and gallant bearing had not yet brought about the bestowal of the wreaths and stars of general officer rank, one officer who in his very person symbolized both the civil and the military virtues of North Carolina. That man was Col. Francis Marion Parker of the 30th Regt. N.C.T., on leave recovering from a severe wound received at Spotsylvania. The legislators came forward and signed a dramatic memorandum extolling Colonel Parker's merits and recommending him to Confederate Secretary of War James Alexander Seddon for promotion to general officer rank. Among the supporting documents attached to this petition was a letter from Brig. Gen. Bryan Grimes to Colonel Parker, written just two weeks before the battle of Cedar Creek, in which Grimes related to Parker a conversation in which Maj. Gen. Stephen Dodson Ramseur had stated to Grimes that he had written a private communication to General Bragg requesting that Parker might be promoted to brigadier general and assigned to their old brigade.

The recommendation of the North Carolina legislators would prove unsuccessful—Colonel Parker's military career came to an end upon the endorsement of General Lee on a petition that Parker's war wounds had rendered him unfit for further active service. However, the legislators' action clearly shows the fine reputation as a soldier Parker had established for himself by the late months of the war.[1]

---

1. The December 1, 1864, petition signed by the Administration's party in the North Carolina General Assembly, together with its endorsements up the military chain of command, and the October 4, 1864, letter to Colonel Parker from Bryan Grimes, are contained in Parker's compiled service record.

Francis Marion Parker (September 21, 1827 - January 18, 1905) seemed destined—by ancestry, birth, upbringing, temperament, position in life, and even his given name—for the role of outstanding regimental commander in the Confederate Army.[2] And surely, had he not fallen severely wounded so many times at the head of his regiment in the forefront of the battle (and had he, perhaps, been from Virginia and not North Carolina), he would have joined the ranks of the generals in gray.

Parker was a representative of the class of slaveholding Southern planters that had the most to fight for—and the most to lose—in the war between the states, and he had the courage, the will, and the leadership ability to lead men into the fight. Of distinguished North Carolina ancestry, Parker was, to put it simply, a member of North Carolina's dominant eastern planter class. A first cousin of one of North Carolina's wartime governors, Henry T. Clark, Parker had a host of connections both in and outside of the army, as his letters make apparent. His deep devotion to the Cause was very much a family affair, and Parker could no more fail in his duty to his state and the South than he could deny his own existence.

Francis Marion Parker was born on September 21, 1827, in Nash County, North Carolina, where his parents were spending the summer away from their home in the town of Tarboro in Edgecombe County. He was the eighth of nine children (of whom six survived into adulthood), and the fifth of five sons (of whom only two survived into adulthood). It is not known how

---

2. There are at least four published biographical sketches of Francis Marion Parker that are drawn upon here, in addition to Parker family genealogical information furnished to me by Frank Parker, Jr., Col. Francis Marion Parker's great-grandson:

Samuel A. Ashe, "Francis Marion Parker," in Samuel A. Ashe and Stephen B. Weeks, *Biographical History of North Carolina from Colonial Times to the Present*, 8 vol. (Greensboro, North Carolina: Charles L. Van Noppen Publisher, 1898), 7:354-361.

D. H. Hill, Jr., *Confederate Military History: North Carolina*, Clement A. Evans, ed., 12 vol. (Atlanta: Confederate Publishing Company, 1899; reprint: Wilmington, North Carolina: Broadfoot Publishing Company, 1987) 7:683-685.

William S. Powell, ed., *Dictionary of North Carolina Biography*, 6 vol. (Chapel Hill, North Carolina: University of North Carolina Press, 1979), 4:16.

"Gen. F. M. Parker, Commanding Third Brigade," *Confederate Veteran*, vol. 6, no. 5 (May, 1898):221-222.

he came to be given the name of South Carolina's hero of the Revolution, the Swamp Fox, but certainly his parents can be said to have been prescient in bestowing the name upon their child.

Parker's father, Theophilus Parker (1775-1849), was a prominent merchant and farmer of Edgecombe County and a devout member of the Episcopal Church, being a vestryman at Calvary (formerly Trinity) Church in Tarboro. Theophilus Parker served as President of the Bank of Tarboro. In 1830, Parker's father owned 39 slaves.[3] His mother was Mary Irwin Toole Parker (1787-1858), the daughter of Capt. Henry Irwin Toole of the 2nd Regiment of the North Carolina Continental Line in the Revolution and the great-niece of Col. Henry Irwin of the North Carolina Continental Line who was killed at the battle of Germantown, Pennsylvania. His mother's ancestors included one of the most influential and important figures of North Carolina's colonial period, John Haywood, who was Lord Granville's surveyor and provincial treasurer of the colony's northern counties.

Frank, as he was called, spent his early youth in the village of Tarboro. Of a strong and robust constitution (which would help him survive three serious war wounds) and full of energy, he took to hunting and a variety of other sports. After a preliminary course in the local schools, Parker was educated at a series of schools established primarily for boys of his class: at J. M. Lovejoy's Academy in Raleigh (where he received some military training), at Dr. Wilson's Caldwell Institute, in Greensboro, at Lincolnton's Pleasant Retreat Academy (alma mater of Robert F. Hoke and Stephen Dodson Ramseur),[4] and at the Classical and Agricultural School for Boys established in the mountains of Wautaga County by North Carolina's first Episcopal Bishop, Levi Stillman Ives.[5]

---

3. 1830 U.S. Census of Edgecombe County, North Carolina.
4. Of the four above-referenced biographical sketches, only the one in *Confederate Veteran* mentions his schooling in Lincolnton. Parker mentions being in Lincolnton in his letter dated June 18, 1861.
5. Bishop Ives' Classical & Agricultural School for Boys at Valle Crucis is discussed in Blackwell P. Robinson, "The Episcopate of Levi Stillman Ives," in Lawrence Foushee London and Sarah McCulloch Lemmon, eds., *The Episcopal Church in North Carolina, 1701-1959* (Raleigh: Episcopal Diocese of North Carolina, 1987), pp. 186-188.

Through close association with his first cousin, Henry Toole Clark (1808-1874), who later became North Carolina's wartime governor from July 7, 1861, to September 8, 1862, and Clark's close association with Lincolnton's Michael Hoke during Hoke's 1844 campaign for governor, Parker became deeply imbued with the principles of the Democratic Party and an earnest adherent of its principles.[6]

His father died as he was about to enter the University, and he returned home and took charge of his father's plantation.[7] In the 1850 Census of Edgecombe County, F. M. Parker, age 23, a farmer, is enumerated in a household with his mother, Mary, age 63. Among others in the household are J. R. Cheshire, a 36-year-old minister of the Gospel; Parker's younger sister, A. C. (Arabella) Parker, age 19; and three teenage girls: S. T. Philips, age 15; M. H. Powell, age 15 and M. C. Tool, age 14. Parker is listed as the owner of 28 slaves farming 300 improved acres producing an annual cotton crop of 27 bales, in addition to the farm's substantial other crops and livestock.[8]

On December 17, 1851, Parker married 16-year-old Sarah Tartt Philips (March 22, 1835 - September 22, 1906). Sally, as he called her, was the daughter of prominent Edgecombe County physician, James Jones Philips (March 12, 1798 - April 10, 1874).[9] Philips' reputation had survived the 1822 North Caro-

---

6. This statement is made in Ashe and Weeks, *Biographical History of North Carolina*, 7:356. The statement might be a late 19th century misunderstanding because Parker's cousin, Henry T. Clark, became a Whig after having been a Democrat. Powell, *Dictionary of North Carolina Biography*, 1:374-5.

7. Hill, *Confederate Military History*, 7:683, states: "His father dying as he was about to enter the university, he took charge of the home farm . . ." In 1849, the year of the death of Theophilus Parker, Colonel Parker turned 22-years-old, a somewhat advanced age for university entrance. It may be speculated that his father's declining health brought him home a year or two before his father's death.

8. The Edgecombe County 1850 Agricultural Schedule states that Parker's farm had a value of $15,000 and contained 600 acres of which 300 were improved. The farm had 8 horses, 5 mules, 7 cows, 3 oxen, 11 sheep, and 100 swine and produced 90 bushels of wheat, 3,500 bushels of corn, 300 bushels of peas, 25 bushels of potatoes, and 75 bushels of sweet potatoes, in addition to 27 bales of cotton.

9. Parker's father-in-law's biography appears in Powell, *Dictionary of North Carolina Biography*, 4:89. The ancestry of the Philips family is discussed in John Bennett Boddie, *Southside Virginia Families*, 2 vol. (Redwood City, California: John Bennett Boddie, 1956; reprint: Baltimore: Clearfield Company, Inc., 1991), 2:350-351.

Sarah Tartt Philips Parker
(March 22, 1835 - September 22, 1906)

19

lina Accident (in which the Federal Vaccine Institute of Baltimore mistakenly sent to Edgecombe County material containing small pox instead of cow pox for the giving of vaccinations by certain physicians, including Philips, resulting in several deaths in spite of the efforts of Philips and other physicians once the error was realized), and he went on to become one of North Carolina's leading physicians. In addition to his medical practice, Philips was a successful planter. By 1860, he would own 53 slaves.[10] He was a respected agriculturist whose opinions in a newspaper controversy over soil analysis with Dr. Elisha Mitchell of the University of North Carolina were considered to be most thoughtful and progressive.

In 1853, 26-year-old Francis Marion Parker left his native Edgecombe County and took up residence on a new plantation just across the Tar River on Fishing Creek near Enfield. Here he would live and plant for the next 52 years until his death. His letters reflect a deep love for his farm. It is important to understand that Francis Marion Parker was that phenomenon so well known from classical antiquity and so much admired by the founders of the American nation, the citizen-farmer-soldier. His letters reflect the fact that his farm was never far from his thoughts. Despite the fame he achieved as a Confederate officer, the principal focus of his life always remained his family and his farm.

By 1860, Parker was master of a thriving Halifax County plantation. He and his 25-year-old wife, had four children by the time of the 1860 census: Mary, age 7; James P., age 5; Theophilus, age 2; and Harriett B., age 3 months. The plantation had a real property value of $6,860, and Parker had personal property valued at $17,860. He owned 21 slaves and 5 slave houses. His plantation had 3 horses, 6 mules, 6 cows, 4 oxen, 10 cattle, and 84 swine, and produced 35 bushels of wheat, 30 bushels of rye, 1,000 bushels of corn, 120 bushels of oats, 27 bales of cotton, 200 bushels of peas, 15 bushels of potatoes, and 300 bushels of sweet potatoes.

The John Brown Raid in 1859 caused a company to be organized in Halifax County called the "Enfield Blues." Parker was elected second lieutenant of the company. The other officers elected were David B. Bell, captain; Montgomery T. Whitaker, first lieutenant; and Cary W. Whitaker, junior second

10. 1860 U.S. Census of Edgecombe County, North Carolina.

20

lieutenant. In June, 1860, the ladies of Enfield held a "fair" on the lawn of the old Burnette Hotel in order to raise money for the purchase of a flag for the company. A bountiful dinner was served and about 1,500 people attended. The proceeds amounted to $80.00, considered to be a nice amount for so small a village as Enfield. A handsome silk United States flag with gold fringe and tassels was ordered from Baltimore for $75.00 and presented to the company by Miss Fannie Whitfield of Enfield upon the introduction of Dr. Henry Joyner, who was later to be Parker's regimental surgeon. Miss Whitfield gave a flowery oration, and presented the flag to Captain Bell with these words:

> I offer it to you from the ladies of Enfield and its vicinity as a simple token of the high respect due from them to you, as their protector. Let it be a silent monitor whispering to you in the gentle tones of the daughters of the Old North State the word Excelsior. Should necessity ever call you to the battlefield, may it wave over heads that will bare themselves to the strife, hands that will be willing to do their part and hearts that will never during life cease their throbbing in the cause of right. But may you triumphantly bear it as the palm of victory, so that America may be proud that between Atlantic's mighty waters and her great chain of Rocky Mountains, there lies nestled in her broad lap two such spots of earth as Halifax and Edgecombe counties, and that there lives upon her bosom such a company as the Enfield Blues.

Two other companies were also present on this occasion, the Scotland Neck Cavalry and the Halifax Light Infantry.

In the spring of 1861, as the secession crisis deepened, the Enfield Blues passed resolutions to change the flag, and Miss Fannie Whitfield was asked to make it over into a Confederate flag. She used the red and white stripes of the United States flag and cut up her own blue silk dress to use as a background upon which she sewed white stars. On the under side, she painted the North Carolina coat of arms, and to this the gold fringe and tassels were added.[11]

---

11. The history of the Enfield Blues recounted here is taken from Kate Riddick, "The Enfield Blues," *Prize Essays Presented to the North Carolina Division* (n.p.:United Daughters of the Confederacy, 1937-38), pp. 105-109.

On April 12, 1861, Fort Sumter was fired upon, and on April 15, President Lincoln issued his call to the states for 75,000 men. This was unsupportable by North Carolina, and orders went out for the Enfield Blues and other companies like it across the state to assemble in Raleigh. On April 27, 1861, the Enfield Blues entrained for Raleigh.

"... the enemy met us there, and they came off second best."
— F. M. Parker

PART ONE
April, 1861 - August, 1861
Raleigh, North Carolina - Big Bethel Church, Virginia

Quarters Enfield Blues
Near Raleigh
April 27/61

Dearest Wife

As you will see from the direction of this note, we are in our Quarters, on the Fair Grounds. We reached Raleigh safely; remained in Goldsboro all night.

I was surprised to see so much enthusiasm as was manifested everywhere, except at Raleigh. All along the road every man, woman, child and little negro seemed brim full of it; shouting and hurrahing, to cheer us as we passed. At some of the depots which we passed I noticed some of the old Ladies in tears; it struck me that they had a proper appreciation of the thing. There are nearly one thousand troops here and more are ordered here.

So far as general movements are concerned, I can give you no information. In fact, I do not think there is any definite plan fixed upon. I hear that the Gov. will establish a military camp at Raleigh, Goldsboro and Weldon; if so, I hope our company will be stationed at Weldon. We number 65 and about 6 more will arrive tonight. Col. Hill,[1] late of the Charlotte Military Academy, who is in command here, complimented the appearance of our company when we marched into the Camp.

---

1. Daniel Harvey Hill (1821-1889), went on to become an important and controversial Confederate general officer, as noted for the sharpness of his tongue as for his coolness under fire . A graduate of West Point class of 1842 and veteran of the Mexican War, Hill taught mathematics at Washington College (now Washington and Lee University) and Davidson College before becoming superintendent of the North Carolina Military Institute in Charlotte in 1859. Assigned to command the camp of instruction at the State Fair Grounds in Raleigh on April 24, 1861, Hill was elected Colonel of the 1st Regiment North Carolina Infantry on May 11, 1861, and promoted to Brigadier General on July 10, 1861, after his regiment's victory at Big Bethel Church, Virginia. Appointed Major

Will you please send my slippers, shoes (best pair), over coat and my pistol moulds, which are in the pistol box, also a clothes brush and all the lead which is in the side board. We are quartered in the building which was used as Floral Hall at the State Fair. It is now filled with the chivalry of the State. The Warren Guards[2] and our company occupy the whole building; and I must say that they are a very quiet, orderly set of men. They have a Chaplain and the two companies unite in prayer every night.

Since I commenced this note, several more companies have come into camp and we now number about 1,200. I promised several of my friends that I would write them but you see from

General on March 26, 1862, he led a division under Joseph E. Johnston at Williamsburg, Yorktown and Seven Pines, and under Robert E. Lee through the Seven Days Battles and at Second Manassas, South Mountain and Sharpsburg. Assuming command of the Department of North Carolina in early 1863, he was promoted Lieutenant General on July 11, 1863. After commanding a corps under Braxton Bragg at Chickamauga, Hill's outspoken criticism of Bragg resulted in Hill's relief from duty. In 1865, he commanded a division under Joseph E. Johnston at the battle of Bentonville, N.C. Following the war, his career included the presidencies of the University of Arkansas and Middle Georgia Military and Agricultural College. Ezra J. Warner, *Generals in Gray* (Baton Rouge, Louisiana: Louisiana State University Press, 1959), pp. 136-137; Johnson, Allen, *et al.*, eds.,*Dictionary of American Biography*, 20 vol. (New York: Charles Scribner's Sons, 1932), 9:27-28; Louis H. Manarin and W. T. Jordan, Jr., eds., *North Carolina Troops 1861-1865, A Roster*, 13 vols. (Raleigh, North Carolina: North Carolina Division of Archives and History, 1966-93), 3:2; William Alan Blair, *Encyclopedia of the Confederacy*, 4 vol. (New York: Simon & Schuster, 1993) 2:775-776; Douglas Southall Freeman, *Lee's Lieutenants: A Study in Command*, 3 vol. (New York: Charles Scribner's Sons, 1942-3) 1:629-630, and 2:54-55, 479, and 715-723; Judith Lee Hallock, *Braxton Bragg and Confederate Defeat* (Tuscaloosa, Alabama: University of Alabama Press, 1991), pp. 91-99; Hal Bridges, *Lee's Maverick General* (New York: McGraw Hill Book Co., 1961) passim; Daniel Harvey Hill, *Bethel to Sharpsburg* (Raleigh: Edwards & Broughton, 1926) passim.

2. The "Warren Guards," like Parker's "Enfield Blues," were in camp of instruction at the State Fair Grounds after serving as a part of the garrison of Fort Macon at the tip of Bogue Banks opposite Morehead City. The company became Company F of the 2nd Regiment North Carolina Volunteers, afterwards the 12th Regiment N.C.T. Manarin and Jordan, *N.C. Troops*, 5:185; Walter Clark, ed., *Histories of the Several Regiments and Battalions from North Carolina in the Great War 1861-1865*, 5 vols. (Raleigh, North Carolina: E. M. Uzzell, 1901), 1:606; Paul Branch, Jr., *The Siege of Fort Macon* (Morehead City, North Carolina: Paul Branch, Jr., 1982), p. 5.

this note that the conveniences for writing are none of the best; they must exercise a little patience. Will you please ask Mr. Hulm[3] to plant the bottom next to the hog pen in corn; that is, all that part of it on the other side of the main or middle ditch. Tell him to manure it with the compost which is made on the same side of the ditch which he will plant. Tell him also to plant the clover lot with white corn. I want a good crop of potatoes made. The articles which I have asked you to send you will please put in [a] box, have it nailed up carefully and write a note to P. H. Johnston[4] at Enfield to direct it to me. If you can not find a box, you must have one made. I wish you to boil a good ham, and bake some good biscuits and send along with the other things; rather hard living up here.

I have been into the city once only, but did not see any of my kin. I have had an invitation from Dr. Richd. Haywood to visit him. I think I shall do so. From the best information which I can get we will not proceed to Washington City short of three months, unless there should be an immediate necessity. Let Mr. Nicholson know this. The reason is that the majority of the companies are not well drilled.

God bless you my dearest wife and my dear little children, kiss them all for me.

Your loving husband,
F. M. Parker

Camp Hill
Near Richmond
May 23 1861

3. The 1860 U.S. Census of Halifax County lists Parker's next door neighbor as 58-year-old farmer Eli Hull whose household included his 50-year-old wife, Claracy, a seamstress, along with sons, Guilford Hull, age 24 and Benjamin Hull, age 23 (see Parker letters of May 28 and June 2, 1861) farm laborers, a daughter, Mary Hull, age 18, a seamstress, and a third son, William Hull, age 15. The Hull household also included Elias Johnson, a 30-year-old shoemaker, and his wife, Lucy Johnson, a 26-year-old seamstress. Eli Hull listed no real property or slaves and can be supposed to have lived on Parker's plantation as a farm manager or overseer.
4. P. H. Johnston appears in the 1860 U.S. Census of Halifax County as a 31-year-old clerk.

My dearest Wife

You will see from the above that our Regt. is encamped near Richmond, on a hill covered by a beautiful grove, which we have called Camp Hill in compliment to our Col. We left Weldon about four o'clock and passed through Petersburg early in the night. You can hardly form an opinion of the crowd of citizens which met us at the depot; the ladies seemed to outnumber the men, and were very enthusiastic; they showered boquets [sic] upon us and but for a mistake in the telegraphic wires they would have provided us with the substantials of life. I saw Mr. Waddell, he is a member of a cavalry troop which escorted us from one depot to the other; I had a few minutes conversation with him; he made kind inquiries about you and the children. We remained in Petersburg but a short time before we proceeded on to Richmond and reached our present encampment late in the night, about 2 o'clock; even at that hour we found crowds on the streets as we marched through, cheering and hurrahing. I think it very likely that it was the general opinion of our Regiment that we would have been in our beds, if we had had that privilege. We have orders to march from the place tomorrow for some point on York river, when we get into camp again I will write you and let you know something of our movements. Mr. Norfleet is here, and has promised to mail this at Enfield, so I thought I would not let so good an opportunity pass without availing myself of it. Cousin Henry Clark met me at Enfield on Tuesday and brought me some cooked provisions and a very kind note from Sister Mary[5]; we have the prayers of so many good people that we must succeed; to say nothing of the justness and righteousness of our cause. At Weldon several of our friends met us to say good bye, among others Mrs. Dr.

---

5. Henry Toole Clark (1808-1874) was a prominent Edgecombe County lawyer and planter who married to his first cousin, Parker's widowed sister, Mary Weeks Parker Hargrave, in 1850. Clark's mother, Arabella Toole Clark, and Parker's mother, Mary Irwin Toole Parker, were sisters, daughters of Revolutionary War Colonel Henry Irwin Toole (1740-1791) and Elizabeth Haywood Toole (1758-1832). At the time of this letter, Clark was Speaker of the North Carolina Senate. Upon the death from tuberculosis of Governor John W. Ellis, Henry T. Clark became governor of North Carolina, serving until succeeded in the governorship by Zebulon Baird Vance on September 8, 1862. Powell, *Dictionary of North Carolina Biography*, 2:374-375. Parker family genealogical material provided by Frank M. Parker, Jr.

Hamite Whitaker; when I went to shake her hand she was very affectionate and kind, and gave me a motherly kiss, which I hope I received in the proper spirit; she was an old friend of my Mother.

And now my very dear wife good bye to you and my children, may the Lord bless and keep you all, is the prayer of your affectionate and loving husband

F. M. Parker

York Town, Va.
May 26, 1861

My very dear Wife

Well, you see we are quartered on the very spot which witnessed the close of the American revolution; it may be the scene of the first act in the drama which seems inevitable. Yorktown is a very old, dilapidated place; I suppose that some of the buildings here were standing during the revolution; at least appearances would indicate the same. Our Regiment left Richmond on Friday last, came by rail road to West-point, on the York river and down said river by steamer and schooners to our present destination.

We marched into this place about midnight and I assure you the town presented quite a dreary and desolate appearance. In addition to its old look, nearly all the inhabitants had fled; the houses were almost tenantless. This arrangement suited the troops exactly for the Col. marched up right into the houses where we quartered for the night and rested quietly and well. The next day we moved about one mile from town, near some springs, where we are encamped in regular military order; the front of each company's tents occupies just as much ground as the company does in line of battle, and then there are streets eight feet wide between each tent, and between two lines of tents, there is a broad street of twenty four feet in width. There is a fine parade ground in front of our tents where the whole regiment manouvers [sic].

So far as our fare is concerned, it is excellent; an abundance of the very finest fish and oysters. I wish you had them; we can get a string of from 10 to 15 fine large trout for ten cents; said string contains enough to feed five persons for a whole day;

then we get the sheep's head, which I regard as about the best fish I have eaten for some time; and still better the drum, which is about as large as four shad. The York river at this point is about two miles wide, and is a beautiful sheet of water, the finest I have ever seen; looking down the river, no land is to be seen, I mean down the centre. The tide affects the river for some distance above this place, and we have the nicest bathing imaginable; the salt water is very bracing, and invigorating, and the boys seem to enjoy it finely; particularly the men from the mountain counties, of which there are four companies in our Regt.[6] We generally carry them down night and morning for the purpose of bathing.

Upon the whole we are pleasantly situated, but not more so than we were in Richmond; we had a fine grove there, and then we were surrounded by some very kind friends; one family particularly, Mr. H. I. Smith; his wife was constantly sending over some little delicacy, and by a sweet little angel, a little daughter about the age of our Mary. Lieut. M. T. Whitaker[7] was quite sick while there, and the little girl came over every day to see him and minister to him. The Lieut. was too unwell to march with us when we left, and we had to leave him with Mr. Smith's family, at his earnest request; he has not joined us yet, but will as soon as well enough. We have fewer on the sick list, just now, than we have had at any time lately. We are all getting on very well.

Please say to Mr. Nicholson that I could not get any such gun as he wished, in Richmond.

Kiss my little children for me my dear wife, and the Lord bless you all, is my earnest prayer.

---

6. This statement is difficult to reconcile because there were only two mountain companies in the 1st Regt. N.C. Volunteers, Co. E, the "Buncombe Rifles," and Company G, the "Burke Rifles." Manarin and Jordan, *N.C. Troops*, 3:24, 35; Greg Mast, "North Carolina Troops in Confederate Service: An Order of Battle," *Company Front* (November/December 1990):9.

7. Montgomery T. Whitaker enlisted for six months in the Enfield Blues in Halifax County at age 35 on April 19, 1861. He was appointed 1st Lieutenant to rank from date of enlistment and afterwards promoted Captain to rank from October 22, 1861. He was mustered out November 12-13, 1861. Manarin and Jordan, *N.C. Troops*, 3:46. M.T. Whitaker, by occupation a farmer, is listed in the 1860 U.S. Census of Halifax County with his wife and five children. He had 39 slaves.

Your very affectionate husband,
F. M. Parker

———————◆●◆———————

Encampment 1st Regt. N.C. Vol.
York Town
May 28, 1861

Mrs. S. J. Parker
Sycamore Alley
Halifax Co.
No.Ca.

My very dear Wife

I wrote you a few days since letting you know that we were here in camp for fear that you may hear reports from our camp which may be exaggerated. I now write to give you a true statement of our position, forces, &c. Our position is a strong one; on our rear a deep and wide ravine and mire protects us; on our left a good brush fence and broken field; in front is the town and to our right we have thrown up a strong breastwork behind which we will await the approach of the enemy; relying upon the justness of our cause and trusting in the kindness of an overruling Providence, we will fear nothing. Yesterday the whole Regiment was very suddenly called out into the field, as we confidently expected to meet the enemy. It would have done any one good to have witnessed the coolness and determination which was depicted upon the countenances of the men, and shown in their conduct; and as Col. Hill rode up and down the line giving us a little encouragement and telling us to be perfectly cool and quiet, it was very apparent that all was right, and that every man was determined to do his whole duty. We remained in line of battle for some time; no enemy showing itself. I was about to conclude that it was a false alarm, until I saw the women, children, negroes and horses come pouring into town, then I concluded that there must be some truth in the report. However, no enemy was to be seen, so a little after sunset the Regt. was ordered to quarters. We slept with our arms by our sides and the men with all their clothes on ready to fall in ranks at a moments notice. But we had no disturbance at all, until about 12 o'clock, when our company was called out to work on the breastworks where we worked steady until day break, throwing up dirt with spades and shovels. The boys have all had their breakfasts and are now lying about resting for whatever duty may be assigned us. If the 1st Regt. is called upon to strike for our rights, you may rest assured that we will give a good account of ourselves. Do not give yourself any uneasiness, my dear wife, on my account; my life at all times is in the hands of the Almighty, I am as safe on the field of battle as any where else; so I hope to trust in his goodness and mercy and do my duty. We have a chaplain in our company, the Rev. Mr. Page, who married a daughter of the Rev. Mr. Wills. Mr. Page holds prayer every night at his tent where the greater part of our company assembles, and seems to be very attentive and to appreciate the privilege which they enjoy. I hope they will be improved thereby.

Please write soon and write <u>twice every week without fail.</u> If you knew how much your letters are prized, you would write often. I hope little Offa is well by this time, and all the rest of you.

Kiss all the children for me; tell them I think of them every day, and want to see them very much. You can explain to Mary why I am away, that I am doing my duty, that I am working to defend you and their and my rights. Home will be so sweet, when our difficulties are settled and we are permitted to return to the bosom of our families, to enjoy our rights and privileges under the glorious flag of the Southern Confederacy.

Remember me to Mrs. Wallace and Ben Hulm; tell Ben that the next time I come home, I hope to be able to look over his crop.

Say to Mr. Nicholson that I was not able to find any such gun as he wished in Richmond; my regards to him, his family and all my friends.

When you write, direct to:

       Lieut. F. M. Parker
       Comp. I, 1st Regt. N.C.Vol.,
       Richmond
       Va.

Wherever we may be ordered, letters will follow us from Richmond. Good bye my dear wife; God bless you and my dear children.

Your affectionate husband
F. M. Parker

———————————◆•◆————————————

Encampment 1st Regt. N.C. Vol.
York Town
June 2, 1861

Mrs. S. J. Parker
Sycamore Alley
N.C.

My dearest Wife

Here I am writing again; if you only write one letter for two of my own, you will do well, but such is not the case, you are very slow in writing; you certainly have not come up to my request, which was to write twice a week. I hope you will do so; it is such a pleasure to get a letter from you. When Dr. Joyner left us the other day, it was almost certain that we should have a brush in a few hours, but there is no evidence of an early engagement just now; the enemy have entrenched themselves about twenty miles below us, which is a sure indication that they do not intend to attack us; and I do not think we will march upon them immediately. Tho' there is a very strong feeling in our Regt. to drive the enemy from Southern soil; nearly all the families from below this have left their homes for fear of the enemy; they have destroyed a good deal of property, such as corn, provisions &c. and have taken a good many negroes.

One thing is certain, whenever we do get a chance at our foes, you may rest assured that they will fare badly. We can not afford to be separated from our families for so long a time; particularly when the fault is not our own.

This is Sunday, we have not performed our regular duties in consequence; have not drilled any, only gone through with the inspection of arms; at first I thought this might have been dispensed with, but then it gave the men employment, which kept them out of mischief and did not [give] them time to become discontented with their situation. It is the history of all campaigns, that confinement to camp is more trying to the good order and morals of an army than any thing else; there is no change in the life; it is a perfect monotony; and hence the men

31

are always eager for any thing which will give them any excitement, even if it is a little brush with the enemy. As I have often told you before, I shall go into battle trusting in the justness of our cause, and the kindness of an overruling Providence. I know we are right, and knowing this we will fear nothing. Our camp has been thick with spies lately; several have been arrested, none tried yet so far as I know; one of the spies is a prominent lawyer of Norfolk; a native of Maine; altho' he has been a resident of the South for several years, his cause has not been altogether approved; in fact, he is now just from Washington City. I think we should be very strict with all such gentry, and handle them with gloves off. The safety of the army depends upon it.

I wrote you by Dr. Joyner, asking you to send my gilt mounted sword to Enfield, to be sent to me; I now ask you to send me one or two pair of linen pants to Enfield to Henry Johnston, to be sent to me by Mr. Gay,[8] who is at home sick but who will join us in a short time. This is all that I want now in the way of clothing. Write me by Gay, send the letter to Enfield; he will get it from there, and do write a long one, get some foolscap paper and fill it up; tell me every thing which is going on about home, how your garden looks, and how Ben's crop looks; tell him to do his best, and establish a reputation as a crack farmer. I think a little talk from you will be of service to him.

Where is Fred now?[9] What Regt. does his company belong to, and where are they ordered?

---

8. There were two privates named Gay in the Enfield Blues: Gilbert G. Gay, age 22, who enlisted at Yorktown, Virginia, on June 11, 1861, and John C. Gay, age 34, who enlisted in Cumberland County on April 19, 1861. Both were mustered out November 12-13, 1861. Manarin and Jordan, *N.C. Troops*, 3:48. The soldier mentioned here must have been John C. Gay.

9. Frederick Philips (1838-1905) was Parker's brother-in-law, the brother of Sally Tartt Philips. The 1860 Census of Edgecombe County lists Frederick Philips, a lawyer, age 21, living at Epinetus Crowell's hotel. He became an outstanding lawyer and judge after the war. Frederick Philips was mustered into the "Confederate Guards," Company I of the 15th Regt. N.C.T. (5th Regt. N.C. Vols.), as a 2nd lieutenant on May 22, 1861. He was defeated for reelection when the regiment was reorganized on May 2, 1862. Appointed adjutant of the 30th Regiment N.C.T. on June 5, 1862, Philips was wounded in the head at Sharpsburg, Maryland, on September 17, 1862, and was again wounded in the left thigh at Kelly's Ford, Virginia, on November 7, 1863. He was appointed Assis-

Say to Mary that I am looking for a letter from her, and shall think a great deal of it, even if it is only two lines. Tell Jimmy to study his book a little every day, and be a smart, good boy. Tell little Offa not to have any more chills, that Pa will be sorry to hear that he is sick.

And you must take care of yourself my dear wife, not only on your own account, but that you may be able to take care of the little ones. Do not give yourself any uneasiness about me; I am getting on very well, enjoy[-ing] pretty good health and our force is constantly increasing at this point; we number now about six thousand men, gallant, brave men who are contending for their rights, their fields and firesides. Remember me kindly to Mrs. Wallace, Ben Hulm, and all our neighbors. I would like to write to them all, but time and conveniences are rather scarce. Good bye my dear wife. God bless you and the children, is the earnest prayer of [your] affectionate and loving husband,

F. M. Parker

PS Direct your letters, by mail, to me
     Comp. I, 1st Regt. N.C. Vol.
     York Town
     Va.

Camp 1st Regt. N.C. Vol.
York Town
June 3/61

My dearest Wife

Your letter reached me this evening. It was so good a letter, and did me so much good, that I thought I would answer it right off; particularly as I have so favorable an opportunity of sending a letter. Mr. Dunn,[10] one of our company, is going home

---

tant Quartermaster (Captain) of the 30th Regt. On March 12, 1864, but later vacated that position due to "nonconfirmation." He was appointed Assistant Quartermaster (Captain) on March 15, 1865, and assigned to duty with Cox's brigade. Manarin and Jordan, *N.C. Troops*, 5:585, and 8:321-322.

10. James Leonidas Dunn, age 23, enlisted for six months in the Enfield Blues in Halifax County on April 19, 1861, as a private. He was mustered out November 12-13, 1861. Manarin and Jordan, *N.C. Troops*,

to see a very sick child and also to recruit for the company; he has told me that he would probably go to see you; I hope he will. It will be a pleasure to you and then to me also when he returns to camp. Your letter today was a very good one, it contained a great deal of very good advice, which I hope to profit by. I have already endeavored to carry out some of the advice which you gave me; and indeed I may say that there has been a great improvement in our whole company, particularly as regards morals. I think that the men are alive to their present situation; they seem to be concerned about their future state, are very regular in attendance on prayers, which we have every night in our camp. I believe I have told you before that Mr. Page[11] is our Chaplain. He seems to be a very good man; he drills, every day, in ranks like the other soldiers, does not presume at all, which of course makes him popular among the men. On Sunday night at prayers, he made a very sensible tho' short talk on the impropriety and sinfulness of taking the name of the Lord in vain. I hope it had a good effect on the men, and believe it did. Our commander, Col. Hill, is a very religious man, he also delivered a few very good and appropriate remarks on Sunday night; among other good things which he said, was this, that bravery which was gotten up by whisky and swearing was not to be trusted and was of little worth. He is very popular with his Regt. altho' he is a very strict disciplinarian; the men all love him, and would fight for him, or follow him any where; when I tell you that he is one of the coolest men I ever saw and a man possessing a great deal of bravery and discretion, you will see at once that he is very efficient. Whenever he has an opportunity, you can rest assured that he will distinguish himself, and I hope his Regt. also. I am sorry to say that Col. Hill is now sick. I earnestly hope he will be up in a short time.

------

vol. 3, p. 48. J. L. Dunn, by occupation a farmer, is listed in the 1860 U.S. Census of Halifax County with his wife and two children. He owned 11 slaves.

11. Jesse H. Page, a Methodist minister, was 30 years old when he enlisted as a private in the Enfield Blues on April 19, 1861. He was mustered out November 12-13, 1861. He was appointed Chaplain of the 17th Regt. N.C.T. and served until resigning July 6, 1863. Manarin and Jordan, *N.C. Troops*, 3:49 and 6:205. Manly Wade Wellman, *Rebel Boast* (New York: Henry Holt and Company, 1956), pp. 19-24 and 54-55. Clark, *N.C. Regiments*, 4:608.

You seem to wish to know something of our position here. It is a very strong one naturally, and then we have fortified it at every point by throwing up breastworks. It would be a very difficult matter to reduce this place, we could defend and hold it against a very superior force to our own. And we are, every day, increasing our fortifications. We do all this work ourselves, have no negroes to help us; our boys say they intend going to ditching when they get back home; that they are getting to be experts at handling the shovel and spade. It goes right tough with some, who have never been used to any thing of the kind before. Today Capt. Bridgers' company[12] was at work near our own, and I could but notice Nathan Mathewson[13] and contrast his present situation with what it was fifteen or twenty years ago; he makes a good soldier. It may be the very thing for him. He certainly looks very well.

I believe there has been no change in the forces of the enemy since I wrote you last. The blockade steamer still lies at the mouth of York river, some eight miles below this point and there she will have to lie. If ever we meet the enemy here we will have to go and look for him; there is no danger of his looking for us. I wrote you last to send me some summer clothes by Mr. Gay; will you please send one of my summer coats, my black

---

12. Company A , known as the "Edgecombe Guards," was commanded by Capt. John L. Bridgers, a 41-year-old Edgecombe County resident, who enlisted for six months on April 18, 1861. He was appointed Lieutenant Colonel, to rank from August 16, 1861, of the 10th Regiment N.C. Troops (1st Regiment N.C. Artillery). He resigned on account of bad health September 28, 1861. Manarin and Jordan, *N.C. Troops*, 3:4 and 1:40. The Slave Schedule of the 1860 U.S. Census of Edgecombe County lists John L. Bridgers as the owner of 101 slaves and 18 slave houses.

13. Nathan Mathewson enlisted as a private for six months in the Edgecombe Guards, Company A of the 1st Regt. N.C. Infantry at age 43 on April 18, 1861. He was mustered out November 12-13, 1861. Manarin and Jordan, *N.C. Troops*, 3:6. Mathewson was afterward mustered in as a sergeant into Co. G, 40th Regt. N.C. Troops (3rd Regt. N.C. Artillery) on March 1, 1862. He was transferred to Co. A, 10th Regt. N.C.T. (1st Regt. N.C. Artillery) on October 8, 1862, and reduced to ranks on October 10, 1862. Records indicate that he was present or accounted for through December, 1864. Manarin and Jordan, *N.C. Troops*, 1:47. Nathan Mathewson appears in the 1860 U.S. Census of Edgecombe County as 41 years old with a wife and two children. He had 5 slaves and two slave houses.

high crown hat, and one of your pillows, by Mr. Dunn. Make a couple of cases for the pillow, out of brown linen; white will not do. I hope you will be good to me and write me a long letter soon, very soon. If you could see me reading your letters over and over again, you would think that I really prized them. Let me know every thing that is going on about home. I am very glad to hear that you are going to Tarboro. I hope and believe you will enjoy the visit. There is one spot I wish you to visit for me, that is my Mother's grave; go there and think of me, and pray for me. Bella[14] gave me Ma's prayer book, when I left Tarboro; I would not part with it under any circumstances. It is a great comfort to me. I hope I may be profited by the use of it. I shall always thank Bella for it. She could have given me nothing, which I would have valued so much. Thank her for me, when you see her. I hope you will not be troubled with my long letter; it is a great pleasure to me to write to you. I feel as tho' I could sit here and write all night; every thing is quiet in our tent now, the other officers are sound asleep; perhaps dreaming of home and their families, perhaps of the field of glory; I am enjoying the real pleasure of writing to a pure, true, loving wife, one whom I love better than any thing else.

God grant that these difficulties may be settled, and that we may all be permitted to return to the bosom of our families. My love to the children, kiss them all for me, speak to them often of me; tell them how I love them; how that I have left you and them, to defend them, to keep the invader from you. Remember [me] kindly to all the neighbors. Say to Mrs. Arrington that Jo[15] is very well and getting on finely. Write soon to your loving and affectionate husband,

F. M. Parker

---

14. Arabella Clark Parker was Parker's youngest sister. She never married. Parker Family genealogical materials provided by Frank M. Parker, Jr.
15. Joseph C. Arrington enlisted for six months in the Enfield Blues as a private in Wake County at age 18 on May 13, 1861. Mustered out November 12-13, 1861, he enlisted as a private for 12 months service in the "Scotland Neck Mounted Rifles," Co. G of the 41st Regt. N.C.T. (3rd Regt. N.C. Cavalry) on January 26, 1862. He was captured at Five Forks, Virginia, on April 1, 1864, and confined at Point Lookout, Maryland. Manarin and Jordan, *N.C. Troops*, 3:46 and 2:229.

P.S. Remember me to Mrs. Wallace and Ben; tell Ben I am very much pleased to hear that he has a good crop.

———————————————•◆•————————————————

Camp 1st Regt. N.C. Vol.
Bethel Church York Co. Va.
June 9, 1861

My very dear Wife

I have after a long trial, succeeded in getting a sheet of paper to write you a few lines. Our Regt. was marched from York Town to this place on Thursday afternoon, a distance of fifteen miles. We were ordered off very suddenly, and brought nothing but our blankets and one day's provisions; we have been here ever since without any tents, and almost without any provisions at least on short allowance; so you see we have seen some of the beauty of a soldier's life. If it had not been for the provisions which we bought from the people in the country, we would have suffered. We were ordered down here to protect the people in this part of the country, against the depredations of the Yankees; they have been committing all sorts of aggressions, such as taking property, breaking open houses, furniture &c; one case in particular was very aggravated; the Yankees went to a gentleman's house below this, and after helping themselves to any thing they wished, they took the preserves of the Lady and threw them all over the parlour carpets; finding a few guns, they seized these; and broke the piano into fine pieces, and destroyed other valuable property about the house.

Yesterday news was brought into camp that a party of Yankees was a few miles below us on a gentleman's farm; Col. Hill ordered one company, and one piece of artillery to put after them, which they did; but there being a large opening all around the house, the Yankees saw our people a great way off and took to their heels; they however succeeded in taking two prisoners, killing three, and wounding several others. Our boys were very bold, they pursued them within sight of Hampton which is near old Point.

We may be attacked at any moment, and we are now (Sunday evening) busily engaged throwing up breastworks to defend ourselves. If these prisoners which we have tell the truth, I think we can whip the Yankees handsomely; as I have before re-

37

marked having right justness on our side, and trusting in a kind Providence. Stern necessity knows no law; we are using the church, near which we are camped, as a store house for corn, fodder, bacon and to confine the prisoners.

I would love to write you a long letter, but this is the only paper which I can get. Whenever I get my trunk I will write you again.

My regards to all my friends. Kiss my dear children for me.

I never knew before how very dear you and they are to me; if ever I get back safely home, I shall never wish to leave you again, unless called away, as I was this time, by duty. If you could only see the destruction of property which we bring about, to say nothing of the Yankees and their doings, you would say keep this war as far from our own soil as possible. Destruction seems to be the ruling spirit of war, both offensive and defensive. This is a beautiful country which we are in, and it does seem bad to have it served as it is done. I can not thank you too much for the letter you sent me by Mr. Whitfield; it was so good a one, it breathed a christian spirit throughout. It is in my trunk at York Town. I wish I had it now to read it over. But I wish I had more paper to write you more; whether it would be interesting to you or not, it is so pleasant to me to sit and write to you. I never tire of it. But you must wait for another letter until I get more paper. Till then, good bye my dearest wife.

Your affectionate husband,
F. M. Parker

Camp 1st Regt. N.C. Vol.
Yorktown June 11, 1861

My dearest Wife

The last letter which I wrote you, was from Bethel Church, some fourteen miles below this place, near Hampton. I will come right to the point at once; the enemy met us there, and they came off second best. Our Regt. was ordered to that part of the county and, finding the ground near the Church a naturally strong position, Col. Hill fell to work defending it by breastworks and other defences [sic], we reached the place on Thursday night, by a forced march from this place, and by Monday morning we were in a tolerably strong position. On Friday and

Saturday evenings, Col. Hill sent out small parties of scouts, which took a Yankee prisoner each time; this incensed the enemy so, that they determined to give us battle, which they did on Monday morning. About seven o'clock our pickets came into the information, that the enemy were only a few miles distant, and were advancing steadily. This news caused the long roll to be sounded, which brought out the whole camp. We fell into the trenches and awaited rather impatiently the coming of the foe. About nine o'clock the ball was opened by a discharge from one of our Richmond Howitzers,[16] which was promptly answered by the enemy with a heavy price of artillery. The cannonading was kept up for some time on both sides with a great deal of singularity until the Yankees got up within range of our rifles and muskets, and then such pipping and snapping as we had, I never heard before; this was mixed up with a boom of the cannon every now and then; after keeping this up for about two hours, it was very evident that the enemy were giving away, they replied with less singularity to our Howitzers with until it finally ceased, the only firing was from the muskets and rifles, this was kept up with great spirit, and with so much effect as to drive the enemy off. It was the opinion of all the field officers that the men were remarkably cool; as far as I could judge, this was particularly the case; there was no excitement at all, every man seemed determined to do his duty, and to do it well.

There was a great disparity as regards numbers; the Yankees had 4,500 men in the field, and we had only 800 in the action, our whole force was only 1,200 infantry, and two troops of Cavalry numbering about 60 each; four companies of our Regt.

---

16. The "battle" of Big Bethel commenced, symbolically enough for the student of the history of the American Union, with a shot fired from a Parrott gun by the grandson of Thomas Jefferson, Major George Wythe Randolph, later brigadier general and Confederate Secretary of War. United States War Department, *The War of the Rebellion: A Compilation of the Official Records of the Union and Confederate Armies*, 70 volumes in 128 parts (Washington: Government Printing Office, 1880-1901), series 1, vol. 2, pt. 1, p. 99. (Hereafter cited as *OR*, followed by appropriate volume and part, all series 1 unless noted); Warner, *Generals in Gray*, pp. 252-3; George Green Shakleford, *George Wythe Randolph and the Confederate Elite* (Chapel Hill, North Carolina: University of North Carolina Press, 1988), p. 61.

did not fire a single shot in the fight, and I am sorry that the Enfield Blues was one of the four; the attack was made on the side opposite to our lines, so we had no sort of chance to get into it. The Edgecombe Guards,[17] one of the Fayetteville companies, the Hornet Nest Rifles[18] and one of the mountain companies, together with a battalion of Virginians[19] did all the work, except for what was done by the Howitzers, and this was a great deal; in fact, the cannon did the greater part of it. Tho' Capt. Bridgers' company did a great deal towards saving the day; so said Col. Hill, and he is authority. Our company and the Buncombe Rifles[20] was more exposed to the cannon of the enemy than any other companies on the field, we were more right in the range of their guns. Every bomb which they threw exploded very near us, sometimes right over us, then either to our right or left, and their grape shot buried themselves in our embankment after passing within two feet of our heads. I tell [you] we did some good dodging; the only way we had to save ourselves was to fall flat on the ground and lie there until the bomb exploded or the shot struck. We could readily tell the report of the Yankee cannons from our own, theirs were much the heavier guns. I have sent you, by Mr. Branch of Enfield, a grape shot which struck our embankment very near me, also a piece of shell. So as to the damage done: to an over-ruling Providence we did not lose a single man, and only six seven wounded; one of these died after we returned to this place; the others are getting on tolerably well; the only one about which there is any doubt, is a member of Capt. Bridgers' company, and a son of Ben Williams of Tarboro.[21] The man who died was also a member of Bridgers' company;[22] there was a dwelling house right in the

---

17. Company A of the 1st Regt. N.C. Infantry.
18. Company B of the 1st Regt. N.C. Infantry.
19. Major Edgar Burwell Montague's Virginia Infantry Battalion. *OR*, vol. 2, pt. 1, pp. 101-102.
20. Company E of the 1st Regt. N.C. Infantry.
21. Charles S. Williams enlisted in Company A, 1st Regt. N.C. Infantry in Edgecombe County at age 24 on April 18, 1861, as a private. He was wounded in the shoulder at Big Bethel on June 10, 1861, and mustered out November 12-13, 1861. Manarin and Jordan, *N.C. Troops*, 3:8 and 718.
22. Pvt. Henry Lawson Wyatt of Company A, 1st N.C. Infantry, achieved great fame as the first North Carolina soldier to fall in the war. He was killed while on his way, with four other volunteers, to burn a house that

range of our guns (cannon) and the enemy seeing this posted themselves behind it, and were troubling our lives considerably, when this man volunteered to go and set fire to the house, he started and got nearly half way before he fell; he received a rifle ball exactly in the centre of his forehead.

The loss of the Yankees was about 500 killed.[23] We had their very best troops to contend against, a part of the famous seventh Regt. of New York was there and the New York Zouaves.[24] It is idle to say that the Northern people will not fight; they fought bravely for awhile; but could not stand the determination, the religion I might say, of the Southerners. But above all I acknowledge an overruling Providence though. His kindness, and mercy moved our arms for the conflict, and gave us the victory; when he is on our side, we will not fear man. While we were lying [in] the trenches and the shot and shell were flying thick around us, and no work to do, it occurred to me that it was an appropriate time for prayer; having command of the company for the day, the Capt. being absent in Petersburg, and the 1st Lieut. sick, [I] accordingly requested Mr. Page, our Chaplain, to ask for the blessings of the Almighty in our cause; I do not

was sheltering Federal sharpshooters. Clark, *N.C. Regiments*, 1:100. Wyatt enlisted at age 19 as a private on April 18, 1861. Manarin and Jordan, *N.C. Troops*, 3:8 and 721. Wyatt's statue, sculpted by Gulzon Borglum, was erected upon the grounds of the State Capitol in Raleigh in 1912. "Dedication of Henry Wyatt Monument," *Confederate Veteran*, vol. 20, no. 11 (Nov., 1912):506-507.

23. Maj. Gen. Benjamin F. Butler, Union commander of the Department of Virginia, reported from Fortress Monroe on June 16, 1861, that the Federal losses at Big Bethel on June 10, 1861, totalled 76 including 18 killed, 53 wounded, and 5 missing. *OR*, vol. 2, pt. 1, p. 82.

24. The 5th New York Infantry, known as Duryee's Zouaves, was commanded at Big Bethel by Col. Abram Duryee. The numerous Zouave regiments in both the Union and Confederate armies, modeled on Algerian light infantry of the French colonial army, often shaved their heads and wore brightly colored uniforms which included baggy pants, short and open jackets and turbans or fezzes. *OR*, vol. 2, pt. 1, p. 89; Ezra J. Warner, *Generals in Blue* (Baton Rouge: Louisiana State University Press: 1964), p. 133; "Zouave" in Mark M. Boatner III, *The Civil War Dictionary* (New York: David McKay & Company, 1959), p. 954. If such a unit seems bizarre from a 20th century vantage point, it must have seemed no less so to a Southern gentleman soldier such as Colonel Parker, based upon his rather strong remarks about the Louisiana Zouaves contained in his letter of June 16, 1861.

think I ever witnessed any thing more solemn.[25] I felt very forcibly the need of His protecting hand; but I was perfectly collected, for as I have told you before, I think I am going right and therefore have nothing to fear.

I am under many obligations to you for another good letter; I am much pleased to see that you are in better spirits than when you wrote before; that is right; keep up my dear Wife; look on the bright side, and if the worse should happen, console yourself with the reflection that all is right. That our arms will prove victorious, I doubt not, tho' many a true heart may fall, many a sad breach may be made in the family circle, many a widow and orphan may be left; we are right our cause is just and must succeed; a kind Providence directing us.

I have received the articles which I wrote for by Mr. Dunn, and have to thank you for being so prompt. You say that Offa and Hattie are sick; it grieves me to hear it, tho I know they are where they will be taken care of well. I hope your next letter will report them entirely well.

———————————◦◦◦——————

Camp 1st Regt. N.C. Vol.
Yorktown
June 16, 1861

My dear Wife

I was very glad to see Mr. Powell, but more so to see the letter which he handed me from you. Your letters always are of great service to me, after reading them I feel moved up to my duty, have a much more satisfied feeling. So if you wish to make me feel pleasant, you must write often, and just such letters as you have written me. Well, the excitement of the battle of Bethel church, is surely over with, except when one of our friends happens to drop in, then of course it is all fought over again, in

---

25. Colonel Parker's calling on Rev. Jesse Page for prayer at the beginning of the battle of Big Bethel is described in Wellman, *Rebel Boast*, pp. 54-55, and was based upon an account of the battle written by Parker in "a newspaper clipping of uncertain date and place." Wellman, *Rebel Boast*, pp. 258 n. 4 and 267 n. 19. I contacted Manly Wade Wellman's widow in searching for the newspaper clipping cited by him, but have been unable to find it.

words. It was truly a great victory which we achieved; the more we learn about, the more are we satisfied of this fact. The number of the loss of the enemy, which Col. Hill reports to Gov. Ellis, is short of the mark considerably; from the best information which we get up to this time, there were about 500 missing. They took nearly all their dead from the field; a citizen of the county, who witnessed the battle, told me that they pressed into service, two carriages, several wagons, and any number of carts to carry the dead and dying back to their camp, and I wish here [to] remark that a cart in this county will hold about three times as much as one of our farm carts.

Two days after the battle, the enemy sent a flag of truce to our camp, to recover a gold watch, sword and other valuables which were taken from one of the field officers of the Yankees who was killed. This of course is a great point gained; flags of truce are not sent to <u>Rebels</u>, but to the enemy; therefore they must acknowledge us as belligerents; a thing which they have not been willing to do heretofore. So much gained.[26]

The recent movements of the enemy are not very plain to us here; the blockade which has been at the mouth of York river, has been removed since yesterday morning, and several vessels have been seen to pass, back and forth, supposed to be carrying troops. I understand that Col. Hill has given it as his opinion that they are looking out for the weakest point to attack, where they intend to concentrate a large force. He has been rather expecting a visit from them at this place, since yesterday; two Regts. slept in the trenches and on their arms last night. Since we returned from Bethel we have been hard at work, strengthening our fortifications here; we have nearly completed the works, and if our friends will delay their visit a little longer, we will give them a lively time when they do come.

There are now stationed here a Regt. from Georgia,[27] one

---

26. Great significance was attached by the South to the flags of truce sent over by the Federals after Big Bethel. See, *Richmond Dispatch*, June 15, 1861, p. 1, col. 4, cited by Freeman, *Lee's Lieutenants*, 1:19.

27. The 6th Regt. Georgia Infantry, commanded by Col. Alfred H. Colquitt, was stationed at Yorktown from May 27 to July 1, 1861. Hewett, Janet B., *et al.*, eds., *Supplement to the Official Records of the Union and Confederate Armies*, 76 volumes in 2 parts (Wilmington, North Carolina: Broadfoot, 1994-1998), pt. 2, vol. 6, pp. 221-230. Noted hereafter as *Supp. OR*.

43

from Alabama,[28] a part of a Virginia Regt. and our own; besides a company of the Richmond Howitzer Battalion, with two rifle cannon and two cannon for grape and shell. The Louisiana Regt.,[29] a company of Howitzers, and the Regt. of Zouaves[30] from New Orleans, have been sent to Bethel Church. A word about the Zouaves, they are the most horrid savage looking set of men, I have ever seen. They are dressed in a jacket of blue flannel; pants of course [sic] red flannel and very loose, which come just below the knee, where they gather close and are confined by leggings of leather; their pants are so very large, that they fall almost to the foot. Their heads are shaved close, and they wear a red cap which fits closely, without any brim whatever, but a long tassel hanging down behind. If ever they were white men, wearing these caps so long has exposed them to the sun until they will pass for dark mulattoes [sic]. An officer in the Louisiana Regt. told me that the officers of the Zouave Regt. were all clever, gentlemanly men who were appointed by the Gov. of the State, but that the greater part of the men were the very offscouring of New Orleans, they look like it. They are very unruly,[31] in fact the only way to organize them is to shoot them down so as not to kill them, but several have been killed in this way, since they left N.O. Altho' they will fight, and place no value on their lives, yet I should not trust them much in battle. But as we have to meet some of the same cattle, I suppose it is well enough to have these along. They say their only wish is to meet Billy Wilson's pets.

---

28. The 8th Alabama Infantry Regt. Commanded by Col. John A. Winston, reached Yorktown on June 13, 1861. *Supp. OR*, pt. 2, vol. 1, pp. 368 and 392.
29. The 1st Louisiana Infantry Battalion, commanded by Lt. Col. Charles Didier Dreux, was composed of five companies attached to the 1st Louisiana Regulars Infantry Regt. at Pensacola, Florida, prior to being mustered into the Confederate service as a battalion at Richmond on June 11, 1861. Arthur W. Bergeron, Jr., *Guide to Louisiana Confederate Military Units 1861-1865* (Baton Rouge: Louisiana State University Press, 1989), p. 148.
30. The 1st Louisiana Zouave Battalion, commanded by Lt. Col. George A. G. Coppens, arrived in Yorktown on the evening of June 14, 1861, and left for Bethel on June 17. *Supp. OR*, pt. 2, vol. 24, p. 673.
31. On the June 1-7, 1861, railroad journey of the 1st Louisiana Zouave Battalion from Pensacola to Richmond, "on account of free access, intoxicating liquors handed to them in abundance by citizens whenever

You ask me in your letter for how long a time have I enlisted; it is for six months from the 13th May last; at the end of that time I shall return home, but how long I shall remain there, the state of the country will determine. I understand a move is on foot to get the 1st Regt. to volunteer their services to the Southern Confederacy for the war; my answer to that, will be to wait until my present term of service expires. The Gov. of N.C. is a western man, thoroughly western;[32] the majority of the companies in this Regt. are from the western part of the State; I do not wish to complain, but great partiality has been exhibited. I do not complain of Col. Hill; he is an honourable, christian gentleman, a brave man and very able officer. But Gov. Ellis and the Adjutant General are not the men for their offices or for the times. I have given my services to my country for six months, my country shall have them longer if necessary. I know the feelings of the officers of the other eastern company; we agree altogether.

We had a serious accident in our company a few days since. A young man[33] who had very recently joined the company, in a fit of derangement shot one of the men, and wounded another; it seems that the young man was of a weak mind, and hearing so much about the late battle and the Yankees coming upon us

they passed together, with a prevailing dissatisfaction for not being paid since in the service, caused all established discipline to drop and become very bad." *Supp. OR*, pt. 2, vol. 24, p. 672.

32. Parker here reveals a bit of eastern North Carolina bias. Gov. John W. Ellis, who was to die on July 7, 1861, was a native of Rowan County in North Carolina's Piedmont section. Ellis was a champion of internal improvements in North Carolina. The long struggle of "westerners" in North Carolina against the control of the State by eastern North Carolina planter-oligarchs (of whose class Parker was a member) dominated much of North Carolina's ante-bellum history. Powell, *Dictionary of North Carolina Biography*, 3:151-152. See, William S. Powell, *North Carolina through Four Centuries* (Chapel Hill: University of North Carolina Press, 1989), pp. 267 *et seq.*

33. Wellman, *Rebel Boast*, pp. 60-62, states that the soldier who shot his comrades was Robert Whitehead, citing a letter from James A. Whitehead in the Duke University Manuscript Collection and a letter dated June 16, 1861, from George Wills in the Wills Papers, Southern Historical Collection, University of North Carolina at Chapel Hill. Wellman states, p. 268, n. 3, that Robert Whitehead was returned to Halifax County and discharged due to insanity, but later recovered at home. Robert Whitehead is not listed in the roster of the Enfield Blues in Manarin and Jordan, *N.C. Troops*, 3:46-51.

45

here, and added to this, Col. Magruder had all the forces at this post drawn up on our parade ground for review. Among these the Zouaves, which excited him more than he was able to bear; the next morning at roll call, without any warning whatever, he shot one of the men clear through his body, and into the arm of another. The man killed was a son of Braswell Britt,[34] the wounded one is a son of Maj. Cherry;[35] it is only a flesh wound. The unfortunate man will be sent to Halifax county. Dr. Pittman, who has been on a visit to us, and who examined him, says that he has strong premonitory symptoms of insanity. Mrs. Bridgers came with Mr. Powell, it was a refreshing sight: a lady. There are none to be seen about here they have all fled. I told Mrs. Bridgers she might have brought you along as company; she told me that she left home so unexpectedly that she hardly had time to bring herself. I should be more than glad to see you, but this is a poor place for women; there are no private houses to be had in town, and then there is no certainty about our movements. We may be ordered from here at any moment. Whenever times get more quiet, I will go to see you, but I can not leave now. I will substitute letters for my presence, as far as they will go and shall hope to be treated similarly. You must do, as necessity has caused me to do, get you some foolscap paper. It is larger than letter paper, and thereby I shall get a longer letter. You say that you have given my sword to Fred; write to Fred and say to him that if he will wear the sword, I shall feel very much grateful, and hope he will do so. He is welcome to that, or any thing else I have. I hope before this, that you have visited Tarboro; you must be certain to go and stay with the folks there. I know they will all be glad to see you and the children; and then you will enjoy the visit. I would remain there long enough to attend church at least on two Sundays. I wish I were with you;

---

34. Braswell Britt was a 49-year-old farmer in Halifax County in 1860 who owned no slaves. He was living with his wife, Elizabeth, one daughter, and five sons including Benjamin F. Britt, age 20, and Lawrence Britt, age 19, both of whom enlisted in the Enfield Blues on April 19, 1861, as privates. Benjamin F. Britt died at Yorktown June 13-14, 1861. 1860 U.S. Census of Halifax County. Manarin and Jordan, *N.C. Troops*, 3:47.
35. John K. Cherry was a 29-year-old clerk living in Halifax County in 1860. He enlisted as a private in the Enfield Blues on April 19, 1861. He was accidentally wounded on June 14, 1861. He later served in Company I, 17th Regt. N.C.T.. Manarin and Jordan, *N.C.Troops*, 3:47 and 674.

think of me. From all I can learn I think we will be stationed at this point for sometime, probably for six months, with, maybe, an occasional march to some point not far distant, whenever we can strike the enemy a blow. We have made this point very strong and if old Abe wishes to try his pluck here, he can be gratified, I think.

I forgot to mention that Mr. Williams, who married Miss Sue Harrison, was of our force on the 10th inst. He is a Lieut. in a cavalry troop from his county, the cavalry had no share in the engagement, tho they have been of great service, as Videttes, scouts, etc. Just before the battle commenced I saw him, he told me that he had been in the saddle all night and had not eaten a mouthful since the evening before. I fortunately found some stewed beef and ship biscuit in our camp and gave him and his Capt. their breakfast; they ate it in their saddles. I have not seen him since.

Remember me to all at your Father's and all the folks in town, I mean the kin. Kiss my little children; tell them to think of their Pa and talk of him, and now good bye my dearest wife. May the Lord bless you all.

Your affectionate husband,
F. M. Parker

Camp 1st Regt. N.C. Vol.
June 18, 1861
York Town, Va.

Mrs. S. J. Parker
Battleboro
N.C.

My very dear Wife

Here I am writing to you again, and nothing particularly to write about; but judging you by myself, a letter will be very acceptable at any time, acceptable did I say, yea highly prized.

I wrote you on Sunday by Mr. Pippen; at that time we were resting from the excitement of the battle at Bethel; we are now busily engaged fortifying our position; there has been a great deal of work done on this place, and if we have a little more time, this will be made a very strong position. It is said to be a very important post and hence they are anxious to make it strong. We are not very well supplied with heavy cannon yet, but I understand these will be sent here soon. I am anxious to see them mounted. The Alabama Regt. and our own, are the only troops inside the works; there are two cavalry companies just outside; but we can be reinforced from Williamsburg above, and the Louisiana and Zouave troops are below us at Bethel church if these latter do not get into a fight. I see no probability of a fight soon, tho' there is no certainty about it. The enemy have been making heavy movements of their forces recently, but what the object is we can not tell; Col. Hill is of the opinion that they are looking for the weakest point to attack, and will concentrate their forces there. It is amusing to see the extracts from the Northern papers relative to the affair at Bethel; they make it out quite an insignificant affair. I guess they feel quite differently about it. It certainly was a great thing on our side; to have successfully opposed five times our number was doing well, particularly well drilled and disciplined troops as they had. The only thing they needed was an officer to lead them. We had two fine efficient officers on the field, Col. Magruder and our own Col. Hill. If the latter is spared he will make his mark in the world; he is the coolest, most collected man I have ever seen, an iceburg [sic] would melt beside him; and he is as brave as he is cool. During the greater part of the engagement the other day, Col. Hill was walking about from the different batteries, smoking his pipe as if he was at his own fireside. His entire Regt. has the fullest confidence in him, they will follow him wherever he leads. There are a great many clever gentlemen in the Regt. of my acquaintance; several from the western part of the State, among them a son of Col. Mike Hoke,[36] who was quite a boy, when I was in Lincolnton. Mr. Williams, who married Miss Ann Harrison, is a member of one of the cavalry companies, stationed near us, I see him occasionally; his health is not good.

---

36. Robert Frederick Hoke (1837-1912) was a native of Lincolnton, N.C., and the son of Michael and Frances (Burton) Hoke. Serving as a 2nd lieutenant of Company K, the "Lincoln Guards," of the 1st N.C. Infantry at the time of this letter, Robert F. Hoke was appointed the regiment's major on September 1, 1861, and eventually rose to be an outstanding Confederate major-general. Johnson and Allen, *Dictionary of American Biography*, 9:126-7; Manarin and Jordan, *N.C. Troops*, 3:51; Warner, *Generals in Gray*, pp. 140-141.

As I have written you before, the morals of the men of our own company have improved greatly since we left home; it is rare to hear any swearing, no drunkenness whatever, card playing, or any thing of the kind. The morals of the whole Regt. is at a high mark. Col. Hill says that he has never seen such a body of men together; he also says that he is not afraid to trust them anywhere.

[The right hand portion of the paper is
cut off in the following part of the letter.]

I reckon you are at your Father's yet. I hope you have enjoyed yourself there and at Tarboro. I wish I could have been with you, but my duty is right here, and here I must remain as long as there is a necessity for it. I know you could not have me at home [. . .] could, your noble nature would despise me [. . .] skulk and not step forward to defend my country [. . .] hours of need. You know that I have not [. . .] sword for glory or honour, it was to defend you [. . .] and my fireside. Whenever the invader is driven [. . .] matters settled upon a sure and sound foundation [. . .] I am ready to lay down the sword and take up [. . .] plow share again. If there should be a lull [. . .] movements, so that I can be spared from the [. . .] I will run to see you and the children [. . .] that time will come I can not tell, nor is [. . .] ing on our movements is somewhat depen [. . .] those of the enemy. I wonder if our little [. . .] much and is she as pretty as ever? I fear she [. . .] me before I see her. And Jimmy and Offa are they sun burned any, or do you keep them too close; keep them from the hottest part of the sun, but let them have it morning and evening; and Mary too, does she progress with her studies, I hope she will make a good sweet girl, one whom her Pa will be proud of; but above all let her be a good little christian. Tell her to write me that letter soon if it is only two lines. I will prize it very highly. You must continue to write me, whenever you feel a little low spirited, sit down and write me, and write a long letter. My kindest regards to all your Father's family, and Dr. Rives'; kiss my little children for me, tell them to think of their Pa, and talk about him often. and now good bye my dear wife. God bless and protect you, is the earnest prayer of your affectionate husband,

F. M. Parker

Camp 1st Regt. N.C. Vol.
Yorktown, Va.
June 23/61

Mr. Nicholson
Dear Sir

Your kind note accompanying the nice present you sent us
has come safely to hand. We thank you kindly for being thus
remembered. With such kind friends at home to cheer us on, we
must do our duty, bravely and cheerfully. And I must here, for
myself, through you, thank these good Ladies in our part of the
country, for such a substantial proof of their good wishes. Bless
the women, with them to cheer us, who would not undergo any
privation or danger? Of course you have all the particulars of
the affair at Bethel Church: I do not think that the loss of the
enemy has ever been put up high enough. From what a private
citizen told me just after the battle, who witnessed the whole
engagement, and from what I could see on the field and the
adjoining woods, such as pools of blood, &c., I confidently
assert that his loss in killed and wounded was fully five hundred. The same man informed me that in their retreat, the
Yankees pressed into service two carriages, several wagons and
any number of carts to carry off the dead and dying; and the
cavalry, who pursued them, reported that they were strewn from
the field of battle to Hampton, a distance of nine miles. At any
rate, we gave them a sound thrashing. Taking the disparity of
numbers into consideration, it was a great victory. We only had
about eight hundred engaged, to four thousand five hundred of
the Yankees. And they were well drilled, well disciplined
troops. You may probably wish to know why the Enfield Blues
were not actively engaged in the fight. The reason is that the
attack was made on the opposite line from ours, at least one
fourth of a mile from us, and we had orders not to leave our
entrenchments unless ordered to do so. When the fight was
nearly over with, it was feared that the enemy would attempt to
flank us on the left, which was our side; to prevent this, Col.
Magruder ordered our company to skirmish up a large swamp
on the left. We did so, and remained scouting in the swamp for
an hour or more after the enemy fired their last gun; so we did

50

not even see a Yankee the whole day. I think the men would have behaved very well in the presence of the enemy, for they were exposed to the whole fire during the engagement, and were remarkably cool. I mean the fire of the cannon; the grape shot fell thick around us and the bombs were bursting around us and over our heads. At first the boys were not much disposed to dodge, but when the shot came very near us, it was difficult to tell who was nearest to mother earth.

Before the action our men seemed unwilling to use the spade and shovel so constantly; but seeing how effectually the trenches screened them from Yankee bullets, they are perfectly willing to do any amount of that kind of work, and even anxious; and by the way, they have done a great deal of it; we have fortified our present position very well, and have done it all with our own hands, not a negro has trenched. We think we can give the Yankees a lively time now, come in what force they please. York Town is a very old, dilapidated place; from all appearances I should say that a nail even has not been driven for years, much less any building, or improving of any kind. This is a fine county too, the soil is excellent, with many means for improving it, yet the people are too lazy and inactive to improve it, or even to cultivate what they plant. From what I have seen I shall always say remove the seat of war as far from my own State and county as possible. Why, sir, there is not a single family remaining in York Town, all have fled; I mean the Ladies; and below this it is just as bad. The county between here and Hampton is almost depopulated. There certainly must be a great sacrifice of property, to say nothing of home comforts and enjoyments. With all the evils, this war has had a good effect on the morals of our men; they have certainly improved very greatly in this respect. As you very well know, we had some pretty hard cases in our company. Well, sir, as for drinking, that is altogether out of the question, there is none to be had, and it is very seldom that you hear an oath or any thing of the kind. There is preaching in camp two or three times each week, the men generally attend punctually and I hope with profit to themselves; they seem to appreciate their situation. I am glad to hear through you that matters are getting on so well at my house. I thank you kindly for your attention, and doubt not but that Mr. Hulm will gladly receive any instructions you may please to give him. Removed as far as I am, I can give no directions at all;

51

the fact is, I can not bring my mind to bear on my business. I hope you will all make fine provision crops this year.

Remember me kindly to every member of your family, and to all my friends. Say to Mr. Moore I should be pleased to hear from him. We are generally kept busy, so much so that it is not at all times convenient to write. As there is no drill or work on Sunday, I have taken this time to write you. I hope you will answer soon.

Very truly yours,
F. M. Parker

Camp 1st Regt. N.C. Vol.
York Town Va.
June 26, 1861

My dearest Wife

I have just received your very kind letter; you are so good to write me such a long letter, that I feel like answering it immediately.

I have written you several letters recently, the last one, I directed to you at home; expecting that probably you had returned from your visit. I am glad to hear that you had a pleasant visit; I hope you will go again soon. I wish I could be there with you. This war has shown me one thing, that is, that my people love me more than I thought they did. Every letter which I get from them, brings with it the kindest, tenderest feelings; now it may be that the war and its surrounding circumstances have brought out kinder, tenderer feelings in me. I hope it has. I see now that I have greatly erred in this respect heretofore. I trust and believe that I will make a better husband now, than I have ever been before.

You complain a little because I did not write by Mr. Powell; I intended to have done so, but Mr. Powell left suddenly, sooner than he expected; I however wrote by Mr. Pippen the day after Mr. Powell left. I am certain I have written you several letters which you have never received. I wrote from Great Bethel, as the Yankees call it, the day before the battle; then I wrote the day after the battle, and sent you a grape shot and piece of a bomb shell which fell very near me, particularly the grape. I sent these by Mr. Branch, of Enfield, and requested him to hand them to Thos. Maner, to be sent to your Father's to you. I have never yet heard that you received either.

You mention having seen Capt. Bridgers in Tarboro. I am glad that the people compliment him, I think he deserves it. It is rumored here that he has been appointed to a field office. I hope it is so, for he does not seem to be able to undergo the fatigues of the command of a company. While I am on this subject I will answer the questions which you ask in your letter.

You wish to know if Capt. Bell[37] is an efficient officer. I must answer candidly that he is not; in the first place he is a little indolent, and then he is not very capable; so far as the stand which the company may take under his command, I can not say. Bell has some influence on account of his means; he is tolerably wealthy; this you know will have its influence. I would greatly prefer a man of more intellectual standing for Captain. I understand that Bell has spoken of resigning, but he has never mentioned the matter to me. Several, a great many, of the men have approached me on the subject, and wished to know if I would accept the office of Capt. if Bell should resign; my answer always has been to wait until he resigned, then it would be time enough to act. I have every reason to believe that I have the entire confidence and esteem of the men; they manifest it many ways. I know you will love them for this.

I see in Col. Hill's second report to Gov. Ellis that he mentions Lieut. Whitaker as commanding Comp. I in the battle at Bethel;[38] this is a mistake which I shall have corrected, as a simple matter of justice to myself. Capt. Bell was in Petersburg, Lieut. Whitaker was sick, and I commanded the company.

It is a simple matter, but I shall have it set right. About my term of service, it will expire about the middle of November. I shall certainly come home then unless there is a strong prob-

---

37. David Barnes Bell enlisted in the Enfield Blues in Halifax County at age 34 on April 19, 1861, and was appointed captain to rank from date of enlistment. He resigned due to ill health on August 31, 1861. He had previously served as colonel of the 35th Regiment N.C. Militia. Manarin and Jordan, *N.C. Troops*, 3:46 and 668. Bell appears in the 1860 U.S. Census of Halifax County as a 33-year-old farmer living with his wife, Margaret, three daughters and two sons. He had 37 slaves and 7 slave houses.

38. *OR*, vol. 2, pt. 1, p. 96.

ability of an immediate engagement; if no fight is on hand I shall be with you then; the state of the country then will decide whether of not I enlist for another term of service. I think that after the Northern Congress meets, we shall have either hot work or peace; it is in their power to decide. I hope it will be peace, an <u>honourable peace</u>. This unnatural war is too bad; I say unnatural for it is so; I can not see what Lincoln is fighting for; he certainly can not expect to subjugate the whole South, nor even conquer a peace [*sic*]. Your letter contained a great deal of good advice, for which I am very thankful to you, instead of its tiring me. I hope you will write me just such another; it encourages me, and makes me feel better.

Now I am on a question which requires very nice decision; you say you wish to come to York Town. You know I should be more than glad to see you; but candour, and justice to you compel me to say that this is no place for a woman; except as a nurse in the Hospital; in the first place there is no private house in York Town, not even a single room which I could get for you; and I should not feel safe for you to be in the country around here. We might have an attack at any time, and then you might be as far away as possible. So upon the whole I think it unadvisable [*sic*] for you to come to York Town. If matters quiet down, and there is no probability of a visit from the Yankees, I may visit you before Nov. I will if I can.

There is a good deal of sickness in Camp just now; measles seems to be the prevailing disease; with some few cases of typhoid fever. I think there has been but one or two deaths yet. I have been generally very well, and hope by prudence to remain so.

I am glad to hear that the children keep well; but am sorry that you have an occasional visit from your old friend the head ache. I wish you could cut his acquaintance altogether.

How I wish I could see you and the little children. God bless you. I think of you very often, and wish to be with you. I should like so much to have little Hattie in my arms now; I wonder if she would know her Pa, or even Offa; the others I know would. Tell Mary I have not received her letter yet, but shall be very glad to get it whenever she writes it. Has Jimmy got to be a farmer yet, or is he a steer driver; I reckon he has fine fun with the calves; tell him to be a smart and good boy.

54

Will you please say to Ben Hulm that as soon as he finishes the crop I want him to go to work on the dam on the creek bank in the low grounds. I have written to Mr. Dunn to give him some instructions and ideas about it, which I hope he will do. When you write, let me know how the crop looks, how the negroes are getting on and how Ben himself does, if he is very attentive.

June 27th: I stopped writing yesterday evening to go on drill, and before I started your letter of the 23rd was handed me, which made me two letters in one day, that was really more than I had a right to expect; it was very evident that I had the best wife of any man in camp, to write me so often. I tell you it makes me a better man every letter I get from you. I am very anxious to see you. Sometimes I feel as if I could not want for the time to come, then when your letters come breathing such a quiet, peaccable, christian spirit, I feel somewhat resigned, but still want to see you just as much. You must not think hard of my objecting to your coming to York Town; this is no place for a woman, as I stated before; in addition to the fact of there not being any accommodations here, I might be ordered off at any moment, and then you see you would be left alone. As I write now there are three Regiments passing our camp, on their way to the lower part of the county; it is reported here that one Regt. of the Yankees is attempting to cross the country over to James River; these forces are sent down to cut them off; our Regt. has not secured any orders yet, nor do I suppose that we will be ordered off unless it be to reinforce those already sent; and surely three Regts. of our men can handle one of the Yankees; the Lord being on our side. When I wrote you last Sunday I mentioned that Lieut. Huske[39] of one of the Fayetteville companies, would read the evening service in one of the tents. I was pleased to hear it and hoped to participate in it, but could not

---

39. Benjamin Robinson Huske was a lawyer residing in Cumberland County when he enlisted for 6 months on April 17, 1861, in the "Fayetteville Light Infantry," Company H, 1st Regt. N.C. Infantry. He was appointed 1st lieutenant to rank from May 21, 1861. He was mustered out Nov. 12-13, 1861. Manarin and Jordan, *N.C. Troops*, 3:41 and 689. Huske later served as captain of Co. D and major of the 48th Regt. N.C.T.. He died in Manchester, Virginia, July 15, 1862, from a wound received at King's School House, Virginia, on June 25, 1862. He is buried in the Presbyterian Churchyard, Hillsboro, North Carolina. Manarin and Jordan, *N.C. Troops*, 11:369; Robert K. Krick, *Lee's Colonels*, 3rd edition rev., (Dayton, Ohio: Morningside Publishing, 1991), p. 202.

because I was busy waiting on two sick members of our company, Oliver Pittman[40] and John Randolph,[41] from Halifax Co. I hope nothing will deprive me of this pleasure whenever I can enjoy it again. Lieut. Huske is a very clever man; is a brother of one of my teachers at Valle Crucis, the Rev. Mr. Huske, now of Fayetteville.

In one of my late letters I requested you to send to Enfield one pair of linen pants to be brought to me by Rev. Mr. Page, of our company; but if you send me a pair by Mr. Powell it will be all sufficient; the fewer clothes here, the better; even the officers are cut down to a very few in case we have to march; so limited are the means for transportation.

One of my friends, Mr. Barnes[42] of our company, told me last night that he intends sending a communication to the Petersburg Express correcting the report of Col. Hill about the battle at Bethel. I will try to have a copy of the paper sent you. I have directed the last few letters which I have written you to Sycamore Alley. I shall send this there also, and request Mr. Moore to have them sent to you if you are still at your Father's. My love to all at your Father's, and to my little children, and

---

40. Oliver P. Pittman, age 28, enlisted as a private in the Enfield Blues in Halifax County on April 19, 1861. He was mustered out November 12-13, 1861. Pittman later enlisted in Company B, 63rd Regt. N.C.T. (5th Regt. N.C. Cavalry) and was appointed 3rd lieutenant to rank from June 12, 1862. He was promoted to 2nd lieutenant to rank from October 1, 1862, to 1st lieutenant to rank from February 16, 1863, and captain to rank from September 2, 1863. He retired to the Invalid Corps on March 31, 1865. Manarin and Jordan, *N.C. Troops*, 3:49 and 2:383. In the 1860 U.S. Census of Halifax County, Oliver Pittman was enumerated along with his wife and two children and owned 29 slaves and eight slave houses. At the commencement of the battle of Big Bethel, Oliver Pittman volunteered to keep watch while the Enfield Blues were led in prayer by Private Jesse Page, a Methodist minister. Wellman, *Rebel Boast*, pp. 54-55, based upon a history of the Enfield Blues published by Francis Marion Parker in an unnamed newspaper (no date given) cited by Wellman, *Rebel Boast*, p. 304 and p. 267, n. 19.
41. John Cary Randolph was a 22-year-old resident of Halifax County when he enlisted for six months as a private in the Enfield Blues on April 19, 1861. He was mustered out November 12-13, 1861. Manarin and Jordan, *N.C. Troops*, 3:50.
42. James H. Barnes was 27-years-old when he enlisted for six months as a private in the Enfield Blues in Wake County. He was mustered out November 12-13, 1861. Manarin and Jordan, *N.C. Troops*, 3:46.

take all for yourself my dear wife. Good bye, and may the Lord bless and keep you is the earnest prayer of your affectionate husband.

F. M. Parker

———————◆•◆———————

Camp 1st Regt. N.C.V.
York Town
July 3rd, 1861

My dearest Wife

Your welcome letter reached me on Monday and I now thank you for it. You are very kind to answer my letters so promptly. Having been on piquet [sic] duty all night, I am excused from duty to day, but this does not excuse me from writing you; on the other hand, I am glad to be perfectly free if it is even for a day; so the first thing I shall go at will be the most pleasant, viz., writing to my wife. You gave me a little scolding for not sending you a letter by Mr. Powell when he was here before; so as soon as he came the other day I inquired of him when he would leave for home; he told me he would remain several days, but in two days he was off. He disappointed me somewhat. I fully intended to have written by him, and you will see that I am not to blame this time. I take the next earliest opportunity of writing. I place very little confidence in this mail and never use it whenever I can send a letter by a friend. Henry Johnston,[43] of Enfield, is here on a visit and says you will receive this very soon, as he will send it by Mr. Maner.

Our company has increased in numbers considerably recently; we number now one hundred and twenty six, which is fully as many as we wish and in fact more than the law will allow us; how Col. Hill will manage with the supernumerarys [sic] I do not know. Among the late recruits whom we have received are two sons of Mrs. Burt,[44] near Ransom's Bridge;[45] they are

---

43. Henry Johnston appears in the 1860 U.S. Census of Halifax County as a 41-year-old farmer with 4 slaves and two slave houses.
44. Three young men named Burt joined the Enfield Blues as privates at Yorktown, Virginia, on June 29, 1861: Alpheus J. Burt, age 19; John A. Burt, age 21; and Robert T. Burt, age 24. Manarin and Jordan, *N.C. Troops*, 3:47.
45. Ransom's Bridge is located at the junction of Nash, Halifax, Franklin

very clever boys; in fact our company, with some exceptions are good men. Yesterday the 5th Regt.[46] from N.C. reached this place. It has the material to make a fine Regt. I have no doubt but that they will give a good account of themselves whenever they may fall in with the Yankees.

The Confederate Guards[47] are among them and are a fine company; they are quartered near us. I shall be with Fred often. He is looking very well; I must think that a camp life agrees with him. He seems to have a great desire to bag a Yankee, says he will not be satisfied with less than eight or ten. From present appearances I would not be surprised if he is gratified soon. Col. Magruder is now very near the enemy, near Newports News [sic], with three Regiments, and is doing everything in his power to draw them out; but so far in vain. It was reported here yesterday that he had gone so near the enemy as to enable his riflemen to pick off two Yankees, while at work on their entrenchments. Col. Magruder is down on a narrow peninsula and there is some danger that he may be cut off from this post; the enemy can land forces on either James or York rivers, and march in behind him, at the same time leaving sufficient force to engage him in front. But he is a bold man, and good officer, and is thoroughly acquainted with this whole country; added to all this he has a fine body of troops with him, the N.O. Zouaves, besides the three Regts. Our own Regt. is expecting to receive orders every day to march in double quick to Col. Magruder's support. I expect General Butler would like to wipe out the stain of the rout at Bethel, but with the same kind Providence overruling us, we will give him another "race over the New Market Course" as Col. Hill rather facetiously [sic] expresses it. I learn that the Yankees have been behaving very well since the tenth of June [and] have been perfectly satisfied to remain within the walls of Fortress Monroe and the entrenchments of Newports News.

In your last letter you ask me a very strange question. You wish to know if I do not want to see you. I think that is right

---

and Warren Counties. William S. Powell, *The North Carolina Gazetteer* (Chapel Hill: University of North Carolina Press, 1968), p. 403.

46. The 5th Regt. was later re-numbered the 15th Regt. North Carolina Troops.
47. The "Confederate Guards" from Edgecombe County served as Company I, 15th Regt. N.C.T.

funny. If I know any thing, I think I know this, that I do wish to see you and the children very much; and I am not getting much weaned either. I suppose we will know in a short time whether or not I shall see you soon. If the Northern Congress will put an end to this cruel, unnatural war, I suppose I may be able to have a short leave of absence before the six months are out; but if otherwise, I am afraid it will be some time before I shall see you. Be assured I will leave, whenever I can. If I can be spared, Col. Hill will know it and will grant me a short furlough.

I received the articles sent by Mr. Powell. I am very thankful for the clothes, particularly the shirts, they are the very things I needed. I managed to keep my white shirts tolerably clean, but then there was no starch in the bosom and you know how badly they must have looked; the coloured ones are decidedly preferable. Yesterday I received two of the same kind from my Mother's old friend Mrs. Harriett Whitaker.[48] She was sending her two sons some of the same and I suppose thought I would like them. Pure kindness prompted her to the act. I never shall forget the parting she gave me at Weldon. It made me feel like I was a child, with a Mother again.

Please thank your good Mother and Aunt Phoebe for the good things they wished to send by Mr. Powell. I feel just as grateful to them as tho' I had received the articles. I am glad you are with your Father and Mother. Of course I feel a great deal better satisfied than if you were at home alone. I wish you to remain there as long as you please. I mean not to go home on account of any business there. Ben Hulm ought to be able to take care of every thing. I was pleased to hear so favorable an account of my crop. I hope it will turn out well. I hear good accounts from the crops generally in No. Carolina.

I hope you will write soon, with a long letter. I am very thankful for the one you last sent me; it was a very good letter. I hope to get many such from you. My love to my little children; tell them their Pa thinks of them often and wants to see them very much. I am really afraid that the younger ones will forget all about me. You must remind them of me.

My love to all at your Father's; I have not seen Fred to day but intend to go over to his camp this evening. Good bye my

---

48. Harriet Whitaker appears in the 1860 U.S. Census of Halifax County as a 66-year-old farmer who owned 66 slaves.

dearest wife, and may the Lord bless you is the earnest prayer
of your loving husband,

F. M. Parker

July 4th—I have seen Fred this morning; he is out with his
company at work on entrenchments; he seems to be the only
working man, among the officers of his company.

———————————◆◆◆———————————

Headquarters 1st Regt. N.C. Vol.
York Town
July 14, 1861

My dear Wife

It is Sunday night; I have finished all the duties of the day;
have had my supper, and while standing out in front of my tent
looking up at the moon, the thought occurred to me that probably you were gazing at the same object and that the children
were playing out in the yard, enjoying themselves; happy little
creatures. Were you thinking of me, thinking of what a life I
must lead here away from every thing like the comforts of
home, except a place to eat and sleep at.

I have had a very soft tender feeling about me all day; or ever
since preaching this morning.

There came in from the country an old gentlemen with his
family of children and grand children. He told me that his
family had not listened to a sermon for two months. They
seemed to appreciate the privilege. Well they might, for they
listened to a very good sermon, delivered by the chaplain of the
Richmond Howitzers, a fine battalion of artillery from Richmond which I have mentioned in one of my former letters.
Among the old gentleman's family were two little girls; one of
them just the size of Mary, and the other a little smaller; and a
little boy about the size of Jimmy. I tell you I felt very much like
going up and kissing the little children; they were the only ones
I had seen for a long time. I thank them very much for coming
to our camp. I found several of the officers out near the
children, among them Capt. Hoke, an old friend of mine from
Lincolnton. I remarked to him that that was a refreshing sight;
he turned round with a great deal of earnestness and said,
Parker, let's go and kiss the children. He too, poor fellow, has

a wife and little ones at home. I can afford to indulge in such thoughts to day; our duty is light; after ten o'clock in the morning we have nothing to do until dress parade, which comes off at sunset. The interim is filled up with attending preaching, reading, and visiting. Tonight I must lay aside all these tender feelings of the heart in some secure place, and in the morning take up the sterner duties of my present life.

I think of you a great deal, I love to do so, it makes me a better man, causes me to enter into many good resolves, which I pray for strength to keep, some of which I do keep. But above all, your letters have a greater effect on me than anything else. The good advice which you give me and the troubles and difficulties which you speak of show me that my situation is not different from that of others. Now, from the rather sad tone in which I have written, do not suppose that I go moping about; far from it. My troubles are all kept within my own bosom. No one knows what is going on within. No doubt the boys think I am happy and contented; they often speak of my looking well, and seeming to enjoy myself. I do enjoy very good health, which is certainly a great blessing. I have been wishing to go to see you for some-time but do not know when I can do so now. Capt. Bell is at home on a sick furlough. His furlough extends to sixty days. When he will return, I can not say. Lieut. Whitaker is also at home to visit a sick family; poor fellow, he lost one of his children lately and his wife and another child are now sick. So you see the company is left with only two officers. Genrl. Hill is very much opposed to the officers leaving their companies, unless under an urgent necessity. If everything should remain quiet, I suppose I may be able to get off once before our six months are out. If I can, I will certainly do so. Whether I go or not, I shall think of you just as often and shall wish just as much to see you and my little children. So you must write me often, and express yourself freely and fully in your letters; they are strictly between us and our God; they are profaned by no other eye.

I received a letter from Sister Mary yesterday; she told me that she had been disappointed by your not coming to see her at the appointed time. I am very sorry you did not go for she would have been glad to see you and you would have enjoyed the visit. You must go and stay some with her as she told me she intended to ask you to do so. Would that I could visit Tarboro once more;

one spot in it rather; you know what I mean. What a great blessing a good Mother is. I feel thankful that my children have such an one.

Sister Mary also wrote me that Brother's little girl, Nannie was dead; it was sad to hear this, but we know that the little one is infinitely better off now than before. She is with her Father in heaven.

I wrote you last week of a skirmish which our forces had with the Yankees and of the great loss to us of an able officer, Lt. Col. Dreux,[49] of Louisiana.

Very recently our cavalry fell in with another party of the Yankees, killing four, wounding one and bringing off eleven prisoners. There was great excitement in the whole camp upon their arrival. The prisoners were brought in a wagon so covered up as not to see anything at all; nor to be seen, which was a great bore to our boys. The object in covering them up was to prevent their getting any idea of our defenses. The day after their arrival, two deserters from the enemy were brought in and to day the whole were sent off to Richmond. There were about one hundred engaged on either side, but the force of the enemy was infantry and ours cavalry; which gave them greatly the advantage. You see another interposition of a kind of Providence. Genrl. Hill is still pushing the defenses forward with vigor. The shovels and axes are never idle. We all thought some time since that the place was well fortified, but we see now how little we knew about it. Positions which were at first supposed to be strong are now discovered to be untenable. More heavy artillery is needed to place on our breastworks; there is a pretty good supply of light artillery for field work.

I see that the Southern Confederacy has issued a commission to our Col. creating him a Brigadier General; this is very proper; he is every way qualified to fill the office, and is deserving it. The only thing to be regretted is that we shall be compelled to give him up from the immediate command of our Regt. Of course the Regt. will form a part of his brigade and will be under

49. Charles Didier Dreux, age 29, a graduate of Transylvania University and a Louisiana lawyer and state legislator, was appointed lieutenant colonel of the 1st Louisiana Battalion on April 1, 1861, and was killed in a skirmish near Newport News, Virginia, on July 5, 1861. Krick, *Lee's Colonels*, p. 123; Columbus H. Allen, "About the Death of Col. C. D. Dreux," *Confederate Veteran*, vol. 15, no. 7 (July, 1907):307; Bergeron, *Louisiana Military Units*, pp. 148-9; *OR*, vol. 2, pt. 1, pp. 188-192.

him, tho' not so intimately connected as heretofore. Genrl. Hill's promotion will create a vacancy in the staff of the Regt. There are several candidates spoken of for the vacant office. Lieut. Col. Lee[50] and Maj. Lane[51] will of course be advanced, so we will have to elect a Major. Capt. Bridgers is spoken of as a candidate among several other captains. Who will be the successful one is more than I can say. I expect my letters are very dull to you; I have no news to tell you, except what relates to our affairs here; you must value the letter as coming from your husband, not regarding the contents too particularly. Tell Jimmy if he was here, he would see more mustering, or, as he expresses it, "playing muster" and hear more drums and fifes than ever he thought of. The little boy who came in yesterday with his grandfather seemed to enjoy it all finely. The Regt. was drawn up for [letter ends here]

———————————◆•◆◆◀━━━

Head Quarters 1st Regt. N.C. Vol.
York Town
July 23rd 1861

My dear Sally

Your very welcome letter reached me yesterday evening. I was so glad to hear from you, and to hear that you were all well, and so much pleased at your promptness in answering my letter,

---

50. Charles Cochrane Lee, a South Carolina native, was a 27-year-old instructor at the North Carolina Military Institute in Mecklenburg County when he accompanied the corps of cadets to Raleigh and was elected lieutenant colonel of the 1st Regt. N.C. Infantry on May 11, 1861. He was elected colonel of the regiment on September 1, 1861, and mustered out November 12-13, 1861. Appointed colonel of the 37th Regt. N.C.T., he was killed during the Seven Days at Frayser's Farm on June 30, 1862. Manarin and Jordan, *N.C. Troops*, 3:2; Krick, *Lee's Colonels*, p. 233.

51. James Henry Lane (1833-1907), a native of Matthews County, Virginia, was a 26-year-old instructor at the North Carolina Military Institute in Mecklenburg County when he accompanied the corps of cadets to Raleigh and was elected major of the 1st Regt. N.C. Infantry on May 11, 1861. Lane was appointed colonel of the 28th Regiment N.C.T. on September 21, 1861. Following the death of his brigade commander, Lawrence O'Bryan Branch at Sharpsburg, Lane was promoted brigadier general effective November 1, 1861. Lane commanded his North Carolina brigade consisting of the 7th, 18th, 28th, 33rd, and 37th Regiments

that I have determined to write to day, or rather begin a letter to day; for it is very seldom that I can finish a letter, without having to attend to several little matters in the mean time; particularly is this the case, now that two of the commissioned officers are absent. Another reason for writing to day is that I have an offer of a friend to take a letter to you, or rather to N. Caro., Mr. Bennett Lyon,[52] who is on a visit to camp. If you could have seen me last night reading your letter, you would have pronounced it "the pursuit under difficulties." I think we had the most violent storm of wind and rain here last night, I ever witnessed; it stormed the whole night. Our tents stood it bravely. I feared they would all blow down, but did not, only leaked a little, tho I managed to keep dry, by covering up head and jeans; this you know, I did not fancy, but it was a choice of two evils. As to reading your letter, I had to take the candle in my hand, bend over it and get a friend to hold his hat just before the candle in order to read at all. I managed to get through with it after a long time; as I had to sleep in my clothes, I placed the letter in my vest pocket, on the <u>left</u> side, and there kept it until morning, when I had a heart of it. This is, like all its predecessors, a most excellent letter. I thank you for it. I hope you will repeat the favour often. Writing to you, and receiving letters from you, is the greatest enjoyment I have; I always feel better from the performance of either.

You ask me how I live in my tent &c. Capt. Bell, the Rev. Mr. Page and I occupy one tent; we sleep on small cots, very comfortable tho; our floor is a dirt one, not a dirty one; from last night's experience, I should say that our tent would stand any rain; the only water which troubled us, was that which beat in at the cracks.

Our bills of fare are very plain, but very good; our friends at home have kept us supplied with hams and vegetables and partially so with corn meal; then we can get chickens here, and

N.C.T. until Appomattox. Lane had a postwar career as a professor of civil engineering at Virginia Polytechnic Institute, Missouri School of Mines, and Alabama Polytechnic Institute at Auburn. Manarin and Jordan, *N.C. Troops*, 3:2 and 8:110. Warner, *Generals in Gray*, pp. 172-173.

52. Bennett Lyon appears in the 1860 U.S. Census of Edgecombe County as a 54-year-old farmer living with his wife Penelope, two sons and two daughters. He had 36 slaves and nine slave houses.

occasionally the commissary furnishes us with fresh beef. So you see there is not much danger of our starving. The men complain a little of the pickle pork with which they are provided. As the hams which are sent from home do not last the men as long as they do the officers, there being only four of us, they have to fall back upon the pork. I tell them it is the best meat they can eat, and set them the example myself. The officers have hired two servants between them, who do our cooking and washing. The men are divided into messes of from ten to sixteen, and they have from one to two cooks to each mess. So you see we live something after the manner of civilized people; we have coffee night and morning; with very brown sugar, for those who use it. We need shelters to cook under very much, but can not get the plank with which to build them, and have to take the open air for it.

At the battle of Bethel we had not even cooking utensils; we fried our meat (Western at that) in our shovels, and made ship biscuit, a very hard dry bread. We had no coffee at all, and this as you know, was a great privation to me, particularly in the morning. If we ever march from our present encampment again, we will know better how to provide for ourselves before leaving camp. As long as we remain here, we shall fare well.

I am glad to hear that you and the children have improved; I do hope you will keep your health, and not suffer at all from any sickness; if you were not with your good Father, I would be uneasy, but I know he will take care of you, and do all that can be done. I never can forget his great kindness.

You say you will visit Sister Mary before you return home. I am glad to hear this, and hope you will stay some time with her, I know she will be glad to see you. I feel sorry for her; I do not think she will be happy in her present position; she is too good a woman to please the fawning sycophants and miserable pretenders among the aristocracy of certain circles. She would a great deal rather be at her home, enjoying the quiet of a country life. She writes me occasionally, and I value her letters highly. I hope she will continue to write me.

Bella wrote me the other day from Wilmington; she told me that she was busy making cartridge bags for the forts. How can we be conquered, when the women take such an active part; no, we can never be conquered, while the hand of Providence is so visible on our side.

This morning about three thousand troops were ordered down in the peninsula, in the direction of and near Newports

65

News; they are a fine body of soldiers, and will do good service, provided they can meet an enemy. The Richmond Howitzers are with these troops; if the occasion offers itself, you will hear a good report from there. They were with us at Bethel; in fact did the greater part of the work there. The Zouaves are also with this column. These I have no great confidence in. They might act as good skirmishers, or would be the very men to throw into an enemy after his lines were broken, but I do not think they would stand a cool, deliberate fire for hours. The object of the movement of these troops I do not know, but suppose it is to have a force convenient to check the enemy, should he make a move from Newports News or Fortress Monroe. We are constantly receiving artillery to place on our works, with the addition of more heavy artillery, and field pieces, and the river being strongly fortified, we think we can give Butler and his rascally crew as lively a time as they would like to have. I do not wish them to come, but if they do come, I shall do my best on them. I am willing to give my life in our cause, but I assure you, I shall sell it as dearly as possible. My own opinion is that we will have no attack here; if we get a fight, we shall have to seek it elsewhere. It has been a difficult matter to write this letter; the boys are so much excited about the great battle near Manassas; wasn't it a great victory? Genrl. Johnston has done some of the best fighting on record; the ten thousand regulars who opposed him should have managed his command very well, according to all the rules of warfare; but justice, a righteous cause, but above all the kindness of an overruling Providence gave us the victory. Surely by this time Lincoln and his minions must know that the Southern people can fight, and that some one "is hurt." But if he is not yet satisfied, he can find another field on which to try his prowess. We must and will succeed.

I went over to see Fred this morning; he looks a little badly, has had a couple of chills, but has broken them with quinine; he is up but not on active duty. I hope he will miss the chills now. Lieut. Sugg[53] of his company is also a little unwell, leaving but one commissioned officer on duty; but for this fact, the Confederates would have been ordered [out] to day; four companies of

53. Redding S. Sugg served as 2nd lieutenant in the "Confederate Guards," Company I of the 5th (later the 15th) Regt. N.C.T. Manarin and Jordan, *N.C. Troops*, 5:585. Redding S. Sugg appears in the 1860 U.S. Census of Edgecombe County as a 15-year-old student residing in the home of P.S. Sugg, a physician who owned 48 slaves.

the 5th Regt. were sent; the Rocky Mount Company being one of them. I rather think they will have some hot work before they return. Genrl. Magruder is getting impatient for a fight; he does not like to be confined too much to camp, but above all he is an ambitious man, seeking military glory. He is one of the finest artillery officers in the world, this is an acknowledged fact; he was in the artillery service of the U.S. Army up to the time that he resigned his commission. In the fight at Bethel the Genrl. aimed several of the Howitzers, and with deadly effect too. He is fond of this branch of the service, and should be connected with it. He has not the qualities to make him a General officer, not a distinguished one. He is too excitable.

I am very sorry to have to report the sickness of Genrl. Hill; he is now suffering with measles; I hope he will not be much sick. Our Lieut. Col. is just recovering from the same sickness. Did ever you hear of so many grown persons having measles; I always supposed it was a disease peculiar to children. The health of the Regt. is not good yet; measles and colds are going through the camp. The deaths are few. The Edgecombe Guards have lost another member; they are unfortunate.

Company I has been favoured so far, tho we have quite a sick man in the Hospital at this time; a case of pneumonia. The poor fellow is quite low. The boys from our own neighborhood are tolerably well; Henry Moore[54] has been in feeble health for some time, tho' he is up. Joe Partin[55] is just out of the measles and looks badly. Joe Arrington is well, and has improved very much since being in camp.

---

54. Henry A. Moore enlisted in the Enfield Blues as a private in Cumberland County at age 24 on April 19, 1861. He was discharged on August 23, 1861. He later served in Company G, 41st Regt. N.C.T. (3rd Regt. N.C. Cavalry), enlisting as a private on January 26, 1862, and being discharged May 5, 1862, by reason of "general debility." Manarin and Jordan, *N.C. Troops*, 3:49 and 700, and 2:232 and 814. Moore appears in the 1860 Census of Halifax County as a 23-year-old farmer serving as the agent for six minors who owned 18 slaves.
55. Joseph J. Partin was an 18-year-old resident of Halifax County when he enlisted as private in the Enfield Blues on April 19, 1861. He mustered out November 12-13, 1861, and later served as 1st sergeant of Company A, 47th Regt. N.C.T. Manarin and Jordan, *N.C. Troops*, 3:49 and 703. In the 1860 U.S. Census of Halifax County, Joe Partin appears as the 17-year-old son of Nelson Partin and wife, Lucinda Partin, who owned six slaves.

I received a letter from Carter Arrington recently also one from Mr. Dunn and also from Mr. Nicholson, they all give me a good report of my crop.

Mr. Nicholson reports every thing going on well, that the negroes seem to be doing their duty. Of course I am pleased to hear all this. I would like to be at home for a little while to see every thing there, and would like it a great deal better to see you and the children, but fear I shall not be able to do so, until my term of service expires; an order was read on dress parade yesterday forbidding the granting of any more leaves of absince [*sic*]. This is hard on those who have not absented themselves at all. So you must put this down as one of the fates of war, and submit to it. I was just thinking of a little trip home as soon as Capt. Bell and Lieut. Whitaker returned, who are both at home sick; but this order is a complete shut down of all my plans. Be patient then my dear wife, a few more months, and we will see each other, if the Lord will.

I hope you and the children will keep well in the mean time. It would almost craze me to hear of your sickness, and not be able to go and see you. Be very prudent then, with yourself and them.

It is now after ten o'clock, all are asleep but myself. I will close now. My love to all your Father's family, to Sister Sue and John and to my little children; kiss each one of them, tell them their Pa thinks of them every day, and wishes to see them, that because he is away from them, away here among rough soldiers, guns, cannon, powder, &c, he has not forgotten his sweet little children at home, no, nor their Mother either; she is first in his thoughts, then the children; tell them to be good and mind their Ma, and every one else whom they should obey.

Write to me soon my dear wife. Good night, and good bye. May the Lord bless you.

Very affectionately your husband
F. M. Parker

———————◆•◆————————

July 24, 1861

My dear daughter

I have asked you several times to write to me and I have never yet written to you. I now ask you to write me a little letter as

68

soon as you can. Capt. Bell received a letter from his little girl not long since; she wrote her Pa a very good letter; the Capt. asked me to read it. She is several years older than you are, and has been regularly at school; now I wish you to write me and be a little sweeter than she is. I will feel very proud of your little letter, if it is only a few lines. Tell me what you do every day, what your brothers do, how they all look and whether your little sister is as sweet as ever. Don't you reckon she will forget her Pa; you will not forget him, will you Mary? Does Jimmy ever ride on horseback. I know he wants his Pa back there to ride him some on Harry. Mr. Carter Arrington wrote me the other day that Bill was driving Harry and Brooks in the wagon. I reckon your Mama is glad to hear this. Would you like to be here with your Pa; you would hear a good deal of pretty music from our fine brass band and a great deal of drumming and fifing, but sometimes you would hear several large cannon fire off, which would scare you; but they would not injure you, they are generally aimed down the river to try their range, as they call it; that is to see how far they will shoot. We have small cannon, called Howitzers, placed on four wheels, to which they fasten horses, so that they can be moved rapidly from one place to another, sometimes they run the horses as fast as they can, and your Pa is getting tired of this noise and clatter of arms; he would rather be at his home, with his wife and children; he had rather have their love than anything else in this world.

Give my love to your Mama, your brothers, and kiss your little sister for me. Tell the little boys they must be good children. I know you will be a good little girl for my sake. I shall be very glad when I get your letter.

Your affectionate Father,
F. M. Parker

Head Quarters 1st Regt. N.C.V.
York Town
July 29th, 1861

My dear Wife

Your letter of the 24th reached me safely. I was very glad to hear from you and to hear that you are all well. It was truly a business letter. I am sorry that you are so troubled with my business. The fact is I have not been able to give my business at home much thought since I have been here, but the barn needed the work which Hilliard[56] spoke of and must be done before the crop is housed. You say that you have ordered the timber, &c. necessary for the repairs, which is all very well; if Hilliard should need any nails will you please order them from Mssrs. Martin, Tannahill & Co. Petersburg. About the meat, I think you will do exactly right to charge Mr. Moore the full Petersburg price for bacon, including the freight. In fact, I do not wish it to go from the smokehouse unless you get this price; and cash at that.

I do not think it best to sell too much meat; after furnishing Mr. Moore, you can use your own discretion about selling any more. I shall wish you to send me a few hams when you get home, say some five or six; after sending this to me, then if you think you have a plenty left, you can sell some to Carter Arrington <u>for the cash</u>. Moses sent me word some time since that he had a good stock of hogs to fatten. I hope he will be successful with them and that you will have a plenty of meat to put away this winter.

My opinion is that bacon will be scarce and dear next year. I should like to be at home for a short time now, but there is no possibility of my doing so. No furloughs will be granted now under any consideration, so you and the children must keep well, or, if you get sick do not let me know any thing of it. This may seem to you a strange request. If I knew that you were sick and could not see you, it would nearly craze me. I hope you will keep well.

The health of this post is not as good as it was when I wrote last. Bilious and typhoid fevers are quite common. In our own Regt. there are upwards of three hundred sick and in the 5th N.C. it is as bad. When I wrote before Fred was a little unwell; he has never given up on account of his bad feelings. He looks a little thin but is taking quinine and I hope will soon be entirely well. We have been unfortunate in our company recently;

---

56. Hilliard was apparently one of Parker's slaves. He seems to have been a skilled carpenter, and Parker was soon to direct his wife to put Hilliard in charge of the management of the plantation. See Parker's letter of Feb. 14, 1862 (p. 129). Hilliard Parker, a 46-year-old mulatto, was recorded as living next door to Colonel Parker in Formosa Township, Halifax County in the 1870 U.S. Census of Halifax County.

within the past week we have lost four men and have several now in the Hospitals. We number 126 men and this morning there were reported for duty only 48 men. We were at first encamped on a marsh which I think is the cause of our present sickness; our encampment had been moved to a high bluff on the river where we can get the benefit of the sea breeze, and I think we will now improve as regards our health. I am very thankful that I have been able to keep well so far; it is very fortunate for the company. Capt. Bell and Lieut. Whitaker are both at home yet, and have been there fully one third of the time that we have been in the service.

I do not feel like writing to day. You will therefore please excuse this poor letter; I will write again soon. My love to all at your Father's, to Sister Sue and John. Kiss the children for me; tell them not to forget their Pa.

The next letter I write you, I may direct it to Tarboro, as I expect you will be there soon. I hope so at any rate.

Write soon.

Very affectionately your husband
F. M. Parker

* * *

Bigler's Wharf Va.
August 5, 1861

My dear Wife

You will ask, where is Bigler's Wharf? My answer is that it is about ten miles up the river from York Town. It is a place which was built up by a very enterprising Northern man. Here he erected several different kinds of machinery, a saw mill, grist mill, a large brick making machine, shingle machine and carried on a large business with the Northern cities. The oyster trade received from him its due attention. He erected a large Hotel and store in one building, together with four or five dwelling houses for families, also a school house, and lastly a very neat building for a church. All this work has been done within the past four years. As soon as the present troubles broke out, this man Bigler took his family and returned whence he came; leaving an agent here, with instructions to make a transfer of all his property here to the Confederate States government. This was accordingly done; and the place is now used as a convalescent Hospital; that is, the cases which seem to improve slowly at the General Hospital at York Town, are sent here, more to enjoy the quiet and ease, which is not known in York Town; a very little medicine is administered here; which I think is better for the men.

Now you may wish to know why I am here. A little more than a week since, I was taken with a chill. I took a little medicine, checked the chills, but the disease turned off on my bowells [sic] and reduced me very rapidly. I was not very sick at any one time, but was very weak all the time; with the advice of Dr. Hines I came to this place yesterday, and have already strengthened and otherwise improved. I hope to be able to return to camp in a few days. Dr. Randolph, the Surgeon at this Hospital, says I must not go until I get entirely well. He is one of the most clever gentlemen I have ever met with. He was a member of one of the Howitzer companies, of which I have before written to you, and took a very active part in the fight at Bethel. [he] Is a nephew of Maj. Randolph, the commander of the Howitzer Battalion, himself a most estimable gentleman. I am very pleasantly situated here, have a nice, pleasant room to myself, in one of Bigler's nice houses. I think these dwellings are more conveniently arranged for house keeping, than any I ever saw; displaying real Yankee ingenuity.

Several members of our company are here; and a good many are in the Hospitals at York Town; to be candid, there is a good deal of sickness in our Regt. our own company has recently lost four members; since then we have moved our encampment to a high bluff on the river, where we get the breeze right out of the Chesapeak [sic], and the sickness has abated somewhat, and I hope will soon disappear. The 3rd N.C. Regt. has also suffered a good deal from chills and fever and measles. Genrl. Magruder now has this Regt., and in fact every Regt. from York Town except the 1st N.C., down in the peninsula near Newports News. It is thought he intends attacking the latter place. If so, you may listen for stirring news from this quarter. It is believed that Magruder is anxious for a fight. Fred is well, and with his company; he had gone before John Battle and Joe reached York Town. John remained in York Town one day, spent the greater part of the day with me, and went on the next morning with Mark Battle and several others, who were too unwell to march when their Regt. was ordered off. How long John and Joe intend to remain below, I do not know; I am afraid I shall not see them on their way back. I assure you I was very glad to see them the other day. I was quite feeble, had been thinking of home and home folks just before they came into my tent. I told Joe I never loved him so well as I did that day. I loved him for himself, and also because he was from home. I reckon I should have loved a cat, coming from home, and you know I have no great affection for them. Do not think that I am low spirited; not a bit of it; but a fellow will think of his wife and little ones when he feels badly.

I once thought if I were unmarried I would not marry during such times as the present, but I have changed that opinion. If it was not for the pleasure of hearing from you and the children, I should feel lonely here indeed. One letter from you is equal to two or three weeks absence; I mean that the pleasure which one letter gives me, counterbalances the pain of a long absence. So administer the antidote to that pain often. My little sickness has put me behind with my correspondence. I intend to catch up with it during my stay here.

Your Father wrote me once by Joe. I was glad to hear that you had gone to Tarboro with the children. I know you enjoyed the visit, and that they were all glad to see you.

When you return home, will you please send me some six or eight hams; have the hams packed in a barrell [*sic*] and the barrell headed up well; send it [to] Enfield, and write Henry Johnston a note requesting him to send it on by the first one coming here. If you could manage to send me some tomatoes I should prize them very highly; you know how well I like them. I also wish you to send the pants which you gave me in the Spring, the same which I sent back home from this place; the cassamere [*sic*] pants. Linen is pleasant to wear, but there is difficulty in having them washed and ironed properly. Please send the pants by the first opportunity.

Why bless me! I came near forgetting to tell you that I slept under a roof, and on a <u>bed</u> last night; the first time in more than two months. It was a long time before I could induce my eyes to close, every thing was so strange.

One thing which Bigler did here I admire very much, and that was to plant a large peach orchard. There are I suppose sixty acres closely planted with peach trees; they look remarkably flourishing, but <u>fortunately</u> for us there is not a peach on them;

there is also a fine vineyard here. It does seem to me that I would have turned Southerner before giving up all this property, so completely fixed up as it was. He owned about 3,000 acres of land.

My love to all at your Father's; not forgetting Sister Sue and John; kiss the children for me, tell Mary I saw yesterday, a young mother surrounded by her children, three little girls one about her size, one smaller, then a sweet little baby in its arms. It was the prettiest sight I have seen since I left home. I hope to see the same sight at home before many months. Good bye, my dear wife, God bless you.

Very affectionately your husband
F. M. Parker

＊＊＊

Head Quarters 1st Regt. N.C.V.
August 8th, 1861

My dear wife

You will see that I am back at camp again, tho a little weak from my recent sickness. As I have a nice chance of sending you a letter, I thought I would write to let you know that I am getting well again. While I was at the convalescent Hospital, an old gentleman of the neighborhood came up in his boat and invited Oliver Pittman and myself to spend the day with him and his family. We accepted the offer, had a delightful sail of about four miles down the river to his house; which we found located very near the river bank, in a shady, pleasant place. We found his family to consist of wife and four children, three girls and a son, the eldest girl a little older than Mary, and of the same name, the youngest a little girl just talking well. This little one and I struck up an acquaintance, which I think will very soon grow into love; she remained with me nearly the whole day; was a very sweet little child; in fact, all the children were very clever, remarkably well behaved and very smart; each one seemed to vie with the other to see who could treat us best.

The lady gave us a very good dinner, all sorts of vegetables. You may be sure I did them full justice, particularly the tomatoes. I really expected to be made sick, but was not. I improved more this day, than any one since I had been sick. I wish you could have had some of the fine fish which loaded the table.

Owing to a severe storm in the afternoon, we were compelled to remain all night which I assure you we did not object to; the next morning we had <u>very fine oysters</u>, taken right out of the water, not an hour before we ate them. There is a great difference in oysters when fresh, and those a long time out of the water. I hope I shall fatten this fall, on oysters. Should I be so unfortunate as to be sick again, I shall strike a bee line for Capt. Busick's house, this is the name of the kind gentleman; and tell Mary the little girl I fell in love with is named Jessie Ida Lindsay Busick. She gave me several little shells for my little girl, which I hope to send to her soon, probably by Mr. Wimberly.

No definite news from Genrl. Magruder yet; it is reported here today that he has burned the village of Hampton; he has had no fight yet.

The health of the two N.C. Regts. is bad yet; there is a great deal of sickness and some deaths. The camp of the 5th Regt. is to [be] moved to a more healthy location, which I hope will improve their health. Their location is now a bad one.

In the letter I wrote to you from Bigler's Warf, I asked you to send me some hams and tomatoes. Will you also send me some butter, if you have it. And with the pants I asked you to send, please send my boots. Well, I missed the Bishop's visit to our camp and was sorry for it. He brought me a letter from Sister Kate, they were all well.

Remember me kindly to all at your Father's and to Sister Sue and John, and Dr. Rives. Kiss the children for me; tell Jimmy to grow fast and be a man, so he can fight the Yankees. Write soon and let me know all about your visit to Tarboro.

Good bye to my dear wife, and may the Lord bless you.

Very affectionately your husband
F. M. Parker

———————◆•◆•◆———————

Head Quarters 1st Regt. N.C.V.
York Town
August 12, 1861

My dear Wife

I write you a short and hurried note this morning to ask you to send the articles which I have written for, to Enfield. I understand that there will be some one coming on from there soon; so you will please send the things to Henry Johnston requesting him to forward them on to me.

Some six or eight hams will be sufficient, a little butter if you have it, my cassimere pants and boots are what I wish sent.

I hope I am getting well, I feel better this morning than I have since I have been sick. I hope, with prudence, to keep well now.

I will write you again soon. Kiss the children for me; remember me to Ben Hulm and the negroes and to all the neighbors. I have sent Mary's shells, which the little girls gave me for her.

Take care of yourself and family; good bye, and may the Lord bless and keep you, is the prayer of your

very affectionate husband
F. M. Parker

———————◆●◆———————

Camp 1st Regt. N.C.V.
York Town
August 15, 1861

My dear Sir

Just about one month ago, I am ashamed to say it, I received a very kind and interesting letter from you; for which I now thank you. About that time the Capt. and 1st Lieut. were both absent at home, consequently a good deal of business devolved on me, particularly as we had a large amount of sickness at that time.

Since then I have not been very well, and added to this is a little laziness, and you have my reason for not writing sooner.

Since you wrote me great events have occurred; the great battle of Manassa [sic] has been fought and won; also the very recent one in Mission. Truly the hand of Providence is visible throughout; it seems as if the Northern people are slow to discover their folly; and are hard to convince of the impossibility of conquering such a people as the Southerners. My own opinion is that, a continuation of the war is the very thing for us; I think we should fight the rascals long enough to cause us to hate them intensely, so as to cut off all intercourse, all trade, and traffick [sic] for the future.

As sure as we get to trading with them again, just so sure will we become subject to them.

August 25: As you will see, there is a considerable interval between the dates of this letter. Our Regt. is now encamped at Ship Point on Pocosin [sic] river, some ten or twelve miles below York Town. We were removed to this point on account of sickness. The Regt. continued very sickly at York Town, with a good many deaths. I think we are very much benefitted [sic] by the move. We are in full view of the Chesapeak [sic] bay, have a delightful breeze, fine shade; but only tolerably good water; and what in my opinion is a good part of the whole matter, our camp is in the midst of an old pine field. After being shut up in York Town for so long a time, the very smell of the woods and country, is refreshing to us. It would not at all surprise me, if the Yankees do not wish, and attempt to share this pleasant place with us; the only danger is from the water side, they can run up within two miles of us, with their vessels, and may give us a little trouble in this way. We would not object to a little excitement just now.

I am glad to hear such favourable accounts from the crops at home, particularly the corn crop. It seems that we are blessed in this respect also.

From a letter which I received from my wife a few days since, I learn that William and Gil are in the service. I was sorry we could not get them in our company. Would have been much pleased to have had them. I hope they are well pleased where they are.

I was prevented from answering William's letter, on account of sickness; Lieut. Whitaker informed him that the authorities had determined not to receive any more recruits into this Regt. Since we left home, two additional companies have been added to us, and the Regt. now numbers nearly 1,400 men. These two latter companies are the Bertie Volunteers; and Dixie Rebels;[57] from Chowan Co.

---

57. The "Bertie Volunteers" were enrolled for active service at Windson, Bertie County, on May 1, 1861, under Capt. Jesse J. Jackocks, and was assigned to the 1st Regt. N.C. Infantry as Company L on June 20, 1861, joining the regiment in late August, 1861. The "Dixie Rebels" were enrolled for active service at Edenton, Chowan County on April 29, 1861 under Capt. James K. Marshall, and was assigned to the 1st Regt. N.C. Infantry as Company M on June 20, 1861, joining the regiment during the first week of August, 1861. Manarin and Jordan, *N.C. Troops*, 3:57 and 61-62.

Remember me to all the neighbors, say to Mr. Wiggins that this is said to be one of the very best points for fishing on this part of the coast; and that if he will come down, I have no doubt but that he will enjoy himself finely. I can take pretty good care of him while here. If he comes, he had better get my sock line from my wife; that will be the very thing for pulling the sheephead, spats, &c. I think the line can be found in one of the bureau drawers at home. Can't you bring him down? I should be glad to see you both; and Mr. Moore also, I guess we can find some widow for him to console.

Remember me kindly to every member of your family.

My love to my wife and children. I shall be pleased to hear from you soon.

Very truly yours
F. M. Parker

Camp 1st Regt. N.C.V.
York Town
August 20/61

My dear Sir

Your kind letter was received yesterday. I thank you for it. I am much obliged to you for forwarding the box for me. It is very gratifying to know that we have such friends at home. I hope the day will come when we can all meet again in social intercourse. But so far as I am concerned, I expect to remain in the service as long as this war continues, be it long or short. My idea is to fight these Yankees rascals until we get to boot them thoroughly so as to cut off and prevent all intercourse and communication with them. So long as we trade with them, we will be their slaves.

I wrote Mr. Dunn some time since telling him that as we had whisky rations now, we would not need his barrell [sic] of brandy, which he do kindly offered us; but unfortunately they have given us the whisky but once. So if you should see Mr. Dunn soon, you can say to him that the brandy will be very acceptable. My kindest regards to old man Jo. Say to him that I hope to get back to have more of our old fox hunts, so he may get his dogs in apple pie order by next winter.

I do not feel very well this morning, therefore you will please excuse this poor letter. Mr. Page can give you all the news. Remember me to all my friends about Enfield.

Very truly yours,
F. M. Parker

"I think there is material in it out of which
a first rate Regt. can be made."
— F. M. Parker

PART TWO

August, 1861 - November 1861
Ship Point, Virginia - Smithville, North Carolina

Ship Point, Va.
August 26, 1861
Head Quarters 1st N.C. Regt.

My dear wife

You will see from the direction above, that our encampment has been removed from York Town. The Regt. continued so sickly there that the authorities thought it best to change our locality. We are now encamped on a point of Pocosin [sic] river, which empties directly into the Chesapeak [sic] bay; we have a fine breeze nearly all the time, which makes it very pleasant; there is one feature about our encampment which I admire very much, and that is we are in the midst of an old pine field, which looks very natural. After being shut up within the bounds of York Town for so long a time, the freshness of the country and the woods is really delightful. The scenery around here too is picturesque; the river winds around the point in three directions and the little sail boats may be seen going to and fro constantly; the regular mail boats (Steamers) can be seen every morning, about sunrise, going from Baltimore to Old Point, and returning the same day; these pass within about eight miles of us. Not sufficiently near, for us to get a shoot [sic] at them. The greatest objection to this place, is the water, there is a sufficiency of it, but it is rather salty. I do not suppose we will have an attack at this place; our move hither is purely a sanitary one. It would not surprise me, if we are not kept here until our term of service expires. I am tired of being moved about. We are distant from York Town only about ten ~~days~~ miles. That will continue to be our post office, so direct your letters as heretofore. And be as good and kind as you have heretofore been, and direct them quite often. I hope you will not feel touched at all by any remarks which I may have made in my last letter relating to the brandy, etc.; as I stated to you then, the Physicians have

81

recommended a moderate use of spirits in this climate; chills are very prevalent here, the Drs. think that the brandy will act as a good "antipragmatic." As you seem so serious about the matter, I will simply say that I hope you have too much confidence in my principles as a gentleman to say nothing of higher and purer principles, to think for a moment that I would be guilty of any excess whatever. No, my dear wife, the love and respect which I bear to you and my children will keep me from acting wrong whenever I know it. So do not give yourself any uneasiness on the brandy question. It has amused me somewhat.

Your interesting description of your matters about home, particularly of the children, was very pleasant to me; every thing relating to home, and those at home receives the greater part of my attention by far. Altho' I am surrounded by war and all its excitements, yet there is a green spot to which my heart turns gladly, and that place is home, sweet home. As to sending Mary to school at Mr. Dunn's, you can use your own pleasure and judgment in the matter. I shall feel perfectly satisfied with any thing you may do in the premises. I think myself that she should be learning now regularly. So far as the family is concerned, I know of none where I would sooner trust a child of mine. Mr. Dunn is a perfect gentleman in every sense of the word. I know him. What has become of Miss Mat. Smith and her school? In your letter you say that Mr. Page is at home and you wish to know why I can not go. Mr. Page is in bad health, and was granted a furlough in order to improve his health. Now the question is had you rather for me to keep my health and remain at my post; or become sick, and have a leave of absence. I know you will say keep well and remain where you are. Mr. Page is a good man and one of my particular friends. I hope you will see him while he is at home. I think it will be the 13th of Nov. before our Regt. will be disbanded. If you have a narrow matrass [sic], such as you had made in Tarboro for your lounges, I should be glad to get it; together with a common bedquilt; nothing fine here will do at all. The mattress I shall need when the weather turns cooler, to place on my cot; that will make me a very good bed. I do not need a blanket. I would like to have my thick black frock coat also; this can be bundled up with the mattress and quilt.

Your Father and Jimmy have not come yet; at any rate not to our camp; they may be in the camp of the 5th Regt.; if so I hope they will extend their visit to ours also. On the return of the 5th from the Peninsula, some time since Fred spent several days with me; he was sick with chills; I nursed him up as well as I knew how. It was a pleasure for me to do so, both on his own account, and because that he was the brother of my wife. I saw him a few days before I left York Town for this place, he was looking much improved in health.

As regards the conversation which was reported to you as having taken place at Enfield, all I have to say is that a certain person there, may judge others by himself; particularly as going to war is concerned. Do not let any such trifles trouble you. I mean the conversation.

Capt. Bell has resigned his office; who will be elected to fill his place, I do not know. I learn that Lieut. Whitaker is making great efforts to secure his election. An election has not been ordered yet, but I suppose [it] will be in a few days. Capt. Bell speaks of coming on home soon. If you can get the matrass [sic] and quilt ready and send them to Enfield I think he will bring them to me. The things had better be put in a box.

It is now nearly twelve o'clock. I will close for the night and will finish in the morning. So good night, my dear wife, pleasant dreams to you.

August 27th: In thinking over things which I shall need; one or two pairs of thick drawers will soon be very acceptable to me; please send them with the other things. I am much obliged to you for sending my boots and pants. I received them through Mrs. Powell. Remember me to all the neighbors; say to Mrs. Arrington that Joe is very well and getting on very well; Joe has greatly improved since he left home; he is a favourite in the company. When you see Mr. Dunn, say to him that Mr. Westray[1] is in good health and getting on very well. I shall never forget Mr. Dunn's kindness. You are fortunate in having such a good neighbor; I wish he was nearer you. Tell Mr. Moore if he will come to see us, I will stop that watering of the mouth, with some good oysters. My regards to Mrs. Wallace and Ben, and to the

---

1. George Westry was 24-years-old when he enlisted as a private in the Enfield Blues on April 19, 1861, in Halifax County. He was discharged November 12-13, 1861. Manarin and Jordan, *N.C. Troops*, 3:50. Westry later enlisted in Company A, 47th Regt. N.C.T.

negroes. Kiss all the children for me; tell them to be good children. Good bye my dear wife; take care of yourself and the children.

Very affectionately your husband
F. M. Parker

———◆◆◆———

Francis Marion Parker was elected captain of the Enfield Blues on September 1, 1861.[2] Parker defeated 1st Lt. Montgomery Whitaker in the election for the position. Whitaker wrote a letter a few days later in which he admitted that a good man had won: "If I am not popular I can't help it . . . the duties of Capt. are very arduous, it is very hard to give satisfaction to so many men. Frank makes a good officer, as good as any in the regiment."[3] Montgomery Whitaker's relative, Corporal George Whitaker Wills, was more biting in his commentary on the company officer elections in a letter to his sister, Lucy: "I think it a shame for me to do, as our company has done, they elected, Lieut. Parker, who was 2nd Lieut., Capt. Over cousin Gomery, who was 1st Lieut, and [Theodore Lucian] Corbitt, who was orderly Sergeant, over (illeg) Cary who was 3rd Lieut. This was ridiculous, it was foul play all the way, done by two or three in the company, who wanted promotion themselves."[4]

———◆◆◆———

Camp 1st Regt. N.C.V.
Ship Point
Sept 1st/61

Mrs. S. J. Parker
Sycamore Alley
N.C.

---

2. Manarin and Jordan, *N.C. Troops*, 3:46; Krick, *Lee's Colonels*, p. 298.
3. Montgomery Whitaker to brother Ferdinand, September 17, 1861, (correspondence in the Southern Historical Collection) quoted in Wellman, *Rebel Boast*, p. 270, n. 20.
4. Letter from George W. Wills to Lucy from Camp Fayetteville dated Sept. 10, 1861. George W. Wills Letters, #2269z, Southern Historical Collection.

My dear Wife

Your Father is now lying on my cot enjoying a fine nap, at least if one may judge from his snoring; and it being Sunday we are a little idle, so I have concluded to fill up the time, by writing to you. Not that I would not take time to write you my dear Wife, not at all; I would suffer other duties to go unfinished in order to have the pleasure of writing to you. But I wish to have a letter ready for Jimmy to take to you, whenever your Father is ready to leave.

I received the box you sent by Ben Arrington, and thank you much for it. The thick drawers I shall soon need, the socks were also very acceptable; the butter is very nice and good, the pickles are excellent, so pronounced by Nathan Mathewson to whom I gave a few to day; and the strawberries are just as nice as those you sent sometime since. I think I like the spiced tomatoes best of all, and the catsup also; this I suppose comes from my fondness for tomatoes generally. In your letter you ask if I do need more shirts; I do not now; I have two brown linen ones, and the two you sent me some time since, besides one or two white ones; this will be sufficient to last me for the balance of my time. I had the misfortune to lose three white ones while at the upper Hospital; now do'nt [sic] scold me for this; it was the fault of the washerwoman. I shall not need any more socks either, I have a plenty, should probably lose some of them, if I had more; it is a difficult matter to take care of clothes here, so I want as few as I can get on with. I sent by one of our men, a few days since, my linen pants and coat and a pair of old pants, the same which I wore in the battle of Bethel; and I send by Ben Arrington a vest and pair of drawers, both tolerably dirty; I concluded you could have them washed a little cheaper than I could.

Our Regt. is somewhat excited just now, in consequence of the reception of the news from N.C.. Butler is in command of the expedition which has invaded our State, and we are anxious to meet him again; particularly on our own soil. With the same kind Providence favouring us, we can show him another Bethel. You recollect he was in command at old Fortress Monroe at the time of the battle, but was too cowardly to be on the field of action. All the company officers of the Regt. have petitioned the President to send our Regt. to Hatteras to repel the invader; I

Dr. James Jones Philips
Colonel Parker's father-in-law
(in his 30's)

hope he will grant the request. Maj. Lane has carried the petition on to Richmond.

At the time Butler's expedition sailed from Old Point, it was thought that this place was the object of attack; we were kept busy here for some time, entrenching ourselves; in fact we have not finished yet, but will in a few days. The authorities intend that the 1st N.C. shall know something of the use of the spade and shovel. There is no doubt but that we have done more work, performed more labour, than any other Regt. in the field.

I am glad to hear through your Father of the fine crops in our State, and particularly of my own crop; he informs me that he learns it is very good. I feel very thankful for this.

By the way, you wish to know what your Father wrote me of Ben Hulm's management &c. He only said that he thought Ben had not used sufficient energy and perseverance in the cultivation of the crop. He said that Ben wanted it distinctly understood that he had the best crop in the neighbourhood. I suppose your Father thought that that might be true, and yet not be any thing extra.

You give me such interesting accounts of of [sic] the children, particularly of little Hattie, that I am more anxious to see you and them. One thing troubles me very much; I have lost the favour of her little face and can not recall it. I can come very near it, but can not fix it certainly in my mind.

My love to Bella, say to her that I received her note and also the little box by your Father and was very thankful for both.

Remember me to Mrs. Wallace, Ben and the negroes, and to all the neighbors. Kiss the children for me. I will write you again by your Father.

Good bye my dear wife. God bless and protect you and yours.

Very affectionately your husband

F. M. Parker

———————————◆●◆————————————

Ship Point
Sept. 4th, 1861
Camp 1st Regt. N.C.V.

My dear Wife

I wrote you by Ben Arrington only the day before your Father left here, and Jimmy promised me that he would go and see you as soon as he reached home, and now I am writing you again so you will be full of news from this point; if I may judge you by my own feelings, you can not hear too often, no not if it was every day.

Capt. Bell is here on a visit; his health not having improved sufficiently for him to rejoin his company. He goes home to day or tomorrow, so I will write by him. In the first place I have a little business I wish you to attend to for me. I wish you to know of Carter Arrington if he has hides enough of my own in tan to make shoes for all the negroes; or how many hides have I. And will you please ask Ben to look in the gin house, and see how much rope and bagging I have; tell him not to loan out any at all. If you have not sent the mattress, &c. to Enfield, will you please do so immediately, as there are one or two of our men now at home, who will return here shortly. Our Regt. is much excited in consequence of the news from Hatteras. Maj. Lane is now in Richmond with a petition from the officers of the Regt. asking President Davis to send us immediately to Hatteras. We would like to meet Butler in our own State, on our own soil; I think we can show him another Bethel. I am satisfied of one thing, viz., that the Yankees will find N.C. quite a different country from this part of Va.; here we have had to watch Virginians as well as Yankees.

I am compelled to draw my letter to a close, as Capt. Bell is anxious to start off.

Remember me to all; kiss the children for me. I will write again soon. Good bye my dear Wife; May the Lord bless and protect you and yours.

Very affectionately your husband
F. M. Parker

Camp Fayetteville
Sept 6th, 1861

My dear Wife

You will think that we belong to the wandering tribes. Genrl. Magruder has not suffered us to remain long in one place. We were getting to be well fixed, and well pleased with our last encampment at Ship Point, when yesterday about 12 o'clock an order came for us to be ready to move in about two hours; so 2 o'clock found us formed and ready to march; these sudden marches cause us to lose a great many things, little conveniences which we had arranged for our comfort. Some of the boys had sent a good many clothes out to be washed, and probably will never get them. I believe they disliked to go away from the nice oysters and fine fish which were so abundant there. I have never seen such a quantity of either. I have often wished that you had some of them. We are now encamped in the woods; have plenty of good water, which is something we have not had, since we have been in Va. I can not suppose that we will remain here long. No doubt but that some important move is at hand; what, I can not say. This moving about so much has taught me one thing, that is that volunteers have a great deal too much baggage. If you have not sent the matrass [sic], you will please not send it at all; for I should have to leave it somewhere. I would like to get that thick coat. If you will send that to Enfield, I may get it soon. I have to leave some of the nice things, pickles &c. you sent me at Ship Point, and I doubt if I [will] get them. So it will be useless to send any thing else of that kind. If I need more meat I can write for it.

I understand that the militia are to be ordered out in our state; if Ben Hulm should be drafted or should wish to volunteer, I wish you to make some arrangement to keep him. Ask Mr. Dunn if he can find some one to take Ben's place in the militia, and let Ben remain where he is. I am willing to help pay for a man to do so. As Ben has been there all the year, I would prefer his remaining. If he is forced to go, and no other arrangement can be made, ask your Father to let Jimmy stay with you; he could attend to putting away the cotton and be good company and protection for you. I dislike to take Jimmy from his school; but I dislike more for you to be left alone. Write me immediately, and answer my last letter, as well as this one. May be Mr. Dunn could prevail on Mr. Partin to give your business at least a partial attention in case Ben leaves. Now if our Jimmy was only large enough to take care of you, I should feel independent.

Mr. Owen is here on a visit to his son; he is looking very well. He got to Ship Point while we were in the field, ready to march. I saw him, went up to him, spoke to him and enquired of his family and friends about Tarboro. I thought he was very formal and over-polite; but after talking with him about 3 minutes he looked at me steadily and exclaimed, Frank! My whiskers disguised me. He seemed glad to see me, has called around to my tent this morning.

If Bella is with you, say to her that I received the little bundle from Mr. Waddell's by Mr. Owen.

My love to Bella, tell her to stay a long time with you. Remember me to Mrs. Wallace and Ben; tell Ben I learn he has a first rate crop, and am glad to hear it. I hope he will beat the neighborhood, particularly in picking out cotton.

Remember me to all the neighbors; tell Mrs. Arrington that Jo is very well. Tell all the negroes I am well. Kiss the children for me.

Very affectionately your husband,
F. M. Parker

Camp Fayetteville, Va.
Sept. 27th, 1861

Mrs. S. J. Parker
Sycamore Alley
N.C.

My dear Wife

Your kind letter by Mr. Bennett reached me, also the one by Sergt. Whitaker.[5] I am very thankful to you for both. I am always glad to hear from you, and to hear that you and the children are well; after reading one of your letters I always feel better, feel more contented, better satisfied with my present lot. Your letter by Mr. Bennett gave me some uneasiness; you seemed to be quite low spirited; I think you must have seen either Mr. Nicholson or Mrs. Arrington, or both. Now cheer up my own dear wife; what if we do have a fight before our Regt. is ordered home, an open field fight at that; do you not know that my head is just as safe on the battle field as it is on my farm. We are always in the hands of a just and righteous Being who

---

5. Theodore Lucian Whitaker was 28-years-old when he enlisted as sergeant on April 19, 1861, in the Enfield Blues. He was appointed 2nd lieutenant to rank from October 22, 1861, and was mustered out November 12-13, 1861. Whitaker later enlisted in Company D, 24th Regt. N.C.T. (14th Regt. N.C. Volunteers). Manarin and Jordan, *N.C. Troops*, 3:46.

will take care of us in his own good way. So do not give way to any evil forebodings. You have stood up bravely so far, hold out a little longer, and if it be the Lord's will we will soon meet again. I do want that time to come very much. Sometimes I become impatient, and feel as tho I can not wait for the time to come; this is not exactly proper, but then human nature can not be led right always. So far as a fight on this Peninsula is concerned, I only gave that as my opinion which of course is not worth much; for in all military matters, only the general officers know what is going on. I based my opinion, expressed to your Father on the movements of troops here. I have not found but one or two men to agree with me in this opinion; so you see there is a strong possibility of my being mistaken. You wish to know if I intend volunteering again. I answer that if my country needs my services, if there is a necessity for me to go, I shall go. You would not have me to remain at home while our fair country, our beloved South is invaded by the banded foe. No, I know you too well, to suppose such a thing for a moment. I think the public should frown, should spit upon those cowards who are now remaining quietly at home, while their own State is invaded. I will also say that at present, I do not consider it necessary for troops to be raised for the winter campaign, as late as we will go home. So will have the winter to spend at home at any rate. Of course this is predicated upon the supposition that the enemy will not carry on operations during the winter. But do'nt [*sic*] let us talk so much about wars, campaigns, &c. Do let me get home, and rest a little first. Oh! how I do want to see you and the children. I have received my mattress and coat, and am using both; they are quite comfortable. I have not received the bacon yet, but will tomorrow probably. I thank you very much for sending it. I hope you have not deprived yourself in so doing.

The butter you sent is very nice, and I thank you for it. About sowing wheat, tell Ben I would like to have wheat sowed, but can not advise him where to sow it; if he can select some good ground on which to sow it, do so. I will see Mr. Manning about the seed wheat, he is here now, to see his son who is sick.[6] I want to sow some 8 or 10 bushels.

---

6. John Manning was a 20-year-old resident of Chowan County when he enlisted in the Enfield Blues at Yorktown, Virginia, on June 29, 1861.

Now you don't know how I prized Mary's letter; it is really a very good one, for a little girl. I shall keep it as long as I live. I have written a little one to Jimmy, and answered Mary's. I have not seen Fred for some time, tho I understand he is improving. His Regt. will soon be quartered near us; I am glad of it. It is a nice ~~place~~ country. Fred has been imposed upon by his other officers; they have been shirking their duty, and leaving it for him.

I shall write you a short letter this morning; I have an opportunity of sending it. I will write again soon. Remember me to all friends. Kiss the children for me. Take care of yourself and them; may the Lord bless and keep you, is the prayer of your affectionate husband

F. M. Parker

Camp Fayetteville Va.
Sept. 29th 1861

Mrs. S. J. Parker
Sycamore Alley
N.C.
Favor of Rev. Mr. Bennett

My dear Wife

I wrote you a few days since by Mr. Taylor; Mr. Bennett leaves in the morning, and I can not let the opportunity pass without writing you again. Writing is the nearest approach I can make to you; it draws me nearer to you and my little children than anything else I can do, nearer probably than thoughts, they are confined to myself, the writing comes from me and goes to you. This is Sunday; Mr. Bennett has preached for us and gave us a good, plain, practical sermon; it was a very earnest one; the old gentleman seems to have his whole heart in this war; he says that if he was not so old, he would shoulder his musket and be found in the ranks, even now if we should be attacked while he is here, he declares he will stand with us. He talks very encouragingly about the result of the war. I do'nt [sic] know that I have ever given you an idea of our life here. Here it is.

Manning was mustered out November 12-13, 1861. Manarin and Jordan, *N.C. Troops*, 3:49.

At present we rise a little after sunrise, attend roll call, after that breakfast; at eight o'clock the working parties go out to throw up breast works; at ten the companies drill for an hour; dinner at twelve; battalion drill at 4 o'clock for one hour; dress parade at 5, which closes the operations of the day. The working parties remain out all day, taking their dinners with them; they return in time to be present at dress parade. This is more a matter of form than any thing else; all orders, either from Genrl. Head Quarters or from the Regimental Head Quarters are read out on dress parade. It is where we hear every thing relating to the Regt. It is then that we have the band out in full, it plays up and down in front of the Regt. A camp life is above all others, most trying to volunteers; they need active service constantly; fighting is the easiest part of our work. There is now a very heavy force on this Peninsula, about 22,000 men. I am afraid there will be suffering among the men this winter. How much better it would be, for them all to be at home.

I have just received a letter from Sister Mary and one from Bella, they were all well. I have learned to day that Fred is quite sick. I shall go in the morning to see him, and shall remain with him a day or two. I hope to find him much better than he is represented to be. I learn he is some distance from York Town, at a private house. I will write you from there tomorrow so that you may know his situation. I am sorry to say to you that Genrl. Hill has left us; he has been ordered back to N. Carolina, I suppose to take charge of the coast defense, or a part of it; you may depend upon it, that if he had been at Hatteras, things would have not resulted as they did. There was treachery there. In your last letter you say that Ben Hulm has had application for employment for another year. I do not see what better I can do, than employ him myself; so therefore please say to him that I will keep him at a fair price, which can be fixed upon when I get home. I have seen Mr. Manning about the wheat; he has none to sell, but says that Mr. Jas. Williams has some very good. If Mr. Nicholson has any to spare, his is also a good kind. I wish to sow some eight or ten bushels. If you have not already ordered rope, you will please not do so. I think I shall use hoop iron. However, I will let you know more about it soon. Remember me to all the neighbors, to Mrs. Wallace, Ben and the negroes; kiss the children for me; tell Mary I feel proud, every time I look at her letter. What did Jimmy think of his. I think he should pick out a heap of cotton for it.

Write soon and let me know how you all are. May the Lord bless and keep you all, is the prayer of your affectionate husband,

F. M. Parker

———————◆◆◆———————

Francis Marion Parker was elected colonel of the 30th Regt. N.C.T. on October 7, 1861, and resigned the next day from his captaincy of the Enfield Blues in order to assume his new command.[7] The 30th Regt. N.C.T. was organized on September 26, 1861, at Camp Mangum near Raleigh. John Bell of Granville County was elected colonel but declined to accept.[8] The 30th was composed of the following companies:[9]

Company A "Sampson Rangers" (Sampson County)
Company B "Nat Macon Guards" (Warren County)
Company C "Brunswick Double Quicks" (Brunswick County)
Company D "Neuse River Guards" (Wake/Granville Counties)
Company E "Duplin Turpentine Boys" (Duplin County)
Company F "Sparta Band" (Edgecombe County)
Company G "Granville Rangers" (Granville County)
Company H "Moore County Rifles" (Moore County)
Company I "Ladies' Guards" (Nash County)
Company K "Mecklenburg Beauregards" (Mecklenburg County)

Following its organization, the 30th Regt. was ordered to report to Brig. Gen. Joseph R. Anderson, Commander of the District of Cape Fear and arrived in Wilmington on September 29, 1861. The arrival of the 30th, about 1,000 strong, at Wilmington, was recalled by John Wesley Bone, who served throughout the war to Appomattox in Company I and who wrote a memoir of his experiences forty years later:[10]

---

7. Manarin and Jordan, *N.C. Troops*, 3:46, and 8:321; Krick, *Lee's Colonels*, p. 298.
8. Historical Memoranda in Compiled Service Records of the 30th Regt. N.C.T. published in *Supp. OR*, pt. 2, vol. 49, pp. 48-56.
9. Manarin and Jordan, *N.C. Troops*, 8:314-423; Mast, "Order of Battle," p. 34.
10. John Wesley Bone (1842-1936) enlisted as private on September 19, 186, in Nash County in what was to become Company I, 30th Regt.

[W]e were pulled into Wilmington, N. C., and got off under the big car shed at the bank of the Cape Fear river. . . . [M]any at this time were greatly under the influence of whiskey and were where they could get plenty more. . . . We were sleepy, tired and hungry, and were off to war. We wanted to fight and the enemy not being very near, some did fight one another. On this present occasion many were put under guard and were guarded by the sober ones. The patience of good and moral officers were tested at this point. I very well remember hearing a very good and moral officer used oaths on this occasion. The men got quiet after awhile and we remained there all day and were given quarters that night in a long building. The next morning we marched out near Oakdale Cemetery, and cleaned up a camp ground and stretched out tents.[11]

The regiment was mustered into Confederate service for twelve months on October 8, 1861, and the next day it was transported by steamboat to Smithville (now Southport) near the mouth of the Cape Fear River and encamped for training and coastal defense near the town.[12]

N.C.T.. He was wounded at the battle of Malvern Hill, Virginia, on July 1, 1862. Returning to duty almost immediately, he fell ill during the advance of his regiment toward Maryland in August, 1862, and apparently missed the battle of Sharpsburg. After participating in the battles of Fredericksburg and Chancellorsville, Bone fell ill with "brain fever" and missed Gettysburg and Bristoe Station. He was present at the battle of Kellyville, Virginia, on November 7, 1863. After being hospitalized for pneumonia at Charlottesville during the winter of 1863-4, Bone was severely wounded on May 12, 1864, at Spotsylvania Court House by being shot through the body. After recuperating at home, Bone rejoined the 30th in the Shenandoah Valley in early October, 1864, in time to take part in the battle of Cedar Creek. He surrendered at Appomattox. Manarin and Jordan, *N.C.Troops*, 8:403; J. W. Bone, "Record of J.W. Bone's Service in the Civil War. Co. I 30th Reg. N.C." typewritten manuscript stated to have been written in 1904 placed in Stanly County Public Library by J. W. Bone's great-granddaughter, Shirley Beal.
11. Bone, "Service," pp. 1-2.
12. Manarin and Jordan, *N.C. Troops*, 8:314. Record of events, Company E, 30th Regt. N.C.T.

My dear Wife

I have been looking and looking for a letter from you, but no letter has come. Here I am surrounded by strangers, and you not writing to me. I would prize a letter very highly just now, from you.

You may wish to know how I am situated here; well, the Regt. is encamped just back of Smithville, on the same ground which Col. Paine's Regt. occupied before leaving for the Mexican war; it is a pleasant encampment, high and dry, and very sandy. We use water from Smithville, have a plenty of it. Now something of the Regt. I think there is material in it out of which a first rate Regt. can be made. The officers, by a very large majority, are <u>very</u> <u>clever</u> <u>gentlemen</u>; men of some means, and standing. Two of the Captains, are nearly fifty years of age;[13] I assure you it makes me feel a little awkward to be commanding such old men. If they were more on the rough and tumble order, were not such nice old gentlemen, I should feel a little easier. I think I shall have a very pleasant time with them. As for the men of the Regt. I can not speak, not having formed the acquaintance of many of them.

Smithville is immediately on the Cape Fear; here a great number of the families of Wilmington spend their summers, having private residences here. The place is considered healthy, I suppose because it possesses the advantages of a fine sea breeze. All night long, the roar of the old ocean may be heard; it sounds grand. There are Barracks here, built by the United States government, capable of quartering a Regt. Col. Iverson's, the 10th Regt., is now occupying these. They are very pleasant quarters. I should have been pleased to have had them myself. About two and one half miles from Smithville, or Fort Johnson, is Fort Caswell, built for the purpose of commanding the inlet to the Cape Fear. I understand it is a strong Fort, well manned.

---

13. Capt. Joseph Green of the "Brunswick Double Quicks," Company C of the 30th Regt. N.C.T. was a 46-year-old Brunswick County resident when he was elected to his office on July 18,1861. Manarin and Jordan, *N.C.Troops*, 8:342. Capt. Robert P. Taylor of the "Granville Rangers," Company G of the 30th, was a 49-year-old resident of Granville County when he was elected on September 7, 1861. Manarin and Jordan, *N.C.Troops*, 8:381. Both Green and Taylor were defeated for reelection when the regiment was reorganized on May 1, 1862.

Between this Fort and Wilmington, there are several other batteries, intended to prevent the passage of Abe's fleet up the river. Other batteries are in the course of construction so that if he delays his visit a few weeks, our people will be better prepared for him. It certainly is a Providential interference, that the Yankees have not taken Wilmington long since; it could easily have been done. Providence favors us in many ways, we know not of. The evening I came down from Wilmington, there were five of Lincoln's vessels lying out the bar, in view. I understand their number varies; sometimes more, then less. There was some excitement here last night; about twelve o'clock, several heavy guns were heard seaward; some thought it was the signal for an attack on this place, but it proved to be the blockade firing into a small vessel which was attempting to run in with a load of fish, and succeeded too. So nobody hurt, so far.

I hope that Offa has gotten clear of the chills long since, and that you are all well. You do'nt [*sic*] know what a hard matter it was for me to part with you the other day. I want to see you and the children now. My love to you and them. Remember me kindly to all at your Father's. Tell Fred to take care of himself and not return to camp too soon. Write me often. Direct to Fort Johnson.

Your affectionate husband
F. M. Parker

————————◆◆◆————————

Camp Walker
Oct. 29, 1861

My dear Wife

Here it is, another mail and no letter from you; have you forgotten me altogether? When I was a little Lieut. you were kind enough to write me often, sometimes every week, but now you do not write at all. I suppose you think I have enough to engage my attention, without any letters. Well, I have a good deal to do, but plenty of time to read a letter from my dear Wife, if I could get one. No one writes me. I mean no particular friend; occasionally I get a communication from the Adjt. Genrl., sometimes from Genrl. Anderson,[14] commanding this military

---

14. The able Brig. Gen. Joseph Reid Anderson, who would be recalled in 1862 to duties of much greater value to the Confederacy managing his

district. Their letters relate only to business. I want a good friendly, chatty, loving letter from you; one which will make me cry when I read it; I can not go to see you, do write and let me hear from you. If you do not, I will send some man from the Regt. to look after you, and see what is the matter with you.

I am getting on tolerably well; everything is raw, and in somewhat confusion. I committed a great mistake in not joining the Regt. sooner after I was elected; they have gone on so long without any directing head, that they think they are nearly free. I hope I am getting matters straight and if the Yankees will let me alone a little longer, I may have a Regt. which will be able to do good service. The Lieut. Col.[15] is a very clever man, but a very silent one; I think he will make a first rate officer; unfortunately he has been sick ever since I have been here. The Maj.[16] is absent at home so you see I have had my hands full; may be it is better for me.

We have had some quite cool weather here; I think you can not send those flannel shirts and drawers too soon. You can direct them to Wilmington to the care of Dr. Drane, and I think I shall get them. It is very probable that some one about Enfield, will be coming down this way soon. If not, send them by express, paying the freight before hand. Henry Johnston will attend to the matter for you. If Ben has not sowed wheat yet, insist on his doing so immediately. It is time it was in the ground. You must have biscuit for the babies, cotton or no cotton.

Well, what has become of Fred? I understand he has been in Tarboro. I am glad he is able to get there. I have no doubt his friends are glad to see him. I hope he will not return to camp too

Tredegar Iron Works in Richmond, was at this time at Wilmington in command of the District of Cape Fear. Warner, *Generals in Gray*, p. 8.

15. Walter F. Draughan, a Sampson County native, was a 40-year-old Cumberland County resident when he enlisted. He was appointed lieutenant colonel on September 26, 1861, and was defeated for reelection when the 30th was reorganized on May 1, 1862. Krick, *Lee's Colonels*, p. 123; Manarin and Jordan, *N.C.Troops*, 8:321.

16. James T. Kell was a 26-year-old Mecklenburg County resident when he was elected captain of what was shortly to become Company K of the 30th on September 13, 1861. Kell was elected major of the 30th on September 26, 1861. He was wounded by a piece of shell at Gaines' Mill, Virginia, on June 27, 1862, and resigned by reason of disability from wounds on August 18, 1863. Manarin and Jordan, *N.C.Troops*, 8:321 and 412. Krick, *Lee's Colonels*, p. 220.

soon. He will be running a great risk to do so. I think he had better remain at home all the winter.

I want you to get some one to live with you; probably Mary Hulm would suit you very well. I think I would try her, say for one or two months at a time.

Remember me to all friends, particularly to Mr. Dunn and family; go to see them. Remember me also to Ben and the negroes, I wanted to see them before I left home but was unable to do so. My love to the children; say to Mary I think it is almost time for another letter from her.

Good bye my dear wife, may the Lord bless and keep you and yours, is the prayer of your

affectionate husband
F. M. Parker

———————————◆◆◆———————————

Camp Walker
Nov. 1st, 1861

My dear Wife

To day I received the last letter, which you wrote me while I was at York Town; it has made me feel so pleasant, that I have concluded to thank you for it, and see if I could not thereby draw a few more lines from you.

Really I can not see why you have not written me. There is a daily mail to Wilmington, and also from Wilmington to this place. Do if you please write me, even if it is only five lines.

I suppose you have heard of the excitement in this part of the State. The people of Wilmington have been very much excited, and I suppose are so yet, in consequence of the sailing of Lincoln's fleet from Hampton Roads. The militia of this county have been called out, so have the militia of several other counties bordering on the coast. I have never thought that the fleet was intended for this part of the coast; they may land about Hatteras, and endeavor to march across the country, so as to attack Norfolk in the rear, or they may be going further South. I suppose every post on the Southern coast now thinks that that is the destination of the fleet. It is well enough to be prepared to meet the vandal rascals whenever they do come. But I do not think there is much chance for a fight here. No laurels for the 30th to win, unless they order us to another field.

Where is my sword, the one I had when I was Lt. Col of the militia? If I mistake not, Fred had it at your Father's. Will you please get it, and send it to me; there is a red leather belt with it, send that also. If the belt is not with the sword, nor at home, it is at Enfield, in Bell & Maner's store. Send the sword and belt, as early as you can conveniently. I want it for my Adjutant.

The little chest, with contents of which I spoke in a previous letter, I hope you will send as soon as you can, also the flannel leggings, and coat. Any thing sent to the care of Dr. Thomas, Wilmington, I shall receive.

Does your father speak of attending the meeting of the stockholders of the R. Road in Wilmington? If he does, he must certainly come down and see me. The Steamer makes the trip daily, so he can very conveniently come.

I must thank you for the letter I spoke of in the beginning of this; it was such a good one, so much good advice. I hope and pray I may be able to carry it out. I know I should be thankful for the many and great privileges and blessings which I have received. It is raining hard tonight but I have a most excellent tent, the best I ever saw; but the poor sentinels on duty, they will fare badly; but they must stand to their post.

Kiss the children for me; good bye my dear wife; God bless you and them is the prayer of your

Affectionate husband,
F. M. Parker

Camp Walker
Nov. 5 1861

My dear Wife

I have received my chest and the contents, for all of which I am very thankful to you. But most of all do I prize the letters from you. I also received a letter by the mail yesterday. It seems that all the good luck is coming on at once. I have waited very patiently for a letter ever since I have been here, but in vain; and to console myself, I have written several to you, which I hope you have received. I hope you do not suppose that I could have let so long a time pass without writing to you. The reading of one of your letters makes me feel good; I feel in a better spirit; they contain so much good advice which I hope and pray I may be able to follow. I like our Lt. Col. Draughan for one thing, he seems to love his wife so well; he is like myself, whenever he receives a letter from home, he has to read it over more than once, and is apt to become a little moist about the eyes also. We got along very well together; for some time we were in the same tent, until I received my own, from the Quarter Master. The Col. is a very clever gentleman; very polite, and a great stickler for etiquette; he likes every thing done in proper form. The Maj. I take to be a very nice man, tho' I have seen but a little of him, he having left for home the day after I reached camp, and is at home sick. There is a good deal of sickness in the Regt. now, mostly from mumps and measles, with a little typhoid fever. There have been a few deaths. You wish to know something of the drilling of the Regt. I have not drilled them in Battalion drill yet, only in squads of eight or ten and in companies. I shall soon however put the Regt. together. We have Dress Parade every evening, which is more a matter of form than any thing else. The companies have all been lined off and assigned their positions in line, so that in case of an attack the Regt. could be formed quickly.

My horse has not come yet, but I look for him this week. Dr. Joyner[17] has not made his appearance yet either. I expect him to day.

I am very sorry to hear of the death of Lucy Johnston. Her Father's family seem to have suffered affliction truly. With regard to getting some one to live with you, I would prefer you to do so, if you can suit yourself. If you can find a good, industrious woman I would hire her. I expect you have heard all sorts of rumors of the Yankees being off our coast; do not be alarmed. I do not think they will attempt to land; if they do, we will whip them back, or give them a right to a small part of our soil, say 2 by 6 feet. We must succeed in the end; our cause is just and justice will be meted out. We have only to put our trust in a Higher power, and use every means within our reach. I wrote you the other day about my old sword, the silver plated

---

17. The 1860 U.S. Census of Halifax County enumerated Henry Joyner as a 40-year-old physician who owned 28 slaves and 7 slave houses. Henry Joyner, a 36-year-old resident of Halifax County, was appointed Surgeon of the 30th Regt. on or about October 21, 1862. He resigned May 1, 1862, and served in the N.C. House of Commons, 1862-65. Manarin and Jordan, *N.C. Troops*, 8:322.

one; if you meet with an opportunity, I wish you would send it to me. I want it for my Adjutant who is a very clever little fellow, was with us in Virginia, was also one of Genrl. Hill's cadets. His name is Carter.[18] If you meet with no opportunity sooner, you can send it when the stockholders meet, which is on the 20th of the month. Tho if you can send the sword and belt to Henry Johnston at Enfield, he will send it to me by one of the Conductors on the R. Road, Mr. Browning.

Tell Mary I think it is time she was writing to me again. Give my love to the children, tell them to be good children. Remember me to all friends, to Ben and the negroes. I suppose Ben has his wheat up by this time. It is fine weather for picking out cotton. Good bye my dear wife, God bless you.

Your affectionate husband
F. M. Parker

On November 6, 1861, the 30th moved from Smithville across the Cape Fear River to Camp Wyatt on Federal Point near Fort Fisher to relieve the 18th Regt. N.C.T.[19] Here the regiment was to remain throughout the winter.

18. Robert M. Carter was a 23-year-old resident of Davidson County when he was appointed adjutant (1st lieutenant) of the 30th Regt. on Feb. 25, 1862, to date from October 16, 1861. He "retired" when the regiment was reorganized on May 1, 1862. Manarin and Jordan, *N.C. Troops*, 8:321.

19. Record of Events, Company E, 30th Regt. N.C.T. The date for the move given in Historical Memoranda is November 5, 1861, but Parker evidences no awareness of such a move in his letter of November 5.

"I shall await the arrival of your potatoes, sausage, etc. with patience,
and shall welcome them with open mouths and good appetites."
— F. M. Parker

PART THREE

November, 1861 - February, 1862
Camp Wyatt near Fort Fisher

Camp Wyatt
Nov. 8th, 1861

My dear Wife

I have to night [sic] written to the Gov. to Genrl. Anderson
and to Adjutant Genrl. Cooper,[1] all on official business; now I
will do the more pleasant part of my labour; write to my dear
wife. It is really a pleasure to write to you, a very great one; in
the first place, I feel I am doing right, in the second place, I am
assured I shall receive an answer, which is by far the more
pleasant part about the whole matter. If I had the time, I would
write you every day, but the days are short and it keeps me busy
to get through with my duties. Since I wrote you last, we have
been moved from our former encampment. On Tuesday just at
night, I received orders to report in with the Regt. with all the
baggage and camp equippage [sic], ready to proceed to
Wilmington. I immediately issued orders to have three days
rations cooked; the men went busily to work and by one oclock
[sic] at night had their provisions all ready; about that time a
second order came to move to this place instead of Wilmington;
so at 2 o'clock I gave the order to strike tents and carry them to
the wharf. After cooking and working all night, we were ready
in the morning to leave, which we did and are now very
comfortably quartered in our new encampment. The ground
was formerly occupied by the 8th Regt. Col. Radcliff's;[2] his
Regt. is now encamped near Wilmington. This is a very windy

---

1. Samuel Cooper (1798-1876) was the ranking general officer of the
   Confederacy and Adjutant and Inspector General throughout the war.
   Warner, *Generals in Gray*, p. 62-63.
2. The 8th, designated the 18th Regiment N.C.T. on November 14, 1861,
   was at this time commanded by Col. James Dillard Radcliffe who was a
   28-year-old Citadel graduate and principal of a military school in

place, being so much exposed to the ocean and river, and it is a tolerably cool one too; if we remain here all the winter, we will have to build huts to live in. The name of the camp was taken from the poor fellow who was killed at the battle of Bethel, Henry L. Wyatt. Little did he ever suppose that he would acquire so much notoriety; alas, he paid dearly for it.

From what we can hear, they are having warm times at Port Royal. I think we shall be able to give the vandals their deserts. When it was known that a Regt. would probably be ordered there, there was a general expression of joy throughout the whole camp. The boys were exceedingly anxious to go, and be in active service. The confinement of a camp life, is very trying to soldiers; the mere fighting a battle is the easiest part of their work.

I received a note from Sister Kate to night in which she says she has written to you to come to Wilmington at the meeting of the stockholders; if you conclude to do so, let me know before hand, and if I possible I will meet you there. If we had remained at Camp Walker, I should have invited you there, and I think you could have spent a short time there very pleasantly; but here there are no accommodations for you, except my own tent. If you can leave home, you would no doubt spend a pleasant time in Wilmington at the time I speak of. If your Father does not wish to come, Mr. Weddle [Waddell] of Tarboro is coming and will take charge of you.

You asked me to let you know how the flannel clothes fit; it has been so pleasant, that I have not put them on yet; they look very nice, and I have no doubt but that they will suit me very well. If you can spare it, I will ask you to send me some bacon. The hams you sent came in the right time exactly. Do not send more if you can not do so well; a little butter will also be acceptable. Any thing sent to the care of Dr. Thomas, I shall be apt to receive. I suppose Henry Johnston will attend to it at Enfield for you.

I received your very good letter, just before leaving Camp Walker, and must now thank you for it. I hope you will continue to write just such good, long letters, full of good advice;

Wilmington when elected colonel to rank from July 18, 1861. He was defeated for reelection at the April, 1862, reorganization of that regiment and later commanded the 61st Regt. N.C.T. Krick, *Lee's Colonels*, p. 312; Manarin and Jordan, *N.C.Troops*, 6:295, 305 and 755.

recollect that I am here surrounded by every thing calculated to take my mind from pure, holy thoughts, and that I need some one to remind me of my duties to my Savior; nothing [letter ends here]

Camp Wyatt
Nov. 10, 1861

My dear Wife

I have just read your letter of the 1st; it has been a long time on the road, but I suppose that is not your fault. Direct all your letters for the future to Wilmington. As I wrote you the other day, we have changed our camp, and Wilmington is now our office. In my last letter I mentioned that Sister Kate had sent you word to come to see her on the 20th, the time of the meeting of the stockholders of the R. Road. If it is convenient and agreeable to you, I think I would come. If your Father does not come, Mr. M. Wadell [*sic*] will be along, and will take charge of you. Or, better still, get Fred to escort you down. I will meet you in Wilmington if every thing is quiet on the coast. Speaking of the coast, I took a long ride on the beach to day reconnoitering; the view is fine[;] nothing to meet the eye but sky and water. I saw the remnants of a great many wrecks; sometimes there would be the hull of a vessel, then the different parts of vessels, scattered about in profusion. There must have been great suffering there. One of these vessels was wrecked only last winter. Our coasts are notoriously dangerous, and at present it may be some protection to us. The pilots about here say, that if the Yankees do not attack us soon, they can not do so this winter. So by the spring we will be better able to repel an attack. The news from Port Royal is not pleasant at all; they will probably be able to manage us on and near the water, but not on land; at any rate they seem afraid to try it.

Have you sent my sword yet; my little Adjutant needs it badly. Mr. Browning, one of the conductors on the Rail Road will bring it, if you will send it to Enfield, to Henry Johnston with instructions to give it to Browning. I should like to have my thick black coat, which is at home. If you come on the 20th, you can bring it. I have another trunk, so you can take yours back with you. Well, I have received my horse at last; he arrived just this evening, is rather a fine looking animal. I think I shall be pleased with him. I wrote you the other day to send some bacon and butter; if you can spare it, will you please do so.

This is a hard country down here; the people are poor, and have nothing to sell in the way of eatables. I believe it is worse than it was in Virginia. If you should send anything, direct it to Maj. Lamb, Qr. Master, Wilmington.

I am sorry to hear from your last letter, that Ben has not sowed wheat yet; it is late for sowing now, the wheat is not apt to be so good, and more liable to the rust and other diseases. I wish Ben to sow rye in the new ground again, and to cut down the bushes, either this winter or next spring. It has been a fine fall for getting out cotton. I hope he has been pushing matters in that way.

I understand the 1st Regt. will soon be in Raleigh. There will be some happy fellows there. My word for it, they will not be satisfied to remain long at home, but will be in service again; particularly as the enemy have invaded our Sister State. I wonder if Mrs. Arrington will be willing to give up Jo again; she had better send Carter off also.

I am writing now nearly alone, every thing is quiet except the ocean. I hear the roar very distinctly; the sound resembles an immense water fall, when you are very near it. It is very grand.

Remember me to all my friends, to Ben and the negroes. Say to Mr. Dunn that I will write him soon.

I am looking for a letter from Mary now, every day. Kiss all the children for me, and take all the love from your husband, who does love you devotedly.

F. M. Parker

On November 10, 1861, a detachment from the 30th under 3rd Lt. Charles T. Stephens of Company A claimed the honor of participation in the first artillery duel on the coast of the Cape Fear in an exchange of a few shots and shell at Anderson's Battery, about three miles above Camp Wyatt.[3]

3. Historical Memoranda of the 30th Regt. N.C.T.

Camp Wyatt
Nov. 14/61

My dear Wife

I wrote you a very hurried note this morning by Dr. Joyner, after reading your letter received by him, the second time, I have concluded to write you again and direct this to Tarboro; where I hope the letter will find you enjoying yourself. I know it will be pleasant to you to be at Church, and among your friends; I very much wish you lived where you could enjoy the privileges of attending church every Sunday. I know you would be happier. It would be much better in every respect, particularly on account of the children. I wish I could be with you tomorrow, ~~Thanksgiving~~ fast day. We have great cause for thankfulness; we have received many and great blessings. We have been altogether too ungrateful, and have seemed to think that these favours and kindnesses were our due. This evening on Dress Parade I had an order read, that tomorrow must be observed as a day of fasting, humiliation and prayer; that all duties would be dispensed with, for the day, except guard duty. And now how shall I spend the day; there will be no religious services of any kind in camp, for the reason that we have no Chaplain among us. There is a Chaplain appointed for the Regt., but he is absent in the County.[4] By the way, I do not fancy the Chaplain much. He is altogether too sanctimonious; uses too many extravagant expressions, where simple language will do. He is a Methodist Preacher; I believe is a graduate of Chapel Hill. He came to me, recommended by all the commissioned officers of the Regt., and I did not feel willing to object to their choice; tho' I believe they are now, rather sick of their bargain. So I must fill up the day, reading and studying. My men will now have two days intermission, for I allow them to wash their

---

4. Alexander Davis Betts, appointed chaplain of the 30th Regt. on October 26, 1861 at age 29, would cause Parker to reconsider his initial poor estimation of the Methodist preacher. Serving the regiment faithfully until the end of the war, he was adjudged "very attentive to his duties." Betts was preaching at Smithville when he received his appointment as chaplain of the 30th and Parker allowed him to attend the Conference meeting in Louisburg before taking up his duties with the regiment. Alexander Davis Betts, *Experiences of a Confederate Chaplain*, W. A. Betts, ed. (Greenville, South Carolina: n.p., 1907), pp. 5-6 and 91; Manarin and Jordan, *N.C. Troops*, 8:322.

Clark, *N.C. Regiments*, 1901

Chaplain Alexander Davis Betts
30th Regt. N.C.T.

clothes, and clean up generally on Saturdays, so that they can come out clean at inspection on Sunday morning. So far I have got on very well with the Regt. tho I now have two very bad cares in the guard house; one of these, I shall have to punish severely. Besides my own Regt. I have control of a company of Artillery from Miss. and part of a cavalry company from this State. So you see we are expected to do a good deal of hard work down here, should the Yankees attempt to land. I have been cutting some roads, over which to move the troops more rapidly, and I now think we could put up a very respectable fight; and I think the officers of the Regt. are of the same opinion, which is a great matter. The Yankees would find us rather weak just now; there is a good deal of sickness in the Regt., measles and mumps.

Well, I suppose you intend coming to see me soon; that is the best news I have heard in a long time. If this reaches you before you have made your plans, let me say to you that I may have to be absent for several days. I am ordered to Newberne to sit on a court martial for the trial of Col. Singletary,[5] and when I shall be able to return, is more than I can say. I have written to Genrl. Gatlin,[6] to relieve me from that duty, but have not heard from him yet. I will write you again in a few days, and let you know when I can meet you in Wilmington. Do not get out of the notion of coming; I do want to see you very much, altho' I can not be with you very long. Col. Draughan is now in Wilmington with his wife. If he had no other recommendation, he has this, that he loves his wife and child dearly. I like him very much. He has a

---

5. George Badger Singletary of Pitt County, son-in-law of former N.C. Gov. Manly and colonel of the 27th Regt. N.C.T., was court-martialled by D. H. Hill and convicted of "conduct prejudicial to good order and military discipline." Singletary resigned Dec. 16, 1861, and was appointed colonel of the 44th Regt. N.C.T. and was killed at Tarrant's Creek, North Carolina, on June 5, 1862. Krick, *Lee's Colonels*, p. 346; Manarin and Jordan, *N.C. Troops*, 8:7.

6. Richard Caswell Gatlin (1809-1896), a native of Lenoir County and an 1832 graduate of West Point, was major of the 5th U.S. Infantry when he resigned in May, 1861, and offered his services to the Confederacy. At the time of this letter, he was serving as brigadier general in command of the Department of North Carolina. Made to shoulder the blame for the losses of Fort Hatteras and New Bern in the spring of 1862, Gatlin resigned his Confederate commission and served as North Carolina's state adjutant general until the end of the war. Warner, *Generals in Gray*, pp. 102-103.

great deal of the old army officer style about him, a little abrupt, but very polite. He is a nephew of Mr. Wells Draughan of Edgecombe. You ask me if I am liked in the Regt. All I can say is, that officers and men show me a great deal of respect, and in some cases the men manifest their partiality for me; to day one of the men, a stranger to me, came up and said to me that his Ma had sent him a baked lamb, and he would be glad if I would take a quarter of it; I thanked him and accepted it, and it was very nice. I afterwards learned the man was a private in a company from Granville County. Now that happens to be a company which I have been pretty strict with; I have sent back to Granville for two deserters from the company. Sensible men do not regard strictness, with impartiality. I generally draw them all to the mark, officers as well as the privates.

To day I happened to stumble upon one of my many cousins; a son of Gov. Dudley;[7] he traced out and claimed the acquaintance himself. He commands the Coast Guard, for about twenty miles along our coast here. This command is also attached to my Regt. So you see with Infantry, Artillery, Cavalry, The Coast Guard, and about a half dozen Pilots, I have a mixed command. I had rather be at the head of my own family at home, than to command the whole, provided every thing would allow of it. But I know this is impossible now; every man has his part to perform, let him do it. I pray that I may have strength and wisdom given me from above, to perform mine faithfully and truly.

Friday, the 15th—I commenced this letter last night, and now will finish it. Our Chaplain has just finished a sermon to the men; he gave us a very sensible talk; I am more pleased with

---

7. Edward Bishop Dudley (1789-1855), a native of Onslow County, was governor of North Carolina 1836-1840. A founder of the Wilmington to Weldon railroad and an advocate for public works, stronger banks, education, and constitutional reform, Dudley was able to capitalize upon North Carolina's 1835 state constitutional revisions, and his gubernatorial administration was the most progressive period in the ante-bellum period of North Carolina history. Powell, *Dictionary of North Carolina Biography*, 2:112-113. Gov. Dudley's son, Edward B. Dudley, transferred to 2nd Co. D, 36th Regt. N.C.T. (2nd Regt. N.C. Artillery) from duty in Coast Guard upon appointment as captain on March 3, 1862. Captain Dudley was captured at the fall of Fort Fisher, North Carolina, on January 15, 1865, and confined at Fort Columbus, New York Harbor, until paroled and exchanged at City Point, Virginia, on March 5, 1865. Manarin and Jordan, *N.C. Troops*, 1:237.

him, after hearing him preach. Yet I think there is rather too much of the artificial about him. I hope he may do great good, and be a blessing to the Regt. He was not of my choosing, therefore I do not feel so much responsibility on that score. I was very anxious to have Mr. Page as my Chaplain. I should have had a warm friend near me. Our whole camp witnessed a very interesting sight this morning; it was a large vessel, which had run the blockade, and was coming up the river to Wilmington; she was sailing beautifully before a fine breeze, with all sails set; her canvas seemed to swell with pride at having eluded the blockading steamer off the bar. This is the second vessel which has come in within the past ten days. The Pilots say this one is loaded with coffee and salt, from the West Indies. There are two inlets to the Cape Fear from the ocean; one at the mouth of the river, which comes up by Ft. Caswell; the other is called New Inlet, which is commanded by Ft. Fisher. If this vessel, of which I have just spoken, had come in at New Inlet, she would have been caught; there is one of the blockade squadron lying off very near; in fact, so near that I could very plainly, with the aid of a glass, see the men on deck, the real live Yankees. Now what do you think of that? It is quite tempting, is'nt [sic] it? So much so, that several of the men have applied to me for permission to go to Wilmington for a couple of steam tugs, and go out and take the Yankee [sic]. I tell them if we can only get the rascals on land, we can use them roughly, but that we do not know much about water. I have however referred them to Genrl. Anderson. I have no idea of getting into such a scrape as Col. Singletary did.

Dr. Joyner came to camp this week but has returned for medicines. He will be back with us soon. We need him very much. He brought the things you sent. I am much obliged for all. The Adjutant is particularly so for the sword. I have a few clothes which I shall put in your trunk, and get you to take back home with you. I wrote you a short note by Dr. Joyner in which I told you to see Mrs. Bennett before you made any bargain with Miss Arnott. I thought probably she might be able to give you some information relative to the young Lady. It will be well enough to know every thing before hand.

I hope you will not get out of the notion of coming to Wilmington. Sister Kate will be glad to see you, and I know I will. Bring Bella with you, I want to see her too.

My love to all at Mr. Cheshires, and at Sister Mary's, and take all for yourself.

Your affectionate husband
F. M. Parker

When you come if you will get that certificate of travelling [*sic*] stock in the Wilmington R. Road, you can come without paying any money. But you may have left it at home.

———————— ◆•◆ ————————

Camp Wyatt
Nov. 15, 1861

Mrs. S. J. Parker
Tarboro
N.C.
If Mrs. P. is not in Tarboro, this letter will be mailed to
    Battleboro, and oblige the writer.

My dear Wife

I wrote you a long letter and sent it to Tarboro by a gentleman who was on a visit to our camp. Here I am writing to you again. I shall write a very short one this time.

I received a letter from Genrl. Gatlin, after I sent off the one to you this evening; saying that he could not relieve me from serving on the Court Martial, of which I wrote you; so I will have to go to Newberne. If it is possible, I will run up from Goldsboro to your Father's, on my return from Newberne. I suppose we will get through with the business of the court in a few days. The court sits on Monday the 18th; so about the latter part of the week, I hope to see you, if nothing prevents. I, however, shall have to get Genrl. Gatlin's permission to do so, and he may refuse. If so, I will write you, and you can come to see me. He will hardly object to that.

I dislike very much to leave my command just now; I am satisfied that the closer an officer sticks to his men, the easier it is to manage them and the better will he get on with the men.

I am sorry to hear that Fred intends to return to camp so soon. I very much fear the consequences of it. I think he should remain awhile longer.

Remember me kindly to every one at your Father's also to Dr. Rives' family and Sister Sue and John. Kiss our children for me. Good bye my dear wife.

Your affectionate husband

F. M. Parker

Newberne

Nov. 22 1861

Mrs. S. J. Parker
Care of Dr. Philips
Battleboro
N.C.

My dear Wife

Still here and with every prospect of remaining two days longer. The court has kept at a three days stand still owing to the absence of General Hill who was a very important witness in the trial. He came on Wednesday evening, so we have had but one day's work.

My object in writing now is to let you know that I have not given out the idea of paying you a flying visit, as soon as I am relieved here. Provided every thing is quiet about Wilmington. Newberne just now, has an abundance of the military; there is here at this time Genrl. Gatlin, Genrl. Hill and any quantity of Colonels, Majors, "et id omne genus." I am tired of so much of the official. I want to breathe some good fresh air, where I can hear a man called by his own name.

By the way I have met with one, who is calculated to take the starch out of the military; no other than John Staton. He is just as matter of fact, as he was, when he was playing the agreeable around Miss Ann E. Lawrence, and other young Ladies, of my acquaintance. John is very clever; he insisted on my going home with him; as an inducement he offered to give me a good fox hunt. I should have gone, if I could have gotten clear of this court.

At present I hope to reach your Father's on Sunday, may be on Saturday night. I can not tell with any certainty; therefore you may expect me when you see me. Remember me to all.

Kiss the babies.

Very affectionately your husband
F. M. Parker

———————◆◦◆◦◆———————

Camp Wyatt
Dec. 5/61

My dear Wife

To day has, I suppose, been observed by you all as a day of thanksgiving; it is very proper that it should be so; we have great cause for thankfulness.

I suppose the turkeys, ducks and the good things of life generally have been discussed freely; well we in camp have fared very well on our little pieces of bacon and turnips. It is now ten o'clock P.M. and I have just finished a very good oyster supper, furnished by one of my friends. I assure you ample justice was done it. Feeling so comfortable, I have thought I would write to you. I have somewhat expected a letter from you before this. I think you might have written by this time. I was in Wilmington yesterday. Sister Kate was looking for a letter from you relative to your cloak. I hope you have written before this so that she may get your cloak soon. I wrote you the other day that I had something like an eruptive disease of my skin, and that the Dr. thought it proceeded from the flannel shirt I wear; the eruption still continues, and is very troublesome; who would ever have supposed that flannel would irritate my skin; but such is the fact. I now wish you to get my silk undershirts from home, and send them to me immediately. I can not endure the flannel. Bundle the two shirts well, and sent them by express, or a rail road conductor to the care of Dr. Thomas. My friend Browning is in Wilmington sick, but I suppose any of the conductors would take charge of the package. I want the shirts as soon as I can possibly get them.

I think my Regt. is getting on better now, with the help of our Medical Staff. I have just commenced drilling in Battalion drill, and the men seem to like it; in fact they are in better spirits generally. They have just been paid off too, this may affect their feelings somewhat. Still we have a good many sick, and would make but a poor resistance to the enemy should they attempt to land. Have you heard that another vessel has run the blockade and reached Wilmington safely? It is a large schooner loaded with wool, lead and copper from Brownsville, Texas.

By the way, will you need any sugar or coffee soon? If you do, I will get it here in Wilmington and send it to you. Or, if you need any thing else, let me know and I will supply you, if to be had here. [***], I do not think you are writing very often; you must spur up. Remember me kindly to all at your Father's; to my children and all the love to yourself from your

affectionate husband
F. M. Parker

———————◆◆◆———————

Camp Wyatt
Dec. 9, 1861

My dearest Wife

How pained and how unhappy I feel after reading your letter. To think that you should have suffered so, and been so low, and I altogether unconscious of it. I do hope that you are feeling quite well now, and will continue to keep well. If I could do so at present I would certainly go to see you right off, but my duty holds me here. And my little girl too, she has been a sufferer. If it were possible I should have greatly rejoiced that you both could have been spared this affliction. Ask Mary, for her Pa's sake, for the love she has for him, to be careful and not use her arm imprudently, to wear it in a sling and be very quiet with it. I would not have it to deform her shoulders for any consideration. I do'nt [sic] know when I have felt so badly, as I have this evening; here I am away from you, and at this moment you may be suffering severely. How I wish to be with you. Do take care of yourself, for my sake. I am thankful to say that my own health still continues to be good. I certainly have had great cause for thankfulness. The eruption I spoke of has nearly disappeared. The health of the Regt. is improving also, and this is a source of gratification to me. The men who were sent home on account of sickness, are constantly coming in. Genrl. Anderson, with one of his staff, are with us to night. I have given up my tent to them, and am now in the Adjutant's tent writing to you. The Genrl. intends to ~~have a~~ review my Regt. in the morning, and have an

115

inspection also. I hope he will find every thing satisfactory. I think this will help the men; it will cause some little excitement, stir them up some. The Genrl. is a fine looking man, and a very clever gentleman, but not a thorough soldier. He asked me to night if I were a married man. I told him yes, and with four little children, and might have added, whom I was very anxious to see.

Sister Kate told me the other day that she had written to you something about the cloak; now I want you to write to her and give her your directions, so that she may have one made for you. I want you to have it.

It is getting quite late now, so I will close, promising to write again soon. I feel very uneasy about you and Mary. Write me again immediately, if you please. My love to all.

Very affectionately your husband
F. M. Parker

Camp Wyatt
Dec. 15, 1861

My dear Wife

I received a very good and very long and very welcome letter from you yesterday. I was so much pleased to know that you were well. I hope you will remain so. I can go on with my duties here with a light heart, when I know that you are all getting on well. The letter from the little girl was a great treat to me, tho I somewhat fear that she will be imprudent in the use of her arm and shoulder; as you say, she is so full of life and spirits, that it will be a difficult matter, to cause her to be sufficiently careful. I hope you will be attentive to this matter and take good care of her. I was very sorry to hear of the misfortune of Sister Sue and John; they have my warmest sympathies. I hope she is getting on very well now.

I certainly must be very forgetful not to have recollected that I gave my silk shirts to Ella. The eruption on my skin is better now. I am wearing cotton shirts next to my body, and the flannel outside. I find it nearly as warm; so far I am getting on very well with the cold weather. Our tents are getting rather airy. The Quarter Master has commenced on the winter quarters, and I suppose will have them completed by the first of Jan. It must be very cold on the Potomac, and in Western Va. I often think of Fred. I hope he will stand the winter well. When you write to him, caution him to be very careful with himself.

I was in Wilmington this week. I found Bella and Mrs. Lewis there; poor woman, she is to be pitied. Bella speaks of coming to see me in camp.

Well, I hope to be with you about the 15 of Jan. You shall hear from me again on this. The only thing of interest about us is the burning of a vessel about twenty miles off the coast on yesterday; we could not see the vessel, but could see the smoke very distinctly; the fire was burning for about 4 hours. If it was a Yankee, it was all right. No blockade had been in sight for nearly two weeks; they may have all gone south. You wish to know something about the behavior of the 30th in the presence of General Anderson. I think we did tolerably well, and that the Genrl. was well pleased; he was somewhat complimentary. I believe you take as much interest in the Regt. as I do. I am glad you do. If the opportunity should ever occur, I hope you will have a greater cause to be proud of it. One of Genrl. Anderson's aids is Lt. Norwood,[8] a son of Rev. Mr. Norwood, who baptized me; I told him I felt some interest [letter ends here]

Camp Wyatt
Dec. 17th, 1861

My dear Wife

Have you thought that just ten years ago we were made one. What a solemn vow we then each made. Have we performed that vow? I suppose that we have had the same difficulties, and the same obstacles to overcome which others in a similar situation have had. What has been the result? Has it been to make us cold and indifferent to each other; or has it knit us more closely

---

8. William Norwood served as aide-de-camp to Brig. Gen. Joseph R. Anderson, with the rank of lieutenant during the Seven Days in June and July, 1862. Joseph H. Crute, *Confederate Staff Officers* (Powahatan, Virginia: Dewent Books, 1982), p. 4; *OR*, vol. 11, pt. 2, p. 880. Parker's letter indicates that Norwood held his position as early as December, 1861. Norwood later served as Brig. Gen. Edward L. Thomas' assistant adjutant-general. Crute, *Confederate Staff Officers*, p. 193. *OR*, vol. 42, pt. 3, p. 1200.

together, and made us feel that we are dependent each on the other? If I know my own heart, and if my feelings do not deceive me, the latter has been the result. I feel very kindly, and very tenderly towards you; to say that I love you with all the strength of an ardent temperament, is saying just what you know. And I feel, and have every reason to believe, that that feeling is altogether returned by you. I am a little afraid that I love you and my little children too well. Nothing would be more in accordance with my feelings, than to be permitted to spend my life quietly, in the bosom of my family. The camp life may take away the little polish which I once may have possessed, but it can never lessen this affection which I have for my family.

I hope that you keep well, and that you are taking very great care of Mary and her shoulder. I have felt very uneasy on account of Mary; she is so active, so full of life, that I fear she may injure her shoulder again; caution her to be very careful for my sake. I am placed just now in a very unenviable position; I suppose there are at least six or eight men coming to me every day, asking for leave of absence; they put up all sorts of excuses; one wishes to go home to attend to a little business, another wishes to go because he has not gone in some months; then again others wish to go and see their wives and children. You may be sure I listen to the wishes of the latter class; they strike me on a sympathetic chord. I have made it a rule to allow all the married men to go home first. So my time will come about the 15 of January I hope. I shall look forward to that time with great pleasure and some impatience. I suppose you will be at home then; I hope so, for I wish to be with you, and at the same time to be at home.

Dr. Joyner has just returned from home; he tells me that he heard through Carter Arrington that Ben Hulm had made me a first rate crop. I am pleased to hear it, and I wish you to let Ben know it. Say to Ben that I have written to Henry Jones that I would hire Tom at a fair price. I shall hire no one else, except Moses. As soon as Ben gets all his crop in, I wish him to finish the dam on the creek. I hope his hogs are in good order; say to him not to keep them on peas in the low grounds too long. Let me know how much cotton he has to pack yet. I think I shall get iron hoops for a part of the cotton. Ben should be very careful in putting the bales away, to keep them raised well from the ground, or else the wooden hoops will rot. I wish him to pack heavy bales. Ask him to have the stock and hogs well taken care of. Also the stock of all kinds, particularly the young stock. Speaking of these things reminds me of the present state of things; our negroes at home are in warm houses, by good fires; while we are away from home in cold tents without any fire. No one knows what he can endure, until the trial is made.

I have before told you of the visit of Genrl. Anderson to our Regt.; tomorrow Genrls. Gatlin and Anderson both visit us, for review and inspection. I have just sent an order, to inform the Captains of this visit, and already it has inspirited and enlivened the men. A soldier in the field likes to be noticed by his superior officers. So we may expect rather big times tomorrow, with two Generals before us. But we have been visited by to day by [sic] the ladies; it was quite a treat to us. There were five of them from Smithville. I believe they made a call on each officer in the Regt.; they popped into my tent about 11 o'clock; very fortunately for me, I was able, through the kindness of Mrs. Joyner, to set before them some very nice cake and cordial. The ladies dined with one of the Captains. They expressed themselves quite well pleased, and say they will come again. Before leaving one of the young ladies played a ladies' trick on me; she came and begged for leave of absence for two of the Lieuts. who wished to accompany them back home. Of course I could not refuse such a pleader; the consequences the Generals will come and find two of my Lts. off on "detached service," as I shall call it. While I am writing I hear some of the men coming with their fiddles and banjos to give me a serenade, so I will stop until they get through.

Well, the serenaders have gone; they gave me really good music; it was just that kind of music which you know I admire, regardless of any measured time or note, coming right out of a musical soul. Then again I appreciate the motive which prompted them to the act, more than I do the music itself. I have been particularly strict of late with regard to my duties, but notwithstanding that the men seem to have a respect and esteem for me. I have not only had the men of the Regt. in the guard house for drinking, but I have arrested and confined a citizen of the county, for selling whiskey to the men. This old fellow was very much surprised when I confined him; he supposed I had no right to interfere with a citizen. I made a right of the necessity of the case. I had no idea of allowing him to sit quietly by the Regt. and poison them with his mean whiskey. We have to act on our own responsibility at times. I believe that the public interest requires the course I have pursued.

I suppose you are now quietly at home; I know you are glad to be there. I hope you have Miss Arnot with you, and that she will suit you well.

Write me soon, and give me all the news; let me know all about affairs at home; how the negroes all are. Remember me to all friends. If you see Mr. Dunn soon, say to him that I will answer his kind letter soon. Remember me to Ben and the negroes. My love to the children, and yourself from

your affectionate husband
F. M. Parker

Camp Wyatt
Dec. 17, 1861

My dear daughter

I was very glad to receive your letter the other day; I was glad that you were well enough to write me and glad that you had not forgotten the promise you made me. I hope you will always recollect every promise you make to anyone, and always fulfill them; but be very careful how you promise any thing; always be sure than you can fulfill your promise.

You don't know how sorry I was when I heard that you had broken your collar bone. I hope, my dear daughter, you will take very good care of yourself, and not injure your shoulder again; if you do, it will give you a great deal more pain than it did at first. When I first heard of your accident, I felt very much like going to see you and your Mother, who was sick about the same time. I hope to be able to be with you about the 15th of January. What must I bring you, when I come? I was on the beach the other day, I saw some pretty little shells and picked some up for you; they had just been washed up by the ocean. If you wish me to bring you anything, you must write me and let me know what it is. Col. Draughan, one of the Field officers of the Regt. has a little girl about your age, I have forgotten her name, but he calls her Sis. He told me the other day that Sis said to her Ma that Mr. Parker must be a good man or else Pa would not think so much of him; her Ma's answer was that her Pa and Mr. Parker

120

must take care of each other. We will try and do this. It is very pleasant to be with people whom we like so well. Col. Draughon is a very clever man and I like him very much. I have consented for him to go home and spend Christmas with his wife and Sis; when he returns to camp, I will then go and see my wife and my little Sis and the other little ones.

I was in Wilmington the other day and saw your Aunt Bella. I was glad to see her. I wish you to ask your Mama if she would not like for me to bring Cousin Mary Lindsay and your Aunt Bella with me when I come. If she would like to have them with her at that time and will write to Cousin Mary, asking her to come with me, I reckon she would like it very much; then Aunt Bella could join us at Rocky Mount. You must ask your Mama to write and let me know all about it.

Now I want you to take care of yourself and be sure and not injure your shoulder again.

Give my love to Ma, Brothers and little Sissy and kiss her for me. I hope you will write to me again soon.

Very affectionately your Father
F. M. Parker

Camp Wyatt
Jan. 19, 1862

My dear Wife

I now comply with a request which you made of me. I do not feel very well to night but will endeavor to write a little. I found the people of Wilmington much excited on account of the expected attack of Burnside. I also learned that Genl. Anderson had telegraphed me at Weldon on Saturday evening, to return to my command without delay, and had ordered all the officers and men back to their Regiments. I made an explanation to him, why I did not come sooner, which was, that I had not received the dispatch. It is very fortunate that I visited you when I did; for at this time no furloughs can be obtained on any account. No one can leave the camp far enough to be without the hearing of the drum; the men complain of this strictness, but I tell them that they are the orders, and must be obeyed. We learned to day that Burnside was at Hatteras, and would probably attack Newberne or Roanoke Island. So we are deprived of the pleasure of a visit

121

from him this time. There is, however, said to be another fleet fitting out, and this may be intended for Wilmington. Now, do'nt [sic] understand me as wishing them to come, by no means; I do not wish an engagement with the enemy; and at the same time, I would not shun it if offered me. I have seen enough of war, to know that a battle is not a very pleasant affair.

I found the Regiment much stronger, than when I left it, and still improving; the men who have been absent sick, are returning to their companies. The men seemed glad to see me back, and I know Col. Draughan was.

I had the pleasure of meeting with Jesse Hargrave and his wife in Wilmington. She is a very clever, modest, lady-like woman. I was pleased with Jesse's choice. I remained a day and two nights in Wilmington, in consequence of the steamer not running down the river. I sent a bundle of flax thread to you, through Mrs. Joyner, which I hope you have received; it is very costly, and scarce. Sister Kate will send the shawl soon. I will send the rice by Dr. Joyner. I am sorry that we will lose him; he certainly will resign. Sure enough I found Col. Draughan and the Adjutant in my house; the Col. is yet with me. The house is very comfortable; there are two rooms to it, which gives us plenty of room. The men are all in their houses also, and are quite comfortable. Just as I told you, they had no sleet down here, nothing but rain. So you see we are in a warmer climate, than Halifax can boast of.

My regards to Miss Martha, say to her that I was so hurried at Enfield that I did not have time to mail her letters, but mailed them in Wilmington.

My love to the children; kiss them all for me and tell Mary to write to me. Does Hattie ever call me now? She is a sweet little thing. Remember me to Mr. Dunn and Dr. Scott.

Take all the love from your affectionate husband
F. M. Parker

———————◆◆◆———————

Camp Wyatt
Jan. 26th, 1862

Mrs. S. J. Parker
Sycamore Alley
Halifax Co.
N.C.
My dear Wife

I have read some today; our chaplain has given us a sermon; I have had dinner, and now I have taken my seat for the purpose of writing you, by far the most pleasant task I can do. I generally am less interrupted on Sunday afternoons than any other time; tho then not altogether free from annoyance. So you will excuse the rambling sort of letter which I am forced to write.

I answered your last letter immediately upon the receipt of it. In that I remarked that I did not wish to hire John (the negro) at the price which Genl. Daniel paid for him. $75 is still the most I will give for him.

As to Miss Martha, I think you had better discontinue her services after her session ends, and in the mean time we will look out for another teacher. I would not be in too great a hurry about the matter, either in letting Miss Martha know that you will not need her services any longer, or in the matter of employing another teacher.

I am sorry that you are so unpleasantly situated; judging by my own feelings, it is any thing but pleasant to be thus separated as we are, and in addition to this, to have those about us who seem altogether devoted to themselves, and take no care or interest in what is going on around them, and who do not strive to make themselves agreeable; must make your life rather dull and lonesome. But my dear Wife, you can fall back upon the satisfactory reflection that you are discharging your duty, and as long as this is the case, we can get on very well. A bright day is ahead, let us look forward hopefully and cheerfully to that; when all these troubles and exciting times will be over, and all of us back with our families at home. I hope and pray for the good time to come soon. But in the mean time, we must cheer up, and bear patiently our trials. Well, so far, nothing reliable from Burnside. We had some heavy practicing from Ft. Fisher last week, which alarmed the country around for some distance; they supposed that the fleet had attacked us. There had been some new guns mounted in the Battery, and they were trying their range. The firing was distinctly heard at Fayetteville; on yesterday Col. Draughan received a letter from his wife, stating that she had been miserable for a day or two, until in fact she received his letter giving an account of the firing. The Col. came into my office after reading the letter, and asked me to listen how saucy his old woman talked; he then read that part of the letter describing her bad feelings, and then how different she felt after receiving his letter. She compared the pleasant part of it, to the "feelings of a mother after the babe is born and all is over." I suppose you can very well imagine how that is. It is naughty in these big guns to be thus frightening our wives, isn't it?

We have had quite a storm on the coast. I very much hope that it has blown Burnside and his fleet to the burning side of somewhere. I suppose the militia in Halifax are being draughted; that is exactly as it should be, that is if they will remain at home, and render a draught necessary. I hope some of those men who have been lying idle may be brought into service now. I think Carter and Mr. Nicholson had better look sharp. I hope Ben will not be taken from the farm. How do the hogs come on? How many have you to kill yet? I did not see Mr. Whitfield at Enfield, and do not know whether he will buy any pork or not. Keep a correct account of the weights of the hogs, in order to know how much is killed.

I wish you would charge Moses with $4 which I paid him when at home, and give him credit for some troughs which he dug; he can inform you all about it. I hope to be able to send you some funds too.

We are getting on tolerably well now; all are in winter quarters, except some few of the officers and they will be soon. My friend Capt. Holmes[9] is temporarily occupying a part of my room. The health of the Regt. is important, the men look well, are cheerful and in pretty good fighting order. Dr. Joyner still speaks of resigning but I hope he will not; this entire Regt. seem to like him. Cummings was down a few days since, he applied for, and has received the appointment of Sutler to this Post. He is now in Petersburg, will be back with his goods &c. soon. Several of my old company speak of joining the Regt. I shall await the arrival of your potatoes, sausage, etc. with patience, and shall welcome them with open mouths and good appetites.

---

9. James C. Holmes was enumerated in the 1860 U.S. Census of Sampson County as a 34-year-old merchant living in Clinton. He was a 35-year-old Sampson County farmer when he enlisted on April 20, 1861, in the "Sampson Rangers," which became Company A of the 30th Regt. N.C.T. Holmes was elected 2nd lieutenant on or about April 20, 1861, and captain on August 3, 1861. He was appointed major on September 3, 1863. Medical records dated April 26, 1864, indicate he was "unfit for duty in the field on account of partial paralysis on the left side, principally affecting the arm, and chronic diarrhoea and general debility." He retired to the Invalid Corps Aug. 19, 1864. Manarin and Jordan, *N.C.Troops*, 8:321 and 323; Krick, *Lee's Colonels*, pp. 196-7.

Remember me to Miss Martha, Ben and the negroes, to Mr. Dunn, Dr. Scott and to Miss Mat.

My love to the children; kiss them for me, tell Mary to write me soon. Take all the love from your

Affectionate husband
F. M. Parker

Have you ever received the thread which I sent through Mrs. Joyner?

Camp Wyatt
Jan. 31st 1862

My dear Wife

You will say why here is Frank writing to me again, troubling me with his letters. Now you see if I could only charge you with the same thing, viz., writing too often, I should like it; but my charge against you is of quite a different character. You do not write enough. I think I shall have you court martialed if you do not do better. I think I can select a court from among the married men of my Regt. who will certainly condemn you. I should be glad to get even five lines from you, letting me know that all are well. So spur up, and do a little better. There is not a bit of news in this part of the world, we have been holding on for some time "watching and waiting" for Burnside; but to no purpose. From the latest accounts we have, there certainly was part of a fleet off Hatteras; but where they are now, no one knows. It seems that the news paper editors have sent them all to "Davy Jones' locker."

How does the draught operate in your country? How does Carter like the idea of trying the tented field at this season of the year. I learn they are paying high prices for substitutes in Edgecombe, as high as $1,000 each; they certainly must not like to fight the Yankees. If Tom Nicholson and some of the Britts' had been draughted also, I should have considered it rich. These men who are dodging their duty, are the very ones who should be forced to go. Such men would not raise a finger to repel an invasion.

I have heard nothing from the sausage, potatoes, &c. yet; they would not be unwelcome customers here just now.

Have you heard from Tarboro recently? and has Sister Mary gone to Raleigh yet? I am afraid she will not be very pleasantly situated there.

Has Ben gotten all his cotton out yet? and how do the hogs come on? You know the provision question is always one of great importance to me. I always feel personally interested. We are having ugly weather here now; the wind is blowing hard from the N.E., a very unpleasant wind always, and then it is raining. I hope it will soon turn to a violent storm, and blow every remnant of the Yankee fleet to pieces. It certainly would be better for them to suffer in that way, than to be shot and cut to pieces by Southern soldiers. What a great misfortune it is that the Northern Government can not see the folly of their way. I suppose they must be blinded for some good purpose. We may be the instruments of accomplishing that purpose. I know one thing. I wish I were at home with my wife and children, and every thing settled as we wish it.

Enclosed I send you some postage stamps; it will be necessary to keep them in some secure place, in order to preserve the mucilage on the back of them. I hope you will use them often; I hope to see them coming back here, one by one. I have some money which I will send by the first safe opportunity. Tell Mary to write me soon. Kiss all the children for me; tell them I want to see them very much. Remember me to all friends.

Good night my dear wife. I send this poor letter full of love from

Your affectionate husband
F. M. Parker

Camp Wyatt
Feb. 3rd, 1862

My dear Wife

Now I have been well treated to night [sic]; two letters from you at a dash; that is something to boast of. You must have an exciting time among the militia in your county; they had better come down and attach themselves to regular volunteer troops at once. Tell Carter I will receive him with open arms in our Regt. Send word to Elias Johnson to come immediately to this place, and join the Regt. if he does not. He will have to go with the militia. He will have to pay his fare to Wilmington; if he will let them know that he is a soldier, they will pass him for half fare on the rail road. It will cost him nothing from Wilmington to the camp. Tell him to call on Maj. Lamb, the Quarter Master and he will send him down the river. You can send as many recruits to us as you please; we will constitute you a recruiting officer, so go to work. If you could hear the fiddle and banjo going, as I do at this time, you would see that the boys here are happy enough.

We are at least, all in winter quarters and are living comfortably; some have stoves, some have not. I have one, which makes my room very comfortable; there are two rooms to my house. I suppose the Q. Master thought the Col. might have company occasionally. One room is intended for office work. There is a little excitement in camp to night in consequence of the departure of a steamer from Wilmington loaded with cotton and naval stores; she will attempt to run the blockade to night, she is bound for Liverpool.

Relative to the negro John, I am not anxious to hire him; but will give $75 for him. Do not wish to go to any trouble about it. If the parties come to you, you can give a note for $75 and take the boy for the balance of the year; if they do not come, say nothing about it.

You ask me something about the conduct of the militia of Raleigh. I have understood that they refused to go after being draughted, and that it required one or two companies of volunteers to quiet them.

I assure you that I am pleased to learn that my box is on the way. It will be heartily welcomed here, or rather the contents will. Dr. Joyner has just received a lot of turkeys; now wo'nt [sic] we live high. Speaking of the Dr. I hope he will not resign. He is very generally liked in the Regt. and is doing very well. I hope you have received your rice before this. I ordered it to be sent to you from Wilmington. I should like to see Jimmy devour some of it. I shall go to Wilmington in the morning on official business, and will attend to your request about the music. Let me know whenever you wish any thing. I hope to send you some coffee and sugar soon. Do you need any molasses?

I have attended to the note of Martin, Tannahill & Co. When you write again, let me know how many hogs there are to be killed yet, whether or not half have been killed, and what is the weight of those already killed. I am afraid you will have none to spare.

Remember me to all friends. Tell Miss Martha the socks will be very acceptable, altho' I have a plenty just now.

Kiss the children for me. And Hattie takes the President to be her Pa, does she? I wish I could see the little girl. Write often, at least twice a week. Have you received the postage stamps yet? Good night my dear wife. God bless you, and yours.

Your affectionate husband,
F. M. P.

". . . please instruct Hilliard to commence planting cotton at least
one hundred yards from the turnip patch fence. . ."
— F. M. Parker

PART FOUR
February 1862 - April 1862
Camp Wyatt - Camp Holmes near Wilmington

Wilmington
Feb. 14th 1862

My dear Wife

I have just learned that Ben Hulm has been draughted; if it
[is] so, and if he has been ordered off; I wish you to put Hilliard
in command on the plantation. Call him in, and caution him of
the responsibility of his position; tell him to do his very best,
that whatever is for my interest is also for his, and I think he will
do very well. I have as much confidence in him; as I have in any
negro; in fact, it will be impossible to get any one at this time
to attend to business. I do not wish to keep any one from going
to defend their country; let every man turn out; now is the time.
I think if you will let Hilliard see occasionally, that you feel
interested in what is going on, it will be of great service to him.
Call him to you, frequently and question him; about the work
&c, what he is doing, how the hands work and any thing else,
which will cause him to think that you take an interest in what
is going on. I will write you again soon. I have been disappointed in not receiving a letter from you.

Mrs. Draughan is here; I have called on her; she is a very nice
lady; [this] must necessarily be so, being the wife of Col.
Draughan.

I hope you are all well. My love to the children. Remember
me to Miss Martha.

Write soon, and often.

very affectionately your husband
F. M. Parker

I have sent you a <u>Valentine</u>.

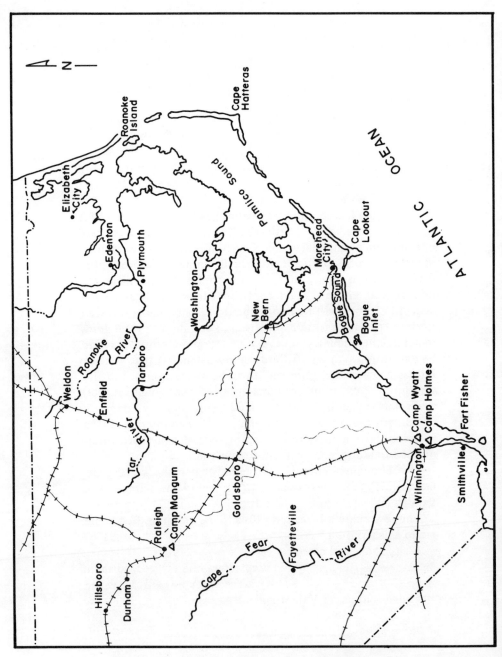

Operations in Eastern North Carolina, 1861-1862

My dear Wife

I received your letter to day, which Ben Hulm mailed at Enfield. It has caused me to feel very restless and uneasy about you. I know that you must feel unpleasant.

I have heard last night that Ben had been draughted, and immediately wrote you to place Hilliard in command; at the same time addressing you, to give Hilliard a good sensible talk, reminding him of his responsibilities, and of the necessity of his doing his best towards carrying on my business. I think he will do very well. I hope he will prove earnest. It is the best I can do, or advise you to do. If I had time to be at home, probably I might succeed in getting some one to attend to my business. I certainly am under lasting obligation to Mr. Harrison for his kindness in this matter, and I hope you will express the same to him. If his habits were different, he would suit very well to attend to the business; but as there is some uncertainty about that, I hardly think he would suit you . However if you feel willing to have him as a member of your family, I am perfectly willing to trust my business in his hands. He is a clever gentleman; would be entertaining as company, and an agreeable member of the family, provided he did not get into one of his frolics. I should feel better satisfied for you to have some one with you, who could take care of you, than for you to be alone.

Mr. Partin might be obtained, in case you do not want Mr. Harrison; Mr. Partin would do very well, but would not remain on the farm constantly, even if he would at all; in fact, I doubt very much whether he will leave home or not. You might write him a note, and know of him whether or not he would attend to the farm for you. I know of no one else who could be obtained besides Mr. Harrison and Mr. Partin. You can do as you prefer in this matter, and it will suit me. If neither can be employed, let Hilliard go on with the business. It gives me a great deal of uneasiness and trouble to think that my wife is so troubled about this matter; I very much wish, it were in my power to alter it. I could do nothing that would prevent any one from volunteering in the defence [sic] of their country; rather than this, all business might go by the board.

Write me immediately, and let me know what you have concluded to do. I do not like to tell you what to do; for I might advise some course, which would not be agreeable to you. I never was more anxious to see you, than at present; so that I could advise with you. If it had been at all possible, I should have gone up the road to day. The court martial, is still in session. I suppose we will be here for several days of next week. I am heartily tired of the business, and am very anxious to return to camp. I want to see Col. Draughan. The news by telegraph to day, is quite cheering; it is reported that we have repulsed the enemy in the West. I hope we shall do something to wipe out the Roanoke Island affair; that is a shameful piece of business; to have surrendered, when only eight men were killed. I must think those men were afraid of being hurt.

All are well at Dr. Drane's and Dr. Thomas'. I am a good deal with Dr. Thomas; he is the same pleasant gentleman he has ever been. I am now writing in his office.

My love to the children; remember me to Miss Martha, and Esquire Duke, if he is with you. Write soon.

Very affectionately your husband,
F. M. Parker

Wilmington
Feb. 15th, 1862

My dear Wife

These are really stirring times. I feel very unplesantly [sic] situated at present. I do not think there is any danger that the enemy will penetrate into your country, but I am very anxious to go with my Regiment to the Roanoke to assist in driving them back. It would be an awful blow to us, should they gain possession of Weldon. If there ever was a time when our government and people should be up and doing, it is at the present; we have been lying idle already too long. I hope for the future that we will show more earnestness in our cause. A great part of our people do not realize that we are in the midst of a great war. The fall of Roanoke Island has cast a gloom over this town; there were a good many there from Wilmington. The Lt. Col. of Col. Shaw's Regt. was one of them.[1] These imprison-

---

1. William J. Price, a New Hanover County resident, was appointed lieutenant colonel to rank from May 16, 1861. He served in the 8th Regt.

ments and loss of life is the price some of us will have to pay for our rights and liberties. I feel that I can very freely make any sacrifice, even to a loss of property, yea and life itself, to gain our independence. What would life be worth were we to be overrun in this struggle? Nothing; therefore, let us turn out as a whole people and drive back and destroy our invaders. Our cause is a just one and must succeed in the end; of this I have no fear. Our court martial is progressing slowly; it is very boring to me; I had great deal rather be in camp with my men. I hope we shall be enabled to get through the business this week, tho' it is somewhat doubtful. I have divided my time somewhat between Sister Kate and Cousin Mary; but for this, I should spend a very unpleasant time of it. The people of Wilmington are somewhat alarmed at the probability of Butler paying us a visit. My own opinion is that he will not come. I think he is destined for Ship Island, or some more Southern part of the country. I am very anxious to hear from you. I hope you will not suffer yourself to be unnecessarily alarmed. You have no need to be so. I have no doubt but that a sufficient force will be sent on the Roanoke to check and drive back our enemies. Have you commenced your gardening or rations yet? It is time, isn't it?

When I got back here I found that the nice sugar I thought of sending you was all sold. Would you not like to have some syrup?

My love to the children, kiss them for me; tell Mary to write me. Remember me to Miss Martha, Ben, and the negroes. Good bye my dear wife, God bless you.

Your affectionate husband
F. M. Parker

———————◆◆◆———————

Wilmington
Feb. 26th, 1862

N.C.T. under Col. Henry Marchmore Shaw. He was captured at Roanoke Island on February 8, 1862, and paroled at Elizabeth City on February 21, 1862, being exchanged in August, 1862. Price resigned on October 10, 1862, by reason of "age," given as 58, and "diarrhoea." His resignation was accepted October 25, 1862. Jordan, *N.C. Troops*, 4:521.

Mrs. S. J. Parker
Sycamore Alley
Halifax Co.
N.C.
Favour of J. C. Arrington

My dear Wife

I did not reach Wilmington till late at night, nearly twelve o'clock. The train was detained on account of some accident, near Weldon, and moreover there was a very heavy load; we had the prisoners from Roanoke Island along; they have been released on parole, and will have to remain inactive until they are regularly exchanged. It will be very galling to true men to have to see their country needing their services; and not be able to render them. No doubt but that a great many of the officers and men of the Regiments [***] will appear this way [***] but whether these two gentlemen have the same feeling is more that I can vouch for. Some of the officers attach a great deal of blame to Col. Shaw; they say that he acted very cowardly; others do not blame Shaw but blame the authority which placed him there, that authority was our great military board which existed during the past year. To say the least of the matter, it was a very unfortunate affair, and will have a very discouraging effect upon our army, I fear. However, we must cheer up and learn our brave soldiers that better things are expected of them. Well I found our perpetual court martial in session still. I hope we will finish our duties tomorrow; I am exceedingly anxious to return to camp.

I found a couple of letters here from you awaiting me. I assure [you] I read them with as much pleasure and avidity as if I had not seen you in a twelve month. I hope you will write often. You write good letters; they have the effect to cheer me up and cause me to feel better after reading them. I do not wish to flatter you, but this is really the truth.

This is a dull, gloomy, rainy day, and one's spirits are apt to be governed by the weather. I feel dull this evening; and therefore not much like writing a long letter; this will, I hope, serve to let you know that I have reached here safely, and that I have not forgotten my dear wife. I am very glad that I remained with you the other night, and only wish that I could be with you all the time. I do so much hope that matters may be so arranged

134

as that we can be together constantly, without any seperation [*sic*]. But to see so much endeavor made to reenlist men for the war, it seems as if there was to be no end to this cruel business. You will see quite a spirited address to the soldiers of the District of the Cape Fear, from Genrl. Anderson. I hope it may have the desired effect. I think the Genrl. is more in earnest now, than I have seen him for some time. You see what effect those disasters [***] It is bad that we have [***] so much for our learning.

Write soon, and let me know what [is] going on. Anything will interest me [***]. My love to the children and to [my dear] wife; remember me to Miss Martha [***].

Very affectionately your husband
F. M. Parker

◆—◆◇◆—◆

While at Camp Wyatt, on February 27, 1862, the "Mecklenburg Beauregards," Company K of the 30th Regt. N.C.T. was joined by a new private, 22-year-old William Erskine Ardrey of the lower Providence community of Mecklenburg County. Ardrey, who would rise to the rank of captain as commander of Company K, would be a faithful and detailed diarist who would chronicle the 30th's career until Appomattox.[2]

---

2. William Erskine Ardrey, age 21, enlisted for six months in the "Charlotte Grays," Company C, 1st Regt. N.C. Infantry (the Bethel Regiment in which the Enfield Blues served) as private on June 24, 1861, at Yorktown, Virginia. He mustered out November 12-13, 1861. Ardrey enlisted as private in the "Mecklenburg Beauregards," Company K, 30th Regt. N.C.T. on February 19, 1862. He was elected 2nd lieutenant on May 1, 1862, and was promoted to 1st lieutenant on September 1, 1863, and to captain on November 7, 1863. He was wounded in the head by a piece of shell June 2, 1864, near Richmond. After being hospitalized, he returned to duty July 7, 1864. Ardrey surrendered at Appomattox. Manarin and Jordan, *N.C.Troops*, 3:15, and 8:412. Taken from the diary of William Erskine Ardrey. The diary is located at Davidson College. It was published in the now-defunct *Matthews News* from about September 1991 to January 1992. I am grateful to Robert K. Krick for calling the Ardrey Diary to my attention and to Capt. Walt Hilderman of Charlotte, captain of the "Mecklenburg Beauregards" reenactment group, for providing me with a copy of the published diary. This is hereinafter referred to as the Ardrey Diary.

Camp Wyatt
March 3rd, 1862

My dear Wife

I will write you a short letter to night, although I do not feel like writing at all. I have been suffering all day with a severe head-ache which almost disqualifies me for writing, or doing almost any thing else. I hope a good night's sleep will relieve my head entirely.

This is very stormy night with us, the wind is blowing terribly; any vessel near the coast will suffer to night. Well, I did not reach camp until last Friday; brought Mrs. Draughan and Lilly with me; found Mrs. Holmes here. The two having been in camp ever since until to day, when they left for for [*sic*] Wilmington; it was quite a treat to have women in camp. I gave up my quarters to Capt. Holmes and his wife. I was much amused at the men going in in the morning to have their passes signed. They thought it was very strange that the Col. had a woman in his house.

Our Regt. is in good spirits just now; the men are reenlisting for the war. I think the whole Regt. will reenlist. This will be very gratifying to me. It shows that they have the proper feeling, and the proper appreciation of our affairs. We need many more troops right now, and I hope will have them soon. The Gov. has promised to send more to this part of the State. There is plenty [of] room for them. I am very sorry to learn, by your letter, that Fred is suffering again. I hope he will soon be back with you all and that he will remain sufficiently long to entirely recover his health. Poor fellow, he must have suffered terribly. I wish I could see him. I feel very much attached to him. He deserves a much better fate than he has met with so far. When he returns home, I will try and get to see him.

I will send you the sugar as soon as I can get it; it is said to be scarce and high, at this time.

I hope you have received the rice, and that it is good.

I suppose you receive your Journal regularly; if so you get all the news from this part of the state. If you wish to subscribe for the Richmond Examiner, you can get Mr. Moore to order it for you. I would take the weekly, if I ordered it at all.

I hope you will encourage Hilliard occasionally by speaking to him of his affairs, by assisting and upholding him in his authority, by taking notice of him and by an occasional little present of some kind. I think he will do better than Ben Hulm did. I hope every thing will move on well.

My love to the children, my regards to Miss Martha, and all the love to yourself from your affectionate husband,

F. M. Parker

Initial enlistments had generally been for twelve months, and enlistments for three years or the war were now sought. Parker turned to Company I and Capt. William T. Arrington to lead the way. J. W. Bone recalled:

> Capt. Arrington, our Captain, was a man that had great influence with his men, and as probably his would be the Company most likely to reenlist first, Col. Parker told Capt. Arrington that if his Company would al reenlist that he would let the whole Company go home at once on a fifteen day furlough, and later on then could have the other fifteen. The Captain went to work and with this inducement son had every man reenlisted. We soon packed the most of our baggage, firearms and amunition down in our quarters, and bade farewell to our comrades and Camp Wyatt for awhile. . . . This inducement helped the most of the other companies to reenlist, but no other company was allowed to go home at a time; this being about the first of March -62. We reached our homes joyfully, which place many had not seen since the first of September, feeling that we knew a great deal about war, but realy had not realized but very little.[3]

Camp Wyatt
March 6th 1862

---

3. Bone, "Service," p. 4.

My dear Wife

I should have received an answer from you, instead of writing you again, but as I did not, and as writing to you is next to receiving letters from you, here goes. We are quite busy, and full of excitement consequent upon the men of this command re-enlisting for the war; two companies have already re-enlisted, and others are nobly engaged at the work. I think every company in the Regt. will re-enlist. The government is offering strong inducements for men to re-enlist, viz., a bounty of $90 and 30 days furlough; of course this will have a great effect with some, others need no such inducement; patriotism prompts them to the deed. As soon as the company re-enlists, [we will have the] privilege of re-electing company officers; of course this puts the officers to work to secure their positions. 1st Lieutenants wishing to be Captains, second Lieutenants endeavoring to be 1st. Lts. and so on; this thing of electioneering will, I fear, have a bad effect on the men. The first company in the Regt. to re-enlist was Capt. Arrington's from Nash,[4] and I assure you he is proud of it, and well he may be; he has been unanimously re-elected Captain, which is a great compliment; for you see the men knew him, and it tells at once that he is a good commander. He leaves with his entire company tomorrow, for home, on a fifteen days' furlough. They are happy fellows tonight. Matters will be in a confused state until we get through with the re-enlisting, and the men all return from their furlough. I see that our Congress is about to pass, what I think a capital law, viz. that no planter shall make more than 3 bales of cotton for himself, and one for each hand which he works; this will entitle me to make only 12 bales cotton. So will you please instruct Hilliard to commence planting cotton at least one hundred yards from the turnip patch fence, and to plant no farther than the barn; let the rows run North and South, or from towards the creek to Carter Arrington's. Tell Hilliard to plant potatoes between the cotton and the turnip patch fence, and also on some of the best spots on the hill near the barn; tell him to select the very best ground in that part of the field for potatoes, and to plant a very large crop. I do'nt [sic] care if he plants 10

---

4. Company I of the 30th. William T. Arrington was 40-years-old when he enlisted in the company in Nash County. He was appointed captain on September 10, 1861. Arrington was killed at Malvern Hill, Virginia, on July 1, 1862. Manarin and Jordan, *N.C. Troops*, 8:401.

Capt. William T. Arrington
Co. I, 30th Regt. N.C.T.
Killed at Malvern Hill, July 1, 1862

acres. Remind him that I want as much of the low grounds cleaned up as possible; not only for this year's crop, but also for the next. I wish only my old kind of cotton to be planted; probably Bill can tell which [it is. It is in the] gin house; by no means do I [want the] seed mixed.

Have you heard any thing more of Fred yet? I feel quite uneasy about him. I wish he was at your Father's.

Your box of provisions, which you sent down, is now doing us great service; we have sausage and bones yet, and they are very nice; it is a little singular that the bones were not spoiled. I also received a box from Bella, with very nice pickles, tomato sauce, catsup, &c. These little remembrances go a great way towards softening our lot, as well as filling our stomachs. I expect to go to Wilmington soon, when I will get the sugar for you. Col. Draughan says that when you parch that Java Coffee, you must not parch it too brown. I suppose he is a connoissure [*sic*].

Remember me to all friends, to Miss Martha. My love to the children; tell Mary and Jimmy I think they ought to write to me. Kiss little Hattie, and take all the love from your affectionate husband

F. M. Parker

Camp Wyatt
March 11th 1862

My dear Wife

How much I do thank you for the good letter you last wrote me; it was worth to me a great deal; it was of more effect than a dozen sermons. I hope you will write just such letters often. I have thought on the subject of your letter, and will think on it. I have a great desire to do what is right, and I flatter myself that it is not so difficult to accomplish it now, as at some former period. I now [*sic*] I am simple and wicked, and have to contend against a great deal; my greatest trouble is my temper; I am ardent, and somewhat impetuous, but I hope by the gentle teaching and kind admonition of a good wife, the best of wives, and the grace of God assisting me, for which I daily pray, that I shall be enabled to overcome this. I repeat I hope that you will write me just such letters as the last one, often.

140

Our Chaplain held communion in camp last Sunday; I wished that I could feel that I had the right to partake of that Holy Sacramant [*sic*]. He also baptized a young man of the Regt. I hope the Chaplain is doing some good; he is not a very able man, but works quietly and patiently among the men.[5]

Have you heard the news from Tarboro, another little stranger down that way. Rather rash people, to be adding to their responsibilities in these hard times, don't you think so?

Mr. Chesire informed me of the event, and went off in one of his glowing statements; his is a happy temperment [*sic*].

I sent you the other day, by Dr. Joyner, some towels; if they are not enough I will send more; you did not say how many you wanted, and I thought I would not get too many. I hope they suited; it was rather a difficult matter to find them in Wilmington. I left orders in Wilmington for a barrell [*sic*] of sugar to be sent you. I suppose it will reach Enfield in a few days. If you will send word to Carter Arrington, he can find out whether or not it has arrived at Enfield.

I gave you some directions about my cotton crop the other day; I now wish to alter those directions; I wish to reduce my cotton crop still more. Will you please say to Hilliard to plant only the piece of land near the gin house; all between the road, and the ditch running below the old gin house. There will be some seven acres or more, and I want him to manure it very heavily, and make over a bale to the acre; tell him to manure it more than he ever saw any land manured, particularly that part on the ridge near to the road; to use good, well rotted manure and put it in thick. If his manure gives out, let him use cotton seed very plentifully. In short, tell him to try his hand on that one piece, and make a brag crop. I also wish him to plant all the land I had in cotton last year, in corn this year, except about 8 or ten acres to be planted in potatoes. I want the hill in rear of Moses' house as far out as my young fruit trees extend, to be planted in potatoes, and then commence at the turnip patch

5. Parker's grudging compliment of Chaplain A. D. Betts certainly appears justified, based upon Betts' own testimony of his work in the regiment while at Camp Wyatt. "I preached often and held prayer meeting in some company almost every night. I copied rolls of companies, noting age of each soldier, where born, postoffice, creed, and to what local church each belonged, married or single, number of children if any, etc." Betts, *Experiences*, pp. 6-7.

fence and plant two or three acres there in potatoes; let the rows run north and south, or from the lane fence towards the mash bed. In addition to this, I want the ground in the lot near the stables planted in potatoes. This will be a large potato crop; so Hilliard will have to bed a large quantity of potatoes.

Tell Moses to take good care of his hogs, to feed them well, and try and have larger hogs to fatten next winter than he did this. Hogs will be scarce again this year, and pork and bacon high. I am afraid I shall bore you with these details of business, but they are points which I think it necessary to give.

We have been very much excited for the past two weeks, on the subject of re-enlisting. Several companies of the Regt. have re-enlisted, and a great many have gone home on 15 and 30 days furlough. Our Regt. is quite thin just now. I shall be glad to welcome all back to camp. My love to the children. Remember me to Miss Martha, and the negroes.

Very affectionately your husband,
F. M. Parker

I wish Hilliard to plant the same land in corn which I selected for him when I was at home in addition to that which I have mentioned in this letter.

———————•◆•————————

Camp Wyatt
March 13th, 1862

My dear Wife

Your welcome letter reached me this evening; in it you express some disappointment at not receiving a letter from me; I thought that I had been tolerably punctual in writing, but for fear of a miscarriage in some of my letters, here goes again; for it grieves me to know that you are disappointed in any thing. And you write me such good letters, so full of good advice that I will do anything to draw one of them from you.

I wish I could get one every week; just such a letter as you wrote me a week ago. I do'nt [sic] wish to flatter you at all, but that letter had considerable effect on me. It breathed such a good, quiet, yet firm Christian spirit.

I am sorry to learn from your letters that little Hattie is not well; I hope her loss of spirits is only temporary. I am very

142

thankful that you and the children have kept so well and I have great cause for thankfulness in my own good health also. I can somewhat appreciate the great blessing which I have enjoyed, from seeing so much of sickness and suffering around me for the past eight or ten months. Our Regt. at the present time is comparitively [sic] healthy; there are no serious cases. The Regt. is still re-enlisting for the war and I think that nearly the entire Regt. will re-enlist. So you are very anxious to know something about the reorganization of the Regt. [***] Well, if all the companies of the Regt. re-enlist and re-organize, then they have the right to re-organize as a Regt. that is re-elect their Field officers. In case they do reorganize I do not fear the result; if they do not re-elect me, I could only retire, and go somewhere else. Dr. Joyner says that if they hold another election for Field officers, that I would be elected by the vote of every officer and private in the Regt. The Field officers tho are elected only by the Commissioned officers. I have every assurance that they like me and none that they dislike me. So far as affairs stand, you can judge of them just as well as I can, I allude to public affairs. I think there must necessarily be some hard fighting this spring. Our recent naval victory was a signal one. I hope we may be as successful on land.

I wrote you the other day, altering some plans previously given concerning the farm, &c. I wish only the piece of ground, in which the old gin house stands, planted in cotton; there are seven acres or more of it; Hilliard can manure it well, and make a fine crop. Tell him to plant all the land which was in cotton last years [sic] in corn this year, except enough for a large potato crop. I want the hill above Moses' house, where my young fruit trees are, planted in potatoes, and several acres next to the turnip patch, besides the lot near the stables, some of the latter he will have to [give up for] early peas, cymblins, &c. You had better have a large irish potoatoe [sic] crop planted also, so as to save corn; try and make a plenty of that, whatever is done. And Moses must take very good care of his hogs also, so as to have larger ones to fatten next winter.

After Hilliard gets his crop planted, I want him to put all his spare force in clearing up the low grounds; after planting as much of that as he can for this crop, then I want more of it cleared up for another year. I hope I shall not trouble you with my business.

143

Have you received any sugar yet? I hope you have, I ordered some sent last week. It is very high now, and I have a strong mind to buy two barrells [*sic*] instead of one, for fear that you may not be able to get it hereafter.

I should like very much to hear from Fred; poor fellow, I fear he must suffer. I hope he will soon be with you all, so that you can nurse him.

My love to the children, kiss them also; remember me to Miss Mat, Miss Martha and the negroes, and be sure to write soon.

Very affectionately your husband,
F. M. Parker

Camp Wyatt
March 14th, 1862

My dear Wife

I wrote you last night, and here I am writing you again. You will wonder what has become of Frank; why is he writing so often. If you recollect in a letter a short time since, you asked me to let you know if I should be ordered off to any point; to day I have received orders to hold my Regt. and the Artillery Company attached to it, in readiness to march at a moment's notice. If we leave here, our destination is Newberne, to meet Burnside's army. I have thus apprized you of this move, as you requested.

I have not time to write more.

My love to the children; kiss them for me. Good bye, my dear wife.

Very affectionately your husband,
F. M. Parker

Wilmington
March 14, 1862

My dearest Wife

I have just read a letter from you, which Dr. Joyner handed me to day. I am here with my Regt. under orders for Goldsboro, and am now awaiting transportation for my command. The news from Newberne is rather bad; we must not give up, or yeild [*sic*] an inch. Some one must be sacrificed in this great struggle; we are contending for a great boon, and must feel willing to pay for it; I feel perfectly [willing] to do so myself. We may fall by scores, but yet our cause will triumph, it is just and right.

If I should fall in this struggle, you have a good Father to take care of you, and above all an Heavenly Father.

But cheer up, all things are governed by His good will. He doeth all things well.

I am pained to hear of Fred's bad health. I hope the good nursing which he will receive will soon restore him to good health.

My love to all at your Father's. Kiss my little children for me and take care of them.

God bless you my dear wife, and shield and protect you and my children, I beg for Christ's sake.

Very affectionately your husband,
F. M. Parker

On March 14, 1862, the 30th Regiment was ordered to the relief of New Bern, North Carolina, which had fallen to Union Brig. Gen. Ambrose Burnside on that day. The 30th moved by steamer to Wilmington, but the orders for New Bern being cancelled, the 30th went to Camp Lamb, near Wilmington.[6]

Camp Lamb
March 18, 1862

My dear Wife

We are still near Wilmington and I do not know when we will be ordered from this place; my own opinion is that if we are not ordered off tonight or tomorrow, that we will be kept here or sent back to the forts below Wilmington. I think the men are all anxious to be sent forward; they seem to be desirous to meet the invaders and drive them from our soil. I think that Burnside should be met and whipped by North Carolinians alone, really

---

6. Historical Memoranda; Record of Events, 30th Regt. N.C.T.; Ardrey Diary.

our people have behaved so badly recently that we should wish to do something to wipe away the stain from our bright name. I hope matters may clear up yet and that North Carolina may have an opportunity of showing what we can do.

My friend, Capt. Browning has promised to take out your barrell [*sic*] of sugar tonight; I also sent by him two prs. shoes for you and one pr. for Mary; I hope they will fit and will suit. I send 1/2 doz. towels. I sent you 1/2 doz. some time since; you never said whether or not you received them. If there is any thing else you want, let me know it and I will send it to you.

The people of Wilmington are becoming very uneasy, and are leaving town in numbers, a great many of the women and children will soon be away from here. I have asked Sister Kate to take Mary and Robley and go to your house; we must do all we can to help our friends and neighbors in these times. I know you will be glad to share your house with them; if they can not get a place in Lexington, I think they will accept my offer.

There is one thing which I wish to call your attention to now; that is, if the Yankees should ever come in your county, I want you to have <u>all</u> <u>my</u> <u>cotton</u> taken out of the way and <u>burned</u>; take it to a sufficient distance from any building so that there will be no danger of setting fire to the buildings. This may seem strange advice, but I want it carried out <u>strictly</u>. I am determined that they shall never have any of my cotton; no, not if they were to pay me one hundred dollars a pound for it.

I hope you enjoyed your visit to Tarboro, and your Father's; I think it will be better for you to visit a good deal.

Remember me to all friends, to Miss Martha and the negroes. Kiss the children for me. Write often and much.

Very affectionately your husband,
F. M. Parker

Camp Lamb
March 22, 1862

My dear Wife

Yours of the 19th was received this morning; I was very glad to get it. I had not heard from you in some time, and was getting quite anxious, and somewhat uneasy about you. I am glad you are safely at home. I do not think you need apprehend any danger where you are at all; there is now between you and Burnside a very strong force of our men; I do not think that Burnside will get much farther into the interior, at any rate not from the direction of Newberne. The next move will be upon Wilmington or Norfolk, which, no one can tell. I hope we will be able to meet him, should he come here. Our force is being strengthened daily. And to day Brig. Genrl. French has assumed command of this District, Genrl. Anderson being ordered to the command at Goldsboro. Genrl. Anderson is a very clever gentleman, a most excellent man, but not a first rate military man. Genrl. French is said to be a good officer, having seen service in the Mexican war, being in some of the most warmly contested battles which were fought. President Davis has a very high opinion of him, and I hope he will do very well here. A large number of people of Wilmington have gone into the interior. Sister Kate, Mary, & Robby will leave next week for Lexington. I think Dr. Thomas' family will go to Louisburg, this is a very unpleasant thing to be compelled to break up, and leave one's home. But it is better that the women and children should get out of the way and let us have fair play.

I have sent you a barrell [*sic*] of sugar, two prs. of shoes for yourself, one for Mary, and a summer hat for Jimmy and Offa, also 1/2 doz towells [*sic*]. I hope you have received these articles, and that they will suit you. If there is any thing else you wish, let me know it, and I will send it to you. I hope the hats fitted the boys; it was all guess work with me.

I hope Cousin Margaret Bell will stay some with you; she is a favorite with me. I am very fond of her.

I wrote you some time since to have but a very little cotton planted. I am still of the same opinion, and if it was not for keeping up seed, I would not plant any at all. Let me know how you get on as a farmer. Write soon and often.

Remember me to Miss Mat, Miss Martha and to the negroes. Kiss the children for me. Good bye dear wife, God bless you.

Your affectionate husband,
F. M. Parker

Have you received Col. Draughan's likeness in a case?

Camp Lamb
March 23rd, 1862

My dear Wife

This is Sunday, and I have not been able to attend church; if it had been convenient I should most certainly have gone; that is one objection I have to war, there is no Sunday in war; we very often have to do on that Holy day, just what we would on any other day. Sally, I feel the need of something which I do not possess; I try to be a good man, and a good christian; I know that I am guilty of no glaring sin; I do not swear at all, I do not drink, I do not bear malice towards any one, and yet I feel that there is something yet wanted to make me feel safe and secure. I would go to the Bishop, and openly take upon myself the vows which my sponsers made for me on Baptism, but I am afraid that I might be guilty of some conduct, or do or say some thing after that, which would cast a reproach on the christian religion. This troubles me very much, and yet I feel that I should do something myself. I feel that I need some one to whom I could unbosom myself freely; oh! how I would like to see you, and spend even a short while with you. Your letters are a great comfort to me, but yet it would be more satisfactory to be with you face to face. I have not mentioned my feelings to any one, nor do I know that I shall. These are such exciting exciting [*sic*] times, that calm, serious conversation is hardly thought of. But to me it is different; this thing has impressed itself on me ever since I have been in the army; the fact of being separated from you and the children, first brought me to think and feel very seriously and then such good advice as I have had from letters from the best of wives, has fastened these sober thoughts on my mind, until I now know that something is necessary to be done. Yes, my dear wife, you can have the satisfactory reflection that you were directly and indirectly the means of bringing me to a true sense of my real position. How I love you for it. If we are allowed to be together in this world, I hope to be able to repay you for it, and if we can be together in the world to come, that will be the reward which you will be satisfied with.

I wrote you yesterday that Genrl. French was in command of this District; he is now on a visit to the Forts at the mouth of the river; I suppose he will return to day; where our next move will be, of course we do not know. I think we will either be kept here, sent to Ft. Johnson, or back to Camp Wyatt.

148

I have recently forwarded you some articles, all of which I hope you will acknowledge the receipt of, so that I may know that you have them; I think I shall send you another barrell [*sic*] of sugar. I am glad to hear that Fred has improved. I hope he will soon be well. Do take him to be more prudent than he was before, and not report for duty too soon. I was satisfied that he returned to camp too soon. No doubt but that he felt well, but was not able to stand the exposure of camp life.

By the way, I see that his Regt. is back in this State. This will be a great temptation for him to join his company too soon. Tell him we will want his services hereafter. There is now a large body of troops in our State, and I would not be surprised if we have some hot work soon. I very much hope that we will be able to drive Burnside from our soil; I think we should do it, and with North Carolinians too.

Dr. Joyner sends his regards to you, and wishes you to say to Mrs. Bennett that he has sent her man Brittain home. If you have any old hams to spare, I wish you would send a few to Mrs. Joyner, with my compliments.

Let me know if I can send you any thing from Wilmington.

My regards to Miss Mat, Miss Martha and the negroes, and my love to the children; kiss them for me, and do'nt [*sic*] let them forget me. Good bye my dear wife.

Very affectionately your husband
F. M. Parker

On March 26, 1862, the regiment moved three miles to Camp French.[7]

Camp French
March 27th, 1862

My dear Wife

You will see that we are on the [***] now from the frequent changes in our camp. Our present encampment is about two miles from Wilmington, near a line of breastworks which have

---

7. Record of Events; Ardrey Diary.

been thrown up for the protection of Wilmington from a land attack. The camp I have named in compliment of Brig. Genrl. French, who is now in command of the Dist. of the Cape Fear and whom I like very much, at least from appearances I think he is a good military man, and that is what we want just now. He is a New Jersey man by birth, but has been living in Mississippi for some years. The Genrl. served gallantly in the Mexican War, fighting side by side in the most warmly contested fights of that war, side by side with President, then Col. Davis, who speaks in the highest terms of him. I think our men have confidence in the Genrl. just from his appearance, for they have seen but a very little of him. I think it probable that Mr. Nicholson may know Genrl. French, also his Aid de Camp [sic], Capt. Haile,[8] who are both ~~from~~ planters from Deer Creek, Mississippi.

We are living in tents again, the Genrl. says, and I think truly, that soldiers have no use for houses; tents are the proper places for them. I feel more at home in my tent and on my little cot, than I did on my bunk and in my quarters. The Genrl. says that he intends moving us every week, until we get clear of all our extra baggage. So you see that he is energetic and prompt and wishes others to be so. It is best for the men, they should not be loaded with baggage.

I wrote you the other day, that I should send you more sugar soon. I will do so whenever the Commissary gets his sugar from New Orleans; he has promised to reserve a barrell [sic] for me. I will send you more Java coffee soon, and that will be the last you will get in some time; so you had better take nice care of it. Let me know if you need any thing else. Please say to Mr. Dunn that salt is worth $4 per bushel now, but that the rail road will take no frieght [sic] now, while so many troops have to be moved. As for his paper, I will try and send him some, but shall not be able to bring it to him in some time. We must drive the invaders from our soil, before we think of home or its pleasures, or rather before we absent ourselves from our duties.

---

8. Calhoun Haile served with the rank of lieutenant as aide-de-camp to Brig. Gen. Samuel G. French from November 1861, to May 1862, when he returned to his regiment, the 20th Mississippi Infantry. He served as captain of Company A of the 20th Mississippi and was wounded at the battle of Franklin, Tennessee, on November 30, 1864. Dunbar Rowland, *Military History of Mississippi 1803-1898* (Jackson, Mississippi: Dept. of Archives and History, 1908; reprint: Spartanburg, South Carolina: The Reprint Company, 1978), pp. 235 and 241.

Sister Kate and Cousin Mary with their children will leave their homes next week; they both dislike it very much. I hope you will never be forced to do this; a home is a good place. I am in hopes that Fred is nearly well by this time; tell him to be very careful of his health. If he feels like visiting, ask him to go and stay with you; it would be very pleasant to both I know. I wish I could be there with him. I assure you that I will be with you at as early a day as possible, but can not [letter ends here]

Camp French
March 29, 1862

My dear Wife

I send home to day my mess chest, with a pr. of my blankets, a little clothing which I do not need, and some empty bottles which I thought might be of service to you, as bottles are scarce now; in the vest pocket is a small post monie [*sic*] for Mary, and a few steel pens; tell her to use the pens in writing to me. Genrl. French is preparing for active, vigorous movements, and that is just what our forces should have been at before. I have been causing the Regt. to get clear of all superfluous baggage, so that we may be prepared to move at a few moments notice. I think we will soon be in that condition.

I received your good letter yesterday, I have read it several times, and the more I read it, the more pleased am I with it. I will try to carry out your advice. I find there are a great many little trials and temptations which arise daily; these need a great deal of care and circumspection in order to be managed, and controlled. I want to be a good christian, and will hope and try and pray to be one. If it was not for you to unbosom myself to I should be in a bad condition. I have no one else, in whom I feel like confiding. I hope these expressions of my feelings are kept within your own heart. If it is possible, I will meet you at Tarboro when the Bishop visits that place. But I am afraid I can not leave my command for some time to come; not until times become more quiet.

Yesterday I received a letter from Mr. Nicholson, asking me to send him a barrell [*sic*] of sugar; will you please say to him that the rail road is transporting nothing now but troops and government stores. If, however, I can send it by some friend, and can get the sugar, I will send it soon. Sugar is very scarce now; that which I sent you, I obtained from the Brigade Commissary (Capt. Drane) and could not have done so, had I not been an officer. I had to give him a certificate that the sugar was for the use of my family. I shall send you another barrell [*sic*], which he has promised me, as soon as it arrives from New Orleans. I shall soon send you some Java coffee, which will be the last I can get you. It is exceedingly scarce. If you have the woolen pants (grey) brought home from Va. will you please send them to me. I want them for my servant. Henry Johnston, of Enfield will forward them for you. You will also find the collard seed you gave me; no chance for gardens now, with the soldiers, at least. [letter ends here]

Camp French
March 30th 1862

My dear Wife

You will see that this is Sunday; I have just received orders to move with my Regt. down on the sound to'morrow, and I thought it best to write you to night so as to let you know of our movements. I am afraid our mail arrangements will be bad, and that I shall not be able to hear from you so often; but you must nevertheless write often, so that when I do get a chance at the mails, I may get a handful of letters.

I expect the place we are going to, is a very pleasant one, you would regard it as such for I hear that fish are abundant in the sound. Fish and oysters are a great part of the living of these people in this country. I have seen Sister Kate and Cousin Mary this evening; they both leave their homes in the morning at 2 o'clock for the up country. I assure you they dislike to go very much. It must be very unpleasant to have to break up ones arrangements. But to us soldiers, it is pleasant; every change is agreeable. It is a great deal best that it should be so; we must not become attached to any one place; we must always be ready to leave our camp at the shortest notice; and the only idea which should possess us, should be to see how quickly we could move. A strong attachment to any place and its surroundings would be in the way of these sudden movements.

Do'nt [*sic*] think that this wandering life will cause me to be restless and uneasy, should I be so fortunate as to reach home again; no, I think I shall be sufficiently amused with tramping about through the country, to remain perfectly satisfied at home when I get there. I hope we will soon be able to drive the Yankees out of our State, so that we can get a furlough occasionally; as long as they remain in our front, there will be no chance for any man to leave, even if he wished it. Last night I sent home my mess chest by Dr. Joyner, who is sick. I also sent the key to you in a letter, which I hope you will receive. The chest contains such things as I do not need now. Genrl. French is reducing our baggage, very properly too. If you will send the pants, I wrote for, (the grey woolens I brought from Va.) to Enfield, Dr. Joyner will bring them to me. I want them for my boy Jim. I sent you by the Dr. a little soap; not that I supposed you personally needed it, but that it would probably be convenient.

Where will you get your negro clothes from this spring? Probably I might send you some cloth for the women's frocks soon. Sister Kate has ordered some from up the country [*sic*] and says I may have a part of it. I expect it will cost 20 or 25 cents per yard. If you can do no better, I will send it to you. Write soon and give me all the news. Remember me to Miss Mat, Miss Martha and the negroes. Kiss the children for me. God bless you my dear wife.

Very affectionately your husband,
F. M. Parker

On March 30 and 31, 1862, the regiment moved five miles to Camp Holmes near Masonboro Inlet.[9]

Camp Holmes
April 2, 1862

My dear Wife

9. Record of Events.

We are at another new encampment as you may see from the direction above. I have named the camp complimentary to Maj. Genrl. Holmes, commanding the Department of N.C. It is a beautiful location for a camp; on a hill, and very near to a large branch of good running water, and about 2 miles from the ocean, within sound of its roar. This is decidedly the best ground for camping, we have had in this State. I think it will be healthy; we are right among the long leaf pines; and you know your Father regards the piney woods as healthy. This is so pleasant a place, that our men say that the Genrl. will not allow us to remain here long.

I sent my mess chest to you the other day; and am glad I did so; we all have too much baggage. I think seriously of sending my trunk also.

Genrl. French has infused a great deal of energy into his command already. He is a good officer.

Wilmington is still our post office; we send our post man up every day; so you may write as much as you please, direct your letters to Wilmington and I will be apt to receive them. I have not had one from you now in several days. Why does'nt [*sic*] Mary write? She commenced so well, that I was in hopes she would keep on; tell her to write to me. I hope your coffee will go up this week. I want you to send me a little bacon when Dr. Joyner returns, 75 or 100 lbs. if you please, hams, shoulders and middlings; weigh the bacon and let me know the number of pieces and the weight. If you have any sausage, or any thing of that kind, you may send a little of that along also. The bacon I shall charge to my mess. I can tell you we are rather scarce on commissary's stores just now, but I understand we will get a plenty of fish soon. When you send for your coffee, you can send the bacon to Enfield. It will be useless to start it from Enfield, unless under the charge of some one; therefore, I wish Dr. Joyner to bring it. In your next letter let me know precisely how much salt you have on hand; I think it best that you should take good care of all you have, as it is now and will be a difficult matter to procure it. I will send you more, as soon as the rail roads will transport it. Salt is now selling at five dollars per bushel.

I have no news at all to give you. The Wilmington Journal will post you.

Our Regt. is in good health, and is getting in good fighting order; but as regards drill and strength, we now number nine hundred and twenty nine (929) aggregate. I hope soon to have one thousand.

Whenever matters become quiet I will go to see you if I can; in the mean time you must write to me, and pray for me and think of me, and you know I will do the same for you. I never knew how to appreciate you, as I do now.

Remember me to Miss Mat and all friends. Kiss the children and keep them mindful of me.

Good bye my dear wife. God bless you, dear wife, is the prayer of your loving husband

F. M. Parker

Camp Holmes
April 4th 1862

My dear Wife

I received a good, long letter from you on [the] day before yesterday; it is useless to say that I was glad to get it, your own experience and your own heart will tell you that it is more than pleasant to receive letters, and particularly such letters as you write me; they are very consoling and encouraging to me, and I hope that this assurance on my part will cause you to write often. Your letters and my own judgment and reflections are the only guides I have in my search after truth. The chaplain which we have in the Regt. is not with us much; and when he is here, he is not of much strength; not a man to inspire much respect or confidence. This is rather unfortunate. I never should have appointed such a man as Chaplain, had he not been recommended so strongly by the Commissioned officers of the Regt. They all regret the course they pursued.

Well, I expect you are busy in your garden this nice, warm spring morning. I wish you much success in your gardening. A good garden is a great help to a family; particularly when provisions are so scarce. You have no idea of the very great scarcity about Wilmington; bacon is selling at 30 cents per lb., beef at 17 to 20 cents; peas at $2.75 per bushel, and other things in proportion, and all very hard to obtain at that. I mention these things to let you know what hard times are ahead of us. Take good care of every thing in the way of eatables, it will be all needed. It is a great satisfaction to me, to know that you have a plenty at home, and I know you will see that none of your supply is improperly used or wasted. And by the way, will you please send me 1/2 bushel peas when you send the bacon by Dr. Joyner. There is another article which is <u>very scarce</u>, and that is paper; not a quire can be bought in Wilmington; it is very hard to be had any where in the Confederacy. I hope you have a supply of that; the paper I brought you from Newberne has not given out yet, has it? I can send you some if you need it; you must be kept in paper, and I will see to it. I sent to Wilmington yesterday for your pins, but not a paper could be had, not one pin.

Col. Draughan has sent to Fayetteville to day for some for you; so I hope to be able to forward them to you soon. Let me know if you want any thing else, and if so you shall have it, if I can get it.

Have you ever received Col. Draughan's picture yet? and if so, what do you think of the old gentleman? He is a good one I assure you, but he wo'nt [*sic*] let me call him old; he insists upon it, that he is as young as I am. I was grieved and surprised to hear that Fred is still so bad off. I should like very much to see him. I hope he will soon be well.

I am much pleased to hear such good reports from you of Hilliard. I have no doubt but that he will do his best. I think a little encouragement from you will be of service to him; he is a good boy. Tell him to clean up as much of the low grounds as possible. Tell Moses to take good care of his hogs; feed them well.

My kindest regards to Miss Mat, Miss Martha and to the negroes, and a kiss to my children, and all the love of an affectionate husband to a good wife.

Yours devotedly,
F. M. Parker

> "Sally, my men fell around me thick and fast,
> and not a hair of my head was touched."
> — F. M. Parker

PART FIVE
April, 1862 - July, 1862
Camp Holmes - Malvern Hill, Virginia

Camp Holmes
April 5 1862

My dear Wife

Well now you have been feeding me well with letters for the past few days. I am afraid you will spoil me unless you continue such treatment. I shall look for a letter most every day. The box has not come to hand yet, but I expect to receive it this afternoon. I assure you it will be very acceptable; we are rather short of provisions down here; it is naturally a scarce country, and the increase of troops has made it more so. While at Camp Wyatt, we had an Artillery Company attached to the Regt., which was ordered to Goldsboro at the same time that the Regt. was; we were halted at Wilmington, and the Artillery sent on; but we now have another Artillery company with us, Capt. Moore's from Wilmington;[1] it is said to be one of the best drilled, and finest Batteries in the service; we are all encamped together, the Regt. on one side of the road, and the Battery on the other.

It is generally considered a compliment to a Regt. to have a Battery of Artillery attached to it. I am glad Genrl. French gave us this one. Capt. Moore is a fine young man, and a perfect gentleman.

In one of your former letters you seemed to be a little uneasy on account of certain things which you had heard relative to the action of one of the captains of the Regt., Capt. [William T.] Arrington is a very restless man and is constantly seeking some change. I do'nt [sic] suppose he has any objection to me, by

---

1. Company E, 10th Regt. N.C. State Artillery (1st Regt. N.C. Artillery), known as the "Wilmington Light Artillery" or "Moore's Battery" was commanded by Capt. Alexander D. Moore. Manarin and Jordan, *N.C.Troops*, 1:89. Moore's Battery joined the 30th Regt. at Camp Holmes on April 8, 1862, according to the Ardrey Diary.

wishing to get out of the Regt. but simply a desire for a change. He has always seemed very friendly towards me, was one of the most active men in my election; and has acted towards me in a very sociable, cordial and confidential manner ever since. A great many reports you hear are not so. It is an easy matter for one to say what another has said, whether the remark has been made [or] not. I do not feel at all uneasy.

I think there is some doubt about the Regt. reenlisting. Some of the companies can not agree as to their officers so the probability is that the Regt. will remain as it is, [until] the expiration of their term of service, which will be [the] 26th Sept. next. Such matters never trouble me in the least. I intend to serve my country in some capacity; as a private, if in no other way. These are no times to squa[bble] over office. I feel certain that I have the confidence [of] my command, and that I do my duty as near as [most] men; and as long as I can keep this feeling, I shall go ahead. I am proud of my Regt.; I have never had a single care before a General Court Martial [yet] having always managed them myself. It is certainly as well disciplined a body of troop as I know of. This may be boasting. I do not intend it as such.

The Regt. now numbers about nine hundred and thirty, and to day I shall send out recruiting officers from each company, by which means I hope to be able to increase our strength to over a thousand, probably eleven or twelve hundred; that will be a fine Regt.

We are now encamped on very good ground, high and dry, with a good branch near which gives us plenty of water; we are about two miles from the sound; should we remain in this part of the country much longer, I shall move our camp nearer the sound, where we can get the benefit of the sea breeze. In examining the country and roads [page(s) missing]

Camp Holmes
April 12th 1862

My dear Wife

It has now been several days, several long days since I have had a letter from you; what is the matter? is the fault with you, or with the mails; my heart tells me that it is the latter; for I

158

believe you would not treat me so badly as to allow almost an entire week to pass without writing me. Particularly when you know from experience, how gratifying it is to receive letters. I have succeeded in getting a few papers of pins for you, from Fayetteville. I expect more soon. I also send you some paper; it is foolscap, but paper is paper now. It is a very difficult matter to get any at all. I shall go to Wilmington to day, to see something about the cloth I wrote you of.

Well the tide of war has at last changed in our favour; I expect we have achieved a glorious victory in the west. Beauregard is generally very modest in his official dispatches; and I look forward to the particulars, to see much more than his dispatch has led us to hope for. We may look for stirring news from the Peninsula soon. Magruder has over 40,000 effective men there, and has several able Generals to assist him, among them our gallant Hill and Genrl. Loring. I sometimes feel as if I should like to be there again. But I shall remain perfectly quiet where I am. I trust in the Lord that we may be successful every where; I feel as if the rascals who are invading us, should be annihilated perfectly, and this is a calm, sober conclusion.

I have received the box of bacon, and it is very nice; you have succeeded in smoking your bacon very well. If I could [get] them down here, I would like to have some peas and potatoes but transportation is so uncertain, that I think it useless to risk it.

I shall enclose twenty ($20) dollars in this letter. I shall send more soon, sometime, early in May.

I have not a particle of news to write you, I can only mention that our men keep well, and are in fine spirits. We are still much pleased with our camp.

Do write soon, very soon, and very often. Remember me to Miss Mat., Miss Martha and all friends and to the negroes. Kiss my children, and keep them mindful of their Pa.

Good bye my dear Wife; God bless and keep you is the prayer of your affectionate husband.

F. M. Parker

———————◄•●•►———————

Camp Holmes
April 13th 1862

My dear Wife

I was in Wilmington on yesterday, succeeded in getting the linen for the boys; had to [pay] pretty high for it; I also sent you some paper, and your pins, which Col. Draughan had brought from Fayetteville; all these things I sent by Capt. Browning to the care of Mrs. Joyner. You will find 50 lbs. good coffee at Mrs. Joyner's also. The Dr. and I bought a bag between us. I also sent by Capt. Browning $20 enclosed in a letter, which I requested him to mail at Enfield. I hope you will receive all these things safely. Write me and let me know if you have. I did not say any thing to Dr. Drane about the cloth Sister Kate was to send me.

Let me know whether or not you need any [***]. I have never heard from you about this salt yet. I have 4 bushels in Wilmington, which I shall send up as soon as convenient. I had to pay $4.67 per bushel; it is now selling at $7.00 per bushel. Every thing is remarkably high about Wilmington; bacon 30 cents. per lb.; beef 20 cents; chickens $1.00 each; butter 75 cents per lb. Now what do you think of that? I do not blame the people for leaving there. The fact is that the Military authorities should take hold of the matter, and regulate the price of every thing for sale.

My dear wife there is a question very near to me, that I have been thinking over seriously for some time. If nothing prevents, I shall go to the Bishop on sunday [sic] next, to take upon myself a vow which was made for me in Holy Baptism. I have thought of this matter a good deal; your letters have enlightened me somewhat on the subject, and I think it a duty I owe to myself, to take the step I shall take, if I am able to do so.

I hope I am not acting presumptuously in so doing. I do it with the fullest sense of responsibility on my part; in fact this has kept me from this step long since. I believe I am doing right, I pray it may be for my eternal good. Of the propriety of the act itself, I have no doubt but that I am fully prepared to receive such a benefit, I am not perfectly certain I do it because [I] believe it right, and I pray so grace for to [act] and so to live, as to prove myself worthy hereafter.

I would be happy to see you, and speak face [to] face, but this pleasure is debarred us now; and there is no telling when I shall be able to leave here.

God bless you my dear Wife, I owe more to you than to any one else on this earth. I hope I [may] live to thank you sufficiently.

We have rather gloomy news from Georgia. We must keep cheerful, always look on the bright side, do our best, and leave the rest in the hands of a Higher Power.

Write me soon and often. Remember me to all friends. Kiss the children, and keep them mind[ful] of their Pa.

Very affectionately your husband
F. M. Parker

Camp Holmes
April 15, 1862

Dr. Drane

Dear Sir

If I am at my present encampment on Sunday or within convenient distance of Wilmington, I shall be with you on that day. My desire is to take upon myself the solemn obligation which my sponsors made for me in Holy Baptism. I am aware of the responsibility of this stop; this knowledge has prevented me from acting sooner, but I think it my duty, and I shall endeavor to perform it trusting in God's help and favor.

Very truly yours
F. M. Parker[2]

Camp Holmes
April 16th 1862

My dear Wife

---

2. This letter is in the possession of the Parker family and not among those in the North Carolina Division of Archives. The Rev. Dr. Robert Brent Drane (Jan. 9, 1797 - Oct. 14, 1862) was the Rector of St. James's Episcopal Church, Wilmington, from 1836 until his death from yellow fever. Dr. Drane was Parker's brother-in-law, being married to his older sister, Catherine Caroline Hargrave Parker. Powell, *Dictionary of North Carolina Biography*, 2:103.

I have received two letters from you recently; you say that you do not get mine; I can not understand this, for I write quite often. There must be some irregularity in the mails. You wish to know if I can not meet you in Tarboro on the 27th. I am afraid it will be impossible for me to be absent now for some time; times are rather uneasy; and every one is expected to be at his post; not even ordinary sickness in a man's family is a sufficient cause for leave of absence to be granted. So, I can not tell when I shall see you. I am more than anxious to see you and the children; but we must wait patiently and quietly. Rest assured that I will be with you as soon as I possibly can. I shall go to Wilmington on friday [sic], and will try and get the articles you have written for. I sent you a few little packages last week, some linen, paper, pins &c., have you received them?

Dr. Joyner remarked to me the other day, that his wife had sent, by mistake, to you some tripoli; if so you had better return it to Mrs. Joyner, by the first opportunity. Say to Miss Martha that I will get her paper and envelopes if I can.

And Billy Arrington is married is he! well, unless he has altered somewhat, he has not much [use] for a wife. I always liked Billy, and wish him well. I am glad you like Cousin Margaret [Bell] so much; she was always a favourite with me. I wish she would stay with you more.

You wish to know something about shirts for the spring for me. I will try it awhile with what I have on hand; so you need not trouble yourself about it at all.

I am glad to hear that Fred is well enough to ride to Tarboro; I hope he will improve fast. It may be very <u>convenient</u> for him to remain about Tarboro for some time. I suppose there is some attraction there. I shall like very much to see him; I hope he will come to see me, as soon as he is able. I think if I were you, I should claim a part of his time myself.

I am sorry you do not receive the Wilmington Journal, I have written to the proprietors about it; and if you do not receive it soon, let me know it. News is very scarce here. Every thing moves on in the usual way. We are expecting to be moved again soon, probably higher up the coast. We have been looking for Genrl. French for a couple of days, to review and inspect the Regt. that will be a little excitement in that. Confined in camp, soldiers look forward to any excitement with pleasure. I hope you get on well with your farming operations. I have no doubt but that Hilliard will do well.

162

Write to me often, and let me know every thing that is going on. Tell Mary to write also. Remember me to all friends. Kiss the children for me, and keep them mindful of their Pa.

Good bye my dear Wife, God bless you and yours, is the prayer of your affectionate husband

F. M. Parker

On April 18, 1862, Parker detached Companies A, D, and H of the 30th for duty in Onslow County, up the coast from Wilmington, to defend against Federal raiding parties. These three companies reached Jacksonville on April 21 after a 57 mile march and moved 9 miles to Hatchel's Mills on April 24.[3]

Camp Holmes
April 20th 1862

My dear Wife

You are really improving in the frequency of your letters; as scarce as paper is, I would be glad if you would write me at least three times a week. I am glad you received the articles I sent you, but I do not understand what you mean by the plaid, unless it is the linen which I intended for the boys clothes, I think that was checked, or figured in some way. You are right when you say that that would be too thick for summer shirts. I intended that for the little boys. I wish you would send my two brown linen shirts, and thin drawers and summer socks. Put them in my little hand trunk, send it to Enfield, and request A. B. Whitaker Esqu to Henry Johnston to hand it to Capt. Browning, who will bring it to me.

Have the key delivered to Henry, so that he can give it to Capt. Browning. I shall send home, a good many of my clothes, in my large trunk. The Genrl. has ordered the baggage to be reduced, and I wish to set a good example. I was in Wilmington on yesterday, but could not get you a hoop skirt. I think I shall be able to send one the latter part of the week. I sent the shoes and a few envelopes; I found no paper, except some which had been torn out of old blank books. May be you can spare Miss

---

3. Historical Memoranda and Record of Events.

Martha some of your paper, and envelopes. Sister Kate has not sent the cloth she promised. I reckon she could not get it. So you had better get your cloth either in Tarboro or Petersburg. Ca'nt [sic] you get Mr. Matthew Waddell to assist you in it.

This morning I shall go to Wilmington to attend Church, and in the afternoon I wish to be confirmed by the Bishop.[4] You know my feelings in this matter. I can but pray for help and strength [to] carry me safely through the trials and difficulties in the way. I do not wish to flatter you my dear Wife, but your kind advice, so constantly and appropriately given, and the fond memory of a good and pious Mother, have led me to this, the most important step of my life.

I hope that my future life will be such as [will] reflect credit on your teachings. I agree with [you] that we may not expect any great change of feeling, upon taking this step. I look upon it as my plain duty, and I shall endeavor so to perform that duty hereafter as to meet with some satisfaction to myself and with a higher reward hereafter.

I think we will soon leave our present encampment. I have already sent three companies of the Regt. under Col. Draughan over to Onslow County, to check the marauding parties of the enemy and in a few days I shall follow with the entire Regt. My post office will still be Wilmington. So I shall receive your letters just as direct.

Write me often, and let me know what is going on, how every thing is going on at home.

Remember me to all friends. Kiss the children; and let them know that their Pa loves them and thinks of them every day. Good bye my dear Wife, God bless you and them.

Very affectionately your husband
F. M. Parker

On April 24, 1862, the balance of the 30th Regiment, excepting Company E which was detached for picket duty around Wilmington, was ordered on a 70 mile march to Onslow County.

---

4. Thomas Atkinson (1807-1881), who resided in Wilmington, was the third Episcopal bishop of North Carolina. Powell, *Dictionary of North Carolina Biography*, 1:62-63.

Passing through Kirkwood, this force marched 12 miles then encamped at Set's. J. W. Bone remembered:

> This was the first march of any considerable distance that we had been called on to perform since we had been in service. We started off in fine spirits, each one loaded with baggage. The roads were very sandy but we soon got upon a plank road, which helped us along in marching, but made our feet very sore. We got to the end of the plank road the first day. The next morning we were sore all over and several began to hire their baggage carried where they could.[5]

On April 25, the six companies marched 22 miles and camped at Golden place. On April 26, they marched 21 miles and camped at Shepherd's store. Their route on Sunday, April 27, took them 16 miles across the New River and through Jacksonville. On April 28, after a seven mile march, these companies were reunited near White Oak River in Onslow County with the three companies that had gone before, and Camp Sanders was established there, being named "complimentary to an old lady whom the Yankees had treated badly." Parker took command there of two companies of cavalry which had previously been sent northward to picket against Federal forces scouting and raiding from New Bern, the "Scotland Neck Mounted Infantry," Company G, 41st Regt. N.C.T. (3rd Regt. N.C. Cavalry), a Halifax County company which contained many of Parker's neighbors from home and former comrades in the Enfield Blues, the "Rebel Rangers," Company A, 41st Regt. N.C.T. (3rd Regt. N.C. Cavalry), a New Hanover company commanded by Capt. Abram Francis Newkirk, and a detachment of artillery.[6]

———————— ◆•◆ ————————

Camp Sanders Onslow County
April 29th 1862

My dear Wife

5. Bone, "Service," p. 5.
6. Historical Memoranda; Ardrey Diary; Clark, *N.C. Regiments*, 2:497.

It has been days since I wrote you, but it has not been my fault. I left Camp Holmes on friday [sic] last with my Regt. and arrived in the present vicinity on sunday [sic] evening. We are now near to Jones county, not far from the enemy. The rascals have been committing raids in this part of the county unchecked; and Genrl. French has sent me down to chastise them, should they come out. I went to day within 18 miles of Newberne without discovering any sign of the enemy. So you see that I am in active service at last; in fact the Genrl. remarked to me, on leaving Wilmington, that he wished me to carry on a partizan [sic] warfare down here.

I have my own Regt., about 200 cavalry, and a part of Capt. Moore's Battery. In fact, all the forces in Onslow county are under my command. Whether we accomplish any thing or not, remains to be seen. Capt. Hills [sic] cavalry Co.[7] is with us; Jo and Ben Arrington[8] are members of that Co. Jo looks better than I ever saw him. There are several members of my old company "I" of the 1st Regt. in Capt. Hill's Co. I have really been so busy, that I have seen but a very little of them yet. Al Wiggins[9] is also among them.

I hope you were in Tarboro on sunday [sic] last; I thought of you on that day, while trudging along at the head of my column, and would have greatly preferenced being with you in church to where I was. I have a strong desire to be confirmed in that church; I mean that building; but I am glad I did not put the

---

7. The "Scotland Neck Mounted Rifles," Company G, 41st Regt. N.C.T. (3rd Regt. N.C. Cavalry) was raised in Halifax County and commanded by Halifax County native and resident Capt. Atherton Barnes Hill who was promoted to captain on October 9, 1861. Hill was defeated for re-election upon the company's reorganization on May 1, 1862. He was later appointed drillmaster with the rank of 2nd lieutenant and ordered to report to the Conscript Bureau. Manarin and Jordan, *N.C. Troops*, 2:227 and 807.

8. Benjamin F. Arrington, after service in 1861 in the Enfield Blues, enlisted in New Hanover County in the Scotland Neck Mounted Rifles on January 1, 1862, as a private. He was appointed bugler September-October, 1864. Manarin and Jordan, *N.C. Troops*, 2:228.

9. Alfred S. Wiggins was a 28-year-old physician residing in Halifax County when he enlisted as private in the Scotland Neck Mounted Rifles on April 23, 1861. Appointed 1st sergeant May 19, 1862, and elected 3rd lieutenant June 14, 1862, Wiggins was promoted to 2nd lieutenant October 7, 1862. He was killed May 17, 1863. Manarin and Jordan, *N.C. Troops*, 2:228.

matter off. There is no telling [now] when I shall have the opportunity, which I enjoyed on the sunday [sic] before I left Camp Holmes. I hope and pray to be enabled to live up to the promises then made. You [pray] for me also. I feel that it is a step I should have taken long since; I should have been a better man. I must endeavor now to make amends for the time past.

I forwarded to you, through your Father, some funds, which I hope you have received. Capt. Browning also promised to take the hoop skirt to you, as soon as one could be had in Wilmington. I am sorry I shall not be able to get any thing for you now. We are nearly 60 miles from Wilmington.

Remember me to all friends, and to the negroes. Kiss the children for me, and tell them to think of their Pa.

Write very often, direct to Wilmington.

Very truly and lovingly your husband

F. M. Parker

On May 1, 1862, at Camp Sanders, the regiment was reorganized with the officers standing again for election. Parker was re-elected colonel and Major James T. Kell defeated Walter Draughan for lieutenant colonel. 1st Lieutenant William W. Sillers of the "Sampson Rangers," Company A, was elected major. Parker regretted Draughan's defeat and felt that "the Thirtieth lost a worthy officer in the person of Lieutenant-Colonel Draughan."[10]

Camp Sanders
May 4th 1862

My dear Wife

It is sunday [sic] afternoon; no duty to attend to just now, so I have concluded to write to my dear Wife. You must not expect to hear from me often now; in the first place, we do not get our mail very regularly, and then I am kept very busy; so much so that I can not write as often as I wish to. Well, the forces in this command have all reorganized, and are now in for the war. Our

---

10. Historical Memoranda; Clark, *N.C. Regiments*, 2:497.

elections took place on the 1st ult. I am sorry to say that Lt. Col. Draughan was not reelected; there was a combination against him, which proved successful[.] The Major was promoted, and one of the Lieutenants elected Major; he is a very nice man, a capital selection, and I doubt not will make a good officer; you may probably have heard me speak of him very favourably, he is Lt. [William W.] Sillers of Sampson Co. Some of the companies of the Regt. have suffered in a change of officers, which I fear will be a drawback to the service.

You have no idea what desolation there is in this country; a great many of the people have left their homes, with no one to look to them. Some of the plantations have not a single person black or white left on them. I was at a very nice place on yesterday, and to see how every thing looked, was enough to make one sad. I was there for the purpose of burning cotton, removing corn, pork &c; it was down very near the enemy, in fact they had been at the very place not a week ago. I have orders to remove all such stores, burn all the cotton, take all the horses and mules which are likely to fall in the hands of the enemy. This is very unpleasant, but it has to be done; if we do'nt [sic] take them, the yankees will; and use them against us too. Al and Tom Wiggins,[11] Ben and Jo Arrington were in the party I had yesterday; these boys seem to enter into these things with a good deal [of] life. There are several members of my old company in the Scotland Neck Mounted Rifles; they too have changed their officers. Capt. Higgs[12] succeeded Capt. Hill; Henry A. Moore is not in very robust health[;] he is wishing to be discharged for disability.

I have not received the trunk you sent me; I expect to get it this week. You have sent rather too many clothes; they will be in my way; the ham &c will be very acceptable. You wish to

---

11. Thomas J. M. Wiggins was an 18-year-old student residing in Halifax County when he enlisted in the Scotland Neck Mounted Rifles on April 23, 1861. He was present or accounted for through February, 1864. Manarin and Jordan, *N.C.Troops*, 2:236.
12. George Andrew Higgs, a Halifax County resident, enlisted in the Scotland Neck Mounted Rifles on April 23, 1861. He was appointed 3rd lieutenant to rank from date of enlistment and was promoted to 1st lieutenant November 4, 1861, and was elected captain at the May 1, 1862, reorganization of the company. He resigned September 13, 1862, by reason of ill health, and his resignation was accepted October 7, 1862. Manarin and Jordan, *N.C.Troops*, 2:227-228.

168

know something about old iron; I think the price which the Government offers is 2½ cents per lb.; if there is no government agent at Enfield, probably you would do well to take the 2 cents cash.

When you write, let me know what is going on about home, how Hilliard is getting on with the farm &c.

I hope you will all keep well; I should dislike to hear of any of you being sick, for I should not be able to go to see you. Rest assured that I will be with you as early as possible.

Remember me to all friends, and to the negroes. Kiss the children for me, and keep them mindful that they have a Pa, who loves them and their Mother devotedly. Write often.

Very affectionately your husband
F. M. Parker

Camp Draughan
May 7th 1862

My dear Wife

As Henry A. Moore has been discharged and will leave to day for home, I thought I would write you by him. Our mails are so irregular here, that I hear you do not receive all my letters. I know I do'nt [sic] get all yours, for I have'nt [sic] heard from you now in some time. I suppose it will cause us to appreciate our letters more highly, but it is not altogether so pleasant to be thus kept from them.

We are still down in Onslow county, on White Oak river, the dividing line between Onslow and Jones counties. So far we have not been able to find any of the enemy; they have drawn in their lines, I suspect for the purpose of moving their troops in some other direction. Wilmington, Goldsboro, or may be York Town. What is to prevent heavy fighting both on the Peninsula and at Corinth, I do not see; great fears are entertained as to the result on the Peninsula; if we should be repulsed there, it will be a heavy blow, but by no means a decisive one; it will only protract the war. I have great hope in Beauregard, in his fortunes. If we should be repulsed at both these points; we may make up our minds for a long, terrible conflict. It is not a very bright picture to draw, but we may do well [to] look it right in the face at once. On the other hand, if we should succeed at these places, it will in my opinion shorten the war. Let us hope and pray for this. These troubles affect me directly; they make it impossible to obtain a furlough. I do not suppose that the General would approve a furlough upon any consideration so you must all keep well, and not render it at all necessary for me to return home; or else, if any of you should become sick, you must not let me know it. This seems hard, but I reckon it is best.

We have had several men from Halifax to join us for the past few days; among them is Tilmon Pullen[13] from our own neighbourhood; now what a good chance there was for you to have sent me a letter, but I suppose you did not know it. Tilmon brought me the gratifying intelligence that you were all well; this he learned from Carter Arrington. Well how do you come on with your farm? have you planted cotton yet, or will you plant any at all? If all your cotton has not been packed, I think it will be advisable to take advantage of rainy days to pack it, so as to have it ready to burn, should such a step be necessary.

I have not received the trunk, with the ham &c. yet, but expect it now every day from Wilmington.

Say to Mary I have not received her letter yet; you must make her write to me. Now I have no news to write you. I am here surrounded by men, horses, &c; my life is somewhat monotonous, but I assure you I have enough to do to keep off the blues, but not enough to prevent me from thinking of my dear wife and children at home.

God bless you all, and may he watch over you and protect you, is the prayer of your

affectionate husband
F. M. Parker

My love to the children, and to all friends. Kiss Hattie for me.

On May 6, the regiment moved to Camp Draughan. On May 8, 1862, a boat came up to Swansboro, and Companies D and H were sent there on a scouting expedition with detachments of

---

13. Tilmon Pullen was enumerated in the 1860 U.S. Census of Halifax County as a 24-year-old clerk living in the household of P. R. Stallings, a 38-year-old seamstress. Tilmon Pullen served as a private in the Enfield Blues. Manarin and Jordan, *N.C. Troops*, 3:50.

170

artillery and cavalry under the command of Lt. Col. Kell.[14] The next day, the regiment received orders to return to Wilmington, taking all boats and fishing smacks found along the New River and the coast to the Cape Fear River at Fort Fisher. After detaching 25 men and one officer for that purpose, the regiment left for Wilmington where it arrived and went into camp at Camp Hall on May 13, after a march in which it encamped near Jacksonville on May 9, ate dinner at Stone Wall Church and camped at Golden place on May 11, and camped at Scott's Hill Church on May 12.[15]

Camp of 30th Regt. N.C.T.
Near Wilmington, May 13th 1862

My dear Wife

Well, you see we are back at Wilmington, and the Yankees did not catch us. The Yankees in that direction are scarce; a couple of them came to Swansboro under a flag of truce the other day, but soon retired. I was very sorry to be ordered back; I can not imagine what is to become of the people in that country; they will be completely over run if some force is not sent there. Genrl. French is as much displeased at our removal as I am. It was the work of Genrl. Holmes, the old gentleman feared we might be cut off down there. We must have been a sleepy set, to have allowed any such thing. When the people found that we were leaving them, a perfect panic seized them; several families followed us off. It is a terrible thing to have the seat of war, or its operations carried on in ones own country. I hope we may be able to keep it from the central part of the State, and from the interior.

I received your note about the cotton cards. Why, my wife is becoming a real manager. I will send the cards if I can possibly find them in Wilmington, and your hoops also.

Is there anything else I can send you; if so, let me know it, and I will cheerfully do so. I shall return the linen pants; I do not need them. I thank you for thinking so much of me, as to send them.

---

14. Historical Memoranda; Ardrey Diary.
15. *Ibid.*

When I was last at home, I told you that I thought I would return some time in April; but here it is May, and no prospect of a furlough yet. I want to see you and the children very much, very much, but I do'nt [*sic*] know when I can leave here; certainly not while matters are in their present position. I do hope to be permitted to spend more time with you; I think we could pass the balance of our lives happily together.

I am glad to hear that Hilliard is managing matters so well at home; he has my confidence and respect. I have no doubt but that a little encouragement from you, will be of great service to him. Make him a little present occasionally; a little money now and then. Tell him to pay strict attention to the corn and potatoe [*sic*] crop; and say to Moses to attend to his hogs well.

Write me often, and let me know what is going on. Kiss the children for me, and keep them reminded of their Pa.

My respects to all friends.

Very affectionately your loving husband
F. M. Parker

Say to Mrs. Arrington that I have brought Ben & Jo back from Onslow with me; they are both well, and in fine spirits; so also are Al and Tom Wiggins. Al probably may take this to you.

F. M. P.

Camp 30th Regt. N.C.T.
May 14th 1862

My dear Wife

Dr. Joyner goes home to night on a furlough to look after his negroes on the Roanoke. Genrl. French regarding that as a matter of some military importance agreed to his leave of absence; I take advantage of his going, to send a few of my superfluous articles; I also send you one pair of cards; they cost <u>eight</u> dollars; the fellow who had them for sale, formerly belonged to a cavalry company which was attached to my Regt. and as a matter of favour he let me have them at that price: ten dollars was his usual price for them. I send a book to Jimmy; Dr. Joyner sends him and Offa a few marbles. I was made proud to receive his letter.

Well my dear Wife things do look a little squally just now; but I trust we will come out right yet. We must fight and fight hard. I will come to see you whenever I can, you may feel certain of that. Keep cheerful, be bright and happy, let come what will.

My love to the children. Remember me to all friends

Very affectionately and lovingly your husband

F. M. Parker

———————— ◆◆◆ ————————

The 30th now began a series of short moves to various camps in the vicinity of Wilmington, moving on the 16th to Camp Drane on Wrightsville Sound.[16]

———————— ◆◆◆ ————————

Camp of 30th Regt. N.C.T.
May 16th 1862

My very dear Wife

On yesterday I applied to Genrl. French for leave of absence for a few days, in order to visit you; he answered me that he could not spare me. So you see I have made an effort, and failed. I suppose the Genrl. thinks that this is no time to be visiting families. I will come as near as possible to a visit, I will write you. In the first place, I wish you to have all the cotton in a condition to be burned at short notice; if it should be necessary to burn it, have it removed far enough from any building, so as not to endanger the building by the fire. I would not have a pound of my cotton to fall into the hands of the yankees for any consideration. I have sent you 4 bushels salt to Enfield. Dr. Joyner promised to let you know it. Take care of all the old salt about your smoke house, particularly that from the pickle pork. If it is washed, it will be as good as ever.

I enquired about your hoop skirt yesterday, and found that it had not been sent on. The merchant told me that they were so high priced, that he would not get one. They charged <u>ten</u> dollars

---

16. Historical Memoranda states the move was made on May 15, but Parker's May 16 letter states the move was being made on the latter date.

173

for the skirt in Charleston. If you wish one at that price, let me know, and I will have it got for you. If there is any thing else you want, let me know; and I will get it for you.

We are moving to day to a new encampment, near the sound; I have no doubt but that it will be healthy there, but we do not remain in one place long enough to tell whether it is healthy or not.

If you can, have those thin cassimere [*sic*] pants, the same which you gave me, which you got from Petersburg; washed, will you please send them by Dr. Joyner; be careful in the washing, for they are full small now.

How do your strawberries come on? If they are ripe, I want you to send Dr. Joyner a nice mess of them; send a plenty, for he is fond of them, and of every thing else good. He told me he intended to go and see you; if he does, you must treat him to the best you have. He has been one of the best friends I have had.

Write me often, and let me know what is going on about home; every thing interests me.

Kiss the children for me. Tell Mary and Jimmy to write to me. Remember me to all friends.

Good bye my dear Wife. God bless and protect you and yours.

Very affectionately and devotedly
your husband
F. M. Parker

Ben and Jo Arrington are both well; so are Al and Tom Wiggins.

———◆◆◆———

Camp Drane
May 17th 1862

My dear Wife

I wrote you on yesterday; but as I have a favourable opportunity of sending you a letter, I have concluded to write a few lines. Tom Battle is here, and will return to day.

You see from the directive of this letter that the Regt. has moved again. I hope our frequent moves will not get us too much in that habit, so that we will move in double quick, when the Yankees get after us. I have not a fine dressed, nor finely equipped Regiment, but I have one which will do good fighting whenever the time comes. And I believe they are itching for a fight. While in Onslow, they were particularly sharp. From all accounts, I reckon we will have a chance at that soon.

Maj. Ker, the Inspector General for the Department of N. C. has to day inspected the Regt., and complimented it, on the condition of arms and accoutrements. Of course this is gratifying to me.

I wrote you in my last, to send Dr. Joyner some strawberries, if yours are ripe; be sure to do it. he has been very kind to me since we have been together.

Will you please send by Dr. Joyner, my Mexican spurs; there is a broad piece of leather belonging to each one, send that also.

I have no news to write. Write to me often; tell the children to write also. Kiss them for me. Good bye my dear Wife. God bless you.

very affectionately your devoted husband
F. M. Parker

On May 21, 1862, the 30th moved to Camp McRae on Masonboro Sound.[17]

Camp McRae
May 22, 1862

My dear Wife

Well you see we have moved again; Camp Drane was not a pleasant one; the water was bad, and then we were too far from the sound to have the benefit of the sea breeze.

We are now on an elevated spot, with good water near, and such a delightful breeze! I wish you could enjoy it at your house. The camp is very near to Genrl. McRae's residence; we have named it after him. We also have the benefit of bathing in salt water, which I have no doubt will be good for the men. It is such a pleasant camp, that I am afraid something will turn up to take us away from it soon, such is generally the case.

---

17. Historical Memoranda; Ardrey Diary.

The General seems to let me have my own way with regard to a camp, and as long as he continues so, I shall certainly remain where we now are.

I received your very interesting letter a few days since. I say interesting, it was, very; it told me of all the little matters about home, just what I wish to know.

You seem to be getting on finely with your garden. I know you will have a nice one. I wish I could be there to enjoy some of your strawberries. But no chance for that I fear.

Mary's note, enclosing a geranium leaf, came safely in yours; it was a great pleasure to me, to be thus thought of by the child; amid all our troubles there is apt to be something bright, something pleasant manifesting itself. I hope she will write again soon. You speak of your Father having visited you, and being somewhat discouraging about the result of the war. Why did you not cheer him up? I am sure matters do not look so gloomy as they did some time since. It will n[ever] do to give up now; we must fight it out; if we have to do it behind the bushes, fences, rocks and [***] of our interior; then is the time when we will avenge ourselves. To think of retiring at this state of the contest is to give up every thing, without having accomplished any thing.

I wrote to Bella the other day, and told her that when Mr. Chesire was ready to move to Franklin, then you would assist him with your teams; which I hope you will do. I think I if were in Mr. Chesire's situation I would go right off.

I received a very kind letter from your Father this evening; it was indicative of his kind heart, and tender feelings; the manner in which he spoke of my little children. He said that all were well at his house. Your Father complimented Hilliard very much, on his good management; I was very much pleased to hear it; it showed Hilliard's real worth for he has every thing his own way, and to hear that he is doing so well, is very encouraging to me.

I know he will take good care of you, and of every thing at home. I have great confidence in him. I wish you to let him know this.

One part of your letter amused me very much, that part of it advising me to take quinine in my whiskey every morning. Do'nt [sic] you know that whiskey is contraband now, and that we can not get it? I will try to take care of myself. I have great

176

cause for thankfulness, for my previous good health. Kiss the children for me. Remember me to all friends. Write soon, and often.

Very affectionately your husband
F. M. P.

———————————◆•◆•—————————————

Camp McRae
May 24th 1862

My dear Wife

Dr. Joyner has returned, but brought no letter from you; he told me he had seen you; that was worth something, but a letter would have been better. You might have slipped one in the pockets of the pants you sent. I shall send my thick drawers, shirts and socks to you, by Dr. Gregory; some of these, I am sorry to say, are not clean; you must make allowances for camp. I also send you the jar, and some bottles.

Well there is no news down this way; every thing is quiet and so it seems every where; tho at this very time Beauregard may be fighting a severe battle at Corinth. I feel very hopeful as to the result of it, whenever it does come off. That odious, devilish order of Butler's, should fire every Southern heart, and move every Southern arm.[18] They are very devils.

I received a very kind letter from Sister Mary last night. Certainly I am greatly blessed, in having such a wife, and such children, and such kin generally. I hope I may ever be worthy of them.

In one of your former letters, you spoke of my good health. I acknowledge such to be the fact, and try to be sufficiently thankful for it. I certainly have been greatly blessed in that respect too.

---

18. Maj. Gen. Benjamin F. Butler's infamous General Order no. 28 of May 15, 1862, enraged the South. Issued in response to insults given to Federal soldiers by women of New Orleans, Butler's order stated that "it is ordered that hereafter when any female shall by word, gesture, or movement insult or show contempt for any officer or soldier of the United States she shall be regarded and held liable to be treated as a woman of the town plying her avocation." President Jefferson Davis proclaimed Butler a felon, deserving of capital punishment. *OR*, vol. 15, pp. 426 and 906-908.

If I have any shoes at home, which are worth sending down here, please send them if you have an opportunity; boots are rather warm. I ~~have~~ do not know whether or not I have any shoes at home, so you can send them, if any.

Write soon, and give me all the news.

Kiss the children for me; remember me to all friends.

very affectionately and devotedly your husband

F. M. Parker

On the evening of May 26, the 30th received orders to move immediately to Wilmington and from there to Fair Bluff on the Pee Dee River near Georgetown, South Carolina. After a forced march of nine miles, the orders were countermanded and the regiment went into camp at Camp Lamb near Wilmington.[19]

Camp Lamb
June 1st 1862

My dear Wife

I think I have written you once since I have been at this camp, but however I will write again. I confess that I have been much disappointed at not receiving a letter from you now for some time; what is the matter with you? why will you not write? Dr. Joyner receives two, sometimes three letters each week from his wife, and here I am with not one this week. I do'nt [*sic*] believe that you love me less than his wife does him; but then I want you to show that you think of me often, by writing frequently.

I looked forward to this day with some pleasure and satisfaction; I intended to have gone to church in Wilmington; but am feeling rather too unwell to turn out in the sun, which is very hot here in this sand.

I hope I shall not spend the day profitless; I have heard a Sermon from our Chaplain, and have read in my Bible and Prayer book. It is a great comfort to be able to read and find out your duty, when you are not able to listen to have it told you.

---

19. Historical Memoranda; Ardrey Diary.

178

My bad feelings have happened at the unfortunate time; not only am I prevented from attending church; but had to decline an invitation from the Genrl. to dine with him to day; he has just sent me a note, saying he was alone, and asked me to join him.

I regret it very much; I like Genrl. French very much as an officer, and think I should admire him as a gentleman; he is one of the most energetic officers I have seen; and he knows very well, what he is about. I have great confidence in him; hope I shall be allowed to remain in his Brigade.

There is one thing certain, he is a fighting man; says he will fight the enemy, in the streets of Wilmington, if necessary. I have cause for liking him, he has always treated me with great respect and confidence. Sending me to Onslow, and then starting me to South Carolina, are evidences.

Well, we are on the eve of stirring events now both in the west, in Va., and in Md. Old Stonewall Jackson is a great one; what is to keep him out of Washington City now, I can not see. I rather guess Lincoln is quaking in his shoes, and will be hunting up his Scotch plaid again.[20] Would'nt [sic] it be a great thing if Jackson were to take Lincoln and Seward and send them on J. Davis & co. as they speak of our President.

If we only succeed at Richmond and Corinth, which I believe we will do; this war is done for; the back bone will be broken. God grant that it may be so. We are bound to succeed in the end, and the sooner, the better.

I see that our North Carolina Regts. have been at work again. Genrl. Branch is an unfortunate man. I think if I were in his situation, I would resign.[21]

---

20. Parker here refers to the disguise in which Lincoln was rumored to have worn as he slipped through Baltimore on his way to Washington to be inaugurated in the spring of 1861.

21. Brig. Gen. Lawrence O'Bryan Branch (1820-1862) was a native of Enfield. A graduate of Princeton, he represented North Carolina in Congress 1855-1861. Elected colonel of the 33rd Regt. N.C.T. on September 20, 1861, Branch was appointed brigadier general on January 17, 1862. Manarin and Jordan, *N.C. Troops*, 9:118. At New Bern on March 14, 1862, he unsuccessfully disputed Burnside's advance before withdrawing to Kinston. John G. Barrett, *The Civil War in North Carolina* (Chapel Hill: University of North Carolina Press, 1963), pp. 95-105. His brigade being transferred to Virginia, Branch was defeated by a superior Federal force at the battle of Slash Church or Hanover Court House north of Richmond on May 27, 1862, suffering heavy

179

Our friend Billy Nicholson has had another horse shot from under him; to be sure he must ride very fine looking horses, so that the enemy mistake him for a Field officer.

I am sorry that Cols. Lee and Lane's Regts.[22] suffered so severely; they must have fought well. It is hard to loose our best citizens, in lieu of those rascally hirelings of the Northern army.

Well, Wilmington has escaped so far, and I doubt very much whether or not it will be attacked. The blockade at the mouth of the Cape Fear has been very much strengthened recently; occasionally they go up and down the coast, and amuse themselves by shelling the entire woods near the coast. This is a very innocent amusement; it does us no harm, and costs the enemy a good deal. On one day [they] threw over two hundred shells. I suppose they are feeling for our camps along the coast. If they will come out; they will find no difficulty in ascertaining our position. May be they think that would not pay so well, as to remain on their gun boats.

We suffered a heavy loss the other day, in the capture of the steamer Gordon;[23] she had a cargo of 5,000 Enfield rifles, and 50,000 lbs. powder, besides other ammunitions of war. She was

---

losses including somewhere between 270 and 300 wounded (including three brothers Robinett in Co. G, 37th Regt. N.C.T. and 731 prisoners). Branch's reverse at Slash Church was not as discreditable as Parker seemed to think for Robert E. Lee complimented Branch upon the action, and the engagement caused a week's delay in McClellan's securing a foothold north of the Chickahominy. *OR*, vol. 11, pt. 1, p. 743. Stephen W. Sears, *To the Gates of Richmond* (New York: Ticknor and Fields, 1992), p. 117. Branch led his brigade with distinction in the Army of Northern Virginia from the Seven Days to Sharpsburg where he was killed on September 17, 1862. Warner, *Generals in Gray*, p. 31; Hill, *Confederate Military History*, 5:298-300.

22. Col. James H. Lane's 28th Regt. N.C.T. and Col. Charles Cochrane Lee's 37th Regt. N.C.T. both suffered heavily at the battle of Slash Church or Hanover Court House on May 27, 1862.

23. A 177 foot wooden hulled sidewheeler of 518 burden tons, the Confederate Navy's blockade runner, C.S.S. *Nassau*, was originally named *Gordon* when first launched in 1851, but was renamed *Theodora* in 1861 and christened *Nassau* when sold to the Confederate government in early 1862. As the *Gordon*, she did good service for the Confederacy as a privateer and by carrying the Confederate envoys Mason and Slidell from Charleston to Cuba in October, 1861. She was captured close to land while running in for Fort Caswell on May 28, 1862, by the U.S.S. *State of Georgia* and *Victoria*. United States Naval War Records Office, *Official Records of The Union and Confederate Navies in the War of the*

captured very near to Ft. Caswell; she was attempting to run in under the cover a thick fog, but very suddenly the fog cleared away, and left her right between two of the blockading steamers: 15 minutes longer of fog, would have put the Gordon nearer the guns of Ft. Caswell, where she would have been safe. How unfortunate! how much I should have been pleased to have had enough of those Enfield Rifles to have finished arming my Regt. with them. I already have one hundred of them in the Regt. also one company armed with the Mississippi Rifle which is also a good one.

My Regt. has done so much moving and marching that the men look rusty and smoky; but I assure you they will do good fighting, if ever they have the opportunity. Genrl. French remarked to me once, that it was the best school for men; that I could make much better soldiers out of them. It was one of the maxims of Napoleon, that want, hardships, privations, and fatigues, made the best soldiers. I believe it is true. At first it is not very pleasant, but the men soon accustom themselves to any of these things.

The telegraph is bringing us all sorts of news from Richmond to day; one part of which, is that Genrl. Hill (my old Col.) has captured a large number of prisoners, and taken several batteries; having cut to pieces four divisions of the yankee army.

For your information, I will state that a division usually consists of about 8,000 men; so you see that is good work. They are fighting to day again. It is said that the President and Genrl. Lee are both on the field. Let us pray that our arms will be victorious; that we may annihilate the invading devils, who would treat our Mothers, sisters, and [wives] as they would the common women of the town. I have perfect confidence that this will be done.

I am a little feverish to day, so you must excuse the rattling way in which my pen has run. Kiss the children for me;

Rebellion, 30 vol. (Washington: Government Printing Office, 1894-1927), 6:738 and 7: 433-4; Stephen R. Wise, *Lifeline of the Confederacy* (Columbia, South Carolina: University of South Carolina Press, 1988), pp. 323-4; Paul H. Silverstone, *Warships of the Civil War Navies* (Annapolis: Naval Institute Press, 1989), p. 225; William Morrison Robinson, Jr., *The Confederate Privateers* (New Haven: Yale University Press, 1928; reprint: Columbia, South Carolina: University of South Carolina Press, 1994), pp. 106-113 and 252-252.

remember me to all friends, and to the negroes. Do if you please dear Wife write oftener to your loving husband

F. M. Parker

———————◆●◆———————

For weeks now the regiment had been hearing stirring news of great events taking place in Virginia, Stonewall Jackson's Valley Campaign, and the battle of Seven Pines. On June 13, 1862, the long awaited orders arrived for the 30th to move to Virginia to join the army of Robert E. Lee facing McClellan outside of Richmond. Parker had apparently gone home to Enfield a few days before the 13th, perhaps with an exacerbation of the fever he mentions in his letter of June 1. The regiment left from Wilmington on the evening of the 13th. En route, half of the cars were left behind, and the engine and the remainder of the cars went two or three miles before discovering the detachment. Goldsboro was reached by sunup on June 14. Passing through Enfield, it was learned that Colonel Parker would rejoin the regiment in a few days. The train arrived at Weldon at 11:00 a.m. At Jarrett's Depot, the ladies sent water to the cars and made loyal demonstrations. Arriving at Petersburg at 4:00 p.m. on the 14th, the regiment was quartered in the market house.

On June 16, the regiment arrived at Richmond at 11:00 a.m., and was assigned to Featherston's Brigade, D. H. Hill's Division. This brigade had been commanded in Featherston's absence at the battle of Seven Pines, May 31-June 1, 1862, by a North Carolinian, Col. George Burgwyn Anderson of the 4th Regt. N.C.T.[24] Anderson was a rising star. Colonel Parker and the 30th Regiment were to serve a brief three months under Anderson's command until his mortal wounding at the battle of Sharpsburg. However, in that brief time, they were to follow him in four major battles, Gaines' Mill, Malvern Hill, Boonsboro, and Sharpsburg, and in those battles to gain that reputation as dauntless fighting men which they retained with only one lapse (the regiment's black and disastrous day at Kelly's Ford, Virginia, on November 7, 1863, in Parker's absence due to his Gettysburg wound) until the end of the war.

24. *OR*, vol. 11, pt. 1, p. 950.

Anderson, a 31-year-old West Pointer (class of 1852, graduating ninth in a class of 41), had served nine years with the 2nd Dragoons on the western plains before resigning his commission in April, 1861. The usual Confederate encomia for a general who fell in battle seem especially sincere for George B. Anderson. Artillerist Edward Porter Alexander, who had served with Anderson at Ft. Leavenworth in 1858, described Anderson as follows:

> He was a six footer of fine figure with specially good legs which gave him a very graceful seat on horseback & his face was as attractive as his figure, with brown hair, blue gray eyes & general good nature in every feature.[25]

At Seven Pines, under the eyes of President Jefferson Davis, Anderson seized the flag of the 27th Georgia and holding it aloft dashed forward amid storms of shot and shell to plant it on the enemy's breastworks. This gallant act won Anderson promotion to brigadier general on June 9, and he received the singular honor of having his commission delivered to him on the field by Confederate Secretary of War George W. Randolph.[26]

The newly-promoted Anderson provided a commander for a new North Carolina brigade. D. H. Hill wanted Featherston out of his division.[27] On June 17, D. H. Hill received permission to assign Anderson to the commands of either Rains' or Garland's Brigade, and that day the 30th received word that it would join Garland's Brigade. However, higher command evidently rethought the organization of the brigades in D. H. Hill's division for on June 23, the 30th was placed in a new brigade under Anderson's command with three other North Carolina regiments (the 2nd Regt. N.C.T. commanded by Col. C. C. Tew; the

---

25. Gary W. Gallagher, ed., *Fighting for the Confederacy: The Personal Recollections of General Edward Porter Alexander* (Chapel Hill: University of North Carolina Press, 1989), p. 154.

26. Warner, *Generals in Gray*, pp. 5-6; Clark, *N.C. Regiments*, 4:445-6; A. M. Waddell, "General George Burgwyn Anderson—The Memorial Address," in *The Southern Historical Society Papers* (reprint:Wilmington, North Carolina: Broadfoot, 1990), 14:392-3.

27. Dowdey, Clifford and Louis H. Manarin, *The Wartime Papers of Robert E. Lee* (New York: Da Capo, 1987), p. 184.

4th Regt. N.C.T. commanded by Col. Bryan Grimes; and the 14th Regt. N.C.T. commanded by Col. Risden Tyler Bennett.[28]) with which it was to serve out the war under Brigadier Generals Anderson, Ramseur, and Cox, successively.

In the meantime, on June 17, while the matter of brigade assignment was being worked out, the regiment encamped five miles east of Richmond on the York River Railroad near the James River. On June 21, the 30th went out on picket near Seven Pines, one-fourth of a mile from the enemy's lines, so close the men could see their balloons and observe their camp and maneuvers by climbing trees. All was quiet until the evening when the 30th, after some confusion in the ranks, advanced 300 yards and opened fire. The enemy replied in kind, and in the ensuing skirmish, before the regiment fell back to the Confederate lines, Captain Grissom and Lieutenant Pitts were wounded.[29]

Now the 30th's war really began. Robert E. Lee was readying a counterstroke against McClellan, who had imprudently exposed his army to destruction in detail by stationing a portion of it, the Fifth Corps under Brig. Gen. Fitz John Porter, in a position separated from the rest of the Union army north of the rain-swollen Chickahominy River. Porter lay in a fortified line along southward-flowing Beaver Dam Creek with advanced forces extending westward to Mechanicsville and Meadow Bridge. While Huger and Magruder demonstrated against McClellan's other four corps south of the Chickahominy east of Richmond out along the Williamsburg Road, Lee planned to attack Porter with a frontal assault by D. H. Hill, Longstreet and A. P. Hill while Stonewall Jackson, arriving suddenly by sur-

---

28. The history of the creation of George B. Anderson's brigade between Seven Pines and the Seven Days can be pieced out from *OR*, vol. 11, pt. 3, pp. 603 and 605; Ardrey Diary; and Thomas J. Watkins, *Notes on the Movement of the 14th North Carolina Regiment* (Wadesboro, North Carolina: Anson County Historical Society, 1991), pp. 4-5. The latter source gives the brigade organization date as June 23, 1862.
29. Historical Memoranda; Clark, *N.C. Regiments*, 2:498. Parker mistakenly states that the 30th took part in the battle of Seven Pines, May 31-June 1, 1862. The regiment was still in North Carolina at the time of Seven Pines. It was in the skirmish on June 21, 1862, that Capt. Eugene Grissom of Company D was wounded and rendered unfit for service. The wounding of "Lieutenant Pitts," along with Captain Grissom on June 21, is mentioned by Ardrey, but I have been unable to identify him in the roster. Manarin and Jordan, *N.C. Troops*, 8:352. Ardrey Diary.

prise from the Shenandoah Valley, fell upon Porter's exposed right (northern) flank and destroyed him. While the plan did not come to fruition due to lapses on the part of Jackson and others, the offensive, known to history as the Seven Days, did succeed in gaining the initiative for the Confederates and removing McClellan's threat to Richmond.[30]

While these great plans were being made, Parker was on his way back to his regiment.

----◆◆◆----

June 25th 1862

My dear Wife

May be you are a little astonished it see that I am still in Petersburg; you may think that I should have gone right on to my Regt. that I should not have loitered by the way; but my dear wife, I have been waiting here for my horse, which only reached here this morning.

I shall leave for Richmond this afternoon, and join my command to night. I drank tea with Mr. Weddull [Waddell?] ~~yesterday~~ last evening; found his family all well; Mrs. Weddull looks a little old I think; she is not quite so lively as she used to be. Mr. Matthew is here yet. I also met Mr. Hoskins from Tarboro; so [I] was among a good many old friends.

There are a good many rumors in Petersburg about the possibility of a fight near Richmond soon, all of which I place no reliance with.

You have a fine day for cutting your wheat, I hope you will have good weather for sowing it, so that you will have good flour. I could get you none in Enfield.

Good bye, take care of yourself and the children. I will write again as soon as I join the Regt.

Kiss the children for me.

very affectionately your husband
F. M. Parker

----◆◆◆----

---

30. Among many fine accounts of Lee's formulation of his plans for the Seven Days offensive, two of the best are those found in Freeman, *Lee's Lieutenants*, 1:494-498 and Sears, *Gates of Richmond*, pp. 174-177.

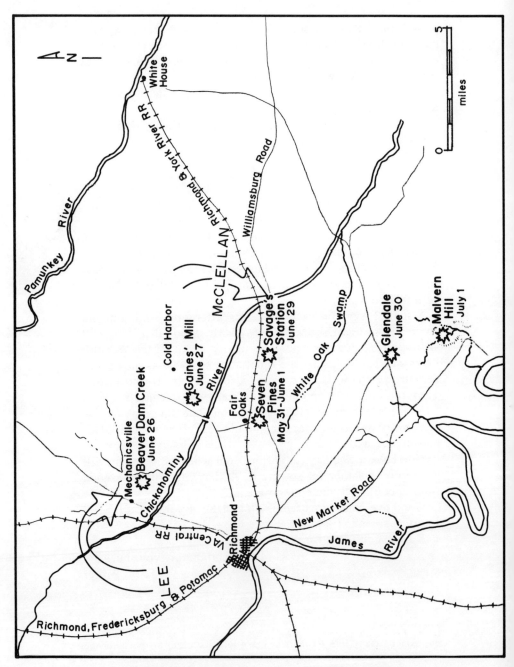

Seven Days Campaign, June 25 - July 1, 1862

186

At 3:00 a.m. on June 26, the 30th Regiment left camp and marched five miles northward up the Mechanicsville Turnpike at the double quick and halted in a beautiful grove of trees near the ruined Mechanicsville Bridge across the Chickahominy where they waited most of the day for word that Jackson had fallen on Porter's flank. The regiment was now on a high hill with an excellent view across the Chickahominy, and the men found themselves under the eyes of President Davis, General Lee, D. H. Hill and others who anxiously awaited the commencement of the attack north of the Chickahominy. At about 3:00 p.m. the impatient A. P. Hill, not having heard from Jackson, crossed the Chickahominy at Meadow Bridge above the 30th's position and commenced the attack on the Federals and began to drive them through Mechanicsville in view of the 30th. At Longstreet's command, after a brief delay in repairing the Mechanicsville Bridge, D. H. Hill threw his forces across the Chickahominy to join in the assault on Porter. The evening of the 26th, Ripley's brigade led the way and suffered heavily in being repulsed in its attack on the Federal fortifications along Beaver Dam Creek. The 30th took position under heavy artillery fire in an open field in support of batteries placed on a hill, and the fire did not slacken until about 10 o'clock that night.[31]

The following day, June 27, the regiment advanced by a circuitous route to take the Beaver Dam Creek line in the left flank, but arrived in the Northerners' camp to find it vacated. In the early morning hours, Porter had withdrawn his forces southeastward to take a strong northward facing position on an oval shaped plateau, whose highest point was known locally as Turkey Hill. Porter's position was of great importance because it covered the Chickahominy bridges—his line of retreat. To the north and west of Porter's new position was Powhite Creek, flowing southward into the Chickahominy. Gaines' Mill, from which the coming battle drew its name, was situated on Powhite Creek. To the south and east of Powhite Creek, along the base

---

31. *OR*, vol. 11, pt. 2, p. 623; Ardrey Diary; Daniel H. Hill, "Lee's Attacks North of the Chickahominy," in Robert U. Johnson and Clarence C. Buel, eds., *Battles and Leaders of the Civil War*, 4 vols. (New York: The Century Company, 1884-89),2:352.. I am particularly indebted to Sears, *To the Gates of Richmond*, pp. 193-248, and Freeman, *Lee's Lieutenants*, 1:506-537 for my accounts of the battles of Mechanicsville and Gaines' Mill.

Sgt. John H. Wells
Co. E, 30th Regt. N.C.T.
Wounded at Gaines' Mill, June 27, 1862

of the northern and western sides of the eminence on which
Porter was posted, flowed southward a second stream, a slug-
gish morass called Boatswain's Swamp, its banks lined with
dense woods.

The 30th Regiment, as a part of D. H. Hill's division, entered
the battle of Gaines' Mill on the left of the Confederate line,
attacking southwestward through Boatswain's Swamp with
Anderson's brigade leading the way. Hill reported that the
Federals were driven out of the swamp after "a short and bloody
contest." J. W. Bone recalled of the attack into Boatswain's
Swamp, "[H]ere was our first fire in regular line of battle, and
it was a heavy one too, but there were no enemies in there."
Emerging from the swamp, Anderson's men found the Union
line strongly posted on the plateau above across an open field
400 yards wide.[32] The Confederate attack had been going on for
several hours and the troops of A. P. Hill and Longstreet to the
right had failed to make much progress. Firing was heavy all
along the line, and at one point the regiment came under heavy
friendly artillery fire from a battery attached to Colquitt's
Brigade.[33] Brigadier General Garland held the Confederate left
and Anderson's brigade was in line next to Garland. Conferring
with D. H. Hill, Anderson and Garland enthusiastically determined to storm the heights, but Hill first sent two regiments of
Elzey's brigade to take an enfilading battery. Col. Alfred
Iverson's 20th Regt. N.C.T. took the battery and held it long
enough to allow Hill's forces to begin their assault.[34] As
Anderson's brigade charged forward up the hill, Capt. Thomas
M. Blount, Assistant Quartermaster of the 4th Regiment serving as an aide to General Anderson, seized the colors of the
30th, galloped forward ahead of the regiment on horseback, and
fell—shot dead from his horse.[35] Unable to withstand this
ferocious assault, the Federals broke and fled. The Army of
Northern Virginia had won the battle of Gaines' Mill, its first
great victory.[36]

---

32. *OR*, vol. 11, pt. 2, pp. 624-625; Bone, "Service," p. 8.
33. Clark, *N.C. Regiments*, 4:444.
34. *OR*, vol. 11, pt. 2, p. 625; *Supp. OR*, pt. 2, vol. 2, pp. 437-438.
35. *OR*, vol. 11, pt. 2, p. 629-630; Ardrey Diary; Clark, *N.C. Regiments*,
    1:268; Manarin and Jordan, *N.C. Troops*, 4:10.
36. D. H. Hill stoutly asserted that his troops on the left of the Confederate
    line had been the first to break the Federal line at Gaines' Mill, claiming

Not all acted so heroically. J. W. Bone recalled in disgust a "commission" officer and some others who did not charge but who stopped at the edge of the field and did not go any further until the battle was over. "If he had gotten his just rights, he would have been Court-Martialed and dismissed; but we charged the enemy and took the field," said Bone.[37]

For two days following their victory at Gaines' Mill, June 28 and 29, the men of the 30th did picket duty along the Chickahominy swamp and feasted on Yankee spoils: "butter, crackers, coffee, hams, beef tongue and whiskey, which we certainly relished and appreciated after our hard marches and fights."[38]

The day after Gaines' Mill, J. W. Bone was assigned to less pleasant duty, a burial detail:

> We were furnished shovels and we went back and followed along where our Regiment fought, and as we would come to the dead men, we would dig a hole by their side and lay them in. If we could get a blanket we would spread it over them and then cover them with dirt. This seemed very bad to us, at this time, but this was war times, and we were regular into it now.[39]

On Monday, June 30, 1862, the 30th Regiment crossed the Chickahominy. Marching through Sunday's battlefield of Savage's Station, the regiment came to a halt north of White Oak Swamp. The men spent the afternoon facing southward without forward movement under desultory enemy artillery fire. Stonewall Jackson failed to force the crossing of White Oak Swamp and allowed McClellan's forces to escape to Malvern Hill, while Longstreet and A. P. Hill launched assaults to the southwest at Glendale or Frayser's Farm.

----

priority over John Bell Hood's Texans who pierced Porter's position over on the Confederate right about the same time. Hill, "Lee's Attacks North of the Chickahominy," 2:356-7. Lee, after reporting the Texans' attack, simply says as to D. H. Hill's assault, "On the left the attack was no less vigorous and successful." *OR*, vol. 11, pt. 2, p. 493.

37. Bone, "Service," pp. 8-9.
38. Ardrey Diary.
39. Bone, "Service," p. 9.

The missed opportunities of White Oak Swamp set the stage for Lee's repulse the next day at Malvern Hill. The field of Malvern Hill was reminiscent of Gaines' Mill, but the piece-meal Confederate attacks of July 1, 1862, were not. The Army of the Potomac was united once again after its "change of base," and Union Brig. Gen. Fitz John Porter arrayed the Union infantry across the brow of Malvern Hill behind rows of artillery placed hub to hub commanding the broad sloping fields of wheat rising to the eminence's crowning plateau from the north. D. H. Hill's troops were in the center of the Confederate position, approaching the Union position directly from the north.

Confederate artillery fire was ineffective that day, and the North Carolinians suffered through a long afternoon. As D. H. Hill's division came within range of the Federal artillery and entered the woods which, as at Gaines' Mill, ran in a semicircle around the northern approaches to Malvern Hill, Brig. Gen. George B. Anderson was wounded and was carried from the field. Col. Charles Courtenay Tew, the 34-year-old colonel of the 2nd Regt. N.C.T. assumed command of the brigade.[40]

Although ordered to do so, D. H. Hill was much disinclined to attack the seemingly impregnable Federal position:

> The Yankees were found to be strongly posted on a commanding hill, all the approaches to which could be swept by his artillery, and were guarded by swarms of infantry securely sheltered by fences, ditches, and ravines. Tier after tier of batteries were grimly visible on the plateau, rising in the form of an amphitheater. One flank was protected by Turkey Creek and the other by gunboats. We could only reach the first line of batteries by traversing an open space of from 300 to 400 yards, exposed to a murderous fire of grape and canister from the artillery and musketry from the infantry. If that first line were carried, another and another still more difficult remained in the rear.[41]

---

40. *OR*, vol. 11, pt. 2, p. 627.
41. *Ibid.*, pp. 627-8.

Pvt. James M. Hobgood
Co. G, 30th Regt. N.C.T.
Wounded at Malvern Hill, July 1, 1862

D. H. Hill questioned Stonewall Jackson as to whether he was really being ordered to assault such a strong position, and Jackson assured Hill that he was. Hill in mid-afternoon received a maddeningly inexact order from Colonel Chilton of Lee's staff ordering Hill's division to advance upon the raising of a yell by Armistead's brigade to Hill's right. After lying in the woods all afternoon, Hill and his brigadiers heard a yell they presumed to be made by Armistead's men and launched the attack at about 6:30 or 7:00 p.m.[42] In any event, the North Carolinians of Anderson's brigade and of the 30th Regiment went forward with impetuosity. 2nd Lt. William Calder of the 2nd Regt N.C.T. in Anderson's brigade wrote:

> Soon the word was passed, 'Up, Second, and at them,' and our Brigade. . . sprang forward through the woods with a shout. We crossed one fence, went through another piece of woods, then over another fence, into an open field on the other side of which was a long line of Yankees. Our men charged gallantly at them. The enemy mowed us down by fifties.[43]

D. H. Hill's opinion of the Confederate charge at Malvern Hill was succinct: "It was not war—it was murder."[44]

J. W. Bone recalled the assault:

> We were the first to charge; we went forward through the broad wheat field (then 3 foot high) under heavy cannonading until we reached the slope. We were ordered to charge up the slope which we did the best we could; the 30th Regiment got through in very good order. We were now almost at the top of the hill, in a broad open field, where the enemy was located and using all their artillery on us to the best advantage, I well remember, just as I reached the edge of the field, I heard a ball hit my left hand companion and he fell

---

42. The time of the assault is given in the report of Brig. Gen. Roswell Ripley whose brigade advanced on the left of the 30th. *Ibid.*, pp. 650.
43. William Calder to Mother, July 4, 1862, Southern Historical Collection, quoted in Sears, *Gates of Richmond*, p. 326.
44. Hill, "Lee's Attacks North of the Chickahominy," 2:394.

dead. I soon had ball shot through my front leg. We charged on until we got to the top of the hill; here we had a broad view of the enemy and they had one of us. We stopped and opened fire; it was a hot place, with lead and iron. In the charge two of the regiments got so badly confused in going up the hill, that they were in no order for the battle and did not do very good service; this being the case, the enemy made their aim at those most exposed. As I loaded and fired I could see the men fall and hear them halloo all around me, but we held our line and kept firing finally I [was] wounded in the hand. About this time Col. Parker saw his situation and that his Regiment was exposed so bad that he ordered a retreat. On hearing this, I made my way down the hill the best I could, expecting to get hit by a ball or piece of shell, but fortunately I was not. About the time I got down the slope a shell bursted over my head and a piece struck a member of my Company by the name of Singleton Langley and shattered his thigh. I went to him and straightened out his leg and put a blanket under his head and left him to make the best of it that he could. I then went on an (sic) got with my Colonel and after more of the Regiment.[45]

While it is unclear from the sources whether Parker had returned to his regiment by the time of Gaines' Mill, it is clear, however, from Bone's account and from that of Parker himself that Parker commanded the 30th at Malvern Hill. Parker recorded that he made the decision to withdraw, after Anderson's brigade had driven the Yankee infantry from their front, when he was informed by Sergeant Major Archibald Francis Lawhon[46] of the 30th that the 30th and part of the 14th were the only troops

---

45. Bone, "Service," p. 10.
46. Arch F. Lawhon appears in the 1860 Census of Sampson County as a 24-year-old schoolteacher living at Warrensville in the household of Lott Rich, a farmer with a wife and four children. Archibald Francis Lawhon, a native of Moore County, was a 24-year-old resident of Sampson County when he enlisted as private on April 20, 1861, in the "Sampson Rangers," which came to be Company A of the 30th Regt. N.C.T. He was promoted to sergeant on August 3, 1861, and to sergeant major on or about May 1, 1862, being transferred to the Field and Staff of the 30th Regiment. On or about March 12, 1863, Lawhon was appointed 2nd

engaged in the charge. Parker, writing nearly 40 years after the battle, recalled an initially humorous, but then tragic, incident of the charge:

It is seldom that a cooler piece of impudence is witnessed than was on this charge. Corporal [Lewis H.] Pipkin,[47] of Company A, the color company, a most excellent soldier, while advancing at charge bayonets, with his right hand, scooped up a pair of new cavalry boots, which were tied together, threw them across his left arm, without taking his eye from the point of his bayonet, or without breaking his alignment. Gallant fellow, he neither brought out his boots or his life. He fell before advancing ten paces further.[48]

The 30th Regiment's most notable casualty, among many, on the field of Malvern Hill was the Colonel's friend, Capt. William T. Arrington. After sleeping in the woods all night and then enduring rain all morning, the regiment marched through ankle-deep mud to a hill a mile east of the battle ground and struck camp on July 2, 1862.[49]

———————————◆◆◆———————————

lieutenant and transferred to Company F, 20th Regt. N.C.T. He was wounded at Chancellorsville on May 3, 1863, again in November, 1863 (probably at Kelly's Ford), and at Winchester, Virginia, on September 19, 1864. He was detailed to command Companies H and I, 20th Regt. N.C.T. in the fall of 1864. Lawhon was appointed adjutant of the 20th after December 31, 1864. He surrendered at Appomattox. Manarin and Jordan, *N.C.Troops*, 8:322 and 329, and 6:433, 485, 502, and 512.

47. The 1860 Census of Sampson County enumerates Lewis Pipkin as a 29-year- old shoemaker living with his 30-year-old brother, Eli Pipkin, also a shoemaker, in the town of Clinton in the household of Thomas M. Clarkton, a 48-year-old painter with a wife and eight children. Lewis and Eli were enumerated in the 1850 Census of Sampson County living in the household of their father, Eli Pipkin, age 63, a farmer. Lewis H. Pipkin was a 29-year-old shoemaker residing in Sampson County when he enlisted as private on April 20, 1861, in the "Sampson Rangers" which was to become Company A of the 30th Regt. N.C.T. He was promoted to corporal on May 1, 1862, and was present or accounted for until killed at Malvern Hill, Virginia, on July 1, 1862. Manarin and Jordan, *N.C.Troops*, 8:330.

48. Clark, *N.C. Regiments*, 2:498.

49. Ardrey Diary.

Encampment Army around Richmond
Near James River
July 3rd 1862

My dearest Wife

Since I wrote you last our Division of the army has fought another terrible battle and won another victory, and thanks to a kind protecting Providence, I am safe. Thank God for me. I never before in all my life knew what it was to be thankful, truly thankful. May my future life show my thankfulness. Sally, my men fell around me thick and fast, and not a hair of my head was touched. Our Brigade, Genrl. Anderson's, was led up to charge a battery of the enemy; owing to the thickness of the wood and the consequent difficulty of preserving the line, my Regt. got in advance of the whole Brigade and went into action wholly unsupported, and was exposed to a cross fire from the Battery and from a heavy force of Infantry; we went at the latter at the double quick and drove the cowardly rascals into the woods; but finding that I was altogether alone, and my Regt. suffering severely, I withdrew them, and rallied for another attempt, but the Brigade being very much scattered, and Genrl. Anderson being wounded he took us from the field. If our Brigade had only been supported I think we could have taken the Battery, tho it was a formidable one, and remarkably well served.

In the engagement on the 27th June we had 16 killed, 60 wounded, and 5 missing. Lt. Col. [James T.] Kell also wounded. In the engagement on the 1st we had 16 killed, 94 wounded, 30 missing. Maj. [Lt. Col. William W.] Sillers severely wounded in the arm. I fear a great many of the wounded will die yet.

The news papers will give you more information about things generally, than I can. Suffice it to say, we have driven the enemy a distance of more than 20 miles, to his gun boats. He destroyed and left on the road a large amount of property; consisting of guns, ammunition, tents, horses, mules, wagons, ambulances, blankets, clothing, &c, &c, &c.

What can make people go to war? To witness the destruction of life on a battle field is enough to put a stop to all such arguments for its future. I mean such arguments as war.

I forgot to mention the death of Capt. [William T.] Arrington. He was killed on the 1st inst. He fell at the head of his company [I].

196

Fighting, marching, and sleeping in the open air, seems [*sic*] to agree with me.

I hope you and the children keep well. Kiss them for me. God bless you and them, remember me to Miss Martha and the negroes.

Very affectionately your husband
F. M. Parker

Pvt. William A. King
Co. B, 30th Regt. N.C.T.
Died of typhoid fever in Richmond, September 8, 1862

> "They obeyed my orders, gave a fine volley, which brought
> down the enemy as grain falls before a reaper."
> — F. M. Parker

PART SIX

July 4, 1862 - September 17, 1862
Malvern Hill, Virginia - Sharpsburg, Maryland

On July 4, commissary and sutler wagons came out to resupply the hungry men of the 30th. By July 6, members of the regiment were on picket duty on the Charles City Road. On July 9, the regiment moved to a camp 15 miles from Richmond, and the next day, July 10, the 30th returned, after "a long, tiresome march past dead horses and Yankees and all of McClellan's fortifications which were skillfully and splendidly arranged and constructed," to the regiment's old camp 4 miles from Richmond.[1] The days that followed were full of rest, eating, drinking, and letters and visits from home. 2nd Lt. W. E. Ardrey of the Mecklenburg Beauregards received a letter on July 20 from his sister Mag stating that "the crops were looking pretty well at home and that everybody had turned out to speculating, cotton was worth 18 cents a pound."[2] Chaplain A. D. Betts was enjoying a visit from his wife and three children, who arrived July 8 in the midst of his rounds of visits to the regiment's many wounded in the hospitals of Richmond. Betts' son Willie (under five years old) joined the ranks of the wounded about 8 p.m. the day of his arrival when he fell six or seven feet from a porch and cut his head fearfully on a brick. Willie did well with his injury, and on July 21, Lieutenant Ardrey noted that "Parson Betts" brought his family out to the regiment's camp from Richmond for a visit.[3]

Significant changes in the command structure were being made. On July 17, 1862, Maj. Gen. D. H. Hill was relieved of command of the division that contained the 30th and placed in command of the Department of North Carolina. In his farewell order to his division, D. H. Hill praised his men for exhibiting

---

1. Ardrey Diary.
2. *Ibid.*
3. Betts, *Experiences*, p. 9; Ardrey Diary.

"all those high and heroic qualities for which the Southern soldier is so remarkable," and then gave the following rather remarkable assessment:

> The troops have ever shown by their quiet and conservative character, their orderly behavior, and prompt obedience that they did not believe whisky, bluster, and profanity and rowdyism to be necessary adjuncts to the soldier.[4]

In the meantime, Colonel Parker was distressed (as usual) by a lack of mail from home.

Camp near Richmond
July 24th/62

My dear Wife

Well really, I do'nt [*sic*] know why I can not get a letter from you. Occasionally, I receive letters from others on business, but not the scratch of a pen have [I] had from you since I have been in Va. At first, I could endure it tolerably well, but now I am exceedingly impatient, and very anxious on your account. I fear that something has happened, that some of you are sick. I have been looking for Fred for some time, with the hope that when he did come, he would bring me a letter, or some message from you; but he has not reached here yet; what can be the matter with you all in the old North State? I should certainly go and see, if I could get away from here; but such a thing as that is impossible; not even a sick man can get off. I have written you a good many letters since I have been here, but do not know whether you have received them. I ordered the Richmond Enquirer to be sent to you; I suppose you receive that regularly, semiweekly; but that will tell you nothing of your absent husband; how much he loves you and his little children at home, and how much he wishes to see you and them. So you must be satisfied with the general news, the paper contains, that is if my letters to you are no more fortunate, than yours to me. For I can not believe that you do not write me; no, I feel certain that there are several letters now in the post office at Richmond for me.

---

4. *OR*, vol. 9, pt. 1, p. 476 and vol. 11, pt. 3, p. 646.

Mr. Price, a neighbour of Mr. Dunn's, called in at my tent yesterday, I had no letter ready for you, so I sent you a card containing the faces of prominent Yankee Generals. On the inside you will see a statement of the loss of my Regt.; this, however, is not very correct, as I prepared it just after the battle of the 1st July. Several of the missing have since come in, and the real ~~state~~ loss of the Regt., is about 182 in killed, wounded and missing. This card was picked up, at one of the camps the Yankees had run from, by Capt. [William T.] Arrington, poor fellow; and given to me. You can give it to the children: that is if Mr. Price ever hands it to you, as he promised to do.

I see that cotton is looking up; 15 cents per lb. is a good price; may be it will get up to 20 cents; that would be equal to making two crops, at 10 cents, which I consider a fair price. If it ever gets to 20 cents, sell what you have on hand and you may be governed by your Father in the disposal of it, at any price. I have not much time to devote to cotton, nor dollars and cents either.

Have you ever received my letter, concerning my mess chest &c. I sent you some money the other day. Have you received that? $70 I think.

I am sorry to report the bad health of my Regt. There are more than 250 present sick, besides a good many in the Hospitals, in and around Richmond; are only about 300 present for duty. That is a small command, is'nt [sic] it?

I am thankful to be able to say that I keep well. The camp is a bad place to be sick at. I certainly have had great cause for thankfulness, on that account. I hope I may contrive to enjoy good health.

My friend Capt. Holmes has just gone off to Richmond in fine spirits; he received a note from Mrs. Holmes, saying that she was in Richmond. How I would like to receive a similar one from you; but that is not altogether practicable; they have no children, to prevent moving about at any time. Now do'nt [sic] get mad with your children, because they keep you at home; that is your duty, to take care of them, and we must strive to render our duty as pleasant as possible, because it is our duty.

I hope and trust to be able to be with you and the children some of these days, when we gain our Independence; then we can enjoy the quiet of home, without any looking ahead at parting, or to the end of furloughs. Kiss my dear children for me, remember me to Miss Martha, and to the negroes. Write soon, and continue to ~~your~~ write to your affectionate and loving husband

F. M. Parker

In some respects these were sad days for the 30th. The days following Gaines' Mill and Malvern Hill, saw the deaths of 27 men mortally wounded in those battles to add to the 34 dead on the field. But for those who were not among the sick or seriously wounded, the 30th's summer idyll continued. On Sunday, July 27, Lieutenant Ardrey and three comrades went huckleberry hunting. July 31 was election day for the soldiers of the 30th who gave Mr. William Johnston of Charlotte a large majority over Colonel Vance for Governor.[5]

Camp near Richmond
August 2, 1862

My dear Wife

It is early in the morning, not yet sunrise, you are not yet up; may be you are thinking of me in your dreams, while I am thinking to you on my paper; if so, I hope the dreams will be as pleasant to you as the writing is to me. It always affords me a pleasure to write to you, I feel, in a measure, as tho I had spent a short time with you.

I have had my breakfast some time since; now for fear that you may think that we are always as smart as this, I will tell you that we were up so early this morning, in order to send off some men down the James River, to throw up breastworks; we sent 250 from this Regt., there are some 800 sent from this Brigade. We had to get them off by 4½ o'clock. So it seems as if the authorities must expect some advance by McClellan; from that direction. McClellan, heretofore has not occupied that part of the country, and hence there are no defences [sic] in that direction. Our boys have an aversion to breastworks; they admire the manner of Jackson's fighting, and are all anxious to be under his command.

---

5. Ardrey Diary.

They had no breastworks to shelter them during the late battles, and they think they got on very well; which the Yankees fought from behind breastworks, and had to leave them. But good breastworks save many a man; I have seen and felt their great utility.

Of course our camp looks quite thinned, and almost deserted. The Surgeon's tent is the most popular place of resort this morning; we have a goodly number of sick, tho the health of the Regt. has greatly improved within the past two weeks. As the weather turns a little cooler, I hope the sickness will disappear. That which we have been troubled with most, has been the summer diseases. The very great quiet of our camp has been broken in upon, for the past day. My former, and favourite, commander, Genrl. French, who now is in command of the District of the Appomattox, at Petersburg, on thursday [sic] night sent down forty pieces of artillery, and opened upon some vessels of the enemy which were lying in the James river. The firing took place between midnight and day break and I assure you it startled us a little, we could not understand it. I learn that the artillery sank four of the vessels; they were transports, and no doubt loaded with stores and supplies for McClellan's army.[6] If we continue this game of destroying their supplies, both here, and in the west, it will have a very worrying effect; and operate sadly upon the enemy.

Well, at last my mess chest has arrived, and I am glad to get it. It came last night, and I have not examined it yet. I am very thankful to you for the contents tho, and assure you that they will be duly appreciated. We are not yet supplied with a cook. I am in [***] for several and hope to get one, at least. Fred, Dr. Gregory and I mess with Capt. Holmes. As soon as Col. Kell and Maj. Sillers return, we will go into a mess of our own. You do'nt [sic] know how well pleased I am with my Adjutant [Frederick Philips]; he is a most excellent one; I would not be without him for any consideration. He [does] very well, and I hope will continue so.

We had a visit from Mr. Wiggins one day this week. He had brought Eugene on to Richmond; to get him discharged from the service; poor fellow, I fear he will lose an eye.

---

6. Brig. Gen. S. G. French's report of this attack appears in *OR.*, vol. 11, pt. 2, pp. 940-942.

I hope you and the children keep well. I feel comparatively easy about you, as long as you are at your Father's.

I have had your news papers (Enquirer & Journal) sent for the present, to Battleboro, instead of Sycamore Alley. Remember me to all at your Father's and Bella, if she [is] with you. Kiss the children for me. Write soon. Good bye, God bless you.

Very affectionately your husband

F. M. Parker

On August 6, a force including the 30th was sent out from the defenses of Richmond to oppose a Union advance from Harrison's Landing in which Malvern Hill was reoccupied and Union forces arrayed in much the same position they held on July 1. The Confederate show of force was successful because during the night of August 6/7, the Northerners abandoned Malvern Hill again and withdrew to their former positions at Harrison's Landing.[7]

Camp near Richmond

August 8th 1862

My dear Wife

Well, we are back to camp again. But you will wish to know where we have been. To no other place than Malvern Hill.

We were ordered there on the 6th, to reinforce Genrl. Longstreet. He reported that the enemy were in force on Malvern Hill, and that if Genrl. Lee would strengthen his flanks, that he would bag the whole Yankee force.

We reached the vicinity of the Heights on the afternoon of the 6th, effecting a junction with Longstreet's forces. I suppose a sufficient reconnaissance had not then been made, to venture an attack on the enemy; and they, having the woods full of scouts and pickets, ascertained our strength, and at 2 o'clock that night retreated back to their encampment at Westover.

The next morning we moved in the direction of the Heights, but were soon informed by our own scouts, that the bird had

---

7. Robert E. Lee's report appears in *OR*, vol. 11, pt. 2, pp. 956-7.

flown, that McClellan had retired with his entire force. Thus a second time, has McClellan been too sharp for us, in the way of a retreat. On this occasion the fault is charged to the 3rd (our own) Division.

Now the question is, at whose door, in the Division; certainly not to the Regimental commanders; for we were formed and ready for the march some time before the hour appointed; neither can the delay be charged to the Brigade commanders; for they did not issue the order until ten o'clock at night; and I suppose they would have issued it sooner, had it been received. The fault then must be in the Division commander; and at present Brig. Genrl. Ripley[8] commands our Division. No Major Genrl. has been assigned to this Division, since Genrl. Hill was ordered to the Department of N.C. Genrl. Ripley, you will recollect, is the officer whom I informed you, had his tent lined with satin. I understand he carried a small <u>sideboard</u> along with him. An officer who spends so much thought, and we must suppose, time also, on such matters, has but little time to devote to his legitimate business. We need energetic, able, commanders, sadly; such men as Jackson & Hill.

After all, it may be good for some of us that the enemy did make their escape; it may be that I might have been a victim to this civil war, on that field; we would necessarily have lost many men but would of course have inflicted a heavy blow on

---

8. Roswell Sabine Ripley was a man who evoked strong reactions, both positive and negative. He was born in Worthington, Ohio, on March 14, 1823. He graduated from West Point in 1843 and was twice brevetted in the Mexican War, for gallantry at Cerro Gordo and for meritorious service at Chapultepec. Shortly afterwards, he wrote a two volume history of the Mexican War. Ripley married into the noted Middleton family of Charleston in 1852 and resigned from the army to engage in business in South Carolina. Appointed brigadier general in the Confederate service on August 15, 1861, he commanded South Carolina and was frequently at odds with his superiors, such as General Beauregard and Adjt. Gen. Samuel Cooper. In a disagreement over the defense of Charleston (in which Ripley was subsequently proven correct), he asked to be relieved. Lee, familiar with his excellent work, at first declined but then gave Ripley a brigade under D. H. Hill. Ripley's brigade fought alongside that of Anderson in the Seven Days, and he was severely wounded at Sharpsburg. From 1863 until the end of the war, Ripley served in North and South Carolina. Following the war, after a brief stay in England, he resided in Charleston and spent much time in New York until his death on March 29, 1887. Warner, *Generals in Gray*, p. 257; Johnson and Allen, *Dictionary of American Biography*, 15:625-626.

the enemy. At any rate, I hope the next time the Division is ordered to any point, it may be more prompt, and not six hours behind time, as Genrl. Longstreet declared that it was on tuesday [sic] in marching from camp to join him. I had a good opportunity of closely inspecting the battle ground of the 1st July. I was over the identical ground which we occupied that day, over which we charged, and from which we were forced to retire. I saw the spot where Capt. Arrington fell; saw the graves of many of my brave men, and I assure you it gave me no pleasure to visit them. Poor fellows, they fell in a glorious cause and deserve a more appropriate resting place, than the road side. Malvern Hill, or Heights, is a series of farms on the James River; there are about 2,000 acres of cleared land together, the different farms separated only by small branches. It is a beautiful country, quite elevated; there are several handsome residences to be seen, all tenantless now; some very much defaced by cannon shot; every thing like a fence is laid low; even the garden palings; this was done to give the enemy a fair range for their guns.

It is pronounced by good military authority to be a very strong position, sad experience teaches us that this is so; tho had our Generals attacked the position simultaneously, and in force, not by detail as was done, we could have carried it on the 1st July, with no greater loss to our army either. But such is the fate of war. The first time we operated against this place we were too fast, the next time too slow; I hope the third time we will hit it just right. I honestly think we will have a fight there soon. A strong force of ours now occupies the Heights, and will hold it.

We are constantly expecting exciting news from the Valley of Va. Jackson and Pope are near each other with large armies.

I have just received a box of provisions: and but for a few of the apples being wrapped in old envelopes, I should not have been able to tell who sent it. They were sent by Sister Mary. I was made to feel mean by the silence of the box. I have not written to her in a long time, and felt rebuked for not doing so. I will write her to day. I received a letter from Sister Bet to day, all are well with her. She mentioned that you had promised to let Mary go with Bella to her house. I think it would be well. I know Mary would enjoy it; and a little change would help her.

I wrote Bella a few days since.

Fred went through with the late march very well; we had no tents, bivouacked in the open air, which, I believe is the healthiest way for soldiers to live. I hope his health will keep good; he makes me a most excellent Adjutant. He has met a great many of his old classmates, and Log Town friends, as he calls them, in the army. He is fine company, is quite lively; tho says he is tired of the war. Who is'nt [sic]?

Our Brigadier, Genrl. Anderson, has returned, he joined us on our way to Malvern Hill. We were very glad to see him back. I particularly, for I had command of the Brigade at that time, and was glad to be relieved of so important a responsibility. The entire Brigade has great confidence in the Genrl. He is a good military man, besides being a very agreeable polite gentleman.

I hope you will write a little oftener than you have formerly done. I will send you a few postage stamps, so that, the want of them, will be no excuse. They are ten cents [a] stamp, of course one will be sufficient. I send all that I have.

Remember me to all at your Father's & to Bella. Kiss the children for me, and keep them mindful of their Pa, particularly the little ones.

If Fred was in, he would probably send some message. he [sic] has gone over to see Capt. [Joseph H.] Hyman,[9] of the 13th [North Carolina] Regt. [Co. G]. I will say that he is very well.

Good bye, God bless you my dear wife.

very affectionately your husband

F. M. Parker

---

9. Joseph Henry Hyman was born on March 24, 1835, and graduated from the University of North Carolina in 1855. He was enumerated in the 1860 U.S. Census of Edgecombe County as a 25-year-old farmer owning 23 slaves and 8 slave houses. He enlisted in the "Edgecombe Rifles," Company G of the 13th Regt. N.C.T., and was elected captain to rank from May 1, 1861. He was promoted to major and transferred to field and staff on October 15, 1862. He was promoted to lieutenant colonel on March 2, 1863, to colonel of the 13th Regt. on June 13, 1863. Wounded on July 1, 1863, at Gettysburg, he rejoined his regiment in the fall of 1863, and served until the surrender at Appomattox. He was a real estate broker in later life and died in March, 1902. Krick, *Lee's Colonels*, p. 205; Manarin and Jordan, *N.C.Troops*, 5:283 and 346.

On August 18, orders were received by the regiment to prepare three days' rations.[10] With McClellan's withdrawal from the Peninsula, D. H. Hill was again placed in command of the division containing the 30th (to Colonel Parker's satisfaction, no doubt).[11] Hill's command was being sent to take part in the fighting in northern Virginia already launched by Stonewall Jackson at Cedar Mountain on August 9, 1862.[12] On Monday, August 19, 1862, the 30th rose at 4:00 a.m. and marched northward up the Brook Turnpike through Henrico and Hanover Counties. On August 20, the regiment camped on the North Anna near Hanover Junction in a spruce pine grove.[13]

⸺⸻ ◄ •♦• ► ⸻⸺

Camp on North Anna river
August 22, 1862

My dear Wife

You will see that we are on the march again. The Division left our old camp on tuesday [sic] morning, marched through Richmond, and took up the line of march for Gordonsville, the rail road not being able to transport us soon enough. We marched one day in that direction during the first night; our orders were countermanded; and the direction of the march changed to this part of the country instead of Gordonsville. The reason of the change in the orders, I understood to be to operate against the enemy, who threatened the rail road about the point. We reached our encampment for the second day, about dark, very much fatigued, in fact almost broken down; we have been in camp probably about two hours, when the order came to get the men in ranks, ready to move at a moments notice. This was soon done, but I assure you I never gave an order more reluctantly. I knew the men were exhausted already, and to march farther that night seemed almost cruel, unless the necessity was urgent. We marched off with the expectation of going only two miles, but marched at least six; and it being on [sic] the night, and dark at that, made the march much more fatiguing. We rested yesterday, and had nice bathing in the river, which is a clear, swift

10. Ardrey Diary.
11. *OR*, vol. 12, pt. 3, pp. 932 and 938.
12. *Ibid.*, p. 942.
13. Ardrey Diary; Betts, *Experiences*, p. 12.

running stream, but <u>not deep</u>; it resembles a mountain stream very much. To day we have orders to cook three days rations which is always indicative of a move; where we will go, I can not say. I think we will be kept somewhere in this country for some time; McClellan's army is at Fredericksburg, and we are now just thirty miles from that place. I suppose we will have to watch him.

This is a rather pleasant country to live in, hilly and broken. It is also a fertile country, and as there have not been many troops quartered near here, we can live tolerably well, for a while at least. I am afraid our intercourse with the outside world will be a little interrupted, that we shall not get our mails regularly; this will be a great loss to me. A letter from you once a fortnight even, is of great value to me, and I do not like to be deprived of so great a pleasure. This must not cause you to cease writing, may be I shall get all your letters at [the] same time. They will be duly prized, whenever received, even if a month old. I was glad to hear that all was going on well at home again. I received a letter from Mr. [***] the other day; he had been over my crop, and did not give me a very flattering account of it; but knowing of the sickness you have had in the negro family, and the high freshet in the creek, I could make due allowance for the shortness of the crop in the low grounds. I hope Hilliard will do a good deal of damming this summer; in fact I told him he might be able to finish it.

I am very sorry to learn that your Mother's health is not so good. If I were you, when I returned home I would visit her often. It will always be a satisfaction and gratification to you. Fred has stood these marches well; tho he was nearly exhausted when we finished the night march. He is very well now; so am I, I am thankful to say. Say to your Father that I have had Mr. Frank Garrett[14] appointed Surgeon to the Regt.; ask him what kind of a selection I have made. The Dr. has not joined us yet. My love to Bella, and all at your Father's. Fred and I were much pleased at the letters from the little girls. Kiss the children for me. Write soon. Fred sends his love to all.

very affectionately your husband
F. M. Parker

---

14. Francis M. Garrett was a 37-year-old resident of Halifax County when he was appointed surgeon of the 30th Regt. N.C.T. to rank from

On August 26, the 30th set out again, hearing reports that Stonewall Jackson was at Manassas. Passing Villa Green on August 27 and Orange Court House on August 28, they camped on the south side of the Rapidan River on August 29. Wading the Rapidan the next morning, the regiment passed over the battlefield of Cedar Mountain during the day. The next day, August 31, it began to rain before dawn. The 30th crossed the Rappahannock and marched all day in the mud, passing the damaged resort of Warrenton, Sulphur Springs. After passing through Warrenton on September 1 in cold rainy weather and marching past the impressive scenery of the Blue Ridge, the 30th saw the heartrending sights of the battlefield of Manassas on September 2 and camped on the Alexandria Turnpike after crossing the Bell River. While crossing the battlefield, Chaplain Betts found a badly wounded Federal with undressed wounds sitting on the field waiting for medical attention:

> He asked me if I thought our surgeons would care for him. I assured him they would. He said he had a wife and two little children in his northern home. His parents were pious and had raised him piously, but he had neglected his own soul. I said: "Brother, Jesus loves you. You came down here to kill my brothers, but I love you." . . . As I was about to hurry away to overtake my regiment he asked me to lay him down! How could I? Where could I take hold? I did the best I could. As I took him by the hand and commended him to God, I think my heart was as tender as it ever was.[15]

On September 3, reaching Leesburg after nightfall, the 30th was cheered incessantly by the ladies and camped just north of the town. The sun came out on September 4, affording the regiment the sight of Sugar Loaf Mountain in Maryland. On September 5, the 30th marched 15 miles north from Leesburg to Lovettsville, and on September 6, the regiment camped on the

September 26, 1862. Garrett resigned by reason of disability on April 1, 1863. Manarin and Jordan, *N.C. Troops*, 8:322.
15. Betts, *Experiences*, p. 14.

south side of the Potomac River near Cheek's Ford. The following day, September 7, 1862, the 30th waded the Potomac as a band played "Maryland, My Maryland," and encamped 4 miles from Frederick, Maryland.[16]

————————◆◆◆————————

Bivouac near Frederick Md.
Sept. 9th 1862

My dear Wife

In Maryland at last; we crossed the Potomac on sunday [*sic*] last, and marched to our present position, which is about four miles from Frederick City. What the plan of our Generals is, I am not able to say. I suppose we will be kept in our present position until our stragglers, which were left behind, shall come up. We have had a terrible march from Richmond; a great many men have been made sick, some have broken down on the road, some have given out from sore feet; from all these causes combined, our ranks have been somewhat thinned; the stragglers are joining us slowly. Fred had been ordered back to the different fords on the Potomac, to collect and bring all the stragglers of our Brigade, to their respective Regiments. Not a very pleasant duty either. He left this morning, and I suppose will be absent for one or two days. You will wish to know how we were received upon entering Maryland; the people are not very enthusiastic in their demonstrations of joy or pleasure; but I suppose are waiting to see what time will bring forth. There are some of the citizens who are very open in their expressions of Southern feeling. A company is now being raised in the City of Frederick, and it is said that the city will turn out at least one thousand men. There are said to be from 20 to 40 thousand in Baltimore ready to join us. If Maryland has any life in her, she now has an opportunity of showing it.

If Maryland, Missouri and Kentucky are really Southern in feeling, and will act at once, this war can be brought to a close in short order; in fact if the war is not closed soon, the most desperate fighting must take place; it must necessarily be so. The very existence of the Yankee government depends upon it.

16. The chronology of the march from Richmond to Frederick is set forth in both the Ardrey Diary and Betts, *Experiences*, pp. 12-15.

Whatever comes, we must make up our minds to do our duty, submit to the consequences. I have always had full confidence in the success of our cause, and in our final triumph; that faith is confirmed by every occurrence which takes place. If we have a fight here in Maryland, and beat them, as we surely will, matters must be brought to a close soon.

All chance of a furlough is now taken away, by the distance from home, if no other reason. When I shall be able to see you, I can not say, but that will not take away the desire to see you. I shall hail with joy, the time when I can visit you and my children. I think of you very often; do you think of me and do you pray for me? I hope you do. I have not had a letter from you in some time, but I do not expect one, now that we are so far from Richmond; but I hope I shall receive them soon. I hope you continued to write. Let me know how you are getting on with every thing. Kiss the children for me. Remember me to Miss Martha, and to the negroes. Good bye my dear Wife. God bless you.

Very affectionately your husband
F. M. Parker

———————◆•◆———————

On September 10, the 30th marched westward from Frederick. The line of march carried the brigade through Middletown in the Catoctin Mountains, and it encamped at the point where the National Pike pierced South Mountain through Turner's Gap, the scene of heavy fighting two days later.[17] The next day, September 11, the brigade continued northwestward through Boonsboro.[18] The regiment marched through a hard rain and encamped 18 miles from Frederick. On September 12, the regiment lay in camp five miles from Hagerstown.[19] On

---

17. Ardrey Diary; George Gorman, ed., "Memoirs of a Rebel, Being the Narratives of John Calvin Gorman, Captain, Company B, 2nd North Carolina Regiment, 1861-1865, Part I, South Mountain and Sharpsburg," *Military Images*, vol. 3, no. 3 (Nov-Dec., 1981): 4-6. It is likely that Gorman is "G." who wrote the Sept. 21, 1862, letter containing an account of the Sharpsburg campaign published in the Raleigh North Carolina *Standard* October 1, 1862.
18. Gorman, "Memoirs," p. 4.
19. Ardrey Diary.

September 13, D. H. Hill ordered Anderson's brigade to the vicinity of Boonsboro at the western foot of South Mountain.[20]

Days of battle were now near at hand in which the Army of Northern Virginia was going to have to fight for its life. In the westward movement from Frederick up and across South Mountain, D. H. Hill's division served as the Army's rearguard pursuant to Special Order No. 191, issued September 9 by General Lee. This order set out in ten paragraphs an audacious plan, typical of Lee, to divide the Army in the face of the enemy by detaching troops under Stonewall Jackson and Lafayette McLaws to capture Harper's Ferry before reuniting at Hagerstown or Boonsboro.[21] Lee's forces in Maryland, even when united, were much depleted by straggling on the march into Maryland, and the Army's individual elements were very weak. D. H. Hill's entire division, for example, mustered less than 5,000 effectives prior to entering the battle of South Mountain on September 14.[22] Special Order No. 191 was lost, perhaps through the fault of D. H. Hill (later stoutly denied by him). It was found wrapped around three cigars in an abandoned Confederate camp on the outskirts of Frederick by an Indiana private, and delivered on September 13 to General McClellan. Possession of this intelligence gave a heavy advantage to McClellan and the Army of the Potomac with a golden opportunity to defeat the Army of Northern Virginia in detail.[23]

The exact sequence of events on the Confederate side, from the time McClellan set his forces in motion upon the finding of the Lost Order on September 13, up to the opening of battle of South Mountain on the morning of September 14, is extremely problematic due to conflicts in the accounts, primarily between those of D. H. Hill and of other officers. Hill stated in one postwar account that during the forenoon of September 13 Gen. J.E.B. Stuart, who was in an advanced position at the gap in the Catoctin Mountains east of Middletown, sent a dispatch to D. H.

---

20. *OR*, vol. 19, pt. 1, p. 1019.
21. *OR*, vol. 19, pt. 2, pp. 603-4.
22. *OR*, vol. 19, pt. 1, pp. 1022 and 1025.
23. McClellan's report to Halleck of the finding of the order appears in *OR*, vol. 19, pt. 2, pp. 281-2. Freeman, *Lee's Lieutenants*, 2:173-4 and 715-723; Stephen W. Sears, *Landscape Turned Red: The Battle of Antietam* (New Haven, Connecticut: Ticknor & Fields, 1983), pp. 89-92 and 112-115.

Hill stating that he was followed by two brigades of Federal infantry. Stuart asked Hill to send infantry to check the pursuit at South Mountain, in response to which Hill sent back the brigades of Colquitt and Garland. In his official report, Hill stated that Stuart had informed him that "two brigades only of the Yankees were pursuing us and that one brigade would be sufficient to hold the pass."[24] On the other hand, Lt. George D. Grattan, who served as Colquitt's Aide De Camp at South Mountain, recalled that Colquitt met Gen. J.E.B. Stuart at the crest of the ridge at Turner's Gap just before dark on September 13 and that Stuart told Colquitt that "no troops were following him but cavalry" and that "Colquitt would have no difficulty in holding the pass with his brigade."[25] Whatever the exact content of Stuart's report, Lee did learn that night that "the enemy was advancing more rapidly than was convenient from Fredericktown" in a manner likely to interfere with the taking of Harper's Ferry and determined to strengthen D. H. Hill's division engaged in holding the mountain passes.[26] Whatever the exact sequence of events, it is clear that, late on September 13, Hill sent the brigades of Garland and Colquitt back to defend South Mountain and moved his other three brigades, including Anderson's with the 30th, up to the vicinity of Boonsboro.

McClellan's first task in capitalizing upon the advantage given him by the Lost Order was to cross the north-south rampart of South Mountain which was pierced by several lightly guarded gaps. The Union forces began moving westward from Frederick on September 13, reaching as far as Middletown. In the early morning hours of September 14, 1862,

---

24. Daniel H. Hill, "The Battle of South Mountain, or Boonsboro," in Robert U. Johnson and Clarence C. Buel, eds., *Battles and Leaders of the Civil War*, 4 vols. (New York: The Century Company, 1884-89), 2:559-581; *OR*, vol. 19, pt. 1, p. 1019.
25. George D. Grattan, "The Battle of Boonsboro Gap or South Mountain," in *The Southern Historical Society Papers* (reprint: Wilmington, North Carolina: Broadfoot, 1990), 39:31-44.
26. *OR*, vol. 19, pt. 1, p. 140. After the war, Lee was reported to have said that "Genl. Hill *ought to have* had all his troops up at the mountain, while in fact part were back in Boonsboro." Memorandum of conversation held with Genl. R. E. Lee [by E. C. Gordon] in Lexington, Virginia, on the 15th of February, 1868, published in Freeman, *Lee's Lieutenants*, 2:717-719.

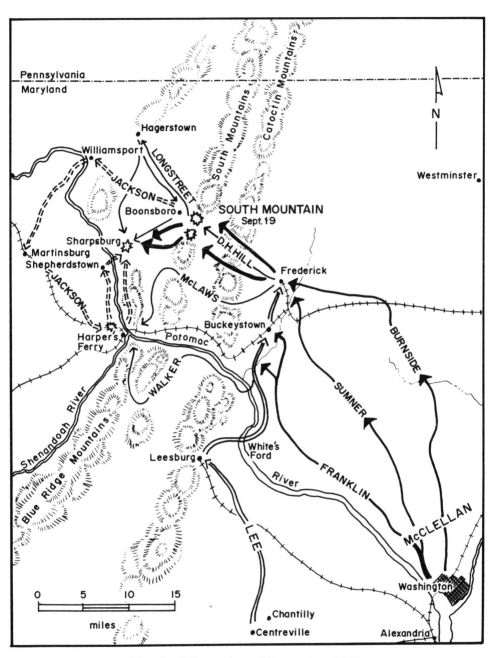

Maryland Campaign of September 1862

215

McClellan put his forces in motion westward from Middletown toward South Mountain. This advance was observed by D. H. Hill while inspecting his defensive positions on South Mountain early that morning.[27] With Colquitt's brigade holding Turner's Gap on his left, Hill ordered Garland's brigade to defend Fox's Gap on the right of his position where the Old Sharpsburg Road crossed South Mountain south of Turner's Gap.[28] Hill also ordered up Anderson's brigade, having determined that Garland's small force could not hold Fox's Gap.[29]

The situation on the Confederate right at Fox's Gap deteriorated rapidly on the morning of September 14. Garland's brigade met a Union force advancing up the mountain along an old road which branched out from the Old Sharpsburg Road to the south and circled to the right of the Confederate position before rejoining the main road at Fox's Gap. Garland's brigade was largely routed, and General Garland himself was killed.[30] The Union forces seized the crest of the ridge south of the Gap.[31]

In response to D. H. Hill's order, Anderson's brigade had set out from camp at 4:30 a.m.[32] Marching up the mountain road from Boonsboro at the double quick to the sound of cannon fire and musketry,[33] the brigade arrived at Fox's Gap at daylight,

---

27. *OR*, vol. 19, pt. 1, p. 458; Hill, "South Mountain," pp. 564-5.
28. *Ibid.*, pp. 561-4.
29. *OR*, vol. 19, pt. 1, p. 1019-1020.
30. Hill, "South Mountain," pp. 562-4; *OR*, vol. 19, pt. 1, p. 1020.
31. *Ibid.*, pp. 458-459. Jacob Cox asserted, "The Kanawha Division carried the crest at Fox's Gap early in the forenoon, while the rest of the army was miles away. General Hill has since argued that only part of his division could oppose us; but his brigades were all on the mountain summit within easy support of each other, and they had the day before them.... Our effort was to attack the weak end of the Confederate line, and we succeeded in putting a stronger force there than that which opposed us. It is for our opponent to explain how we were permitted to do it." Jacob D. Cox, "Forcing Fox's Gap and Turner's Gap," in Robert U. Johnson and Clarence C. Buel, eds., *Battles and Leaders of the Civil War*, 4 vols. (New York: The Century Company, 1884-89), 2:583-590. As noted above, Lee felt that D. H. Hill should have had all of his brigades up on the mountain.
32. Betts, *Experiences*, p. 15.
33. Clark, *N.C. Regiments*, 1:244.
34. Gorman, "Memoirs," p. 4-5; *OR*, vol. 19, pt. 1, p. 1020; Hill, "South Mountain," p. 567; Gorman states that Anderson's brigade was in position at the Gap at sunrise, contrary to D. H. Hill who says in his official report that, "Anderson's brigade arrived in time to take the place

shortly after the rout of Garland.[34] Hill entrusted Anderson with the defense of the Old Sharpsburg Road.[35] George B. Anderson divided his brigade upon arriving at the Gap. He took the 14th and 30th Regiments to the left or north of the pass and directed Colonel Tew to take the 2nd and 4th Regiments to the south of the road, or to the right, facing Frederick.[36]

In the fierce fighting which went on into the afternoon, the 2nd and 4th Regts. N.C.T. were in the advance in the assaults made by Anderson's brigade around Fox's Gap. While the Confederates did not manage to drive the Northerners off South Mountain, they did succeed in keeping them from penetrating the Gap. The 30th was not engaged with any visible part of the enemy's forces at any time during the battle of South Mountain. The regiment suffered less than 20 casualties. However, the men became exhausted on account of the rapid movements up and down the mountain in the heat of the day during the battle.[37] Colonel Parker could hardly keep his men awake even under enemy fire.[38]

In the late afternoon of September 14, when D. R. Jones' division came up at last as a relieving force, Anderson's brigade fell back to Boonsboro.[39] Early on September 15, the 30th fell back from Boonsboro across Antietam Creek to a hill near the

of the much demoralized troops of Garland," and in Hill, "South Mountain," p. 567, "It was more than half an hour after the utter rout and dispersion of Garland's brigade that G. B. Anderson arrived at the head of his small but fine body of men."

35. *OR*, vol. 19, pt. 1, p. 1020.
36. Clark, *N.C. Regiments*, 1:245.
37. *OR*, vol. 19, pt. 1, pp. 1050-1051. The 30th's official report, written by Major Sillers, states that the loss was one captain and three privates wounded and 15 privates missing. A review of the 30th's roster in Manarin and Jordan, *N.C.Troops*, 8:321-423, found that the losses at South Mountain were one mortally wounded, three wounded (including Capt. Jesse Johnson Wicker of Company H) and 10 captured.
38. Hill, "South Mountain," pp. 579-581.
39. Accounts of the battle at Fox's Gap on September 14, 1862, from the Confederate point of view appear in *OR.*, vol. 19, pt. 1, p. 1020-1021; Hill, "South Mountain," p. 567-8; and Gorman, "Memoirs," p. 4-5. Historical narratives of the battle appear in Sears, *Landscape Turned Red*, pp. 114-149 and Freeman, *Lee's Lieutenants*, 2:166-183. An entire book is devoted to South Mountain: John Michael Priest, *Before Antietam* (Shippensburg, Pennsylvania: White Mane Publishing Company, Inc., 1992).
40. Betts, *Experiences*, p. 16.

1st Sgt. James W. Wells
Co. E, 30th Regt. N.C.T.
Wounded at Sharpsburg, September 17, 1862

small town of Sharpsburg.[40] The men of Anderson's brigade lay on their arms all night, sleeping on "beds of clover." "Our brigade had piled their knapsacks on the mountain & in retreating at night, all was lost. So we lay on the earth with nothing but the blue heavens for a covering."[41] September 16 was spent under desultory artillery fire in line of battle outside of Sharpsburg.[42]

At daylight on September 17, 1862, Anderson's brigade was awakened by the sound of heavy musketry and cannon fire on its left.[43] They moved northward to take up position in a sunken road. Now truly the regiment's day of trial was at hand. For fate had decreed that Colonel Parker and his men were to take center stage on this, the bloodiest day in American history by holding the center of the Confederate line. The sunken road would be known forever after as the "Bloody Lane."[44]

The configuration of the land at the position of Anderson's brigade and the 30th was unusual, presenting advantages and problems for both defenders and attackers. From the brigade's left flank, held by Col. C. C. Tew's 2nd Regt. N.C.T. adjacent to the 6th Alabama of Brig. Gen. Robert E. Rodes' brigade, the sunken road bent back to the right and ran generally eastward downhill and through the position of Col. Risden Tyler Bennett's

41. James W. Shinn of Company B, 4th N.C. Regt. N.C.T. "Notes written during the war," p. 137, Osborne Papers #567, SHC. These notes were copied by James W. Osborne from "The Record book of Jas. W. Shinn's Notes & Commentaries of The war between the 'Rebs' & '_____' for the Liberty & Dignity of 'The South.'" The author was James W. Shinn who was a 27-year-old physician residing in Rowan County when he enlisted as private in Company B, 4th Regt. N.C.T. on June 3, 1861, for the war. Shinn was promoted to orderly sergeant on August 20, 1861, appointed 2nd lieutenant to rank from July 22, 1862, and promoted to 1st lieutenant to rank from February 11, 1863. He died March 14, 1863, at Baker's Mills, Rowan County, of disease. A "talented and noble soldier," he was greatly distinguished for courage at Sharpsburg. Manarin and Jordan, *N.C. Troops,* 4:26 and 738; Clark, *N.C. Regiments,* 1:270.
42. Betts, *Experiences,* p. 16; Gorman, "Memoirs," p. 6.
43. *Ibid.*
44. The accounts, as usual, conflict as to the time the 30th and Anderson's brigade took up position at Bloody Lane. Parker recalled that the position was occupied "during the night of the 16th." Clark, *N.C. Regiments,* 2:499. Major W. W. Sillers of the 30th reported, "Our position was taken, I suppose, about 8:30 a.m." *OR,* vol. 19, pt. 1, p. 1051. Shinn, "Notes," p. 139 says "Anderson's brigade changed position in an old road early in the morning. . ."

14th Regt. N.C.T.. From there it continued eastward, through the position of the 4th Regt. N.C.T., uphill to the position of the 30th. The terrain to the regiment's north allowed the enemy to get within a short distance before coming into sight. Major Sillers reported:

> In front of the right wing of our regiment, and at a distance of not more than 50 paces, there was a ravine which, extending diagonally to the left, gradually narrowed down the level space in front until in front of the extreme left of the Thirtieth there was not more than 30 paces of level ground.[45]

Colonel Parker noted that the regiment "was much exposed by reason of our position on the crest of the hill." On the left or opposite flank of Anderson's brigade, Generals Lee and D. H. Hill—inspecting the line and urging that it be held lest disaster befall the army—were reassured by the valiant words of Col. John B. Gordon of the 6th Alabama: "These men are going to stay here, General, till the sun goes down or victory is won."[46]

In thirty to forty-five minutes, the Yankees made their appearance, crossing the ravine and advancing up the hill toward the 30th. A well directed fire broke their line and drove them back.[47] Colonel Parker recalled:

> I have never witnessed a more deliberate nor more destructive firing. I cautioned my men to hold their fire

---

45. *OR*, vol. 19, pt. 1, p. 1051. The position of the 30th is shown looking toward the east from about the position of the 4th Regt. N.C.T. in the full page color picture published in Richard M. Ketchum, *The American Heritage Picture History of the Civil War* (New York: American Heritage Publishing Co., Inc., 1960), p. 236. The 30th's position can also be clearly seen in the background from a point farther west, beyond the bend in the sunken road, looking west, in James Hope's 1889 painting "After the Battle, the Bloody Lane—Battle of Antietam, Maryland, 1862." Hope's painting is published in Harold Holzer, and Mark E. Neely, Jr. *Mine Eyes Have Seen the Glory: The Civil War in Art* (New York: Orion Books, 1993), p. 197; James M. McPherson, ed., *The American Heritage New History of the Civil War* (New York: Viking Penguin, 1996), p. 227.
46. John B. Gordon, *Reminiscences of the Civil War* (New York: Charles Scribner's Sons, 1903), p. 84.
47. *OR*, vol. 19, pt. 1, p. 1051.

until I should give the command, and then to take deliberate, cool aim; that I would not give the command to fire until I could see the belt of the cartridge boxes of the enemy, and to aim at these. They obeyed my orders, gave a fine volley, which brought down the enemy as grain falls before a reaper.[48]

About this time, Brig. Gen. Ambrose R. Wright's Georgia brigade of Maj. Gen. Richard H. Anderson's division came up to the support of the 30th.[49] Major Sillers recalled the fighting after the arrival of Wright's Brigade:

The enemy continued to make his appearance, first on one hill, then another, but always at long range. The line was ordered to advance, and halted on the edge of the ravine. Here a hot fire was kept up for a few minutes. Soon the line was ordered to take its first position, and did so.[50]

While the firing was very hot, Courier John F. Bagarly[51] from brigade headquarters reported to Colonel Parker that General

---

48. Clark, *N.C. Regiments*, 2:500.
49. *OR*, vol. 19, pt. 1, p. 1051.
50. *Ibid.*
51. Clark, *N.C. Regtiments*, 2:499-500. Parker refers to the messenger as "Courier Baggarly." John F. Bagarly was a 30-year-old resident of Davie County when he enlisted in the "Davie Sweep Stakes," Company G of the 4th Regt. N.C.T. at Camp Pickens near Manassas, Virginia, on August 2, 1861. He was assigned to extra duty for most of the war as courier with the field and staff of the 4th Regt. and, apparently with the succession of 4th Regt. colonels who had risen to command the brigade. Manarin and Jordan, *N.C. Troops*, 4:12 and 76. Bagarly was cited by Brigadier General Stephen D. Ramseur for his conduct as a brigade headquarters courier at Chancellorsville. *OR*, vol. 25, pt. 1, p. 998. At Cedar Creek, while serving as Brig. Gen. W. R. Cox's brigade headquarters courier, Bagarly let General Ramseur have his horse (with Cox's consent) after Ramseur's own horse was shot, Ramseur refusing to take shelter. Shortly thereafter, Ramseur received his death wound. William R. Cox, "Major-General Stephen D. Ramseur: His Life and Character," in *The Southern Historical Society Papers* (reprint:Wilmington, North Carolina: Broadfoot, 1990), 18:254. John F. Bagarly survived carrying messages through the hottest parts of many fights to surrender at Appomattox. "Paroles of the Army of Northern Virginia," in *The Southern Historical Society Papers* (reprint:Wilmington, North Carolina:

Turner and Bridgers, *History of Edgecombe County, North Carolina*, 1920

Adjt. Frederick Philips (postwar)
30th Regt. N.C.T.
Colonel Parker's brother-in-law

Anderson was wounded and had left the field, that he was unable to find Colonel Tew, of the 2nd Regt., the brigade's senior colonel, and that he was therefore making this report to Colonel Parker, he being next in command. Parker instructed his regimental adjutant and brother-in-law, Lt. Fred Philips, to proceed cautiously down the line, observing what was going on, and if possible, to find Colonel Tew, on the brigade's opposite flank, and carry Bagarly's report to him. The difficulty of traversing Bloody Lane at this point in time would seem to have been insurmountable. However, Lieutenant Philips set off and, after receiving several shots through his clothing, came within hailing distance of Colonel Tew and gave him the report. Philips asked Tew to give some indication that he was heard. Colonel Tew, who was standing erect, lifted his hat, gave Philips a polite bow, and fell immediately from a head wound.[52]

The death of Colonel Tew occurred about 11 o'clock a.m.[53] Adjutant Philips fell with a head wound himself on his return journey to the 30th's position, traveling from the left to the right of the brigade along Bloody Lane. Colonel Parker now attempted to go to the left of the brigade. He had not gone ten paces when he was struck by a minié ball in the head and was taken from the field.[54] The wounding of Colonel Parker took place at about 11:30 a.m.[55] Chaplain Betts examined Parker at the brigade hospital two miles in the rear when he was brought in about noon along with Adjutant Philips. Betts noted:

> A rifle ball passed over Colonel Parker's head, cutting away a narrow strip of skin and plowing a nice

Broadfoot, 1990), 15:256. A. M. Waddell, "General George Burgwyn Anderson—The Memorial Address," in *The Southern Historical Society Papers* (reprint: Wilmington, North Carolina: Broadfoot, 1990), 14:392-3.

52. Clark, *N.C. Regiments*, 2:499-500. Parker's account indicates that the fighting at Bloody Lane had been going on for a considerable period of time when Tew fell. John B. Gordon stated that he was standing next to Colonel Tew when he fell and that "[T]he first volley from the Union lines in my front" fired the fatal ball. Gordon, *Reminiscences*, p. 89. Fred Philips wrote of this incident in a letter dated August 25, 1894, to H. Heth misfiled in the 3rd North Carolina file in the John M. Gould Papers, Dartmouth College Library, Hanover, New Hampshire.
53. Gorman, "Memoirs," p. 6.
54. Clark, *N.C. Regiments*, 2:500.
55. *OR*, vol. 19, pt. 1, p. 1051.

little furrow in the skull, leaving the membrane that covers the brain visible but uninjured. What a narrow escape![56]

Major Sillers assumed command of the 30th upon the wounding of Colonel Parker. The situation deteriorated rapidly for the Confederates. While no mention was made by Parker or Sillers of any problems caused by Wright's brigade in its reinforcement of the North Carolinians in Bloody Lane, 2nd Lt. James W. Shinn of the 4th Regt., holding Bloody Lane on the 30th's left, recalled a chaotic scene following Wright's reinforcement of the 4th's line:

> Wright was drunk & and <u>tried</u> to order our Brigade forward, but the commanders choosed to await Anderson's orders as we were under cover & preferred to let the enemy come up. Another Brigade came up & pushed into the road on our brigade & created some confusion.[57]

It was about this time that Generals Wright and Anderson were wounded.[58] Command of the brigade now devolved upon the next senior officer, Col. Risden Tyler Bennett of the 14th Regt. N.C.T.[59] Things were beginning to look bleak for the Confederates.

---

56. Betts, *Experiences*, p. 16.
57. Shinn, "Notes," p. 139. Shinn's statement that Wright was drunk finds no support in other sources. While advancing with the 3rd Georgia toward the sunken road on the morning of September 17, Brig. Gen. Wright's iron gray horse was hit squarely in the breast by an enemy shell which exploded inside the horse and threw Wright 10-15 feet in the air. Wright, however, came down on his feet. C. H. Andrews "General Wright at Sharpsburg," Atlanta *Journal* Nov. 2, 1901. When 200 yards from the enemy, later determined to be the Irish Brigade, Wright received a wound passing through the muscle of the leg below the knee. "Wright (who was still lying on the field, and desired himself to be carried forward to give the command on a litter) advanced the Brigade nearer the enemy at a charge Bayonet who broke in confusion." Report of William Gibson, colonel 48th Georgia. comdg. Wright's Brigade, Charles H. Andrews Papers, #2849, Southern Historical Collection, and *Supp. OR*, pt. 2, vol. 3, p. 570. Also see, "Letter from Wright's Brigade" dated Oct. 1, 1862, in Augusta *Daily Constitutionalist*, October 18, 1862.
58. Shinn, "Notes," p. 139.
59. *OR*, vol. 19, pt. 1, p. 1047.

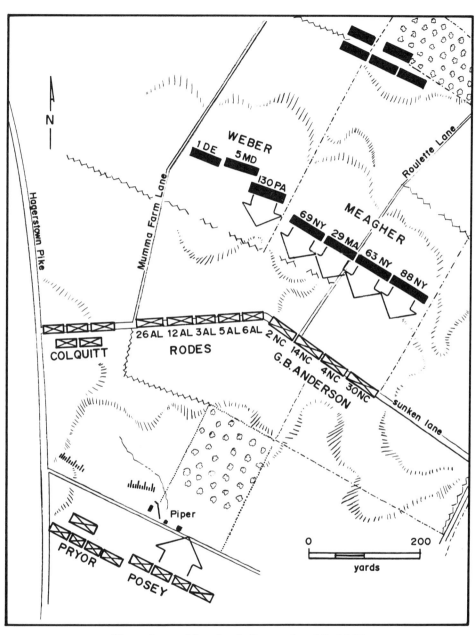

Sharpsburg, Maryland, September 17, 1862
G. B. Anderson's brigade in the Bloody Lane

As the Union troops came over the rim 30-50 yards in front of Bloody Lane, they were able not only to shoot down upon the Southerners lying packed in the sunken road in front of them, but also to fire obliquely into the crowded ranks on the road as well.

The loss of brigade and regimental commanding officers was particularly debilitating. Not only General Anderson and Colonels Tew and Parker had fallen by this time. The 4th Regt., with Col. Bryan Grimes disabled by a wound at South Mountain three days before, began the day commanded by Beaufort County's Capt. William T. Marsh of Company I, the "Pamlico Rifles." When Captain Marsh was mortally wounded, Iredell County's Capt. Edwin Augustus Osborne of Company H took command until he was wounded. The command of the 4th then devolved upon Iredell County's 22-year-old 2d Lt. Franklin H. Weaver, also of Company H. When Weaver fell mortally wounded bearing the regimental colors, the 4th was left without an officer. "[T]he men needed none except for general purposes," the regimental historian Captain (later Colonel) Osborne recalled.[60]

Brigade after Yankee brigade had been fed into the Confederate killing machine for three hours or more, and the fields to the north of Bloody Lane were littered with the blue-clad dead. But now the disadvantages of the terrain, the Northerners' pressure, the confusion attendant upon the loss of so many commanding officers and the disorderly reinforcement of the line by Wright and others combined to cause the Confederate line at Bloody Lane to break.

Lieutenant Shinn of the 4th recalled:

> The minié balls, shot & shell rained down upon us from every direction except the rear. We were ordered to fall back & many men took this chance (from all Regts) to leave the field entirely.[61]

From Col. R. T. Bennett's perspective, the break in the line on his brigade's right was a rout occurring when masses of troops from Major General R. H. Anderson's division rein-

---

60. Clark, *N.C. Regiments*, 1:247.
61. Shinn, "Notes," p. 139.

forced the line and then "broke beyond the power of rallying after five minutes' stay." Colonel Bennett's judgment upon his fellow regiments was harsh: "In this stampede, if we may so term it, the Fourth North Carolina State Troops and the Thirtieth North Carolina Troops participated."[62]

Major Sillers reported that he withdrew the 30th about 300 yards upon determining that both flanks of the regiment were uncovered.[63] From this position the regiment twice charged the Federals.[64] To the left, Colonel Bennett's regiment was compelled to fall back by the collapse of the brigade's line on his right and the mistaken retreat of the 6th Alabama on the left caused by a misunderstood order.[65] After retreating some distance, Colonel Bennett, with a handful of men of the 14th, commandeered a single piece of artillery near the Hagerstown Pike, opened on the advancing Yankees and drove them back.[66]

The Confederate line in Piper's swale south of Bloody Lane were weak and disorganized. "In falling back & running back the Regts. & Brigades became mixed up, & was not regularly organized that day."[67]

The fate of the Confederacy hung in the balance on September 17, 1862. A more aggressive commander than McClellan would have pushed through the Confederate center to Sharpsburg and destroyed Lee's army. But McClellan did not do so and the scratch line occupied by the surviving soldiers of the 30th held until dark.[68]

The next day, September 18, the brigade received rations about 9:30 a.m. and was then called into line by Gen. D. H. Hill who made a speech, calling the men "the Faithful Few" and

---

62. *OR*, vol. 19, pt. 1, p. 1048.
63. *Ibid.*, p. 1051; Shinn, "Notes," p. 139, recalled that the 4th "withdrew over a quarter of a mile and formed."
64. *OR*, vol. 19, pt. 1, p. 1051; Shinn, "Notes," p. 139, also recalled two charges on the Yankees after the retreat from Bloody Lane.
65. *OR*, vol. 19, pt. 1, pp. 1037-8 and 1048. Gorman, "Memoirs," p. 6.
66. Capt. T. D. Beall, "Reminiscences about Sharpsburg," *Confederate Veteran*, vol. 1 (1893):246.
67. Shinn, "Notes," p. 139.
68. Several accounts of the battle of Sharpsburg have been drawn on in reaching an understanding of the action at Bloody Lane, including: Freeman, *Lee's Lieutenants*, 2:203-225; Sears, *Landscape Turned Red*, pp. 236-254; Priest, *Antietam*, pp. 136-191.

warmly commending their courage and fortitude during the previous day's battle. [69]

The 30th Regiment N.C.T. before the battle of Sharpsburg numbered about 250.[70] It suffered 77 casualties (30.8%) in the battle: 9 killed, 6 mortally wounded, 1 mortally wounded and captured (a total of 16 fatalities), 40 wounded, 20 captured, and 1 wounded and captured.[71]

69. Shinn, "Notes," p. 140; Clark, N.C.Regiments, 1:249.
70. OR, vol. 19, pt. 1, p. 1052.
71. See casualty list at end of this book.

PART SEVEN

September 18, 1862 - Christmas, 1863
Fredericksburg, Chancellorsville,
Gettysburg, and Kelly's Ford

After lying on the battlefield of Sharpsburg all day on September 18, the 30th Regiment left the field at midnight and crossed the Potomac "without molestation."[1] Colonel Parker presumably started for North Carolina, probably by wagon, but his journey southward from Sharpsburg is not documented. On September 20, the regiment encamped near Martinsburg. Out of rations, the men ate green corn.[2] On September 22, Lt. Gen. Thomas Jonathan "Stonewall" Jackson rode by the regiment's camp to the soul-stirring music of the 14th Regiment's fife and drums. That night, Chaplain Betts lay beside his horse gazing at the stars thinking of his wife and children and the words of the Psalmist: "What is man that thou art mindful of him."[3] On September 27, the regiment broke camp and marched through Martinsburg and Bunkertown, encamping near Bunkertown.[4] Here the 30th was to remain until October 25.

A time of rest and recovery began in which the men occupied themselves with reading mail, shooting squirrels, visiting, and preparing for the continuation of the war. On Sunday, September 28, Chaplain Betts preached to the regiment a sermon which contained a summary of the recent battles.[5] On October 16, D. H. Hill conducted a grand review of his division.[6] On October 25, the regiment broke camp and spent the night tearing up the tracks of the Winchester & Harper's Ferry Railroad below Charlestown in a cold rain.[7] On October 27, the 30th marched through Berryville, and on October 31, the regiment waded

1. Ardrey Diary.
2. *Ibid.*
3. *Ibid.*; Betts, *Experiences*, p. 17.
4. Ardrey Diary.
5. *Ibid.*
6. *Ibid.*
7. *Ibid.*; Betts, *Experiences*, p. 20.

across the Shenandoah River at Berry's Ferry and crossed the Blue Ridge at Ashby's Gap reaching the village of Paris.[8] The men enjoyed the spectacular views, and Chaplains Betts and Powers of the 30th and 14th Regiments found two or three hours to walk up a mountain with a fine view and pray together up there.[9] On November 3, the regiment took up the line of march for Front Royal, arriving there on the morning of November 4.[10] On November 6, pickets were posted under command of Major Sillers on Jackson's May 23, 1862, battlefield. The enemy advanced, but no major attack was made, and D. H. Hill finally ordered a withdrawal across the Shenandoah River after nightfall. Wading the river in the bitterly cold weather was very hard on the barefooted men of the regiment. On November 9, Hill withdrew his division westward to Strasburg. The division remained in the vicinity of Strasburg for the next 10 days, marching out to tear up railroad tracks on November 11.[11]

Gen. D. H. Hill assigned Col. D. H. Christie of the 23rd Regt. N.C.T. of Iverson's brigade to command the brigade of G. B. Anderson, who died on October 16 in Raleigh from the effects of his wound at Sharpsburg. In November, however, Hill assigned the 4th Regt.'s able Col. Bryan Grimes to the brigade command upon Grimes' return to the brigade after recovering from an injury suffered from a horse kick received while crossing the Potomac into Maryland on September 5.[12]

On November 20, Hill's division marched for Fredericksburg, heading south through Woodstock and New Market, then eastward across Massanutten Mountain and the Blue Ridge Mountains and through Madison Court House. An encampment three miles from Gordonsville was reached on November 24. Here, rawhide moccasins were made for the numerous barefooted men. On November 26, the men marched through Orange Court House and reached a point within 12 miles of

8. Ardrey Diary; Betts Experiences, p. 20.
9. *Ibid.*
10. Ardrey Diary.
11. *Ibid.*; Betts, *Experiences*, pp. 20-21; William M. Norman, *A Portion of My Life* (Winston-Salem: John F. Blair, 1959), pp. 150-152.
12. Pulaski Cowper, *Extracts of Letters of Major-General Bryan Grimes to His Wife Written While in Active Service with the Army of Northern Virginia* (Raleigh: Alfred Williams & Co., 1884), reprint edited by and with new material by Gary Gallagher (Wilmington: Broadfoot Publishing Company, 1986), p. 21.

Fredericksburg. From November 28 to 30, the brigade encamped near Guinea Station and, from November 30 to December 12, near Port Royal, guarding that crossing of the Rappahannock.[13] It had now been less than five months since the 30th's
arrival in Virginia from North Carolina, but the extremely
eventful interval had been taken up with fighting four major
battles and marching with only brief respite from Richmond to
invade Maryland, followed by maneuvers in the Shenandoah
Valley and a trying late fall route march from Strasburg to
Fredericksburg. These men were now veteran soldiers. Pvt. J.
W. Bone remarked on their appearance:

> We were a very hard looking set of soldiers, the men
> had lost, thrown away and worn out about all that they
> started from Richmond with in August, and as I have
> said before we did not get much besides our rations
> while in the valley.[14]

On December 12, the brigade was ordered to Hamilton's
Crossing where, on the morning of December 13, it took position along the railroad near the Hamilton House. The brigade
was in this position for the next two days, and while not directly
engaged in the great battle of Fredericksburg, the men saw the
fight and suffered casualties from artillery fire.[15] The 30th
Regiment's losses numbered 1 mortally wounded, 14 other
wounded, and 1 captured in the battle of Fredericksburg.[16]

Following the battle of Fredericksburg, the 30th and the rest
of its brigade went into winter camp near Corbin's Crossroads,
nine miles from Guinea Station, and began picketing the Rap-

---

13. The 30th's route from Strasburg to Fredericksburg appears, from the
summary account in the 30th's Record of Events and Bone, "Service,"
p. 13, to have been the same as that of its fellow regiment of the brigade,
the 4th Regt. N.C.T.. The 4th's route of march is described in detail in
Norman, *A Portion of My Life*, pp. 153-154. Bone, "Service," p. 13,
mentions the making of footwear by cutting out pieces of rawhide which
were tied to the feet with strings. These homemade shoes soon dried out,
however, and rubbed the feet raw after about a day unless a new piece
of rawhide was obtained.
14. Bone, "Service," p. 13.
15. Cowper, *Letters of Major-General Bryan Grimes*, p. 25; Norman, *A
Portion of My Life*, p. 155; *OR*, vol. 21, p. 644.
16. See casualty roster at the end of this book.

Capt. William Caswell Drake
Co. B, 30th Regt. N.C.T.
Resigned, January 5, 1863

232

pahannock River.[17] On this duty the regiment was engaged until spring. Many long, cold and lonely hours were spent by the men pacing up and down the bank of the river. Pvt. J. W. Bone was relieved on picket duty one night by a thinly clad man who asked him for his overcoat. Bone did not want to come out of it, but knew what hardship the man faced and let him have it. The officer in charge remarked, "You gave your coat at a very hard time," but Bone, in retrospect, did not regret the act for the man was killed in the very next battle fought by the regiment.[18]

The morale of the regiment suffered in the weeks after Fredericksburg. Ten men deserted from Company I on January 11, 1863, and sixteen men deserted from the regiment on January 27.[19]

Stephen Dodson Ramseur was assigned as the 30th's new brigade commander on November 6, 1862, following George B. Anderson's death, but Ramseur was not sufficiently recovered from a severe wound, suffered at Malvern Hill, to be able to report for duty until January, 1863. Personally selected by General Lee for the post on account of his skill and fighting spirit shown in the Seven Days, Ramseur was certain to lead his men to where the fight was the hottest.[20]

The long months of convalescence from his wound received at Sharpsburg having passed, Colonel Parker returned to the regimental camp on April 10, 1863, and resumed command of the 30th on April 11. Apparently he now wore a sponge on the crease across his skull. Parker was serenaded by the 4th Regiment Band and gave a little address. A response was given by Capt. D. C. Allen of Company H.[21]

---

17. Cowper, *Letters of Major-General Bryan Grimes*, p. 27; Norman, *A Portion of My Life*, pp. 163-164; Bone, "Service," pp. 13-14.
18. *Ibid.*, p. 15.
19. Ardrey Diary.
20. *OR*, vol. 19, pt. 2, pp. 698-9; For a discussion of Ramseur's promotion and appointment to and assumption of command of George B. Anderson's brigade, see, Gary W. Gallagher, *Stephen Dodson Ramseur: Lee's Gallant General* (Chapel Hill: University of North Carolina Press, 1985), pp. 46-50.
21. Ardrey Diary.

Camp near Hamiltons Xing
April 11th 1863

My dear Wife

You see I am back at camp; I reached here safely on yesterday, found Fred at the depot with my horse, was received in a very complimentary manner [by] my Regt. All seem glad to see me; I am pleased at being back with them once more, but yet my heart is left at home; I long too [sic] be back with you. I have thought several times, that I have not acted as I should have done. I now wish that I had taken service in our own State. If I find, upon trial, that I can not stand the service, I shall certainly resign. There are so many men sneaking from the service of their country, now when their services are so much needed, that I am almost ashamed to retire from almost any cause.

Every thing is remarkably quiet here; there is no movement of the enemy to be discovered. There are various opinions about the probability of a fight here. My own opinion is, that if we get a fight at this point we will have to cross the river for it. Things are remarkably quiet in N. Carolina, and at Charleston. I hope that Genrl. Hill will bag the whole force at Washington, and that Genrl. Beauregard will drive back and sink every Yankee vessel at Charleston. I sent you from Petersburg by Henry Jones, the books for Mary; and from Richmond by Maj. Taylor, your cabbage seed, and some receipts which I hope you will take care of. I owe nothing in Petersburg now.

I hope that Hilliard is going on well with his planting operations. He should endeavour [sic] to plant the low grounds as soon as the land is dry enough.

Too much bread can not be made this year. You have heard various rumours [sic] about the suffering of the men in the army; I tell you I never saw men looking better; they all look hard, and fat enough for good work.

Rations are rather scarce; but the men manage to get along on them; I am sorry to say that we have a good many desertions from the army. Several from my own Regt.

I told you that I should feel better after reaching my Regt. than I did in Richmond; I do, but yet I want to see you and the children very much. I hope you will keep very well, and be sure to write to me often. Direct your letters to Genrl. Ramseur's Brigade, Genrl. D. H. Hill's Division, Richmond, Va. Kiss the children for me. Good bye.

234

your affectionate husband
F. M. Parker

Hd. Quarters 30th Regt. N.C.T.
Camp near Hamilton's Xing
April 12th, 1863

My dear Wife

Well I am here writing to you so soon again. It is sunday [*sic*] night, Fred is out, and I have nothing too [*sic*] do; so I thought I would while [*sic*] away the time by writing you.

I am yet considerably home sick; I fear it will take some time to break me into the harness again. My long stay with you was so pleasant, that I wish for it again. God grant that these difficulties very soon be honourably [*sic*] settled, and that we may be all at home with our families. I know you join me in this wish.

I find several changes in the Regt. during my absence; there are many new officers, the old ones having been dropped. Among others is Kearney [W.] Arrington; he was elected a Lieut. in the company formerly commanded by Capt. [William T.] Arrington [Company I]. He seems to be a very clever young man. [He] is rather shy; has not called on me yet; I met him coming off Dress Parade this evening, and told him he must come to my tent and sit with me.

From what I can see so far, the Regt. has been greatly improved in company officers, and I shall expect better things of it for the future. To day, Lt. Col. Hyman, Capt. Frigna, and Lt. Nicholson [***] came over to see us. They all seemed to be in fine spirits. Hyman says he must have a wife, so when you see Miss Minnie, tell her to look sharp. Our Brig. Genl. is quite a young man, not more than twenty-seven; he is a very strict disciplinarian. Drills very hard. I never expect to be under the command of such a man as the lamented Anderson. He was a fine officer, and a perfect gentleman.

You will find a box at Enfield containing my suit of uniform, your pair of blankets, and a few ~~blankets~~ bottles. I have returned the blankets and clothes for fear I should lose them, and the bottles, that you might return them to us filled with something good.

235

I wish you would have my horse cover, the one which Bill had, mended up, if it needs it; may be there will be a few leather straps to sew to it, Isham can do that part of it; after mending the cover, send it to me by the first safe opportunity. probably Dr. Joyner can have it sent on for you. My horse looks badly, and I wish to fix him up a little. Now how are your and my little children getting on? Is Mary as anxious to get off to school as ever; and does she bring home a report every friday [*sic*] afternoon? Does snap his eyes [page missing]

Hd Quarters 30th Regt. N.C.T.
April 14, 1863

My dear Wife

I did expect to day, to have received a letter from you; I have been disappointed. I know of no reason why you should not have written. You certainly knew where to direct your letters; so now you must make up for all deficiencies, and write often. My object in writing so soon is to ask you to send my black hat, by the first safe opportunity; the one I have here is too low in the crown, to allow me to wear a piece of sponge on top of my head, and this I consider very necessary. It may be that Dr. Joyner is coming on soon; if so he can bring the hat for me, and my horse cover also, which I requested you to send, in a former letter.

The weather remains quite cool here yet; there was a white frost this morning, the sun is warm in the day, but the nights are cool. The roads, however, are getting in fine order, and I can not understand why some movement from "FJ" Hooker's army is not made. The two capitals are for fighting Joe. For the past two days they have taken their pickets off their lines, immediately in our part; but they have been sending up a balloon, I suppose, to reconnoitre [*sic*].

Cowardly rascals, they are afraid to come into our lines for the purpose of finding out any thing. Well, we whipped them around Richmond, with their best General, and their balloons in the bargain, and with the help of God, we will whip them here.

I believe every one seems to be perfectly confident of success, at this point and at Charleston.

236

Before you receive this, you will have gone to Tarboro. How much I should delight to be with you on that interesting occasion. I will be with you in thoughts, and you must remember me in your prayers. I know you will.

I sent you, a few days since, my uniform suit, and your blankets. I was afraid I should loose my clothes, and I had no use for the blankets. I hope you have received them.

If you have not already done so, I would advise you to sell all the lard you have to spare; I think it will fall in price.

Write me often, and let me know how every thing is getting on; all details about the farm will interest me much, but all particulars about you and the children will interest me more. I want to see them very much. I thought about them on sunday [sic] last; thought that if I had been at home, Offa would have asked me to "come Pa les' walk about some." Well, I hope I may have the opportunity of walking with the little fellow often yet.

Kiss them all, and tell them I think of them often, and of their Mother oftener.

Tell Mary and Jimmy to write to me. Remember me to Mr. Dunn and family, and to Mr. and Mrs. Bennett when you see them. Fred is asleep, or else he would send his love to you.

very affectionately your husband,
F. M. Parker

Hd. Quarters 30th Regt. N.C.T.
April 19th 1863

My dear Wife

It is sunday [sic] afternoon, I have nothing to do, am all alone, Fred and the Maj. have rode over to Genrl. Pender's Brigade to visit some friends; so I have concluded that I could use my time in no better way than by writing to my dear wife. I have thought of you a great deal to day; you were in Tarboro, at church, at the church of your choice, among your own people; how pleasant, what a great privilege it is! how little we are apt to value such privileges, until deprived of them. I know you had a good sermon from the Bishop, and I know you enjoyed it. I hope you carried the children with you, at least Mary and Jimmy, and Miss Mat also. I have heard a sermon myself to day, from our own chaplain, Mr. [Alexander Davis] Betts, and I think it was rather a better sermon than he usually gives. I think he is exercising more influence over the men now, than formerly; he certainly is a good man, and means well.

Now my dear wife, it does seem to me that I have written you very often, since I left you, and have received only one letter from you. I am sure that it requires some time for a letter to come from N.C. to this army, and therefore you must write often and regularly; at least twice a week. The mail is brought to me every day for distribution, and I examine it very carefully, to see if I can find more for myself. Fred says that he never saw a man write so much as I do. I tell him if he had a wife, he would write too.

Genrl. Pender called on me yesterday; I have not seen him before in two years; he is looking very well. He is regarded as a no. one soldier, by those who know him. Edgecombe has cause to feel proud of him. I wish very much, that my Regt. was in his Brigade.

In your letter, you said that you had sold some hams to Dr. Joyner. Now ca'nt [*sic*] you spare the Government some bacon? By reducing your women, field hands too, to 3 ½ lbs. per week; and the men to 4 lbs, their present allowance, and with your beef, your garden, your surplus milk &c. I should think that you might be able to spare some. I leave this matter to your consideration. Do'nt [*sic*] be governed by what others do, but act upon your own ideas of patriotism and duty. If the soldiers, ~~can~~ your husbands and brothers, can live upon ¼ lb. per day, surely the negroes can do so likewise. This is a subject which I am afraid, the people have not properly considered.

Speaking of your cows, does Jim turn the milk cows in the new ground? I had the fence put up for that purpose, and that alone; no other stock should be allowed to run in there with them. By that means, I hope you will get a plenty of nice milk.

I asked you, in a previous letter, to have my horse cover sent me. If you have not already done so, you need not sent it now. I do not need it. But I do very much need my hat. [letter ends here]

Parker was perceived at this period to be taking a greater interest in religion than formerly. Chaplain W. C. Powers of the

14th Regt. N.C.T. reported to the Chaplains' Association of the Second and Third Army Corps on April 20, 1863, that "his regiment being absent, he had been preaching for Brother Betts in Thirtieth North Carolina, where a large number were concerned, among them a prominent officer (the colonel), a man of large influence at home, but heretofore unconcerned.[22]

———————————◆◆◆————————————

Hd. Quarters 30th Regt. N.C.T.
April 21st 1863

My dear Wife

I am afraid you will think that I do nothing but write to you. Now if I could have a little of the same thought about yourself, may be I could get a letter now and then. I have received only one from you yet. I continue to hope for better things.

Our chaplain, Rev. Mr. Betts, leaves home this morning, on a ten days furlough; he will pass through Weldon, on his way back to the Regt. in about ten days from this date, and has kindly promised to bring back my hat with him. Now if you will send the hat to Dr. Joyner, he will send it to Weldon for Mr. Betts, and I shall get it in that way. If there is a hat box about the house, send the hat in that; if their [sic] is none, you can wrap the hat up carefully in paper, and mark it for me. I hope I shall get it, for the one I have is too low in the crown, for summer; I can not place a piece of sponge in it; I hope you will send the hat to Dr. Joyner as soon as you receive this; so that he may have ample time to get it to Weldon, for Mr. Betts.

I wrote you such a long letter on sunday [sic] last, that I have not a bit of news to write now. I can say, however, that the weather has changed from balmy spring, to blustering winter. Yesterday and to day have been cold and very disagreeable, with a good deal of rain.

This country is much colder, than where you live; the trees have not even budded here yet; the grass is just beginning to spring up. Our poor horses are glad to see this, for their forage, like the men's rations, are quite short. In speaking of the allowance for your hands, in my last letter, I remarked that I

22. J. William Jones, *Christ in the Camp or Religion in the Confederate Army* (Atlanta: The Martin & Hoyt Co., 1904), p. 520.

thought you could reduce the quantity of meat issued to them. 3 ½ lbs. of good bacon, without much bone, say middling for instance, is enough for the men, and 3 lbs is sufficient for the women; particularly as your vegetables will soon be coming on, and your milk &c.

Of course, if you weigh a piece with much bone in it, you must give some more weight, in order to make up for the bone. I am satisfied that this allowance will be sufficient; it will be more then, than your neighbours give to their hands. By this reduction, you may have some bacon to spare to the government and let none but the government have it; no speculators, nor agents for any one, none of any kind, should have one pound, if I were you.

When you write me, please give me the date of my "will." There is [an] addition which I wish to make to it, and Fred says that it will be better to have the date of the will; give me the full date.

I wish Mr. Betts would pass Enfield; I should like to send you some money.

I hope you will write soon, and write often. I do get so much comfort and encouragement from your letters. Kiss the children for me. Tell them I think of them very often, and their Mother too.

I dreamed of you all last night; only a dream; this morning dissipated it all. Remember me to all friends. Good bye, may the Lord bless you all.

very affectionately your husband
F. M. Parker

On April 24, 1863, Ramseur, assuming the presidency of an examining board, left Parker in temporary command of the brigade which set out in a pouring rain to take up picket duty on the banks of the Rappahannock River.[23]

23. Ardrey Diary; William Calder letter to Mother, May 10, 1863, Calder Family Papers #125, Southern Historical Collection, University of North Carolina; Parker letter dated April 27, 1863, below.

On picket, Rappahannock
April 25th 1863

My dear Wife

You see from the above, that we are now on the outpost, doing picket duty. It is not very pleasant either. We went on duty yesterday, during a pretty heavy rain, which lasted nearly the whole day. It is clear and right cool to day.

This is certainly a magnificent country; the valley of this river is a very fine soil; none of the farms are now kept up, all devastated by war, cruel war; there is a good deal of wheat, however, which is altogether exposed to stock of all kinds; then there is any amount of fine clover; were it not for the latter, our poor horses would fare badly, as they receive no forage at all, only a little corn. This an old settled part of Va., is consequently a very open country. Some of the elevated positions give a very commanding view of the country. At least a half dozen residences and farms can be clearly seen, from one point; and the residences are so handsomely, and tastefully fitted up too, I mean the grounds. The buildings themselves are generally fine specimens of architecture, generally built of brick, and altogether indicate a good deal of wealth.

There must be wealth in so fertile a country as this. It is a great pity that all this fine country should be so desolated by war. The inhabitants are all refugees. Doubtless they often turn to their deserted homes, with longing hearts. These people have suffered much. You, who are removed from the seat of war, can have no idea of what has been suffered. God grant that you may never feel it. Just on the opposite side of the Rappahannock is the residence of Mr. Seddon, a brother of the Sec. of war; the house is a large one, built of brick, on a very high hill, and as all the dwellings do, faces the river. The farm lies all around and below the house; in the yard, are several falls or terraces, which are regulated by the rising of the ground. The whole is covered with a beautiful grass, and presents a very fine appearance from the distance. Stop; there is one thing to mar the beauty of the whole; and that is the presence of the detested, thriving abolitionists. Mr. Seddon's house is the Hd. Quarters of a Cavalry Brigade, we can see them very plainly. They picket on one side of the river, and we on the other. Until very recently, the pickets on both sides were allowed to talk to each other; there is now an order forbidding it. Our boys are very anxious to pick off the

241

Yankee pickets, but that is also contrary to orders. To show you how they destroy property, I will mention that they have even taken Mr. Seddon's family carriage down to the river, to protect their pickets in case of bad weather; yesterday, while it was raining so hard, our boys were walking their post while a rascal of a yankee was smug and dry in his carriage; and no doubt laughing at us. But I have said enough about the miserable scoundrels.

In my last letter to you, I advised you to reduce the allowance of meat which you give to our hands. [***] 3 ½ lbs. to 3 lbs a week. This quantity will be sufficient. By this means you will be able to spare the government some bacon, and recollect to reserve enough to send me some occasionally, as opportunity may offer. I see that other counties in our state are moving in this matter. I hope Halifax will also.

At present we are living tolerably well; the supplies I brought from home are not yet exhausted; then we buy a fine fish occasionally.

But I tell you the rations of the men is short; ¼ lb. of bacon is a small allowance for a soldier, for an entire day; particularly as they get nothing else.

I hope your garden, and farm, and pantry, and every thing else is going on well. Let me know all these matters in detail, when you write; every thing of the kind interests me.

I hope you have received my letter requesting you to send my hat to Enfield, to be sent to Weldon for Mr. Betts to bring back to me. I shall not need the horse blanket. So you are still uneasy about my horse are you? why, he is as gentle as I would have him. He never misbehaves with me. It was only those boys that caused him to perform so.

Now Sally the mail is just run, and no letter for your husband. I commenced writing this, before the mail came, hoping to get a letter from you, but am awfully disappointed.

Here I am, away down here in plain hearing of the Yankee drums, and seeing the rascals every day, and then ca'nt [sic] hear from my wife and little ones. Make Mary write, if you ca'nt write yourself.

Fred and I both keep well; he looks as well as I have ever seen him; sends his love to you and the children. Kiss them for me; I would ask you to kiss yourself, let Hattie do that for me.

Good bye, the Lord bless you all.

very affectionately you husband
F. M. Parker

Hd. Qrs. Picket post
Rapphannock river
April 27th 1863

My dear Wife

I received your letter of the 23rd on yesterday, and right glad
was I to get it; out here on our picket post, with nothing to
interest us, nothing to do but to watch a few Yankee pickets on
the opposite side of the river; the least thing interests us, in the
way of reading, but when that reading is in the shape of a letter
from a dear wife at home; one who we know loves us, as only
woman can love, then it is, that we can fully appreciate such
favours. We will remain on outpost only two days longer; when
we will return to camp, but even then, I shall hope to get more
letters from you. You certainly can not complain of my not
writing to you. I have written several letters since being in
camp; if you have not received them, charge it to the mails. I am
sorry you have not received your Enquirer; I certainly ordered
it sent to you, as the receipt will show. I have written to the
Editors, and hope that they will have the matter attended to.

About the receipts you spoke of, I did not send Mr. Waddell's
receipt among the first bundle; I overlooked it; but have sent it
in a letter, since. As for Martin, Tannahill & Co. it was a note
which I owed them, and I think I destroyed the note after paying
it, as I usually do. So you have not lost any of the papers, my
dear Wife. If Mr. Garnett has not paid for the corn yet, you must
charge him for it, in my large book, charge him $12.00 per bhl;
when Dr. Joyner settles for the bacon you have sold him, ask
him to deduct $35.00; that is what I owe him. Have you sold
your lard yet? I think I would sell it, if I met with a favourable
[sic] opportunity.

Now you want to know something of my condition; my head
has not troubled me any yet. I had a very severe cold, soon after
getting to camp, which made my head a little sore; but as the
cold went away, my head became all right. I think I have
nothing to fear now, but the sun and hot weather; if I can get the
hat I wrote for, I think I can get on very well with my piece of

sponge. So I am afraid there is no danger of my having to return home on account of disability.

I am becoming better satisfied now, than when I first returned. There is nothing like a little hard work, to keep people straight. I hope I shall get along very well now. I am not well satisfied with the Brigade I am in, but will try to get along as well as possible. I should like much better to be in Genrl. Hill's Division in N.C. or in Genrl. Pender's Brigade, in A. P. Hill's division.

Genrl. Pender called on me the other day; he is a very clever gentleman besides being a first-rate officer.

Genrl. Ramseur is now President of an examining board, this leaves me in command of his Brigade.

My duties so far are rather light, but yet I would prefer to be with my own Regt. I hope the Genrl. will not be absent long from his command. As to the probabilities of a fight. [***] I think they are very weak. There is no movement here on the part of the enemy manifest.

I hope every thing is getting on quietly at home, and that you will make a fine crop this year.

Kiss the children for me. Write often, and let me know every thing which is going on.

Good bye, my dear Wife, God bless you all.

very affectionately your husband
F. M. Parker

———◆●◆———

On Wednesday, April 29, the brigade received word that the Federals were across the Rappahannock, and division commander Robert E. Rodes positioned Ramseur's brigade on the south bank of Massaponax Creek guarding the ford near its mouth.[24] In this position the brigade was shelled by an enemy battery on the opposite shore, with no one being able to expose himself without being fired at and a few men being lost. The sharpshooters were placed in rifle pits along the river bank and a brisk fire was exchanged with the enemy's sharpshooters.[25]

24. *OR*, vol. 25, pt. 1, p. 939; Calder to Mother, May 10, 1863, Calder Family Papers.
25. *Ibid.*; *OR*, vol. 25, pt. 1, p. 995.

The next afternoon, Thursday, April 30, again under Ramseur's command, the brigade marched toward Fredericksburg by a circuitous route, attempting to keep out of sight of enemy artillery but being spotted and shelled twice. Just before dark, the brigade reached a commanding hill near Hamilton's Crossing from which the men could observe a "very pretty little artillery duel." The small portion of the night allowed for rest was passed sleeping in the bushes on wet blankets.[26]

Before daybreak, in the early hours of Friday, May 1, Ramseur's brigade formed up and began a march which carried the troops from Hamilton's Crossing by the Military Road to its junction with the Fredericksburg & Orange Court-House Plank Road, then up the Plank Road for two miles.[27] Just after daybreak, the troops were lying by the road resting when a shout of "Stonewall's coming!" was heard, and a cheer was taken up along the whole line. Soon the "old hero" came dashing by, his horse at full speed and his hat in hand, followed by a single courier. Stonewall's head swiveled back and forth, "as if it were on wires."[28] To 1st Lt. William M. Norman of the 2nd Regt., "[h]e seemed to be anxious to cast his eyes at every soldier as he rapidly rode by, as if to say, 'There is heavy work ahead.'"[29]

After marching seven miles of the journey westward, Ramseur was detached and ordered to report to Maj. Gen. Anderson.[30] About 3 p.m. Ramseur's brigade advanced upon the enemy up the Orange Plank Road with Posey's Mississippi brigade on the right and Wright's Georgia brigade on the left.[31]

---

26. *Ibid.*, pp. 939 and 995; Calder to Mother, May 10, 1863, Calder Family Papers. The exact date on which Ramseur resumed command from Parker does not appear in the *OR*, but Ramseur begins the use of the first person in his report with respect to the brigade's move toward Fredericksburg on April 30.
27. *OR*, vol. 25, pt. 1, pp. 939 and 995 (where Ramseur states that his brigade was aroused for the march at 3 a.m.); Cowper, *Letters of Major-General Bryan Grimes*, p. 28; Calder to Mother, May 10, 1863, Calder Family Papers, where Calder states that "At two o'clock we were called up hurriedly, and ordered to fall in. In five minutes all were in line, and the march commenced." Watkins, *Movement of the 14th North Carolina*, p. 9, says the men were allowed to sleep until 3 a.m..
28. Calder to Mother, May 10, 1863, Calder Family Papers.
29. Norman, *A Portion of My Life*, p. 169.
30. *OR*, vol. 25, pt. 1, p. 995.
31. *Ibid.* The time of 3 p.m. for the opening of the fight is given in the Ardrey Diary. The troops are shown to be in position at 1:30 p.m. in John

The sharpshooters, with Ramseur in personal command, took the advance. The Federals fell back in confusion for about two miles, littering their way with knapsacks, canteens, haversacks, guns and accoutrements. The Confederate advance was finally halted about 6 p.m. when the foe was encountered in force in their front and the sharpshooters were outflanked on the left by a battery and a line of skirmishers.[32] It was reported that Jackson said that the skirmishing was "beautifully done."[33]

On Friday evening, May 1, as the sharpshooters came out of the woods, Lieutenant Calder witnessed a famous scene: "I saw a sight that many in our Confederacy would like to see. Lee and Jackson, side by side, surrounded by their staff. They appeared to be discussing some subject, and Lee was writing an order upon the pommel of his saddle."[34] Night closed in, and the men of the brigade lay down in the leaves to sleep in line of battle.[35]

Saturday, May 2, was a very pretty day.[36] General Lee had decided to divide his army, sending Stonewall Jackson on circuitous flank march to the west and then north in order to fall on the Federals' right flank. Rodes' division, including Ramseur's brigade and the 30th Regiment, headed the column with Colquitt's brigade in the lead stepping off about 5:30 a.m.[37] The Confederates, largely hidden from the Union forces by the forest, marched westward to Catherine Furnace, then southwest down the Furnace Road and north up various byways and the Brock Road across the Orange and Germanna Plank Roads to the Turnpike, reached by Jackson's lead elements about 2:30 p.m.[38]

Bigelow, Jr., *The Campaign of Chancellorsville* (New Haven: Yale University Press, 1910; reprint: Dayton, Ohio: Morningside House, Inc., 1991), Map 14. Bigelow discusses this action at p. 248.

32. *OR*, vol. 25, pt. 1, pp. 940 and 995; Calder to Mother, May 10, 1863, Calder Family Papers.
33. *Ibid.*
34. *Ibid.*
35. Norman, *A Portion of My Life*, p. 170; Calder to Mother, May 10, 1863, Calder Family Papers; Bone, "Service," p. 15; Ardrey Diary.
36. William Whatley Pierson, Jr., ed., *Whipt 'Em Every Time: The Diary of Bartlett Yancey Malone* (Jackson, Tennessee: McCowat-Mercer Press, 1960; reprint: Wilmington, North Carolina: Broadfoot Publishing Company, 1987), p. 78.
37. Bigelow, *Chancellorsville*, p. 274.
38. *Ibid.*, pp. 274-289 and Maps 16 and 17.

The way grew warm as the day wore on with the trees holding the heat down on the road.[39] Many men of the 14th Regiment fell out by the wayside during the march.[40] Ramseur's brigade halted about three o'clock and was given a good long rest time.[41] As the Confederate brigades arrived, Jackson deployed them in readiness for attack in a line perpendicular to the Turnpike facing east. Sometime around 5 p.m. Jackson ordered the advance to begin on Howard's unsuspecting Eleventh Corps which formed right wing of the Army of the Potomac and hung unprotected in thin air, with Union soldiers lounging about and off guard in the late spring afternoon.[42]

As the Southerners went forward, Ramseur's brigade was on the Confederate right in the second line with orders to follow Colquitt's brigade, the unit in the first line ahead. During the advance, Colquitt halted his brigade to resist a supposed Union attack on his right flank, based on the sighting of a small body of enemy cavalry, and sent word to Ramseur who advised Colquitt that he would protect the flank while Colquitt continued the advance in conjunction with Rodes' other brigades. Ramseur moved about a half a mile to the right, but did not find a single Yankee, and thus his brigade was, as Rodes put it, "necessarily deprived of any participation in the action." Ramseur returned to the division line and, moving by the left flank, took up position behind Colquitt whose men were resting in line of battle near Dowdall's Tavern.[43]

The Federal army had been caught by surprise and driven back. It suffered from an incompetent high command. However, these Northerners were made of stern stuff and able to

---

39. *Ibid.*, p. 276 and Calder to Mother, May 10, 1863, Calder Family Papers.
40. Watkins, *Movement of the 14th North Carolina*, p. 10.
41. Norman, *A Portion of My Life*, p. 171.
42. Rodes says that his division formed line of battle at 4:00 p.m. and that the advance began at 5:15 p.m.. *OR*, vol. 25, pt. 1, p. 940. Lt. William Calder of the 2nd Regiment says the advance began at 5:00 p.m.. Calder to Mother, May 10, 1863, Calder Family Papers. For a discussion of the conflicting times given for the beginning of Jackson's advance on the evening of May 2, 1863, see Bigelow, *Chancellorsville*, p. 295.
43. *OR*, vol. 25, pt. 1, pp. 942 and 995. The positions of the Confederate brigades at the time of the commencement of the attack on May 2 are shown on Bigelow, *Chancellorsville*, Map 18. Bigelow (p. 308) states that Ramseur and Colquitt halted near Dowdall's Tavern and Bigelow Maps 21-24 and Plan 3 show Ramseur's brigade in this position from 7:15 p.m. on May 2 until 5 a.m. on May 3.

rebound from a momentary reverse. Defensive positions were being strengthened as the night passed. The advantage of surprise was lost to the attackers. On the morrow, the Confederates would have to take the offensive in the tangle of woods ahead and fight as fierce a battle as they ever fought. And they would have to do so without their legendary Corps commander, for shortly after 9:15 p.m., Lt. Gen. Thomas J. "Stonewall" Jackson was shot and mortally wounded by North Carolinians of Lane's brigade while reconnoitering the Union lines.[44]

In the forest east of Ramseur's brigade, toward Chancellorsville, the Union forces were busy during Saturday night, May 2/3, strengthening their position. The 123rd New York of Col. Samuel Ross' Second Brigade, a part of Brig. Gen. Alpheus Williams' First Division of Slocum's Twelfth Corps, lay with the 3rd Maryland between its right flank and the Orange Plank Road. Sgt. Rice C. Bull of the 123rd New York remembered:

> As soon as we were given a place in the new line we commenced to cut the timber in our front to make a barricade, trees as far away as fifty feet or more were cut to fall parallel to our front. This formed an abatis with the larger logs piled up so as to make a breastwork. By three in the morning we had strong protection that saved many lives when we were attacked the next day.[45]

The 5th New Jersey in Brig. Gen. Gershom Mott's Third Brigade of Maj. Gen. Hiram Berry's Second Division of Sickles' Third Corps was positioned to the rear of the 123rd New York, and Pvt. Alfred Bellard recalled that "all night long chopping was going on in our front."[46]

---

44. *Ibid.*, pp. 317-319.
45. K. Jack Bauer, ed., *Soldiering: The Civil War Diary of Rice C. Bull* (Novato, California: Presidio Press, 1977), pp. 52-53. The 3rd Maryland and the 123rd New York continued fortifying their position until the Confederates opened fire on the morning of May 3. *OR*, vol. 25, pt. 1, pp. 698 and 705.
46. David Herbert Donald, ed., *Gone for a Soldier: The Civil War Memoirs of Private Alfred Bellard* (Boston: Little, Brown and Company, 1975), p. 212. Rice Bull of the 123rd New York in the Sixth inaccurately identified the Third Corps Mott/Sewell New Jersey Brigade behind his regiment's position as the Sixth Corps New Jersey Brigade, Bauer, *Soldiering*, p. 56.

2nd Lt. William Calder of the 2nd Regt. N.C.T., gave a simple but accurate description of the formidable Union position that the Confederate forces west of Chancellorsville, including Ramseur's men, faced at dawn on Sunday, May 3, 1863:

> During Saturday night, the enemy had not been idle. They had felled the trees in the woods, so as to impede our progress, and built breastworks of logs. In the rear of this breastwork, on a commanding hill, they had entrenched themselves, and planted a great many guns. In addition to this a line was formed nearly at right angles to the other, as to flank our line when we should charge the breastworks. These were the formidable obstacles our men had to overcome, and right well did they accomplish their task.[47]

Two significant re-positionings of the Union forces in front of Ramseur's brigade south of the Plank Road took place during the middle of the night and the early morning hours of Sunday, May 3. The Union forces may have been thrown in disorder but they had plenty of fight left in them. About midnight, Third Corps commander Daniel E. Sickles, whose troops lay in the vicinity of Hazel Grove, attempted to regain the ground lost in the flight of the Eleventh Corps. By launching a night attack with Ward's and Hayman's brigades of Birney's division northward, he attempted to surprise the Confederate forces astride the Plank Road. The chaotic moonlit assault veered too far to the east and only brushed the Confederates while slamming into Alpheus Williams' Union Twelfth Corps division and setting off a fierce battle between friendly forces. Sickles, however, did succeed in firmly linking up with the Twelfth Corps on his

---

47. During the late afternoon May 2 Confederate flank attack, the sharp-shooters were ordered to serve as brigade provost guard in the rear of Ramseur's men. The sharpshooters became separated from the brigade, probably due to Ramseur's futile move to the right in pursuit of a phantom enemy flanking force, and Calder did not succeed in rejoining the brigade until Monday morning, May 4—thus missing the hardest fighting at Chancellorsville, which occurred on May 3. However, Calder's letters contain vivid descriptions of the May 3 fighting. Calder to Bob, May 5, 1863; Calder to Mother, May 7, 1863; Calder to Mother, May 10, 1863, Calder Family Papers. The passage describing the Union position is taken from Calder's May 10, 1863, letter.

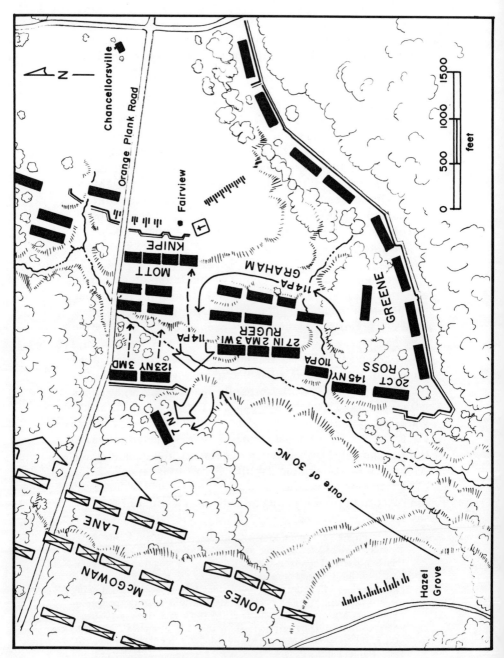

Chancellorsville, Virginia, May 3, 1863: 9 to 11 a.m.

right and taking a more advanced position on the strategic eminence of Hazel Grove.[48]

The enhancement of the Union position on Hazel Grove by Sickles' night attack proved pointless however, because at dawn Hooker ordered Sickles to abandon this position and withdraw to the east toward Fairview in order to form a more compact defensive line around Chancellorsville.[49] Col. Edward Porter Alexander, acting commander of the artillery of the Confederate Second Corps, made a reconnaissance of the Hazel Grove position during the night of May 2/3. This was of essential importance in the Confederate seizure of that commanding eminence within 90 minutes after daybreak. Porter commented many years after the war, "There has rarely been a more gratuitous gift of a battle-field. Sickles had a good position and force enough to hold it, even without reenforcements, though ample reenforcements were available."[50]

The morning May 3 Confederate assault along the Plank Road began at sunrise as the lead brigades south of the road, consisting of Lane, McGowan and Archer in line from left to right, charged eastward. Ramseur's brigade formed a part of the third Confederate line and did not advance until about 9 a.m. after the battle had been in progress for about three hours.[51] The alignment of the Confederate brigades in the assault on the morning of May 3 was depicted schematically by E. Porter Alexander as follows:[52]

---

48. *OR*, vol. 25, pt. 1, p. 409; Bigelow, *Chancellorsville*, pp. 325-327; and Ernest B. Furguson, *Chancellorsville 1863: The Souls of the Brave* (New York: Alfred A. Knopf, 1902), pp. 208-211. Sickles' (or Ward's, as Union writers commonly refer to it) night assault around midnight on the night of May 2/3, 1863, is a dramatic example of a rare Civil War maneuver. The resulting chaos clearly shows why night attacks were scarcely attempted—the fact that it took place at all shows how desperate the Union commanders considered their position to be following Jackson's flank attack.

49. *OR*, vol. 25, pt. 1, p. 409.

50. Edward Porter Alexander, *Military Memoirs of a Confederate* (New York: Charles Scribner's Sons, 1907; reprint: New York: Da Capo Press, 1993), p. 345. Alexander reported his reconnaissance and the taking of Hazel Grove in *OR*, vol. 25, pt. 2, pp. 822-823.

51. *Ibid.*, p. 995. Rodes states that the Confederate attack of the night before was renewed "about 6 a.m.." *Ibid.*, p. 943. Samuel Ross of the 20th Connecticut reported that the attacks on his regiment began about 5:30 a.m.. *Ibid.*, p. 699.

52. Alexander, *Memoirs of a Confederate*, p. 343. The Confederate align-

Thomas	Pender	Heth	Plank Road	Lane	
					McGowan
					Archer
Nichols	Paxton			Warren	Jones
Iverson	Rodes			Ramseur, Doles, Colquitt	

Archer's brigade angled off to the right heading southeast toward Hazel Grove, just as Sickles began his evacuation. At 6 a.m., Archer caught Graham's brigade (except for the 105th Pennsylvania which was corduroying a road for the artillery across the low swampy ground between Hazel Grove and Fairview to the east[53]) of Birney's division, the tail end of Sickles' Union Third Corps, as the brigade was formed in close column by regiments preparing to withdraw. Archer hurried Graham's Federals on their way off Hazel Grove with the 141st Pennsylvania fighting a rearguard action, not its last of the day.[54] Graham's brigade retreated through the Union defensive line established during the night of May 2/3, after Jackson's flank attack had run out of steam, from a point to the right front of Hazel Grove (where the ground begins to rise, from between the confluence of two branches of Scott's Run, northeastward toward the Fairview cemetery) running more or less due north to the Plank Road.[55]

---

ment is also clearly explained in *OR*, vol. 25, pt. 1, p. 1011.

53. *Ibid.*, pp. 414 and 421.

54. *Ibid.*, p. 925 (Archer's report); p. 414 (Graham's report); p. 426-7 (Col. Henry J. Madill's report, 141st Pennsylvania).

55. The disposition of the Union forces south of the Plank Road is carefully delineated in Bigelow, *Chancellorsville*, Plan 3 on p. 344. The only regimental position accurately marked by veterans on the battlefield is that of the 27th Indiana on the north side of Berry-Paxton Drive. Donald C. Pfanz, "History through Eyes of Stone: The Story of the Monuments in Fredericksburg National Military Park" (November, 1983), (bound typescript in Visitors Center at Chancellorsville, Virginia), pp. 121-126. The marking of the position of the 27th Indiana is important because it made a valiant stand on the morning of May 3, holding its own position after the rest of Ross' brigade retreated and thereby anchored the Union line which ran north from its position to the Plank Road. The 27th's courageous fight is probably the reason why at least one of its veterans wanted to insure that the position it held on the battlefield was memorialized. An argument can and will be made that the position of the 7th New Jersey of the Mott/Sewell Brigade is not correct on Bigelow,

In all of the confusion following Jackson's surprise attack and the resulting nighttime reorientation of the Federal defensive positions from an east-west to a north-south axis, brigades were split up to fill gaps in the new line. Ruger's Third Brigade of Alpheus Williams' First Division of Slocum's Twelfth Corps (with the 27th Indiana, 2nd Massachusetts and 3rd Wisconsin aligned from left to right) was placed in the Union line between elements of Ross' Second Brigade of the same division. Ross' 145th New York and 20th Connecticut were positioned on Ruger's left flank, south of the 27th Indiana.[56] Between Ruger's line and the Plank Road lay Ross' other two regiments, the 123rd New York and the 3rd Maryland whose right flank touched the Plank Road. These regiments, as noted above, had been able to fortify their position during the night with a low breastworks of logs and an abatis of fallen trees.

The initial Confederate attack spearheaded by the brigades of Lane and McGowan succeeded in driving back the Union troops just south of the Plank Road. The 3rd Maryland gave way before the 123rd New York did, but shortly after the action began,[57] pressure on the right flank and a lack of ammunition compelled the New Yorkers to retreat as well, leaving among others the wounded Sergeant Bull near the stream bank.[58] Col. William J. Sewell's New Jersey brigade took the place of the retreating 3rd Maryland and 123rd New York.[59] Sewell later reported:

Chancellorsville, Plan 3—it being too far to the Union left. The case for the placement of the 7th New Jersey closer to its own brigade will be made infra (see footnote #83). A regiment of Zouaves fell back through the position of the 27th Indiana early in the morning of May 3, and this regiment was almost certainly the 114th Pennsylvania, known as the "Collis Zouaves." Edmund Randolph Brown, *The Twenty-Seventh Indiana Volunteer Infantry* (Monticello: E. R. Brown, 1899), p. 330.

56. *OR*, vol. 25, pt. 1, pp. 698-699.
57. Sewell states that the second line was attacked 15 minutes after the first. *Ibid.*, p. 473. However, the history of the 115th Pennsylvania (of Sewell's brigade), in Samuel P. Bates, *History of the Pennsylvania Volunteers, 1861-5*, 10 vol. (Harrisburg, Pennsylvania: Singerly, 1869-1871; reprint Wilmington, North Carolina: Broadfoot, 1993), 6:1210, states, "At daylight on the morning of the 3rd, the first line was attacked, and after maintaining its position for an hour, was driven back upon its supports."
58. *OR*, vol. 25, pt. 1, pp. 473, 698 and 705. Bauer, *Soldiering*, p. 58.
59. *OR*, vol. 25, pt. 1, p. 473.

It has been the fortune of this brigade to have participated in many hard-fought actions, but former experience was nothing in comparison to the determination of the enemy to carry this position.[60]

Sewell's New Jersey men advanced to defend the line being abandoned ahead with the 8th New Jersey's right flank on the Plank Road,[61] and the 115th Pennsylvania on the left flank of the 8th New Jersey.[62] The 5th New Jersey also took over part of the position vacated by the first line,[63] and the 2nd New York and 6th New Jersey also advanced into the action.[64] In a fierce struggle, the first Confederate line (the brigades of Lane and McGowan) was outflanked and driven back to the Slocum Log Works, and the second line (consisting of the brigades of Warren and Jones, from left to right, south of the Plank Road) was fought to a standstill, even after Paxton's (Stonewall) brigade was brought south of the Plank Road from left to right to assist in the attack and Paxton was killed.[65] The fierce fighting south of the Plank Road now began to reach a climax as Sickles ordered Graham's brigade back into action to relieve Ruger whose troops were running out of ammunition.[66] In its early morning retreat from Hazel Grove through the line formed by Ruger and Ross, Graham's brigade, or at least its rear element formed by the 141st Pennsylvania, passed through the narrow cleared space, not three or four rods in width, which joined the northern edge of the cleared land of

---

60. *Ibid.*
61. *Ibid.*, p. 480.
62. *Ibid.*, p. 482.
63. *Ibid.*, pp. 391 and 473.
64. *Ibid.*, pp. 476-7 and 481. The exact positions of the 2nd New York and 6th New Jersey are not given in these reports.
65. Determination of the exact sequence of the Confederate attacks on the morning of May 3 defies even the most careful analysis of the sources, but the general outlines of the action can be discovered by reading the following Confederate reports in *OR*, vol. 25, pt. 1, pp. 799-800 (Lee), p. 888 (Stuart), pp. 902-905 (Hamilton, commanding McGowan's brigade), p. 917 (Lane), pp. 943-945 (Rodes), pp. 952-953 (O'Neal), pp. 967-968 (Doles), pp. 995-997 (Ramseur), pp. 1005-1006 (Colston), pp. 1013-1014 (Funk), p. 1026 (Vandeventer commanding Jones' brigade), pp. 1032-1033 (Brown commanding Colston's brigade) and pp. 1037-1038 (Williams commanding Nicholls' brigade).
66. *OR*, vol. 25, pt. 1, p. 391.

Hazel Grove farm with the southern edge of the cleared land of Fairview farm. It was a gap in the woods lying along the deeply worn channel of the stream—a tributary of Scott's Run—that runs southward along the foot of the eminence at Fairview on which the Union artillery was formed in a bristling Malvern Hill-style mass formation of guns fortified with lunettes.[67]

Following its retreat, Graham's brigade reformed south of the Plank Road directly behind the Fairview graveyard. As soon as the Confederates appeared on the eastern crest of Hazel Grove, the brigade charged again into the battle, heading back parallel to (and just north of) the brigade's early morning retreat. In this advance, the alignment of Graham's regiments was, from left to right, 105th Pennsylvania, 114th Pennsylvania, 68th Pennsylvania, 57th Pennsylvania, 63rd Pennsylvania, and 141st Pennsylvania.[68] Graham's advance carried the Pennsylvania brigade westward back toward the Confederates, but to the right of Graham's former position, closer to the Plank Road. Graham's men moved down the hill from Fairview, across the low ground bordering the stream below and west of Fairview, and up to the edge of the woods. In these woods the

---

67. The Collis Zouaves (114th Pennsylvania) evidently fell back through the position of the 27th Indiana. Brown, *27th Indiana*, p. 330. The detailed topographical description recited here is found in David Craft, *History of One Hundred Forty-First Regiment, Pennsylvania Volunteers, 1862-1865* (Towanda, Pennsylvania: Reporter-Journal Print Co., 1885), p. 75-6. It seems most likely that the layout of the field and woodlines at the time of the battle in 1863 was very similar to that mapped on the 1925 survey done in preparation for the creation of the National Military Park—now on file at the Chancellorsville Battlefield headquarters. The configuration of the open land around Hazel Grove and Fairview was shaped more like two rectangles with adjoining corners than like a broad lane running between the two heights. Clear and very accurate maps, according to the above stated notions, can be found in Gallagher, *Ramseur*, p. 63; and in Augustus Choate Hamlin, *The Battle of Chancellorsville* (Bangor, Maine: Hamlin, 1896), Map 9. The Hotchkiss map, "Sketch of the Battles of Chancellorsville, Salem Church and Fredericksburg, May 2, 3, and 4, 1863," in the *OR Atlas* probably gives an inadequate portrayal of the woodlines between Hazel Grove and Fairview. The new "Chancellorsville Battlefield Map" (Orleans, New York: McElfresh Map Co., 1996) does a better job of depicting the shape of the Hazel Grove and Fairview clearings or fields, but most likely, based on Craft's description, shows the connecting opening between the two clearings to be too wide.

68. *OR*, vol. 25, pt. 1, p. 414. Craft, *141st Pennsylvania*, p. 77.

1st Lt. James W. Badgett
Co. G, 30th Regt. N.C.T.
Wounded at Chancellorsville, May 3, 1863

Confederates were drawn up in line of battle to receive the Pennsylvanians, and the contest raged fiercely for two hours.[69] As the Federals advanced into the open forest, they discovered the Confederate line in position on a crest in the woods. Colonel M'Knight of the 105th Pennsylvania was shot through the head and instantly killed. Lieutenant Colonel Watkins of the 141st Pennsylvania on Graham's opposite flank was knocked off his horse by the concussion of an exploding shell, from which he was able to recover after being momentarily stunned, and to press on with his regiment.[70] They opened fire at about 150 yards, driving the Southerners off the crest and up another ridge in their rear to a line of log breastworks—probably Slocum Log Works.[71] By the time Graham re-entered the woods, the second line of Confederates must have been in the fight because the 68th Pennsylvania captured the flag of the 10th Virginia of Col. E. T. H. Warren's brigade of Colston's division, the second brigade from the right in the Confederate second line.

On Graham's left, the 27th Indiana anchored the Union line.[72] Col. Silas Colgrove did not retire the 27th Indiana along with the other regiments of Ruger's brigade, which withdrew after running out of ammunition. Instead, they continued to hold the place in Graham's line that should have been held by the 114th Pennsylvania, the Collis Zouaves, as the second regiment from the left in Graham's brigade.[73] Throughout the morning, the left of the 27th Indiana was strengthened by the

---

69. *Ibid.; OR*, vol. 25, pt. 1, p. 420.
70. Bates, *History of the Pennsylvania Volunteers*, 6:784; Craft, *141st Pennsylvania*, p. 77.
71. *Ibid.; OR*, vol. 25, pt. 1, p. 414.
72. Rice Bull of the 123rd New York in Bauer, *Soldiering*, p. 55, mistakenly said that the 27th Indiana and the 2nd Massachusetts were located to the right of the line of his regiment. In fact, the 2nd Massachusetts and the 27th Indiana were in line to the right of the 123rd New York with the 3rd Wisconsin in between on the left flank of the 123rd New York. Brown, *27th Indiana*, pp. 328-329.
73. Craft, *141st Pennsylvania*, pp. 77-8; *OR*, vol. 25, pt. 1, pp. 414, 420, and 710-713. Ruger reports that his brigade withdrew due to lack of ammunition after being engaged "about two hours." *Ibid.*, p. 709. Col. Samuel Quincy of the 2nd Massachusetts, in position on the right flank of the 27th Indiana reported being relieved "by fresh troops" after running out of ammunition. Quincy saw in his front what was reported to him as being the flag of the 1st South Carolina of McGowan's brigade, the

257

brave fighting of 200 men of the 110th Pennsylvania of Bowman's brigade of Whipple's Third Division of the Third Corps left under Colgrove's command the night before.[74] In addition, during the action three companies of the 107th New York were moved into a gap which had developed between the right of the 27th Indiana and the left of the 2nd Massachusetts.[75]

The exact time at which Graham re-entered the fight is uncertain. Finley Curtis, Jr., of the 1st North Carolina of Warren's brigade witnessed a desperate charge against his unit by a regiment of Zouaves, most likely the 114th Pennsylvania.[76] As the fighting raged, General Graham ordered the Collis Zouaves to move to his brigade's right flank where the 141st Pennsylvania was under pressure on its right flank due to the withdrawal of the 3rd Maryland and 123rd New York. A flank movement under fire is an extremely difficult maneuver, but the Collis Zouaves did manage to get to Graham's right flank. The end result, however, was not a happy one. Graham reported, "They [the Collis Zouaves] did this [made the move to the

---

second regiment from the right in that brigade according to J. F. J. Caldwell, *The History of a Brigade of South Carolinians* (Philadelphia: King & Baird, 1866; reprint: Morningside Bookshop: Dayton, Ohio, 1984), p. 114.

74. *OR*, vol. 25, pt. 1, p. 713. To the left of the position of the 27th Indiana beyond the 145th New York and 20th Connecticut on the 27th Indiana's left flank, Doles' Georgia brigade was breaking through a line held by Greene's brigade of Geary's Twelfth Corps Division. *OR*, vol. 25, pt. 1, pp. 758-9 (Greene's report) and pp. 967-8 (Doles' report).

75. *Ibid.*, p. 718.

76. Finley Paul Curtis, Jr., "Chancellorsville," *Confederate Veteran*, vol. 25, no. 7 (July, 1917):303-5. Finley Paul Curtis, Jr., was not a member of the 2nd Virginia, the Stonewall Brigade, as stated in James I. Robertson, *The Stonewall Brigade* (Baton Rouge: Louisiana State University Press, 1963), p. 188. Rather, Curtis belonged to the 1st North Carolina as did his brother, Lt. L. J. Curtis, mentioned in Curtis' *Confederate Veteran* article. (Manarin and Jordan, *N.C. Troops*, 3:158). The charge seen by Private Curtis was most likely the charge of the 114th Pennsylvania reported by Col. Charles H. T. Collis in *OR*, vol. 25, pt. 1, p. 423. Disgusted with the flight of the Collis Zouaves a short time later, General Graham stated that Colonel Collis' report was "a complete romance from the beginning to the end," *Ibid.*, p. 425. But perhaps Graham was at least partially incorrect and there was some factual basis for parts of Collis' report? Graham himself notes the gallantry of Major Chandler and Captain Eliot of the 114th Pennsylvania in an attempt to take a stand of enemy colors, probably the same attempt mentioned by Collis. *Ibid.*, p. 415.

brigade's right flank]; formed and fired one volley, when they broke and fell back."[77] Alfred Bellard of the 5th New Jersey, located to the right, saw them go:

> Before long a regt. of Red Legged Zouaves who were on the left of the first line broke, and running past our Regt. their officers called upon us to fire into them. We did not obey the order. The Red Leggs started the rest, and soon after all the troops on our left had fallen back thus leaving us in a bad position.[78]

The rout of the Collis Zouaves caused the withdrawal of Graham's entire line.[79] In the course of this withdrawal occurred one of those astounding incidents which makes the Civil War so endlessly fascinating. Union Col. Henry Madill of the 141st Pennsylvania saw his regiment being driven back by the Confederates. He was carrying the national colors and, sticking the flag staff into the ground, he began to sing "The Battle Cry of Freedom:"—"Rally 'round the flag, boys! Rally once again." The regimental historian recorded that "most nobly did the boys

---

77. *Ibid.*, p. 414.
78. Donald, *Gone for a Soldier*, p. 214.
79. Oddly, the 114th Pennsylvania was the only Union regiment other than the 27th Indiana (which had an outstanding record on May 3, 1863) to erect a monument on the May 3, 1863, Chancellorsville battlefield south of the Plank Road. Col. Charles H. T. Collis led the regimental delegation and gave the dedication speech on May 3, 1899—36 years to the day after the battle. The 114th Pennsylvania monument sits just south of Route 3, a short distance east of the Chancellorsville Visitor Center. Contrary to the inscription on its face, Colonel Collis admitted in his speech that the monument was not located where the 114th fought, an area farther south of the Plank Road and not adjacent to it. Pfanz, "Monuments in Fredericksburg National Military Park," pp. 115-120. The irony is that the regiment that performed the best on May 3, 1863, and the one that performed the worst, were the only ones to erect monuments on that part of the battlefield. With that said, it must be stressed that in spite of running at the end, the 114th did do some hard fighting that day, and returned to do it after the initial early morning retreat from Hazel Grove. Many units, both Union and Confederate, had mixed records that day. Following the fierce action in which his regiment captured five colors, Col. Louis R. Francine of the 7th New Jersey retired from the field after losing his voice, "having fought his regiment gallantly up to that time, but inopportunely now taking with him some 400 of the brigade," according to the New Jersey brigade commander, Col. William J. Sewell. *OR*, vol. 25, pt. 1, p. 474.

respond; for many of them joined in singing the stanza, and without a word of command they formed their line, and faced the enemy as firmly as ever." After about 15 minutes, the 141st withdrew across the low ground and past where the batteries had been on Fairview.[80]

At the time of the flight of the Collis Zouaves, the Mott/ Sewell New Jersey Brigade became heavily engaged with Ramseur's brigade.[81] When the Confederates began their May 3 morning assault, Ramseur's brigade was aligned perpendicular to the Orange Plank Road with its left on the Plank Road and with the 4th, 2nd, 14th and 30th Regiments aligned from left to right. As noted above, Ramseur formed part of the third Confederate line of assault troops and advanced to the support of the second Confederate line about 9 o'clock, three hours after the Confederate attack began.[82]

The Mott/Sewell Brigade's 7th New Jersey had been having a glorious morning up until this time. Detached from its brigade about 5 a.m., the 7th was assigned to a gap in the Union line forward and to the left of its brigade's reserve position. Finding the morning's Confederate attacks diverging to the regiment's right and left, the 7th advanced beyond the Union line, wheeled right, and took position on a "knoll" in the woods a short distance from the Plank Road. From this vantage point they opened fire on the flank of successive Confederate brigades seen surging down the road, including the Stonewall Brigade and Ramseur's brigade.[83] In the course of the fighting, the 7th

---

80. Craft, *141st Pennsylvania*, p. 79.
81. Capt. Samuel Hopkins of the 7th New Jersey, like Alfred Bellard of the 5th New Jersey (see footnote #78), described the flight of the Collis Zouaves past his position and identified them as such. Samuel Hopkins, Diary and Journal ("The Battle"), manuscript, Alexander Library Special Collections and Manuscripts Department, Rutgers University, New Brunswick, New Jersey, pp. 54-55. I am grateful to Paul Lader, Esq., of Marlton, New Jersey, historian of the Mott/Sewell New Jersey Brigade, for telling me about the Hopkins manuscript.
82. *OR*, vol. 25, pt. 2, p. 995. Rodes states that the Confederate attack of the night before was renewed "about 6 a.m." *Ibid.*, p. 943. Samuel Ross of the 20th Connecticut reported that the attacks on his regiment began about 5:30 a.m. *Ibid.*, p. 699.
83. The exact position of the 7th New Jersey is difficult to determine. According to Colonel Francine, his regiment was detached from Mott's brigade about 5 a.m. and "under orders from Major Tremain of General Sickles' staff, filled up a gap occurring between Birney's right and our

260

immediate front." *OR*, vol. 25, pt. 1, p. 478. Capt. William R. Hillyer of the 7th New Jersey recalled: "At 4 A.M. we were aroused and moved a few rods to the front, where our division had been placed across the plank road in the edge of the woods. Our regiment was detached and placed in a gap in the first line where no breastworks had been constructed, and there was no material at hand for any defensive barrier. The gap was in the line of the 1st Division, and about half way from the plank road to the eastern edge of the timber. The woods were open in front of us, no undergrowth obstructed our view through the forest of large pines. The ground sloped gently up for say 200 yards, and there the skyline was visible between the trees. We had been here but a short time when just at broad daylight, about 5 A. M., the rebel yells on our right and left told that the struggle had begun." William R. Hillyer, D.C. MOLLUS Paper No. 55 (1904), p. 138. Hillyer also states that the 7th New Jersey held a part of the Union line between the segment assaulted by the Confederate troops charging down the Plank Road to the 7th's right and those fighting on Hazel Grove farm to the 7th's left. As a result, "for perhaps a couple of hours, no enemy appeared in the front of the regiment, so that what little firing was done by the 7th N. J., was at a right oblique when the charges were made, but it was not effective as we were too far away. By the topography of the field it came to pass as these [Confederate] brigades started upon that charge, as each of them did from the line of breastworks on the other side of the wood, yelling as they ran, those regiments having Hazel Grove as their objective, bore to the right and became separated from those moving down the plank road. Thus a wide gap of several hundred yards was opened and no troops appeared in front of our position as stated above." *Ibid.*, p. 148. Bigelow, *Chancellorsville*, Plan 3 on p. 344, places the 7th New Jersey on the right of the 27th Indiana, but this seems too far to the left, taking Hillyer's description of the position at face value. The most likely place in line for the 7th New Jersey is between the right flank of Ruger's brigade (held by the 3rd Wisconsin) and the left flank of the 123rd New York of Ross' brigade. Sickles' report that the 7th New Jersey "on the left" vied with the 5th New Jersey "in repelling the rebel masses" (*OR*, vol. 25, pt. 1, p. 391), and the account by Alfred Bellard of the 5th New Jersey that the 7th New Jersey was on the left of the 5th (Donald, *Gone for a Soldier*, p. 214), indicate that the 7th was immediately on the left of the position taken by the New Jersey brigade when the front line (i.e., the 123rd New York and the 3rd Maryland) retreated. Capt. Samuel Hopkins of the 7th New Jersey provides clear evidence that the 7th New Jersey was on Graham's right flank in Hopkins Diary & Journal, Rutgers University, pp. 53-58. According to Captain Hillyer, Francine advanced into the woods in his front, swung to the right parallel to the Plank Road and proceeded to spring an ambush on the right flank of each Confederate brigade charging down the Plank Road, including the Stonewall Brigade and Ramseur's brigade. Hillyer, D.C. MOLLUS Paper No. 55, p. 149-153 and map on p. 139. Col. A. L. McDougall of the 123rd New York complained that troops of the "Third Brigade" on his left advanced out of the line and moved in front of the 123rd in pursuit of the retreating enemy, interfering with the 123rd's line of fire. *OR*, vol. 25, pt. 1, p. 705. This may have been the 7th New Jersey (of the Third Brigade,

New Jersey managed to capture one flag each from five different Confederate brigades, the colors of: the 21st Virginia of Jones' brigade, the 18th North Carolina of Lane's brigade, the 1st Louisiana of Nichols' brigade, the 2nd North Carolina of Ramseur's brigade, and "some Alabama regiment."[84] The flag and a large number of the men of the 2nd North Carolina were captured after 9 a.m. in a fierce melee in which the 7th New Jersey fell upon the Carolina regiment's right flank which was unsupported because Ramseur's 14th North Carolina and three companies of the 2nd had been compelled to halt some 150 or 200 yards in the rear of the 2nd for fear of being outflanked themselves.[85] Alfred Bellard saw a "fight for the colors" between a member of the 7th New Jersey and a Confederate color bearer, probably that of the 2nd.[86] It was probably shortly after this encounter that Parker and the 30th arrived on the scene to save the day.

Parker and the 30th had been on detached duty while the main body of Ramseur's brigade fought along the Plank Road. Ramseur's North Carolinians had advanced about one-fourth mile from their 9 a.m. starting point when Maj. W. J. Pegram, commanding Walker's artillery battalion, applied to Ramseur for support for his battery, which had been newly installed to the right front on the commanding eminence of Hazel Grove (abandoned by the Union army in the early hours of May 3). Ramseur detached the 30th Regt. for this purpose and ordered Colonel Parker to advance obliquely to Pegram's position and to rejoin the brigade after his support was no long needed or to engage his regiment as circumstances might require.[87]

Second Division, Third Corps) and McDougall's reference to the "Third Brigade" is most likely to Ruger's brigade, the Third Brigade, First Division, Twelfth Corps. The 123rd New York was a part of Ross' Second Brigade, in the same division with Ruger's brigade.

84. *Ibid.*, p. 478. The roll call of the regiments whose flags were captured by the 7th New Jersey is a clear indicator of the jumbled alignment of the Confederate brigades.

85. *Ibid.*, pp. 478 and 996.

86. Donald, *Gone for A Soldier*, p. 214-215.

87. *OR*, vol. 25, pt. 2, p. 996. Ramseur is clearly mistaken when he states in this report that he ordered Parker "to advance obliquely to his front and left" because Pegram's position at Hazel Grove was to Ramseur's front and right, not left. Later in his report, Ramseur does refer to Pegram's Battery as being to his right.

Colonel Parker and the 30th proceeded to Hazel Grove as ordered, but he was too much the fighter to stay in a defensive position long. One of the fiercest battles of the Civil War was raging in the forest to the east and northeast of Hazel Grove as wave after wave of Confederates swept down the axis of the Orange Plank Road and crashed against the Federals defensive positions. Parker was not about to sit this fight out, but rather decided to join the Confederate attack then reaching its climax along the Plank Road and in the woods on either side of it. Finding Pegram's artillery in no danger and waiting until Pegram thought the danger had passed,[88] Parker took advantage of the discretion he had been given and advanced to rejoin Ramseur, directed by what he took to be his firing. Parker and the 30th probably headed northeast from Hazel Grove.[89] The 30th was now presented with an opportunity to add luster to its reputation by administering the coup de grace to the Yankees while also saving the balance of Ramseur's brigade from disaster.

Parker and the 30th moved forward into an extremely disordered and confused situation in which the dead and wounded were strewn through the forest, and bits and pieces of regiments and brigades were scattered about like so much flotsam and jetsam. By the time of 30th's advance from Hazel Grove, sometime after 9 a.m., the Federals still had plenty of fight left in them, but the Union line had been severely weakened by the sledgehamer blows of three long hours of Southern assaults.

As Parker moved north toward the sound of Ramseur's firing, the 30th came upon a considerable body of Confederate troops lying in a confused mass in an irregular way observing

---

88. Maj. W. J. Pegram did not mention Parker nor the assignment of the 30th Regiment for his batteries' protection, but Pegram did complain that the lack of skirmishers in his area allowed the enemy to carry off their guns from his immediate front. *OR*, vol. 25, pt. 2, p. 938. Parker mentions that he only advanced when Pegram thought the danger had passed. Clark, *N.C. Regiments*, 2:501.

89. The account given here of the actions of the 30th Regiment on the morning of May 3 after leaving Hazel Grove is based on three first-person accounts written by Colonel Parker—appearing in: *Ibid.*; James I. Metts, "The Thirteenth (sic) North Carolina at Chancellorsville," *The Sunny South*, August 17, 1901, publishing a letter from Parker dated January 15, 1898; Parker letter, May 29, 1891, Ramseur Papers, North Carolina Division of Archives and History, Raleigh.

no alignment. Upon inquiry, Parker was told that these were men of Brig. Gen. John R. Jones' Virginia brigade of Brig. Gen. Raleigh E. Colston's division. Being told that General Jones was not on the field, Parker then asked why they did not go forward—telling them that every man was needed at the front. The recumbent Virginians replied that they had no orders to advance. Parker invited them to join him in charging a line of breastworks which he had discovered on his right, but not a man joined him.

The soldiers of the 30th Regiment moved over the Virginians. It is not reported whether Parker's men let fly any taunts, but surely they must have felt just as their fellow brigade members of the 2nd Regiment did—one of whose number reported of their similar advance over the backs of reclining Virginians, "The brave chivalric Virginians lay flat on the ground, and the 'tar-heels' whom they so often ridicule walked over them to glory and to victory!"[90]

---

90. Calder to Mother, May 10, 1863, Calder Family Papers. As previously noted, Calder was separated from Ramseur's brigade on May 3 and did not take part in this sanguinary assault. This is one of the earliest written uses of the term "tar-heel" by which North Carolinians are now known. Ramseur's official report of the battle of Chancellorsville stated that in the advance on the morning of May 3, following Parker's detachment, the main body of his brigade, like Parker, encountered Virginia troops of Jones' brigade and also of Paxton's Stonewall Brigade lying upon the ground behind captured breastworks. When these troops refused to advance, Ramseur obtained J.E.B. Stuart's permission to run over them. *OR*, vol. 25, pt. 2, p. 996. "Forward boys, walk right over them," Ramseur said. When the command was given, Col. Bryan Grimes of the 4th Regiment, by his own account, put "his foot on the back and head of an officer of high rank, in mounting the work, and, through very spite, ground his face into the ground." Cowper, *Letters of Major-General Bryan Grimes*, p. 32. The official reports of Jones' brigade, made by Col. A. S. Vandeventer and of its component regiments, the 21st, 44th, 48th, and 50th Virginia Infantry Regts., indicated that Jones' brigade took refuge behind the captured log barricade after an initial attack and later joined in the final successful assault that resulted in the capture of the Union artillery position at Fairview. These reports do not mention the refusal to advance with Parker or with Ramseur. *OR*, vol. 25, pt. 1, pp. 1025-1031. Even before Ramseur's official report was written on May 23, 1863, reports circulated that Ramseur had remarked that the Stonewall Brigade had disgraced itself on May 3 through its failure to advance with him. Col. J. H. S. Funk, commander of the Stonewall Brigade wrote to Ramseur protesting that he was mistaken. Letter dated May 9, 1863, from Funk to Ramseur, *Supp. OR*, pt. 2, vol. 4, pp. 693-4.

2nd Lt. Archibald A. Jackson
Co. H, 30th Regt. N.C.T.
Killed at Spotsylvania Court House, May 12, 1864

Advancing a short distance, the 30th attacked the log breast-works and drove the enemy from them. At the works, Pvt. Archibald A. Jackson of Company H, the Moore County Rifles, found evidence of the bloody repulses the Virginians had suffered before the 30th's successful assault:

> I noticed one Brest work we charged wher we had to move the ded back to have room up at the workes, but our loss was much smaller than the Yankes so you may draw some Idia of the harrows of this awful war.[91]

After resting long enough to get his men in good trim, Parker fell upon a heavy Union column that was attempting to take Ramseur in the right flank and rear. The 30th took some 300 to 400 of the enemy prisoner.[92] It is not known which troops these were, but most likely elements of all the Union forces in the area, including those of Graham's, Ruger's, Ross' and Sewell's

---

Ramseur replied to Funk with a good-natured letter dated May 22, 1863, in which he expressed to Funk his great satisfaction with Funk's "statement of facts" in his letter and offered to correct the impression that his men ran over the Stonewall Brigade by having Funk's letter published to his troops at Dress Parade. *Supp. OR*, pt. 2, vol. 4, pp. 689-691. Ramseur, however, persisted in making the assertion that his brigade ran over a "small portion" of Jones' and Paxton's brigades in his official report dated the very next day. Allegedly, Ramseur offered to correct this statement in his report when it was brought to his attention by Col. William Terry of the 4th Virginia of the Stonewall Brigade in May, 1864, but he was killed at Cedar Creek before he could do so. William Terry, "The 'Stonewall Brigade' at Chancellorsville," in *Southern Historical Society Papers* (reprint: Wilmington, North Carolina: Broadfoot, 1990), 14:364-370.

91. A. A. Jackson to Dear Sister, May 15, 1863, from Camp near Fredericksburg, Va., quoted with permission of owner, Chapel Hill Rare Books, Doug Odell, proprietor. Archibald A. Jackson was a 26-year-old Moore County resident when he enlisted on August 15, 1861, in the Moore County Rifles, which became Company H, 30th Regt. N.C.T. Mustering in as a corporal, A. A. Jackson was promoted to sergeant in February, 1862, and elected 2nd lieutenant on the reorganization of the regiment on May 1, 1862. Wounded at Gettysburg, Pennsylvania, on July 1, 1863, he returned to duty that same day. 2nd Lt. A. A. Jackson was killed on May 12, 1864, the same day as his younger brother, Pvt. Burgess C. Jackson, also of Company H. Manarin and Jordan, *N.C. Troops*, 8:391 and 395.

92. *OR*, vol. 25, pt. 1, p. 996.

Pvt. Burgess C. Jackson
Co. H, 30th Regt. N.C.T.
Killed at Spotsylvania Court House, May 12, 1864

brigades.[93] Parker then moved in the direction of Chancellorsville. Being so far in advance of any other Confederate troops, J.E.B. Stuart took the 30th for Yankees and opened fire upon them with two artillery pieces. Parker and his men were saved by the action of one Captain Randolph, of Stuart's staff, who ran his horse down the Plank Road near enough to Parker and the 30th to satisfy himself that they were Confederates and reported such to his chief.[94]

For his actions on May 3, 1863, Parker was thanked by Ramseur and commended in Ramseur's official report of the battle:

> Colonel Parker, of the Thirtieth [North Carolina], who was detached during the fight of Sunday to support a battery, and having accomplished that object moved forward on his own responsibility, and greatly contributed to wrest the enemy's stronghold at Chancellorsville from their grasp, as well as prevent their threatened demonstrations upon the right of my brigade. . .[95]

---

93. The timing would indicate that the prisoners should have come from the Mott/Sewell New Jersey Brigade, but the casualty returns show only 48 prisoners. Ruger lost 68 prisoners, Ross lost 201, and Graham lost 194. *Ibid.*, pp. 178, 179, and 184.

94. General Rodes, Parker's divisional commander, reported that the final advance on Fairview was made by the 30th Regt. N.C.T. in conjunction with the Stonewall Brigade. Colonel Parker vehemently denied that the Stonewall Brigade was anywhere to be seen nor joined the 30th in the advance: he stated, "If the Stonewall Brigade joined me any time that day, I never knew it." Metts, "The Thirteenth (sic) North Carolina at Chancellorsville," *The Sunny South*, August 17, 1901. He had earlier stated, "I insist that the Stonewall brigade was nowhere near us." Parker letter, May 29, 1891, Ramseur Papers, North Carolina Department of Archives and History, Raleigh, North Carolina.

95. *OR*, vol. 25, pt. 1, p. 997. I long ago concluded that Ramseur's thanking Colonel Parker for his actions on May 3 in attacking the Union troops moving on Ramseur's right flank and rear was one of Parker's proudest moments of the war. Parker, always the soul of modesty, mentioned Ramseur's thanks in a manuscript letter that I was privileged to read in the summer of 1976. The letter fell from a book I was reading in the apartment of Judge Frank M. Parker, the colonel's grandson, in Raleigh. When I showed the letter to Judge Parker, he told me he thought that it should go to the North Carolina Collection at the University at Chapel Hill and would take immediate steps to see that it went there. Unhappily, 21 years later, in researching this book, I have been unable to find the letter in the North Carolina Collection or the Southern Historical

Whether the Union troops which broke under Parker's surprise attack from Hazel Grove were the 114th Pennsylvania, the 141st Pennsylvania, or the 7th New Jersey, it is clear that the 30th arrived on the scene at a critical moment in the battle and at a weak point in the Federal line where Graham's Pennsylvania brigade and the Mott/Sewell New Jersey Brigade adjoined.[96] General Ramseur acknowledged his debt to Colonel Parker. It would not be the last time that Ramseur's brigade and the 30th Regiment North Carolina Troops saved the day in a major battle of the Civil War.

The fight had been a bloody one indeed. The losses of the 30th Regiment were heavy: 22 killed, 15 mortally wounded, 75 wounded and 3 captured of whom 2 were wounded.[97] As a very rough estimate, perhaps two thirds of the roughly 30,000 total casualties of both armies at Chancellorsville were suffered in only four hours, between 6 and 10 a.m., on the morning of May 3, 1863, in the forest along the Orange Plank Road just west of the Chancellor House and Fairview. It is sobering to pause and realize that the May 3, 1863, morning casualties at Chancellorsville were of the same order of magnitude and intensity as those suffered by Great War combatants on the Somme on July 1, 1916—and the Confederate and Union forces had no machine guns! Captain Ardrey recorded, "The fields were literally covered with the dead and dying."[98]

Collection at Chapel Hill or the North Carolina Division of Archives and History at Raleigh. The rendering of thanks to Parker by Ramseur is also mentioned in Parker's biographical sketch, undoubtedly composed from information obtained from the colonel himself. Hill, *Confederate Military History*, 5:683-685: The division under the command of General Ramseur of R. E. Rodes had a conspicuous part in the flank attack where Jackson received his mortal injury, and on the following morning the Thirtieth supported Pegram's battery and then moved through the thick woods and assailed the enemy behind breastworks, making a hand-to-hand fight in which the bayonet was used freely, and capturing many prisoners. Subsequently it encountered a flanking column which it drove from the field, protecting Ramseur's brigade from disaster, for which General Ramseur personally thanked the gallant colonel.

96. David Gregg McIntosh, "The Campaign of Chancellorsville" in *Southern Historical Society Papers* (reprint: Wilmington, North Carolina: Broadfoot, 1990), 40:88 stated that the 30th struck Graham's brigade in the flank.

97. See the casualty roster appended to this book.

98. Ardrey Diary.

From May 3 to May 6, the 30th Regiment lay in its entrenchments, and on May 7, upon Hooker's withdrawal across the Rappahannock, the regiment returned to the camp at Hamilton's Crossing from which it had set out slightly more than a week before. Here the 30th was to remain until June 4, mourning its dead and writing letters home.[99] The day after the 30th arrived back in camp, Mecklenburg County's Sgt. Aaron Leonidas DeArmond,[100] a regimental elder at age 36 (senior even to Colonel Parker by seven months) wrote his wife this graphic description of the Sunday, May 3, 1863, battle:

> . . .as the son rose uppon our heads a sabbath morning, we were sheld by the yankys and at that time the command was going to forced forward [questionable reading]. [That] was the cry by our Generalls and we made a desperat charg upon the yankys and capt Ther bristworks after a despert hard fout battle; and at that time Milton Rea[101] and Wilee Hartis[102] was shaut

99. *Ibid.*
100. Aaron Leonidas DeArmond (born Feb. 15, 1827) enlisted in the "Mecklenburg Beauregards," which became Company K of the 30th Regt. N.C.T., on September 13, 1861, mustering in as sergeant. After being reduced to ranks at some point during the period May-September, 1862, DeArmond was captured at Sharpsburg, Maryland, on September 17, 1862. Paroled on September 21, 1862, he was wounded in the arm at Fredericksburg, Virginia, on December 13, 1862. Being promoted sergeant prior to July 1, 1863, DeArmond was captured at Kelly's Ford, Virginia, on November 7, 1863. After confinement at Point Lookout, Maryland, he was transferred to City Point, Virginia, where he was received for exchange on March 20, 1864, and, after a furlough at home, rejoined his company near Richmond on June 10, 1864, just prior to the 30th's joining Early's Army of the Valley in the Shenandoah Valley. DeArmond was mortally wounded at Snicker's Gap, Virginia, on July 18, 1864, and died August 19, 1864. Family oral tradition tells that the family received word that Sergeant DeArmond was on the way home by train, but "[w]hen they met the returning train they found he had died in transit." Manarin and Jordan, *N.C. Troops*, 8:415; "To Hold Sweet Communion: Letters and Diaries from a Confederate Sergeant Aaron Leonidas DeArmond," copyright ©1982 by Martha R. Brown, quoted with permission of Martha R. Brown, Winston-Salem, North Carolina, great-granddaughter of Sgt. Aaron Leonidas DeArmond.
101. James Milton Rea was a 24-year-old resident of Mecklenburg County when he enlisted in the "Mecklenburg Beauregards" as private on September 13, 1861. He was killed at Chancellorsville, Virginia, on May 3, 1863. Manarin and Jordan, *N.C. Troops*, 8:419.
102. Wilson L. Hartis was 27-years-old when he enlisted as private in

Rea was shot in the left eye and Hartis was shot betwean the eyes after we chast them out of that bristwork I thought we had routed them completely but we had hardly commenced drivan them and persued themtill they gut our Generalls whear they wanted us then they open the battrys uppon us and then we ware ordered to make a charg uppon their battery and it was an affel time the yankees oppen on us with canester and grape shot and I tell you it did slay our men rappedly but thanks be to God, I was shealded by his allmity power and by his assistance our battry caused their yankys battry to seas firing, and we captured ther battry and they hist a flag of truse and there was about 2 thousand of the yankys surrendered at the time we ware chargin that battry Robert Barns[103] was shot by a grape shot in his bowls he lived one day and knight Jake Wetherspon[104] rec'd a wound in his thigh with a grape shot and he is still living but is not expecten to live - his thg was broak Oh my dear I tell you it was a affel time s I evr saw in my life the woods cot on fire and it burnt the leaves of the ground and it burnt up a many a man Oh it was a affell site I evr saw my dear I never will forget the day that holy sabat day it was the hardis days work that I evr done in my life. I tell you we completely routed them.[105]

Mecklenburg County in the Hornet's Nest Rifles, Company B, 1st Regt. N.C. Infantry on April 18, 1861. Mustering out November 12-13, 1861, Hartis enlisted as private in Company K, 30th Regt. N.C.T. at Camp Wyatt, North Carolina, on January 18, 1862. He was promoted to corporal in 1863 and was killed at the battle of Chancellorsville, Virginia, on May 3, 1863. *Ibid.*, 3:10 and 8:417.

103. Robert C. Barnett enlisted in Mecklenburg County in the Hornet's Nest Rifles, Company B, 1st Regt. N.C. Infantry, as private on June 24, 1861, and mustered out November 12-13, 1861. He enlisted at age 22 as private in Company K, 30th Regiment N.C.T. at Camp Wyatt, North Carolina, on February 10, 1862. Barnett was killed at Chancellorsville, Virginia, on May 3, 1863. *Ibid.*, 1:9 and 8:414.

104. M. J. Witherspoon was an 18-year-old Cabarrus County resident when he enlisted in Company K, 30th Regt. N.C.T. at Camp Drane, North Carolina, on May 26, 1862, for the war. He was wounded at Chancellorsville, Virginia, on May 3, 1863, and died May 7, 1863. *Ibid.*, 8:422.

105. Aaron Leonidas DeArmond to Dear wife from Hamilton's Crossing, Fredericksburg, Va., May 7, 1863, in DeArmond Diary.

Colonel Parker wrote his wife a detailed account of the battle on May 8, but that letter did not find its way into the collection of letters in the North Carolina Division of Archives and Records in Raleigh. On May 9 Parker felt led to write his wife again.

———————◆·◆·◆———————

Hd Qrs. Ramseur's Brigade
May 9th 1863

Mrs. S. T. Parker
Sycamore Alley
Halifax Co.
N.C.

My dear Wife

I wrote you on yesterday,[106] but really I feel like writing to you again; I suppose you will not object to reading the letter, if you do, just hand it over to Mary and let her read it. If I may judge you by myself, I think you will be glad to get a letter every day. I gave you rather a detailed account on yesterday of the part which my Regt. bore in the recent fights. There are many little incidents which I do not now recollect, but which would be both interesting and instructive. I have never seen so great [a] slaughter, as I saw on the field of sunday [sic]. At the breastworks the enemy would be lying on one side, and our men on the other; some dead, some dying, others badly wounded. I noticed the colour [sic] bearer of one of our Regts. lying cold, the top of his flag staff shot away, but the gallant fellow was grasping the part which was left, with both hands.[107] I called my own

---

106. The letter of May 8, 1863, to which Parker refers here, as well as one of May 7 referred to in Parker's letter of May 10, are lost.
107. The 7th New Jersey of the Mott-Sewell Third Brigade, Second Division, Third Corps, captured the flag and a large portion of the 2nd Regt. N.C.T. of Ramseur's brigade, along with the four other regimental colors. *OR*, vol. 25, pt. 2, p. 472. Alfred Bellard of the 5th New Jersey witnessed and depicted a hand-to-hand fight for the colors between a Confederate color bearer and a soldier of the 7th New Jersey, perhaps resulting in the gruesome aftermath viewed by Parker. Donald, *Gone for a Soldier*, p. 215, with illus. on p. 217. The actions of the 7th New Jersey on the morning of May 3 were recounted by Hillyer, D.C. MOLLUS Paper No. 55.

colour [*sic*] bearer to witness the scene. Poor fellow, it was not long before he too was shot down, and has since had a leg amputated. A second man took the flag, he too was struck down; but not killed; the third one bore it safely through the remainder of the day, but ran a narrow risk, he had a ball put through the top of his hat.

I have never seen men fight better, nor behave more nobly. I shall not be afraid, for the future, to lead my men anywhere. For the reason which I gave you in my letter of yesterday, my Regt. did not suffer as much as the others of the Brigade; but it suffered enough surely. Our loss is 25 killed, 99 wounded, and only one missing; there were a large number of slightly wounded, who are now on duty again, these we take no account of.

How thankful I feel that I was not struck. Fred and I are both safe. Every day I live, gives me additional cause for thankfulness for the great mercies which I receive at the hands of the Lord. That I may so live, as to show my thankfulness, is my earnest prayer. The matter which I mentioned to you, in my letter of yesterday gives me trouble. I pray that I may be forgiven, and that I may have strength for the future, to resist all temptation. This is a life of trial, and happy is he, who goes through with it safely.

Soon after reaching camp, from home, I sent back to you, to the care of Dr. Joyner, my new uniform, and your pair of blankets; have you ever received them? if not, please send down at once, and enquire [*sic*] of Dr. Joyner something about it. I put the uniform and blankets in a box; and sent them by Mr. Barnes of Nash Co. If Dr. Joyner has not sent my horse cover from Enfield, please ask him not to do so; I do not need it now; and [Brig.] Genrl. [Robert E.] Rodes says I must get a light coloured hat; he thinks that a black hat will keep my head too warm. He says that he felt very uneasy about me in the sundays [*sic*] fight. He seems to be much concerned about me. Genrl. Rodes is in command of our Division; there is a probability that he will be promoted to Maj. Genrl. Our own Brigadier is a very gallant officer. He broke himself completely down in the fights.

If you have many strawberries, I wish you would send Dr. Joyner a nice mess or two, with a plenty of ice; and whenever you have an opportunity, I want you to send the Dr. some ice; it will keep him cool during the warm weather. You ca'nt [*sic*] show him too many little favours [*sic*]; he has been exceedingly kind to me. I want you to teach my children to regard him in such a light, as one of my best friends.

Fred and I would like very much to get hold of some of your good butter, but I fear we will not have the opportunity of doing so.

If there is any chance to do so, please send me a couple of pillow cases, for a medium sized pillow. I would prefer the cases to be made of some dark material. I need these very much.

Do'nt [sic] to let me know about my uniform at once, I feel uneasy about it.

Tell Mary I have answered her letter, and now she must write me another.

Say to Jimmy that he must get up early every morning, salt his sheep at least twice a week, and sometimes go with Moses to feed his hogs. And what can little Offa do? he must help to feed the chickens. Kiss them all for me, and Hattie too.

God bless you and them, Sally. Write often.

your affectionate husband
F. M. Parker

Hd. Qrs. Ramseur's Brigade
May 10th 1863

My dear Wife

I have written for the last four days, every day. But a young man has just come in to get a pass to N.C. and thinking this a good opportunity of sending a letter, I have concluded to write again. I have just written a little to each of the children, thinking it would please them. I wrote you yesterday to send me by the first opportunity a couple of pillow cases, of medium size, and of dark material. I also wish to know if you have ever received my new uniform and your blankets, which I sent back soon after reaching camp. I sent the box containing them, to the care of Dr. Joyner, by a Mr. Barnes of Nash Co. I feel a little uneasiness about it.

Well, matters have quieted down to their old status. We have gotten off nearly all our wounded, I am glad to say. Our Brigade is thinned very much; we lost heavily.

The loss in my own Regt. is about 125; this does not include the slightly wounded, we have a number of these.

How does your farming operations come on? try and make as much corn as possible, and meat too. Insist upon Hilliard's planting the low grounds, until the first of July; I allude to that part of it, which he will clean up; and let him clean up as much as possible.

I reckon you have a very nice garden; plenty of strawberries and cream, with ice. I want you to send Dr. Joyner a nice mess; and send him a supply of ice, whenever you have an opportunity. The Dr. is a great friend of mine.

Let me know if the Richmond Enquirer goes regularly to you now, and the other paper also.

Mr. Betts did not return to the Regt. by the way of Weldon, so I have not received my hat yet. If I can do so, I will get another, of a lighter colour [sic]. I shall not need my horse cover at all; [I] am sorry I wrote for it. Has Halifax county taken any steps towards furnishing supplies to the Government? I am certain that by reducing your negroes to ½ lb per day for the men, and less for the women, that you can spare some bacon. If matters get quiet, I think I shall send Wyatt to you for another supply of bacon &c. Fred sends his love. Remember me to all friends. Good bye; write soon, and often.

yours lovingly,
F. M. Parker

Hd Qrs. Ramseur's Brigade
May 16th 1863

My dear Wife

You will think three things, viz. that paper and ink are plentiful, that I have plenty of time, and that I am fond of writing to you. But if it affords you as much pleasure to hear from me, as it does me to hear from you, then you will not complain of my frequent writing. I am a little interested in my present writing. Maj. [William W.] Sillers will start his servant tomorrow for N.C. He will return, passing Enfield on monday [sic] or tuesday [sic] next, probably on monday [sic] evening.

My purpose in writing to you, is to ask you to send me some butter, some tea and a little coffee, and about a bushel of sweet potatoes. Send a good deal of butter, if you have it on hand; you can also spare a good deal of tea, also a little coffee. If you have any thing nice about the house, you can throw it in to fill up. I shall not want any meat now, I may send for some soon. You can send these things to Enfield on monday [*sic*] morning to the care of Dempsy Bryan, I will ask him to attend to them for me. If you have no sweet potatoes, I reckon you can get some from Mr. Nat Harrison. I do not need any summer clothes now. I wish you would have my thin cassimere [*sic*] coat washed and mended, if it needs it, and get me 6 stars to go on the collar; as the collar of a falling one, the stars will have to be placed on the lappell [*sic*], or falling part of the collar.

Dr. Joyner sometimes goes to Wilmington or Richmond; if you will ask him, he will get the stars for you. I do not want you to send this coat just now. I may have an opportunity of getting it soon; in fact I do not need it now.

I shall have to send for my horse soon and can get any thing I may need then.

Tell Jimmy he must have my horse in good condition, by the time I need him. To day, we had some company, Lt. Col. Hyman, Maj. Engelhard and Capt. Scales,[108] all from Genrl. Pender's Brigade. Col. Hyman wished to say to Miss Minnie that Fred was the prime mover in all those tales about the snaps, &c., but that he will be very thankful for snaps or almost anything else to eat.

These gentlemen seemed to be in fine spirits. Maj. Engelhard told me that his wife was not well when he heard from her last. I do'nt [*sic*] know of any thing that I will prize more, that you can send me, than a letter in the box with the butter. I am always, under all circumstances, glad to get your letters.

---

108. Joseph Henry Hyman (1835-1902) of Edgecombe County, an 1855 University of North Carolina graduate, was promoted to colonel of the 13th Regt. N.C.T., Pender-Scales' brigade, on June 13, 1863, and was wounded in the foot at Gettysburg. Krick, *Lee's Colonels*, p. 205. Joseph Engelhard (1832-1879), an 1854 University of North Carolina graduate who attended Harvard Law School, practiced law in Tarboro before the war. After serving in the 33rd Regt. N.C.T., he was appointed assistant adjutant-general of Pender's division in May, 1863, and held that post until the surrender at Appomattox. Powell, *Dictionary of North Carolina Biography*, 2:157-8. Erasmus D. Scales, a resident of Rockingham County, enlisted in the "Yanceyville Grays," Company H of the 13th Regt. N.C.T. on May 30, 1861. He was appointed commissary sergeant and transferred to the regimental field and staff on June 10, 1861, thereafter being promoted assistant commissary of subsistence (captain) on November 14, 1861. He was promoted to assistant brigade commissary on June 13, 1863. Manarin and Jordan, *N.C. Troops*, 5:284, 286 and 363.

I hope that every thing is getting on well at home. Let me know how the oats, corn, and every thing looks. I expect you will have a fine crop, and a fine garden too. I wish it were possible for me to enjoy it with you. Your company would be of more interest, than the garden.

Tomorrow, I shall go to hear a sermon from the Revd. Mr. Friend, an Episcopal minister who is a refugee from Port Royal Va. He will preach at Grace Church, which is distant from our camp a few miles. I know I shall enjoy the privilege of worshipping in a church.

Be sure to let me know if you have received my uniform and your blankets, which I sent back some time ago. Kiss the children for me. Remember me to all friends. Do write often.

very affectionately your husband
F. M. Parker

Some time since, I sent to you, in a letter, Offa's fine crest piece, which Bella gave him; have you ever received it?

F. M. P.

I have sent a saddle to Enfield by the Maj.'s boy; please have it taken home when you send the things to Enfield. This saddle is to bring my horse back with, so hold on to it, until I send for the horse. If you can do so, please send me the pillow cases, I wrote for.

———————————◆•◆———————————

Hd. Qrs. 30th Regt. N.C. T.
May 21st 1863

My dear Wife

For several days now I have had no letter from you. I know you have written, and that the fault is in the miserable mismanagement of the mails. On yesterday no mail at all came to Hamilton's Crossing. This is very bad. If I could get hold of the guilty party, I would make him suffer.

Well, Genrl. Ramseur has returned, and I am again with my Regt. where I had much rather be. The Genrl. returned sooner than we expected him, in fact much before his furlough [would] have expired. It may be that he has returned too soon for us now. It is reported that Genrl. D. H. Hill had made a request, that our

Brigade be sent to N.C. and that Genrl. Ramseur was opposed to leaving this army; be that as it may, one thing is certain that troops are being sent to N.C. A Georgia Brigade, Genrl. Colquits, leaves to day. There is a great deal of dissatisfaction in the Brigade, in consequence of the alleged action of Genrl. Ramseur. It certainly would have been pleasant to have gone to the old State again, but [it] may be that all things are for the best; at any rate, we must think so. I might have seen you and the children a little while at Enfield, but I have no idea that any leave of absence would have been granted me. I made application on yesterday to detail a man of my Regt. to send for my horse, but the detail was disapproved. I suppose Genrl. Lee wants every man now that he can get. I will try and make some other arrangement to get my horse. In the mean time, if the horse is needed at home, he can be used; in fact I would prefer that he should be worked moderately; but let them be very careful, lest the gear should rub the hair off at any place. I wrote you the other day by Maj. Sillers' boy. I hope you received the letter, and that we will get the few little things I wrote for.

When the supply, which the Maj. has sent for, is consumed, I think I shall draw on your smoke house, and on your peas, for an additional one. I think our cooks are a little wasteful, but these things can not be well regulated here in camp.

I intended to have written you last night, when I could have given you a much better letter, than now; but I was suffering very much with that same tooth ache. I am feeling better of it this morning.

On yesterday our entire Brigade attended Divine services. We had a most excellent service from Rev. Dr. Hague, of Richmond, a Presbyterian minister. He is a very eloquent man, gave us a fine sermon.

A few days since I called to see Mrs. Haughton, who is here attending to her son Capt. Lord, who, I fear, is mortally wounded; poor woman, she is in much distress; seemed glad to see me, was very cordial towards me. She enquired [sic] after you and the children.

Remember me to all friends; say to Mr. Dunn that he has not answered my letter yet. Kiss the dear children for me; tell them I think of them very often.

I will write again soon. Encourage Hilliard to plant as much corn in the low grounds, as possible. I mean in that part which he will clean up this spring. Write soon, and often. Good bye, my dear Wife; God bless you all.

very affectionately your husband
F. M. Parker

———————◆◆◆———————

Hd. Qrs. 30th N.C.T.
May 25, 1863

My dear Wife

I have written you recently, but I hope another letter will not be objectionable to you, certainly not, if I may judge you by myself. I have just learned that the impressing officers for the government, are impressing horses for service. I write to say ~~to say~~ to you that if one of such officers should visit my house, that you inform him that I have no pleasure horse, no horse except what is needed on the farm for the ~~prodct~~ cultivation of the crop, except the one which I shall send for soon, and which I need for my own use in the army; and I wish you to object to his being taken, and if necessary, have the horse locked up in the stable and kept there. I hope and believe that none of the impressing officers will visit you, for any such purpose; but if they should, you must state to him candidly how you are situated, and then be firm in standing to what I have recommended. If necessary, send for Mr. Dunn, he will assist you in this matter. I suppose you are as much excited at home, with regard to the fate of Vicksburg, as we are in the army; some are gloomy and despondent; others are full of hope, and confidence; I am in the latter class; I do not believe that Vicksburg can be taken, except by the greatest loss of life, more by a great deal, than the yankees are willing to suffer. I look for very brilliant successes in the south and west, provided we drive the enemy back at Vicksburg.

Who knows, but that under the blessings of God, that this attack on Vicksburg, may be the turning point in the war, and the beginning of the end. God grant that it may be so, and that we may be able to conquer a speedy and honourable [sic] peace, an everlasting peace. How tired I am of this now; how I long to be at home with you and the children, never more to be thus separated. I know that your heart receives this feeling. We certainly will well know how to appreciate home with all its endearments, after this war.

Mrs. Holmes is here on a visit to the Capt. [James C. Holmes] he really seems to enjoy it much. I have excused him from all duties with his company, while his wife is here. I make a self

279

case of the matter; if you were any where near me, I know very well that I should want nothing else to attend to.

But what is proper in one, is not at all advisable in another; Mrs. Holmes has no children, and can readily leave home, and move from point to point. Now do'nt [sic] wish that you had no children; no, the dear little creatures are too great a blessing to be deprived of.

I have not seen Mrs. Holmes yet, but will call on her tomorrow; she has sent me a bottle of nice wine; I must go and thank her for it. I suppose that you sent your box to Enfield, to day for Maj. Sillers' boy to bring to me. We shall prize it highly, I assure you. We appreciate all such little favours. A few days since, I received a small box from Sisters Bet and Mary, sent by one of my men who was returning to his company. We go on picket on wednesday [sic], and my opportunities for writing will be bad, so you must not look for too many letters then. I am much pleased to tell you that there is a prospect of our having Dr. Garrett as our Surgeon again. We will welcome him most heartily. I hope he will be able to come.

And now what shall [I] say to the children? ask Mary if she brings home a report every friday [sic]; and if it is a good one, I hope it is.

Does Jimmy ever go with Moses to feed his hogs, or to salt the sheep? and has he quit snapping his eyes, I hope so. Does Offa ever fall in the branch now, and get himself dirty? and does little Hattie get any dirt on her clothes? Bless them, all these little things I think of, while thinking of them.

And how do you come on raising chickens? and how does your garden and crop look? Very well, I expect. You must let me know all about these things when you write again, which I hope will be soon, very soon. I had a letter from Bella the other day; she said you spoke of visiting Tarboro soon, I would certainly do so, if I were you.

We are getting more N.C. troops in this army. [Brig.] Genrl. [Junius] Daniels' [sic] Brigade arrived here a few days since. Gaston Lewis[109] and Joel[110] are in this; so is Carey Whitaker[111]

109. William Gaston Lewis (1835-1901) of Rocky Mount was one of those unsung heroes of the Confederate service who rose from 3rd lieutenant to the rank of brigadier general through his own considerable abilities. A graduate of the University of North Carolina and civil engineer in the ante-bellum period, he was enumerated in the 1860 U.S. Census of

and other of my friends. I have seen Gaston and Joel, but none of the others. It was in the place of this Brigade, that Genrl. Hill wished ours; there is but little prospect of our leaving here. May be it is all for the better. The army has never been whipped, and the men feel as if it can not be; but our losses are terrible sometimes. Please have my cassimere [sic] coat, and the thin cassimere [sic] pants all ready as soon as you can; see that the buttons are all tight on the pants. You know I am a terrible fellow on buttons.

Be sure to carry out my instructions about my horse. Remember me to all friends. Kiss the children for me. Write soon to
your affectionate husband
F. M. Parker

————————

Edgecombe County as a 24-year-old merchant living in the household of Robert Wimberley, a 50-year-old farmer who owned 50 slaves and 22 slave houses. Lewis enlisted at age 25 in the "Edgecombe Guards," Company A of the 1st Regt. N.C. Infantry, on April 18, 1861, and was appointed 3rd lieutenant. He was promoted to 1st lieutenant on September 7, 1861, and mustered out November 12-13, 1861. He was appointed major of the 33rd Regt. N.C.T. and after distinguishing himself at the battle of New Bern, North Carolina, on March 14, 1862, he was promoted to lieutenant colonel on April 25, 1862, and transferred to the 43rd Regt. N.C.T.. He was appointed acting commander of the 43rd on July 3, 1863, and promoted to brigadier general on May 31, 1864. Lewis was wounded and captured at Farmville, Virginia, on April 7, 1865. Manarin and Jordan, *N.C. Troops*, 3:4, 9:118 and 10:293; Warner, *Generals in Gray*, pp. 186-187. Hill, *Confederate Military History*, 5:328-330.

110. Joel Lewis was enumerated in the 1860 U.S. Census of Edgecombe County as a physician living at Cromwell's Hotel, the same establishment in which Colonel Parker's brother-in-law and adjutant of the 30th Regt., Fred Philips, resided. After serving as a private in Company I, 15th Regt. N.C.T., Lewis was appointed assistant surgeon of the 43rd Regt. N.C.T. on January 29, 1863. He was present or accounted for until resigning on January 6, 1865. Lewis was paroled at Greensboro, North Carolina, on May 1, 1865. Manarin and Jordan, *N.C. Troops*, 10:294.

111. Carey Whitaker was listed in the 1860 U.S. Census of Halifax County as the owner of five slaves (one a fugitive) and one slave house. Cary W. Whitaker, who enlisted on April 19, 1861, at age 29, after serving as 1st lieutenant of the Enfield Blues, Co. I, 1st Regt. N.C. Infantry, with Parker, was elected captain of Company D, 43rd Regt. N.C.T. on January 24, 1862. He was present or accounted for until wounded at or near Charles Town, West Virginia, August 21, 1864. He returned to duty November-December, 1864. He was wounded in the hand at the fall of Petersburg, April 2, 1865, and died of gangrenous wounds at Danville, Virginia, April 19, 1865. Manarin and Jordan, *N.C. Troops*, 10:323; Wellman, *Rebel Boast*, pp. 234 and 255 (where Cary Whitaker's death date is given as April 20, 1865).

On May 29, 1863, Generals Lee, Longstreet, and Ewell conducted a grand review of Rodes' division.[112]

On Picket
Sunday morning May 31st 1863

My dear Wife

We have just come from the picket lines, where we were called about 12 o'clock last night, to repel a supposed attempt of the enemy at crossing. We have had our breakfast, and I now sit down to write to you, as that is the most pleasant duty which I could perform; having already read some in my bible. In a former letter I think I mentioned to you, that there were some very good Southern Ladies living opposite to our picket lines, who gave us valuable information of the plans of the enemy, just prior to their crossing in the last fight; on yesterday the same ladies came to the river bank, attracted the attention of our pickets, and made signals of the intentions of the enemy, by crossing a couple of pieces of paper which they had in their hands, and them pointing up and down the river, meaning that the Yankees would cross both above and below this point. From this, and other information, which our Generals received, there was quite a stir among the troops last night. My Regt. was under arms about 12 o'clock and marched to the river bank and other Brigades were posted at convenient points.

I will here remark that our Regt. is in reserve; the other three Regts. of the Brigade being on the line constantly. We are about a mile from the river, encamped in a beautiful place, cool and shady, with excellent water. We went to the river, remained the balance of the night, found and left every thing remarkably quiet. The enemy evidently are on a move of some kind, but what that move is, we here do not know yet.

---

112. Ardrey Diary. A humorous account of the effect of the ladies present at this grand review is given in the letter of Capt. James I. Harris of Company I, included in an appendix to this book.

My own individual opinion is that Hooker is going to the Peninsula, to try McClellan's old route to Richmond. Others think that he is falling back to the fortifications around Washington City. I suppose a few days will tell what is going on.

I mentioned to you the other day that Genrl. Lee would review this Division, and that we would not be present. But the day before the review Genrl. Ramseur sent me an order to bring up three Regts. of the Brigade, leaving one in the lines. So I left the 14th N.C. and took up the others. We had a very warm, dusty time of it; but the men were very quiet and patient. I suppose the honour of being reviewed by Genrl. Lee, compensated for all the fatigue, incident thereto. The review passed off in fine style. Besides Genrl. Lee, we had Genrls. Longstreet, A. P. Hill, and Early; all, officers of note in the world. Our corps [Jackson's] is now commanded by Genrl. Ewell; he is a fine officer; what to us, is a good recommendation, is the known fact that Genl. Jackson had a very high opinion of him. Genrl. Ewell lost a leg at the second battle of Manassas. He has an artificial leg, and rides very well. I hope he may fill the place, made vacant by the loss of the great, the noble Jackson.

The daily papers of yesterday were silent as to Vicksburg; I do hope and pray that Vicksburg may stand; it would be a sad blow to us, should it fall, but no cause for despondancy [*sic*]; we can not expect to succeed in every engagement. It is true that this army, the army of Northern Va., has <u>never</u> been whipped, so some of the other armies must fail. We must put our trust in God, do our entire duty, and continue to look upward and onward. Every thing will yet be right. I feel certain of that; I may not live to see the end, but you and my children will enjoy the peace, and protection, and liberty, for which I am fighting; this alone is sufficient to urge us on. I feel that I have many reasons for sticking to my post of duty. I hope that I may have the health and strength to faithfully perform it. It is very bad, and a great trial to be thus separated from you and the children, and for so long, but when I look forward to the time when I shall return to you, with peace smiling on our beloved country, and no wars, nor rumours of wars to disturb the quiet which we so much desire, it causes me to be somewhat satisfied with my present situation. If on the other hand, I should fall, should never return to you again, you would have the proud satisfaction to know that I fell in the discharge of my duties, and the consolation, I hope, that I had died as a Christian soldier should die; in fact that all things are in the hands of a good Being above, who

[page(s) missing]

Baptist, the Methodist, a few Presbyterians, and one or two primitive Baptists. I am much pleased to see all this; it makes a man a better soldier if he is a good christian; this is the result of my experience, and it was the expressed opinion of the noble, the glorious Jackson.

We return to camp tomorrow, that is if we do not scare up a fight before we get off. It has got to be a maxim in our Brigade that when we go on a picket, something unusual must happen, either a rain, a snow, a review or a fight. Our last tour brought us the rain and the fight; this one has produced, so far, only the review, and I will be perfectly satisfied with that alone. If nothing happens, I will start Wyatt on Tuesday or Wednesday to N.C. for my horse.

You complain of the dry weather. Tell Hilliard to plow deep while it is dry and to plow often. Tell him to work on the low grounds, clean it up, whenever he has a chance. I suppose he has sheared your sheep before this.

Kiss the children for me. Write often.

Very affectionately and sincerely yours
F. M. Parker

In speaking of the minister who preached today, I do not wish to detract from the services of Mr. Betts, our chaplain; of course he has done all this work.

———————————◆◆◆———————————

Hd. Qrs. 30th N.C.T.
June 2nd, 1863

Mrs. S. J. Parker
Sycamore Alley
N.C.
By Wyatt

My dear Wife

We are back in camp again, having gotten off picket without any fight. Every thing is very quiet.

I shall start Wyatt for N.C. this morning to bring my horse to me. He will go by your house, and then to Tarboro for a day or two.

If you can get a pair of saddle bags, I want Wyatt to bring my uniform back with him; I think the coat can be folded so as to be brought without injuring it much. I would prefer to have it brought in a box, but do not know of any one coming on soon. If William Nicholson is still at home, may be he would bring it for me; the uniform could be folded and wrapped in a small bundle so as not to be of much trouble. If he is there, I wish you would ask him to bring it for me. If he consents to bring it, have it done up in strong paper, so as to come as safely as possible. But if you ca'nt [*sic*] send the clothes any other way, I wish you would send them by Wyatt. Whether Wyatt brings the clothes or not, I would like to have a pair of saddle bags; they will be very convenient to carry clothes in, should we be on the march. I send one of my bandages; I wish you would put some new strings to it. I also send back your jars, bottles, &c. The things you sent were very nice, and very acceptable.

I send my thick shirts and drawers[.] I wish you would send me one good shirt by Wyatt; one will be sufficent [*sic*].

You complain of my letters not reaching you in time; the reason of this is that our letters have to go to Raleigh to be distributed, and hence they are long in getting to your office. You are very kind in writing so often. I hope you will continue to write.

Say to Hilliard that I want him to plant peas every where that he has corn; the peas will not interfere with the oats which he will sow at the last plowing.

Enclosed I send $ 20 which I wish you to hand Wyatt when his starts back with the horse, to bear his expenses back. I want him to bring my halter, the bridle I had made in Wilmington, and the saddle I sent by Maj. [William W.] Sillers' boy.

I send to Hattie the picture of a yankee private, which I picked up on the field of Chancellorsville; it will amuse him a little; also a little pin, the likeness of McClellan. Fred sends this to Offa. Kiss all the children for me. Remember me to all friends. Good bye, God bless you all.

very affectionately your husband

F. M. Parker

----◆◆◆----

On June 3, 1863, the 30th received orders to prepare for a long march and company commanders were told to make requisition for four months' supply of clothing for their companies.[113] The fateful march toward Pennsylvania was about to begin, and Ramseur's brigade was to lead the invasion of the North. Ramseur and his regimental commanders, including Colonel Parker, began the Gettysburg Campaign with a sterling reputation in the Army of Northern Virginia, a reputation which they were only to enhance in the weeks ahead. On June 4, Gen. Robert E. Lee wrote Gov. Zeb Vance, urging recruitment to fill the brigade's thinned ranks, and giving Ramseur and his colonels what was, for Lee, very high praise indeed. "I consider its brigade and regimental commanders as among the best of their respective grades in the army. . ."[114]

The 30th entered the Gettysburg Campaign with an estimated strength of 278.[115] On June 4, the 30th was aroused at 3 a.m., and along with the rest of Ramseur's brigade broke camp and marched 16 miles westward through the poor and barren country of Spotsylvania County to Spotsylvania Court House.[116] On June 5, the brigade marched 21 miles before camping near old Vedierville. On June 7, they marched 19 miles, crossing the Rapidan at Somerville Ford, reaching Culpeper Court House and going into camp 4 miles beyond. The brigade was ordered out to support Stuart at Brandy Station on June 9, but arrived after the Federal withdrawal.[117]

---

113 Ardrey Diary.

114. *OR*, vol. 27, pt. 3, pp. 871-2.

115. John W. Busey and David G. Martin, *Regimental Strengths and Losses at Gettysburg* (Hightstown, New Jersey: Longstreet House, 1986), p. 168.

116. Ardrey Diary.

117. *Ibid.*; Memoir of Julius L. Schaub, Co. B, 14th Regt. N.C.T., handwritten memoir, 44 pages in length, in Troup County Archives, LaGrange, Georgia, p. 14. "1st Sgt. J. L. Schaub" appears in the roster of the 14th Regt. in Manarin and Jordan, *N.C. Troops*, 5:411 and 724, under the guise of "1st Sgt. J. L. Shoup," a phonetic spelling of his name. "Sgt. Schaub" is mentioned as an authority on the 14th Regiment in Watkins,

On June 10, the brigade broke camp and marched north toward Winchester, marching 10 miles and camping at the Hazel River near Gourd Vine Church.[118] A 15 mile march on June 11 carried the brigade (via Gaines' Crossroads) to Flint Hill, and on June 12 the Blue Ridge was crossed at Chester Gap during a 17 mile march in which they passed through Front Royal, forded the Shenandoah, and went through Cedarville to Stonebridge.[119] Marching through Millwood to Berryville on June 13, the brigade drew up in line of battle upon confronting a group of Union troops who precipitously withdrew—abandoning 200 sick men, large white Sibley tents, and quartermaster's stores and supplies. Capt. John C. Gorman, of the 2nd North Carolina wrote:

> Our whole brigade partook of a hot dinner of beans and pork, baked beef, and fresh loaf bread furnished ready for eating by our accomodating [sic] Yankee friends. Every soldier filled his haversack with the pure bean coffee, sugar, and other camp delicacies.[120]

The brigade marched on past Berryville to Summit Point where it camped for the night, having covered 20 miles that day.[121] The following day, June 14, Ramseur's brigade led the rapid 19 mile march of Rodes' division through Smithfield, Bunker Hill and Darksville and its headlong assault upon the Federals drawn up in Martinsburg—resulting in the capture of five artillery pieces along with their caissons and horses and

---

Movement of the 14th North Carolina, p. 33, and his death and service with the 14th is noticed with suitable encomium in F. M. Longley, "Commander J. L. Schaub," *Confederate Veteran*, vol. 20, no. 4 (April, 1912):179. In using Schaub in this history, the assumption is made that the 14th and the 30th were together at all times unless there is specific evidence to the contrary.

118. Schaub, "Memoir," p. 14; Record of Events.
119. Schaub, "Memoir," pp. 14-15.
120. George Gorman, ed., "Memoirs of a Rebel being the Narratives of John Calvin Gorman, Captain, Company B, 2nd North Carolina Regiment, 1861-1865. Part II: Chancellorsville and Gettysburg," *Military Images*, vol. 3, no. 6 (May-June, 1982):24.
121. Ardrey Diary; Schaub, "Memoir," p. 15; *OR*, vol. 27, pt. 2, pp. 547-8. The action at Berryville, Virginia, and the rest of the Gettysburg Campaign, is discussed in detail in the August, 1863, letter of Capt. James I. Harris of Company I, included as an appendix to this book.

many other stores.[122] On June 15, the Army of Northern Virginia crossed the Potomac at Williamsport with Ramseur's brigade in the lead.[123]

A halt at Williamsport was deemed absolutely necessary by General Rodes due to the condition of his men's feet and their lack of shoes,[124] and here Ramseur's brigade remained for two days. Moving two miles beyond Hagerstown on June 17, the men then encamped for another four days, resting and enjoying visits with the townfolk and especially the ladies. "Hagerstown is noted for the pretty ladies," recorded Lieutenant Ardrey, who also recalled that on June 18 he "[d]rew rations of molasses, butter and whiskey, etc." The men found many Southern sympathizers in Hagerstown. Ramseur had his headquarters in the female seminary. On June 22 or 23, the brigade marched 13 miles through Middleburg to Greencastle, Pennsylvania, where they rested on June 24.[125]

———————————◆◆◆———————————

Bivouac near Green Castle, Penn.
June 23rd 1863

My dear Wife

Well, you see now, that we are an invading army, instead of one for defence [sic]; we are only a few miles in Penn. what our object is, or how far in this direction we will go, I can not say; we are on the direct route to Harrisburg, the Capital of the State, and are about one days march from Chambersburg, a town of some six or eight thousand inhabitants. Our cavalry have already been in Chambersburg, but whether they still occupy it or not I do not know; it is reported that there is a large amount of stores there, and I think it probable that we will go there; so far, we have not even seen a militia man; the Dutch of Penn. must be a cowardly set.

———————————

122. Ardrey Diary; Schaub, "Memoir," p. 15; *OR*, vol. 27, pt. 2, pp. 548-550.
123. Record of Events; Schaub, "Memoir," p. 15; Ardrey Diary.
124. *OR*, vol. 27, pt. 2, p. 550.
125. Ardrey Diary; Schaub, "Memoir," pp. 15-16. Schaub and Ardrey are in conflict: Ardrey dates the move from Williamsport to Hagerstown on June 17 while Schaub says June 19. Ardrey says that the march to Greencastle, Pennsylvania, was made on June 23, while Schaub and Rodes (*OR*, vol. 27, pt. 2, p. 551), say June 22.

We are entirely destitute of any news of the operations of the balance of the army; you must recollect that only Genrl. Ewell's corps is operating here; and only Rodes' Division in this particular section. The other two Divisions of the corps, Early's and Johnson's are operation on another route. If there is any thing like a general engagment [sic], of course the whole corps will be concentrated.

We are perfectly ignorant too, of the fate of Vicksburg; in fact, we are isolated so far as news is concerned. I suppose that you do not hear from our operations either, for I do not suppose that the papers would publish any thing if they knew it. I would give twenty dollars for a letter from you; I have been hoping that Wyatt would overtake us, and that I should get a letter by him; but so far, I have been disappointed, and I hardly expect him at all now. I am sorry that I did not start him for my horse sooner, I should like very much to have the horse with me.

If the horse is yet at home, tell Hilliard not to feed him high, that he must not be kept too fat, and I want him worked a little also.

Since we entered the valley of the Shenandoah in Va. up to the present time, we have passed through the most magnificent country I have ever seen; it is all a lime stone soil; such fields of wheat and clover, I never looked at, and such cattle too; these people certainly must have lived like lords, before this war. We are now in the Cumberland Valley, between the Blue Ridge and the Alleghany [sic] mountains. It is certainly the finest country I have ever seen. I hope you are all keeping well at home, and that every thing is getting on well; by this time you have cut your wheat, and I suppose the crop is nearly made, so far as cultivation is concerned; I hope you will make a fine one.

Kiss the children for me, and keep them mindful of their Pa. If you can not get a letter to me, you can pray for me, which may be of more service to me.

I have written this letter hurriedly, but I do'nt [sic] know when I shall be able to have it mailed. Good bye, God bless you all.

very affectionately your husband
F. M. Parker

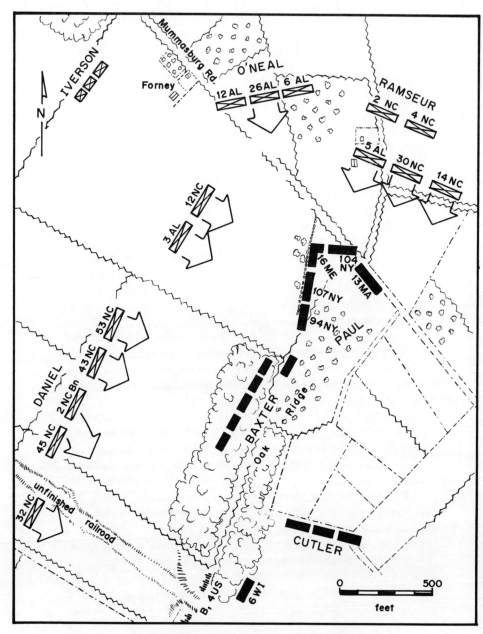

Gettysburg, Pennsylvania, July 1, 1863
Ramseur's final attack on Paul's brigade (approx. 3:45 p.m.)

Continuing up the Cumberland Valley, Ramseur's men marched 14 miles on June 24, passed through Chambersburg, and encamped two and a half miles beyond it. There they remained until June 27.[126] The brigade's line of march on June 27 carried it through "the little villages of Leesburg, Jackson, and Hockensville" to Carlisle.[127] Encamping at the famous Carlisle Barracks, the men enjoyed plenty of good things to eat (abandoned by the Union garrison who left upon their approach) and letters from home.[128] On June 29, the Confederate flag was hoisted up the Carlisle Barracks flag pole and speeches were made by Generals Trimble, Rodes, and Daniels, complimenting the North Carolina troops "that they had raised the Confederate flag in greater latitude than any other Southern troops."[129]

On June 30, the brigade turned southward, marching 22 miles through Paper Town and Petersburg to camp at Heidlersburg.[130] On July 1, they made a morning march of 14 miles straight toward the sounds of battle. During the march the brigade was positioned in the rear of the division train as a guard.

Arriving northeast of Gettysburg near Oak Hill at about 1 p.m., Ramseur advanced after a 15 minute rest. Detaching the 2nd and 4th Regiments to the support of O'Neal's brigade, Ramseur hastened with the 30th and 14th to the support of Iverson's brigade which he found annihilated on the field. Being warned by two officers to avoid Iverson's line of advance, Ramseur made a rapid flank march to the left and swept down from the northwest upon the right flank of the Union First Corps troops of Gabriel Paul's brigade who held a stone wall along the Mummasburg Road—the right flank of a position shaped like an inverted "V." Ramseur led the charge in person on horseback, and had his horse shot out from under him during the attack. The 30th hit the stone wall head on while the 14th, on the 30th's left, wrapped around the Union right flank. At the

126. Once again, Schaub and Ardrey are in conflict with Schaub dating the march through Chambersburg on June 24 and Ardrey on June 25. Rodes (OR, vol. 27, pt. 2, p. 551), gives the date as June 24.
127. Ardrey Diary.
128. Ardrey Diary.
129. Ardrey Diary.
130. Record of Events; Ardrey Diary; Schaub, "Memoir," p. 16.

moment of victory at this stone wall, as the Northerners broke and fled, Colonel Parker was shot in the face, receiving a serious wound through the nose.[131] Capt. James I. Harris of

---

131. *Ibid.*; *OR*, vol. 27, pt. 2, p. 587. The Confederate assault by Ramseur's brigade and other elements of Rodes' division on the afternoon of July 1, 1863, was made in a southwesterly direction toward and across the Mummasburg Road against Union First Corps forces of Brig. Gen. Gabriel Paul's First Brigade of Brig. Gen. John C. Robinson's Second Division holding an untenable position on both sides of the apex of a northward pointing triangle. Some descriptions of Ramseur's attack include accounts by Rodes (*OR*, vol. 27, pt. 2, p. 554); by Ramseur (*Ibid.*, p. 587); by Colonel Parker (the name of the author of the letter mistakenly transcribed as A. M. Parker) of the 30th (letter dated May 29, 1891, in a typescript in the Ramseur Papers in the North Carolina Division of Archives and History, Raleigh); by Maj. W. W. Sillers of the 30th (*OR*, vol. 27, pt. 2, p. 591); by the 30th's Adjt. Fred Philips (letter to David Schenk dated October 27, 1891, typescript in the Ramseur Papers, NCDAH); by Col. Bryan Grimes of the 4th Regt. (*OR*, vol. 27, pt. 2, pp. 589-590); by Col. Risden Tyler Bennett of the 14th Regt. (letter to Judge Philips dated May 28, 1891, in typescript in the Ramseur Papers, NCDAH); and by 2nd Lt. William Calder of the 2nd Regt. and of the Brigade Sharpshooters (Calder to "My Dearest Mother," from Camp near Hagerstown, Maryland, July 8, 1863, Calder Family Papers). Ramseur came up just after the disastrous repulse of Iverson's brigade in which that unit had walked into a trap and was virtually annihilated. This Confederate catastrophe, in which Iverson's dead lay in rows as if on parade, is discussed in Gerard A. Patterson, "The Death of Iverson's Brigade," *Gettysburg Magazine*, no. 5 (July, 1991):13-18. Ramseur was apparently saved from a similar disaster by the quick thinking of 2nd Lt. James Crowder of the 23rd Regt. N.C.T. of Iverson's brigade, and a Lieutenant Dugger of another regiment who ran back to Ramseur and advised him not to advance over the ground on which Iverson's men were slaughtered, but rather to move to the left and take the Federals in the flank. Clark, *N.C. Regiments*, 2:237, and Watkins, *Movement of the 14th North Carolina*, p. 14. (I am grateful to my friend and fellow historian, Greg Mast, for introducing me to the problems posed by Ramseur's move by the left flank prior to his July 1, 1863, attack.) Just before the attack, Col. Gilbert Prey of the 104th New York of Paul's brigade saw the Confederates passing into the McLean timber. William F. Fox, ed., *New York at Gettysburg*, 3 vol. (Albany: J. B. Lyon Company, 1900-1902), 2:757. Once underway, that attack carried all before it. In his May 28, 1891, letter, Adjutant Philips (brother-in-law of Colonel Parker) states: "General Ramseur formed the 14th and 30th Regiments at right angles to the rock wall, under cover of some pines on the edge of a hill, and as we reached the open field he wheeled the line to the left and sent us forward in a run to attack the enemy in this position. There was no faltering. Every man was at his post, and some of the gallant men of the 12th N.C. Regiment of Iverson's Brigade which had been driven back joined us. The attack was especially fierce.

Company I recalled, "Just at this time Col. Parker was wounded by a shell—he passed on telling us that he was wounded but to move forward." Chaplain A. D. Betts recorded:

> The ball entered just below one eye and came out just below the other, cutting the nasal tubes. When I knelt by him and prayed for him and his wife and children, he seemed to strangle with the blood. I stopped praying and held my arm lovingly till he was quiet.[132]

Parker's adventures of the day were not yet over. Ramseur's wounded horse was put just in the rear of the hospital tent in which Parker was housed on the evening of July 1. When she finally dropped dead that night, the horse very nearly fell on Parker, completely overturning the tent.[133]

In the meantime, the 30th pursued the enemy into Gettysburg only to see them take an immensely strong defensive position south of the town on Cemetery Hill. On the evening of July 2, the 30th advanced with the rest of Ramseur's brigade to take part in an assault on Cemetery Hill and the word was "North Carolina to the rescue." Ramseur's attack was aborted once its obviously suicidal nature was determined,[134] and the brigade

---

General Ramseur led the charge and he was the only officer in the field who had a horse under him. The fine gray mare upon which he rode fell from bullet wounds within a few yards of the stone fence. Col. Parker of the 30th Regiment was badly wounded in the face just as we reached the wall. The bullet ridden flags of the 14th and 30th were planted there, and for a few minutes the fighting was terrific. The 2nd and 4th Regiments moved promptly up on our right and the retreat of the enemy assumed the character of a rout." In his May 29, 1891, letter, Colonel Parker states: "When he [Ramseur] formed his line it was at a right angle to the [rock] wall. As soon as we cleared the small pines, Ramseur wheeled the line to the left, and then sent us forward at the double quick, or, rather, run. It must have been a grand sight to one who was not too intimately connected with the movement. Ramseur could handle troops under fire with more ease than any officer I ever knew." This charge is discussed in Warren W. Hassler, Jr., *Crisis at the Crossroads: The First Day at Gettysburg* (University, Alabama: University of Alabama Press, 1970), pp. 98-100; Gallagher, *Ramseur*, pp. 71-73; and David G. Martin, *Gettysburg July 1* (Conshohocken, Pennsylvania: Combined Books, Inc., 1995), pp. 386-393.

132. Betts, *Experiences*, p. 39.
133. Parker letter, May 29, 1891, Ramseur Papers, NCDAH.
134. According to the 2nd Regiment's Capt. John C. Gorman, Ramseur crept

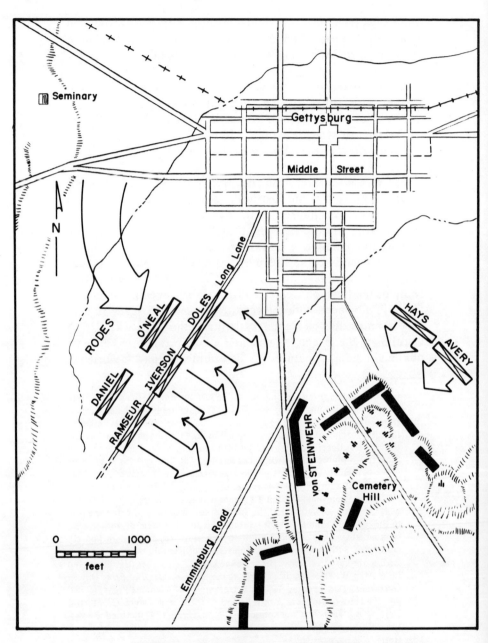

Gettysburg, Pennsylvania, July 2, 1863
Rodes' division attacks Cemetery Hill (approx. 8 p.m.)

294

spent July 3 lying in Long Lane just north of the field of the Pickett-Pettigrew-Trimble Charge, observing that grand and fatal assault at close range.[135] During the night, the brigade was withdrawn to a position near its first day's fight and a Union hospital where it spent July 4.[136]

Before daybreak on July 5, the Confederate retreat began with Rodes' division as the rearguard of the army. The brigade camped that night at Fairfield and continued across the mountains by Monterey Springs and Waynesboro to Hagerstown which they reached on the evening of July 6.[137]

In the meantime, the desperately wounded Colonel Parker was being conveyed southward lying in the foot of a buggy driven by Col. Risden Tyler Bennett of the 14th Regiment, also wounded but still able to drive (Bennett was shot in the groin, but the ball's force had been broken by "heavy osnaburg underwear"). They reached Martinsburg where they were nursed in the private home of Mr. Anderson for five weeks before moving on to a hospital in Richmond and then to home. Parker returned to command the regiment after six months of convalescence on January 21, 1864.[138]

After arriving at Hagerstown on July 6, the 30th Regiment, now under the command of Lieutenant Colonel Sillers, rested and held the extreme left of the army near Williamsport. The 30th and the other regiments of Ramseur's brigade re-crossed the Potomac during the night of July 13/14, wading through knee deep mud for 300-400 yards before fording the river, with orders to swing their cartridge boxes around their necks as the water came up to their armpits. They then marched another three miles through the rain before falling down in exhausted sleep.[139] The 30th broke camp about 11 a.m. on July 14 and

---

forward in person in order to reconnoiter the strong Union position before the attack was called off. Gorman, "Memoirs pt. 2," p. 25.
135. *OR*, vol. 27, pt. 2, pp. 587-8. The events of July 2 and 3 are described in detail in the August, 1863, letter of Capt. James I. Harris, appended to this book.
136. Schaub, "Memoir," p. 18; Harris letter in the appendix.
137. Record of Events; Schaub, "Memoir," p. 19.
138. W. A. Smith, *The Anson Guards* (Charlotte, North Carolina: Stone Publishing Co., 1914), p. 275-6; Ardrey Diary; Betts, *Experiences*, p. 53; Compiled Service Record of Francis Marion Parker.
139. Schaub, "Memoir," pp. 19-20; Harris letter in the appendix; Record of Events; Ardrey Diary.

moved to a camp near Martinsburg. On July 15, the brigade moved southward and encamped near Darksville, where it remained for a week, moving to Winchester on July 22. The following day, July 23, featured a 37 mile march in which the 30th advanced to Manassas Gap, formed in support of Wright's brigade (then in line of battle confronting the enemy), and then marched through Front Royal and 10 miles beyond toward Luray. The next six days were spent in marching through the Luray Valley, crossing the mountains at Thornton Gap and marching through Sperryville, to Madison Court House, arriving on July 29. The next day 2nd Lt. Archibald A. Jackson of Company H wrote his sister a fairly cheerful assessment of his condition and that of his company:

> Arrived yesterday. I have bin marching nerley all the time seinse we left Fredericksburg the 2 of June but I have held out finley tho if has taken some off that big lazey fat off of my bones. . . . The helth of the company is very good. We have 26 men present for duty. We get plenty to eat if we could get more salt.[140]

On August 8, the brigade went into camp near Orange Court House to rest and recover from the Gettysburg Campaign.[141]

While the 30th had fared somewhat better than the other North Carolina units at Gettysburg, its losses were still heavy by any standards:

Killed 4
Mortally wounded 6
Mortally wounded and captured 1
Wounded 27
Captured 23
Wounded and captured 9
TOTAL CASUALTIES 70 (approximately 24%)

---

140. A. A. Jackson to Dear Sister, July 30, 1863, from Camp near Madison Court House, quoted with permission of owner, Chapel Hill Rare Books, Doug Odell, proprietor.
141. The itinerary of the 30th and Ramseur's brigade from the Potomac to Orange Court House is taken from the 30th's Record of Events; Schaub, "Memoir," pp. 20-21; and the Harris letter in the appendix.

The days of rest and recovery in August, 1863, were accompanied by news from North Carolina of the Holden-inspired peace movement. This was greeted with disgust, at least by Capt. James I. Harris of Company I of the 30th:

> I am sorry to see that my old adopted state has so far yielded to an ambitious traitor's influence, as to give thought, much less expression to sentiments so conflicting with our prescripts and so destructive to our interests. Holden ought to be hung and every rascal who utters disloyal sentiments to the South ought to be shot.[142]

In addition, perhaps in part in reaction to Gettysburg and to the news from home, a great revival swept the army in general and Ramseur's brigade and the 30th in particular.[143] A. D. Betts

---

142. *Ibid.* The flames of sentiment in favor of peace and desertion from the army were being fanned in North Carolina by one of its leading newspaper editors. After supporting Zebulon V. Vance for governor in 1862, William W. Holden (1818-1892), editor of the North Carolina *Standard*, turned against his own erstwhile protege after Vance had firmly declared his intent to prosecute the war to a successful end. Confederate defeat at Gettysburg, with heavy North Carolina losses, added fuel to the flames. By August, 1863, Holden-inspired peace meetings were being held across North Carolina. The situation became so serious that Governor Vance travelled to Richmond to consult with Jefferson Davis about Holden. Georgia troops of Benning's brigade passing through Raleigh wrecked Holden's newspaper office on September 9, 1863. For discussions of the opposition in North Carolina, led by Holden, to Confederate government actions and policies, see J. G. de Roulhac Hamilton, *Reconstruction in North Carolina* (New York: Columbia University Press, 1914; reprint: Gloucester, Massachusetts: Peter Smith, 1964), pp. 39-50; Georgia Lee Tatum, *Disloyalty in the Confederacy* (Chapel Hill: University of North Carolina Press, 1934), pp. 110-119; Edgar E. Folk and Byrum Shaw, *W. W. Holden, A Political Biography* (Winston-Salem: John F. Blair, 1982), pp. 151-170; William C. Harris, *William Woods Holden: Firebrand of North Carolina Politics* (Baton Rouge: Louisiana State University Press, 1987), pp. 127-136; Joe Mobley, ed., *The Papers of Zebulon Baird Vance*, 2 vol. (Raleigh: North Carolina Division of Archives and History, 1995), 2:xviii-xx; and Horace W. Raper, "William W. Holden and the Peace Movement in North Carolina," *North Carolina Historical Review*, vol. 31 (1954):493-516.

143. Jones, *Christ in the Camp*, p. 325. One chaplain wrote "Without a doubt, in hundreds of instances, the shock of battle has been sanctified to the saving of souls." *Ibid.*, p. 328.

returned to the regiment on August 14 from a visit to Richmond with 50 Testaments and Psalms, thirteen Bibles, one hundred "hymns," and other materials which were put to good use. Prayer meetings were held almost every night. Chaplain Betts noted many penitents and frequent conversions in his diary.[144] On Sept. 2, W. E. Ardrey of Company K noted in his diary:

> We are having a great religious revival in the camp now, under the preaching of Rev. Powers, chaplain of the Fourteenth Regiment North Carolina Troops, and a member of the South Carolina M. E. Church, South. Over two hundred penitents every night, preaching every day and night under a large brush arbor made by the soldiers, surrounded by torch lights at night. It is a grand sight to see about two thousand soldiers attending every service and not a single lady in the congregation. I never have witnessed such spiritual interest before, several hundred have connectied [sic] themselves with the church.[145]

On September 5, Chaplain Betts made this brief notation in his diary:

> Self-denial. Furlough in my pocket; but feel it my duty to remain at my work. Much encouraged by frequent conversions.[146]

A grand review of the Second Corps was conducted by Ewell on August 26 and by Robert E. Lee on September 1 when Ardrey of the Mecklenburg Beauregards recorded the following:

---

144. Betts, *Experiences*, p. 43.
145. Ardrey Diary. Chaplain George B. Taylor reported preaching to the Doles-Cook Brigade (also in Rodes' division) near Orange Court House in September, 1863, in "a large amphitheatre of log-seats, with a pulpit in the centre, covered with an arbor, and flanked on either hand by a platform, whose blazing lightwood illuniated [sic] every face in the vast congregation." Taylor described, "[t]he sea of upturned, earnest faces, and the songs swelling from hundreds of manly voices and making the forest resound." Jones, *Christ in the Camp*, p. 333. Of all the scenes in the famous history of the Army of Northern Virginia, those of the Great Revival along the Rapidan River in the fall of 1863 are the ones the author of this book would most like to have seen.
146. Betts, *Experiences*, p. 44.

Grand review of the second army corps by Gen. R. E. Lee, commander in chief. The three divisions arrived on the field about 9 o'clock and were formed in order according to rank of the lieutenant generals, Gen. Early's division in front, Gen. Johnston in rear, and Gen. Rhodes in the center. Each line was about three miles long. We opened ranks, presented arms, the drums were beating, the bands playing and down the lines. Then he took his position in front and the three divisions passed review. It was one of the grandest sights that we ever witnessed in our lives. The army was in fine condition and made a fine appearance. We felt proud of ourselves and our country.[147]

On September 14, 1863, the 30th moved to Morton's Ford on the Rapidan River and went on picket duty. Here the regiment remained for nearly four weeks. On October 9, the regiment broke camp at 5 a.m. and marched northward past Orange Court House with the rest of Ewell's and A. P. Hill's corps in an attempt by Lee to outflank Meade and bring on an engagement.[148] On October 10, the brigade marched 27 miles, through Madison Court House and across the Robinson River, camping 16 miles beyond. On October 11, Ramseur's men marched for 10 miles, camping on the Sperryville Pike 5 miles from Culpeper Court House. On October 12, they crossed the Hazel River at a burnt bridge and overtook the enemy at Warrenton Springs at 3 in the afternoon. Sharpshooters were called to the front, but after a brief skirmish, the Federals retreated, and Ramseur's men crossed the Rappahannock and encamped at 9 p.m. Taking up the march at daylight on October 13, line of battle was formed when the enemy was met at Warrenton Court House, but the bluecoats retreated and the North Carolinians went into camp a mile further on. Breaking camp before daylight on October 15, Ramseur's men met the Union forces at 8:30 a.m. and went into line of battle, advancing under artillery fire. The sharpshooters were hotly engaged and drove off the Yankee cavalry. After marching in pursuit, the brigade went into camp near Bristoe Station. On October 16, the brigade marched to the

147. Ardrey Diary.
148. Record of Events.

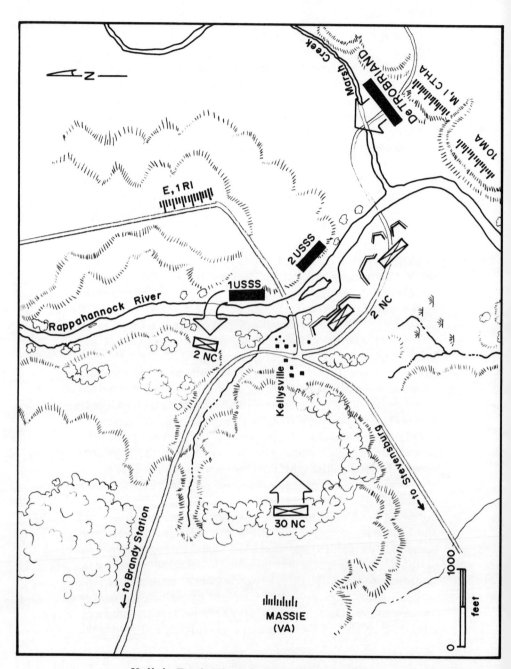

Kelly's Ford, Virginia, November 7, 1863

300

37th mile post on the Orange and Alexandria Railroad and began destroying that railroad, burning its crossties and bending its rails. Thomas J. Watkins of the 14th Regiment noted, "The boys seemed to enjoy this sport."[149] This continued through October 17, with the brigade encamping near Warrenton Junction. On October 18, they marched to Rappahannock Station then camped. On October 19, Ramseur's men left camp at 3 a.m., crossed the Rappahannock in a hailstorm and went into camp, tired, wet and sore, near Kelly's Ford.[150] The futile Bristoe Station Campaign had cost the 30th Regiment nine casualties: killed: 1; mortally wounded: 2; wounded: 5; and captured: 1.[151]

On October 21, the brigade moved camp to near Mountain Run, about one mile from Kelly's Ford, and commenced building winter quarters. Chaplain Betts built a chapel on October 23 and 24.[152]

The men of the 30th Regiment might well have anticipated that a season of peace and quiet was setting in, but they were wrong. On November 7, two and a half weeks after the regiment went into camp, the 30th's greatest military disaster of the war occurred, the so-called battle of Kellyville or Kelly's Ford, Virginia.

The setting of the catastrophe has changed little in the intervening 133 years and can still be seen today. Maj. Gen. Robert E. Rodes described the scene well:

> The Second and Thirtieth North Carolina Regiments, of Ramseur's brigade, were on outpost duty at the river, the former, numbering about 332 effective total. . . . [T]he bulk of the [2nd] regiment was placed partly in rifle-pits and partly deployed, so as to command Kelly's Ford and the site of the enemy's pontoon bridge, used on their former crossing. The Thirtieth North Carolina Regiment, numbering about 500 men, was in reserve protecting the solitary battery (Napoleon) under my

149. Watkins, *Movement of the 14th North Carolina*, p. 19.
150. Betts, *Experiences*, pp. 46-47; Schaub, "Memoir," pp. 21-23; and *OR*, vol. 29, pt. 1, pp. 410-411. The Ardrey Diary's dates for the Bristoe Station campaign appear confused.
151. Casualty list of the 30th appended to this book.
152. Betts, *Experiences*, p. 47; Schaub, "Memoir," p. 23.

Cpl. Lawson Knott
Co. G, 30th Regt. N.C.T.
Captured at Kelly's Ford, November 7, 1863

command. The battery and regiment were about three-quarters of a mile from the river in the edge of the nearest woods to the ford.

At Kelly's Ford the bluffs are on the enemy's side [of the Rappahannock], close to the river, and encircle the ground which my outpost force was compelled to occupy. On our side the land for a mile or more from the river bank is cleared and slopes gently to the river.[153]

Five months later, Adjt. Peter W. Arrington described the events of November 7, 1863:

[O]ur regiment being the reserve picket at the Ford supporting the 2nd N.C.T. was ordered to the front as the enemy had advanced in heavy force and was about to cross the river. The regiment under command of Lt. Col. Sillers who had been promoted upon the resignation of Lt. Col. Kell. Advanced about a mile thorough [sic] an open field under a heavy fire of the enemies infantry and artillery attempting to take a position on the banks of the river. In advancing we had to cross a fence that ran obliquely to our line of battle which kept the Regt. very much broken and together with the fact of there being a residence immediately in our front encircled by railings with a garden fence of the same kind, which while it necessarily separated the men, afforded them but little protection. The Lt. Col. after passing the obstructions found it necessary to halt and reform but before he had time to accomplish his purpose, he received orders to withdraw. He ordered the fall back and though wounded and lame made every effort to get all the men to the rear as there a number of buildings on the premises into some of which men had been sent to annoy the enemy by discharging their pieces from the windows etc. while behind others they sought protection with a considerable loss the most of whom were captured. The enemy consisting of one corps crossed the river. We fell back a short distance, deployed as skirmishers for the protection of our artil-

153. *OR*, vol. 29, pt. 1, p. 631.

lery but in a short time Col. Bennett of the 14 N.C.T. commanding Brigade ordered the Regs to be deployed on a line farther to the right when the enemy were advancing and this time we stopped and held them in check until night came to our relief. It was here that our adjt. (now q.m. [Fred Philips]) received a very painful wound through his left thigh. Lt. Col. Sillers comdg the Regt rec'd a wound thorugh [sic] his lungs from which he died two days afterwards in Gordonsville. T'is with the deepest sorrow I record the death of this Christian Citizen, noble soldier and generous friend. Beloved by the entire command, he was a grand and earnest advisor, a good disciplinarian, and a kind friend and perhaps the strongest sentiment of his good heart was his lack of coruption [sic] and devotion to duty. Gentle, quiet, and unassuming, his great affection for kindred, friends and country was as much a part of himself that it seldom found his mouth in words and a stranger would never have fathomed the depth of feelings which lay a deep and powerful current beneath the surface of his Christian character. But alas he is lost alike to his country, his kindred and to us. The Regt withdrew on the night of the 7th from Kelly's Ford and on the night of the 8th reached their old camp at Morton's Ford . . .[154]

General Rodes, the divisional commander, was very harsh in his judgment of the 30th's actions on November 7, 1863, at Kelly's Ford:

> The Thirtieth North Carolina, going to the assistance of the Second, was speedily broken and demoralized under the concentrated artillery fire which swept the ground over which it had to march. . . .
> The Thirtieth did not sustain its reputation. It arrived at the mills [on the south bank of the Rappahannock at Kelly's Ford] in great confusion and became uncontrollable. Its leader, Lieutenant-Colonel Sillers, behaved gallantly and did his duty, but many of his men refused utterly to leave the shelter of the houses when

---

154. Record of Events.

he ordered the regiment to fall back. All who refused were of course captured, and hence the large number of prisoners from this regiment.[155]

Careful analysis of the engagement at Kelly's Ford leads one to lay blame for the disaster not upon the gallant men of the 30th, but rather upon the faulty orders of their high command— leaders who failed to foresee the slaughter pen created by the terrain at Kelly's Ford whereupon encircling Union troops on the high ground north of the Rappahannock could overwhelm the 2nd at the Ford and slaughter the 30th advancing to its support. Robert E. Lee indirectly reprimanded Rodes with a typically understated remark for ordering the 30th to advance to the Ford—a reproof all the more stinging, doubtless, for its mildness: "It was not intended to attack the enemy until he should have advanced from the river . . ."[156] Certainly Ramseur could not be blamed as he was absent from the brigade on wedding leave upon November 7.[157] It is doubtful that Ramseur, had he been present, would have led his men into such a trap. The 30th's gallant conduct on so many other occasions shows plainly that responsibility for the disaster at Kelly's Ford cannot easily be laid upon the regiment, and Rodes' comment about the 30th failing to maintain its reputation is patently unfair.

The 30th Regt. N.C.T. suffered its heaviest losses of the war at Kelly's Ford, a total of 181 casualties, including 5 killed, 5 mortally wounded, 20 wounded, 150 captured (10 of whom were wounded), and 1 deserter.[158] The deserter, Pvt. J. N. Ballenton of Company C, was a 38-year-old resident of New Hanover County who on June 14, 1863, was "taken from his shop by a file of men without being allowed an opportunity of seeing his family." He never fired a gun and took the first opportunity of deserting and came into the Union lines at Kelly's Ford on November 8. He was confined at the Old Capitol Prison in Washington, D.C., on November 10, 1863, and died in hospital in Washington on March 13, 1864, of "variola confluenta."[159]

155. *OR*, vol. 29, pt. 1, p. 632-3.
156. *Ibid.*, p. 612.
157. Ramseur to Ellen Ramseur, November 24, 1863, Ramseur Papers.
158. See the regimental casualty roster appended to this book.
159. Manarin and Jordan, *N.C. Troops*, 8:343.

305

Pvt. William H. Peed
Co. D, 30th Regt. N.C.T.
Captured at Kelly's Ford, November 7, 1863

The 30th remained in its old camp at Morton's Ford on the Rapidan for about three weeks. On November 27, word was received that Meade's army was across the Rapidan to the east, and Rodes' division broke camp and marched eastward, first forming line of battle with its right resting near Zoar Church and then just west of Locust Grove. Ramseur's brigade initially formed the division's right flank adjoining Early's division, but was later moved to the division's left flank—partially covering a wide gap between the divisions of Rodes and of Edward Johnson. About 12 o'clock at night, Rodes' division fell back westward from Locust Grove and began entrenching along the north-south ridge just west of Mine Run. Here, from November 28 to December 1, under occasional artillery fire, the Confederates awaited a Union assault which never materialized. On December 2, Ramseur advanced to find the Union forces in retreat across the Rapidan.[160] The Mine Run Campaign cost the 30th only two men captured.[161] The brigade returned to its position at Morton's Ford on December 3, and there it remained in peaceful winter camp for five months until the beginning of the Wilderness Campaign in May, 1864, interrupted only by a Northern sortie across the river at Morton's Ford on February 6, 1864.

Christmas, 1863, brought a time of inward reflection for the men of the 30th who had now been in the army for more than two years and who had seen so many of their comrades fall. William Erskine Ardrey, the new Captain of Company K, the Mecklenburg Beauregards (promoted following the death of Capt. John G. Witherspoon at Kelly's Ford, at which time Ardrey had been on leave back home) reflected sadly:

> The true history of the past year can never be written. Thousands of our brave soldiers have poured out their life's blood and their bones to bleach on the battle-fields, and their names will pass into oblivion, only as the poor widowed mothers will in after years around the hearth stones of the dear old homes tell the sad story to the orphan children. We trust the war cloud will soon

---

160. *OR*, vol. 29, pt. 1, pp. 876-879 (Rodes' report of the Mine Run Campaign) and pp. 886-887 (Ramseur's report).
161. See the regimental casualty roster appended to this book.

pass off and peace will soon be restored, and we all can return to our dear homes and our loved ones, never to hear of war or rumours of wars again in our dear Southland.[162]

---

162. Ardrey Diary.

PART EIGHT

December, 1863 - February, 1865
Morton's Ford, Wilderness & Spotsylvania,
Valley Campaign, and Petersburg

While the 30th was inconclusively marching and fighting along the Rapidan and Rappahannock Rivers in the months following Gettysburg, Colonel Parker was on convalescent leave at home. On December 10, 1863, he was examined by the regimental surgeon, F. M. Garrett, who found Parker still unfit for duty for at least another 30 days on account of wounds received at the battles of Sharpsburg and Gettysburg, ". . .any exposure to cold produces severe inflammation in the wounds."[1] On January 21, 1864, Parker returned to the 30th and resumed regimental command. "We were all so glad to see him, he had been absent a long time," commented Captain Ardrey.[2]

Hd. Qrs. 30th N.C.T.
Jan. 22nd 1864

My dear Wife

You see that I am at my post again; the command seem[s] to be pleased to have me with them, and I am glad to be back; now do not understand me to mean that I prefer to be here, rather than with you and the children, far from it. I had to night rather be under my own roof, and with my family, than to be in President Davis' place; but it [is] just as well to make ourselves contented and pleased with our duties, as be constantly grumbling about them.

I spent one day in Richmond; I subscribed to the daily Sentinel for you; also to the Illustrated News up to the 1st of April 1865; the Sentinel for only six months. Every thing is remarkably high in Richmond. The News is now twenty dollars

1. Compiled Service Record.
2. Ardrey Diary.

per year; the daily Sentinel thirty. I had to purchase some tin ware for my use in camp, it cost me a great deal.

I ordered four sacks of salt to be sent from Petersburg; if you should get them, please let Mr. Pullen know that he can have the three sacks I sent home by <u>Stanly</u>; that which I sent up by Moses is of a better quality and should be kept, so is that which you will receive from Petersburg. Mr. Pullen can have the three sacks I bought in Enfield, for just what they cost me, viz. twenty ($25) five dollars per bushel. Why did you let me forget the peaches Mrs. Burnett sent me; and by the way, I wish you to thank Mrs. Burnett for me. We put no butter in my box either; well, you can send the peaches, and a little butter and some peas by Blount when he comes on.

Will you please tell Hilliard <u>not</u> to take any peas to Enfield to Capt. Whitaker. I have not saved more than the law allows me to keep. I can tell you that rations are scarce up here; we eat but two meals per day. I have'nt [*sic*] your potatoe [*sic*] pudding to sit down to now. The men all look remarkably well. I have no doubt but that a light diet is better for them while in camp.

I handed $300 to Mr. Bridges to be sent to Tarboro for you. I handed him $700 to invest in stock of the Danville R.R. company for us.

It is getting pretty late, so I will close. I wish I could peep in upon you and the dear children to night. Kiss them all for me, and believe me very affectionately your husband

F. M. Parker

———————— ◆ ————————

Hd. Qrs. 30th N.C.T.
Jan 26th 1864

My dear Wife

This is the second letter I have written you since I returned to camp; I am becoming very anxious to hear from you. I wonder if you wish to see me, as much as I do you. I often think of the many hasty words I have given you, and think of them with sorrow and [page torn]; but you must know that I do love you [page torn], and knowing this, you must forgive my many irregularities of temper. I hope to get back with you before very long, to see if I can not control my temper better.

You may wish to know something of our encampment; we are on rolling ground, some eight or ten miles this side [of] the Rapid Ann [Rapidan], with a very high ridge to hide us [from the] view of the enemy; by ascending this [ridge] we can have a full view of their entire encampment; I have not gone on this ridge yet, but intend doing so soon. There is nothing doing in camp now, but the ordinary camp duties. The men are being furloughed now very liberally; twelve from every hundred arms bearing men are allowed to go home. The poor fellows appreciate it, and they richly deserve it. I hope by this system of furloughs that all the men will get home this winter. The army is in fine health and spirits; if the croakers at home were near so true, our affairs would be in a better condition. Our rations are short; we eat only two meals per day; do'nt [sic] you reckon this goes hard with me? but it does not, I get on with it very well. I take breakfast about 9 o'clock A. M., and the other meal about 3 P.M. Would'nt [sic] this be a good idea for the [people at] home to adopt. I will send you a copy of [Genrl.] Lee's order, on the short rations. By the way, I brought no butter with me, please send some by Blount, also the peaches Mrs. Burnett sent me. And thank her for them for me. My trunk is so nearly worn out, that I wish Hilliard to make me a neat, strong box to keep my clothing in. Tell him to take a poplar log to the mill and have it sawed, one half [page torn] the other, and to make a box for me two feet [by one] foot deep, and one foot wide; to put the hinges, [clasp], and iron bands for the corners, which were made for [my] mess chest. I have a pad lock here to go to it. I bought some needles for you in Richmond, will enclose them in this letter.

Tell Mary that I prize the little gourd she gave me, as much as any thing I have; water drinks sweet out of it. I am getting on very well; my provisions are holding out very well, and Dick Hicks is a good cook; he can make a better biscuit than any woman you have; he cooks my peas well done for me too; altogether he pleases me very well; I hope he will continue as he has commenced.

This is delightful weather with us; tell Hilliard he must push his plows to the utmost now, while the weather is good; tell him also to take all the leather in the gin house, and put it in the dairy. When you want your shoes made, let [Hilliard] get the patterns from Isham and cut them [out] for you.

The religious state of feeling in the [army] is very good. Our Chaplain has erected a very comfortable log chapel in which to worship; he holds services several times during the week; [the] men seem very attentive and much in earnest.

You may probably wish to know something of the fate of the Pitt boys; two [of] them Jack and [page torn], with Price, are sentenced to [page torn] on the defenses around Richmond and to wear a ball and chain during the war, and for the first seven days of each month, to be placed in stocks. Buck Pitt, for gallant conduct at Sharpsburg, is released and restored to his company.

I find Peter Arrington here as Sergt. Major of the Regt., he is one of the cleverest young men I know of, and a fine business man. Nearly all the officers of our Brigade have their wives with them. Genl. Ramseur, Col. Grimes, and Maj. Williams.[3] How would you like to come on?

Now how do my children come on? how is Pa's baby, and does she miss her Papa very much? and how is the steer driven, does he drive Pete about the house as much as ever? and my little boy, what is he up to? and [my] little gal too, is she spinning now, or is she busy [with] her books? I hope she will learn both to spin [and] her books also. Has Miss 'Ginny come back to you yet? I hope so, for I should dislike for you to be by yourself.

Write me at once, and let me know how every thing is getting on; write often.

I wrote you last that I had left with Mr. Bridgers $300 to be sent to N.C. for you; I made a mistake, I deposited [it in] Richmond, and took out tax certificates [instead]. These certificates will be received for taxes for this year. I also left $700 with Mr. B. to invest in stocks of the Danville R.R. Co. for me. If you need money, use the interest bearing note which you have, but be sure to collect the interest on it. Kiss all the children for me. Good bye.

---

3. Buckner D. Williams was a 28-year-old resident of Warren County when he enlisted in the "Nat Macon Guards" (which became Company B, 30th Regt. N.C.T.), being appointed 1st lieutenant on or about August 16, 1861, and asst. quartermaster (captain) on September 26, 1861. He was promoted to brigade quartermaster on or about November 20, 1863, and subsequently served in that position on the staffs of Brig. Gens. Stephen D. Ramseur, and William R. Cox. Manarin and Jordan, *N.C. Troops*, 8:322 and 334. Crute *Confederate Staff Officers*, pp. 45 and 61.

your affectionate husband
F. M. Parker

Let Hillard make the box in time for Blount to bring back with him.

As the month of February, 1864, began, the 30th was on picket on the Rapidan at Morton's Ford. Captain Ardrey was reading Wilkie Collins' *No Name*.[4] About 9:00 a.m. on the morning of February 6, the Federals crossed the Rapidan at Morton's Ford. The 30th skirmished with the enemy near the Morton House until Brig. Gen. George H. Steuart's brigade arrived to relieve the regiment. The Confederates were soon in fortifications and ready for battle. Ramseur recklessly exposed himself, riding so near the enemy's lines that they fired a volley of 15 rifles at him, but he escaped. Since Ramseur was wearing a civilian overcoat, a Confederate battery near the 30th refused his order to fire until he pulled off his coat and showed them his epaulettes. Artillery and sharpshooters were engaged all day. The Union forces recrossed the river that night. The next day, the two armies faced each other across the river. "It was certainly a grand sight," Captain Ardrey recorded. General Lee rode up and down the lines several times through the cold and unpleasant weather.[5]

Morale suffered in the bad winter weather, especially as news reached the army about the hardships and growing sentiment for peace back home in North Carolina. Forty-two-year-old Pvt. James L. Green of Company H, who had farmed on Brushy Creek in Cleveland County before enlisting in August, 1863, wrote his wife about a mass desertion that occurred in late February, 1864:

> When we were down on picket, five of our men out
> of the 14 left and went over to the Yankey & 4 out of the
> 30 left & went to the Yankeys, all out of this brigade,
> & two of them was out off my company & I was not

---

4. Ardrey Diary.
5. *Ibid.*; Freeman, *Lee's Lieutenants*, 3:333-334; *OR*, vol. 33, p. 142.

Pvt. James L. Green
Co. H, 30th Regt. N.C.T.
With twin son, George Green

314

Mary Ann Griffin Green
With daughter, Susannah E. Green

315

close too them when it took place. One of them was my best friend. Hunter was my great mate. Hunter & Branch were the men's name that deserted.[6]

On February 28, Rodes' division was sent on a long tiring march in pursuit of raiding Union cavalry under the command of Kilpatrick. Kilpatrick escaped southward and the 30th returned to its camp near Orange Court House. Pvt. James L. Green described the march to his wife:

I had to go on a March some twenty or more [miles]. It was a rain[in]g and a-freezing when I started. It rain all day long & at knight. It a pretty smart snow & we had to ly out and take it. I suffered a good deal with the cold.[7]

Captain Ardrey recalled, "It was extremely cold and we were badly exposed to the bad weather. Our camp seems like home to us."[8]

———————◆•◆◆———————

Hd. Qrs. 30th N.C.T.
March 12th 1864

My dear Wife
When I wrote you last I spoke something of the probability of my being home in a short time. I now only see how much folly there was in my thus expressing myself. In the first place, I have not yet heard from the application I made for leave of absence;

6. Letter from J. L. Green to Mary A. Green, March 4, 1864, in Irene Roach Delpino, *A Broad River Digest* (Philadelphia, Pennsylvania: Omega Press Inc., 1990), p. 272. The two deserters mentioned by J. L. Green by name were Pvt. A. L. Branch, a 43-year-old from Harnett County who enlisted on September 28, 1863, and Pvt. J. R. Hunter, Sr., of Union County who enlisted on September 24, 1864, at age 40. Branch deserted February 25-26, 1864, and Hunter deserted February 28, 1864. James L. Green was captured on May 12, 1864, at Spotsylvania Court House, Virginia, and died at Elmira, New York, on October 4, 1864, of "chronic diarrhoea." Manarin and Jordan, *N.C. Troops*, 8:392-395. I am grateful to Tim Greene of Charlotte for directing me to the James L. Green letters.
7. Delpino, *A Broad River Digest*, p. 272.
8. Ardrey Diary.

but worst of all, Genrl. Lee has issued an order forbidding all leaves of absence to officers, and furloughs to men, for a season; the reason given for this, is that the rail roads are needed for transportation. Whether for Government supplies, or troops is not known. I suppose the order forbidding furloughs will be revoked soon. I hope so at any rate, for we have a good many men yet, who have not gone home in a long time; and who really should go home.

But one thing is certain, that I will for the future, take the news of my leave of absence to you in person, not send it by mail. I confess it has been a sore disappointment to me. Pete Arrington says that I have not been the same man since I made an application for the leave of absence. I had anticipated a season of enjoyment with you and the children; but like all our other calculations, this has failed, at least for the present; it may be in a few weeks that I shall be with you.

Say to Mary that I have received her letter, and will answer it soon. I am very proud of my little girl. Is'nt [sic] it almost time for Jimmy to be writing me a letter? I should be delighted to get one from him.

At last, we have had rain, which causes the roads to be very muddy. I think there is a probability of having more rain or snow soon; so the weather will keep every thing quiet for some time to come. I am afraid that you are giving yourself up to sad feelings too much; I think you had better visit some; go over and see Mrs. Dunn, she will talk you into a lively humour [sic].

You must not write such gloomy letters to me; you will cause me to have the same feelings and views. We must leave every thing in the hands of that Good Being who is able to take care of us.

Our prospects were never brighter, than at present. The army is in the best spirits; surely the people at home should not be despondent.

Now you must write me soon; and with a good, cheerful, long letter. Kiss the children for me.

May the Lord bless and keep you all.

very affectionately your husband
F. M. Parker

Tell Hilliard to use my horse, Harry well; not to have him skinned or rubbed by the plow gear.

Hd. Qrs. 30th N.C.T.
March 17th 1864

My dear Wife

I have recently written you, but I suppose that is no reason why I should not write you again; certainly not, if thereby I can [***] from you a letter in return. Well, I have pretty well given up the hope of getting a leave of absence. Soon after I made the application, Genrl. Lee put a stop to all such proceedings; why, I do not know; the order suspending furloughs, was said to be temporary, but it seems to hold on tolerably well. It is said to be owing to the amount of transportation, which has to pass over the rail roads in Eastern North Carolina; thus no furloughs are allowed just now; but it does seem to me that the roads could soon dispose of any thing to be transported. How long the state of affairs will continue, I can not say. If I can I will go home, but you need not expect me by any means. It is as great a disappointment to me, as it can be to you, but we must learn to bear disappointments. There is nothing certain in the world, except sin and suffering.

I see that the papers are starting the recognition question again. I place no confidence in any thing of the kind. Should France send a minister resident to Richmond, that would not open our ports, nor drive the armies of the enemy from our soil; we must continue to fight, trusting in the justness and righteousness of our cause, and above all in the help of a Just Judge above. I think we have every thing to cheer us up at this time. I am in hopes that the year will end the war.

Well, how does Fred come on? has he become used to the married state yet? I expect he looks forward to the time of leaving his wife, with a good deal of displeasure.

Will you please say to him for me, not to be in a hurry to get back; even the first of April need not [***] him; let his wife know this, and I'll be bound she will manage to retain him. He certainly should not return until he is fully able for duty. If I do not succeed in getting home, I shall send Dick Hicks home for the purpose of bringing back my horse, with Fred; as I understood him to say he should return on horseback.

This is St. Patricks day; the great day with the Irish and the day on which they plant their potatoes; I hope you have planted

318

all yours by this time. I suppose that Hilliard will soon commence planting corn; he certainly should do so by the latter part of this month. The ground is warm and dry, and will be in order to plant early; say to him to plant the low grounds as early as they are in order to plant. And to be sure to have them in good order <u>before</u> he does plant them; the ground is much easier managed before, then after planting; sometimes it is necessary to break the [***] several times, before planting. The great object this year, should be to produce as large a provision crop as possible.

By retaining Stanly there Hilliard might get on very well. In your next, let me know how the wheat and oats in the low grounds, are doing; which or not they are growing. I hope that the crop of wheat will be a fine one, so that you will have a plenty of good flour.

Tell Hilliard to be sure and plant as much of the fresh land in the low grounds, as possible; I mean that which was cut down last winter; it will produce fine corn, if not interfered with by a freshet. I hope I shall not trouble you [page(s) missing]

Governor Vance visited the Army and reviewed Ramseur's Brigade on March 28. Vance gave a four hour long address which greatly pleased the soldiers. Chaplain Betts noted that Vance addressed the North Carolina troops as "Fellow Tar-Heels!" Pvt. Walter Raleigh Battle of Co. F, 4th Regt. N.C.T. wrote his mother on March 29 an interesting account of the speech:

> Yesterday there was a grand review of all the North Carolina troops that in this Corps, by Gov. Vance, including the Cavalry. After the review the troops were all arranged around a stage erected for the purpose in the camp of the Thirtieth Regiment, and he addressed them with a speech of three or four hours in length. He had the whole assembly in an uproar in less than two minutes after he arose. He said it did not sound right to him to address us as "Fellow Soldiers," because he was not one of us——he used to be until he shirked out of

319

the service for a little office down in North Carolina, so now he would address us as "Fellow Tar Heels," as we always stick.[9]

The weeks passed. On March 30, Capt. Seaton Gales, Ramseur's assistant adjutant general, gave a fine lecture in the hall of the 14th Regiment on the moral effects of war. Captain Ardrey noted, "It was certainly a fine address, but it seems that there is not much morality in war, especially to old soldiers."[10]

The men faced the coming campaign with grim determination. On April 5, 1864, 2nd Lt. Archibald A. Jackson of Moore County wrote a manifesto chiding a friend for involvement with the peace movement, defiantly stating in Biblical cadence, "[A]s for me I shal serve Jefferson Davice and Bobb Lee for where-soever they goeth Abraham nor Grant can not come."[11]

On April 11, Colonel Parker left the regiment on leave of absence for 14 days.[12]

Desertion continued to be a problem. On April 28, 1864, Pvt. James L. Green of Company H wrote his wife about witnessing the execution of three men belonging to the brigade and also recounted some of the hardships he was enduring:

> I will say to you that I witnessed a sene yesdardy that I never saw before. I saw three men tied to a stake and shot for disertion. They was marched to the stake by a band of music. The preacher then prayed and they got on their knees and lent their back agains the stake and was tied fast, and they pulled off their hats and they blind folded them, and when the guns fired their heads droped. It looked like they was shot most all to pieces. I never want to see such a sight again. It seemed like I

---

9. Betts, *Experiences*, p. 57; Walter Raleigh Battle to Mother, March 29, 1864, Hugh Buckner Johnston, ed., "The Civil War Letters of George Boardman Battle and of Walter Raleigh Battle of Wilson, North Carolina" (typescript in Wilson County Public Library, Wilson, N.C., 1953), letter no. 27.
10. Ardrey Diary.
11. Unaddressed letter from A. A. Jackson dated April 5, 1864, from Camp 30th NC Troops. Permission to quote this letter given by the letter's owner, Chapel Hill Rare Books, Doug Odell, proprietor.
12. Ardrey Diary.

could not stand it. . . . They put all kinds of punishment
on the soldiers here for disertion. Some wears Barrel
Jackets. Some wears a Ball & chain and put to hard
labor during the war & some rides wooden Hosses and
every other punishment they can think of. . . . My fare
is short. We get one quarter of a pound of Bacon, 1 ¼
corn meal and a little sugar and coffee and rice per day.
I am very often hungry, but I make out the best I can .
. . . I don't have any idea that I can stand the hard
marching we will have to do and drilling. They drill us
very hard. They drill us four hours per day.[13]

This letter was written for Private Green by Pvt. A. T.
Campbell of Moore County who had enlisted in 1861 at the age
of 32. After being captured at Gettysburg, Campbell had been
confined on David's Island in New York Harbor, before being
exchanged in August, 1863. Apparently a bachelor, Private
Campbell appended a note to Green's letter:

Mrs. Green after my respects to you and your family
I will say that I have a notion to go home with Mr. Green
when the war ends & I want you to pick me out a nice
mountain girl for a sweet hart.[14]

Private Campbell would dream in vain of life after the war
with a nice mountain girl. Campbell would be captured at
Spotsylvania Court House with many of his comrades on May
12, 1864, and would die at Elmira, New York, of pneumonia on
March 22, 1865.
The warm spring sun dried the earth. As April, 1864, turned
into May, the soldiers knew that fighting was not far off. The
30th Regiment, as May began, was on picket duty at Raccoon
Ford when word came that the enemy was crossing the river on
May 3 and 4.[15] The war was on again.

13. Delpino, *A Broad River Digest*, p. 273.
14. *Ibid.* Delpino has transcribed the name as A. J. Campbell, but the most
    similar name on the roster is that of A. T. Campbell. Manarin and
    Jordan, *N.C. Troops*, 8:393.
15. Watkins, *Movement of the 14th North Carolina*, p. 21; *OR*, vol. 36, pt.
    1, p. 1081.

Ramseur's brigade remained in place holding the line of the Rapidan from Rapidan Station to Mitchell's Ford for a couple of days before being ordered to rejoin the corps. Ramseur took position en echelon on the left flank of Maj. Gen. Edward Johnson's division. On the morning of May 6, Ramseur was ordered to the Confederate center, arriving on the right of Daniel's brigade of Rodes' division south of the Orange Turnpike near the Chewning Farm just in time for his brigade's skirmishers to repulse a large Union flanking force from Burnside's corps. They drove the Union troops back about a half mile and enabled Ewell's corps to connect with that of A. P. Hill. [16] The losses of the 30th at the Wilderness were relatively light (1 killed, 4 wounded and 2 captured),[17] but the action of Ramseur's brigade on May 6 was important.

The race between Lee and Grant to Spotsylvania Court House was already underway when Lee ordered Ewell to march southward from the Wilderness via Shady Grove Church toward that fateful courthouse.[18] The hot, tiresome, and hurried march on May 8 to the vicinity of the courthouse resulted in many stragglers, but Ramseur's brigade arrived just in time late that afternoon to reinforce the Confederate line at a critical moment.[19]

Ramseur's brigade took position on the western face of the Mule Shoe salient above Spotsylvania Court House. Here the brigade engaged in heavy skirmishing on May 9, 10, and 11. Lee's arrangements to evacuate the position miscarried on May 12 when Union forces stormed into the apex of the salient in the early morning, virtually destroying Maj. Gen. Edward Johnson's division, cracking open the Confederate line and threatening to

---

16. Watkins, *Movement of the 14th North Carolina*, p. 21. *OR*, vol. 36, pt. 1, p. 1081; Bone, "Service," p. 27; Ardrey Diary. Ramseur mistakenly states that the repulse of the Union flanking force by his brigade took place on May 7. The correct date is May 6, 1864. Gordon C. Rhea, *The Battle of the Wilderness, May 5-6, 1864* (Baton Rouge: Louisiana State University Press, 1994), pp. 326-330.
17. See casualty roster appended to this book.
18. *OR*, vol. 51, pt. 2, p. 902. William D. Matter, *If It Takes All Summer, The Battle of Spotsylvania* (Chapel Hill: University of North Carolina Press, 1988), p. 76.
19. Watkins, *Movement of the 14th North Carolina*, p. 22; Ardrey Diary; Walter Raleigh Battle to "My dear Folks," May 14, 1864. Johnston, "Letters of George and Walter Battle," letter no. 28.

roll it up in either direction. It was truly a war-winning moment of opportunity for the Union. At the moment of supreme crisis, Ramseur and his men were thrown into the breach. It would have been hard to find a better brigade for the necessity of the hour.

In the early morning darkness Ewell, very much excited, rode hurriedly up to the brigade's position, on the salient's western face below the breakthrough, and asked the identity of the troops. After determining that the men belonged to Ramseur's brigade, Ewell rode off and orders were sent for the brigade to move out of the works and doublequick to its right (northward) behind Daniel's brigade to the vicinity of the McCoull farmstead.[20]

The gallant and hard-hitting Ramseur deployed his brigade facing generally northward, parallel to the two lines of works which the enemy had taken. Ramseur's four veteran regiments, each commanded by a talented colonel, were arranged from left to right as follows: Risden Tyler Bennett's 14th Regt. N.C.T., Bryan Grimes' 4th, William Ruffin Cox's 2nd, and Francis Marion Parker's 30th. The men were ordered to lie down and Ramseur prepared his men to retake the fallen positions.[21]

Before making the charge, Ramseur told the men that if any did not think he had the nerve to make the charge, he could fall back to the rear and would not be punished. Few took advantage of the offer.[22] As the men were forming for the charge under heavy fire, Ramseur said to Colonel Parker, "Colonel, we have got to charge those works and get them back." Parker replied, "We can do it."[23] It was also while forming for this charge that Pvt. Tisdale Stepp of the 14th Regt. began singing "The Bonnie Blue Flag." He was promptly joined by the men standing around him. Private Stepp was shot by accident by a man in the rear rank before the charge commenced.[24]

---

20. Schaub, "Memoir," pp. 26-27; letter of J. L. Schaub, Co. B, 14th Regt. N.C.T. to "Comrade" O. C. Whitaker, dated June 5, 1909, Julius L. Schaub Collection MS#93, Troup County Georgia Archives, LaGrange, Georgia. Kershaw's brigade extended rightward to take Ramseur's place in the line. *OR*, vol. 36, pt. 1, p. 1072.
21. *Ibid.*, p. 1082.
22. Watkins, *Movement of the 14th North Carolina*, p. 23.
23. Bone, "Service," p. 28.
24. Clark, *N.C. Regiments*, 1:723.

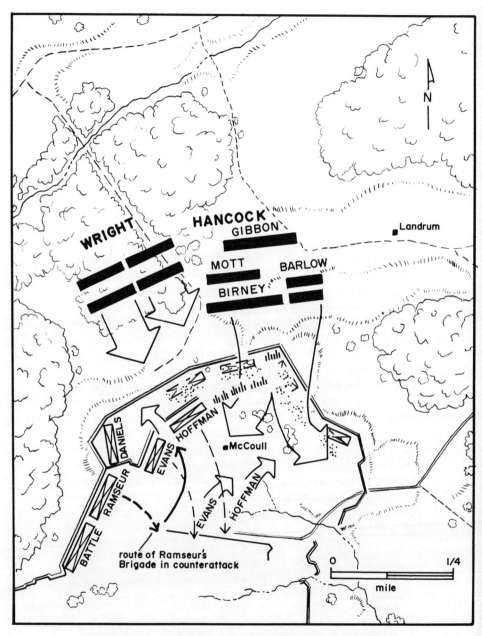

Spotsylvania Court House, Virginia, May 12, 1864
Early morning advance of Ramseur's brigade

Ramseur gave orders that the men were to move slowly, not firing and keeping their alignment, and when the command "Charge" was given, the men were to advance on the run shouting "Charge!" and not to stop until they had reached the farthest line.[25] On command, Ramseur's men charged northward, retaking both lines in front of the brigade, driving the Union forces over the outer Confederate works. "Ramseur on his fiery steed looked like an angel of war."[26] Ramseur's brigade retook a portion of the Confederate works along the northwestern shoulder of the Mule Shoe from Doles' salient running downhill toward the toe of the salient, but only the North Carolinians got as far as the point where the modern park road cuts through the line of Confederate entrenchments. Unfortunately for the Southerners, Ramseur's brigade did not extend far enough to the right to be able to retake the toe of the salient, and the Union troops holding the elevated knoll at the apex of the salient (known to history as the Bloody Angle), were well positioned to pour a destructive enfilading fire down upon Ramseur's men.[27]

The fighting now reached a level of savagery unparalleled in the war. Frequently the contest was hand-to-hand. The struggle was especially severe on the front of the 30th which was nearest to the Bloody Angle. The 30th's adjutant, Peter W. Arrington, was captured by being dragged over the works by his hair.[28] Numerous counter-assaults were launched by Grant. A Union soldier captured the flag of the 30th by stripping it from the staff while the color bearer held the pole:[29]

> The enemy charged our lines in columns, trail arms most of the time. I presume it was Grants idea, that the rear ones would press the front ones over our works. They frequently got on the works. In one of their charges they got the color of the 30th N.C. but the one who first got hold of it, did not carry it far. But some one in the next charge would take it, a short distance to go as the other fellow did. After repeated failures, they

25. *OR*, vol. 36, pt. 1, p. 1082.
26. Clark, *N.C. Regiments*, 1:257.
27. Schaub, "Memoir," pp. 27-28.
28. Clark, *N.C. Regiments*, 1:723.
29. Ardrey Diary.

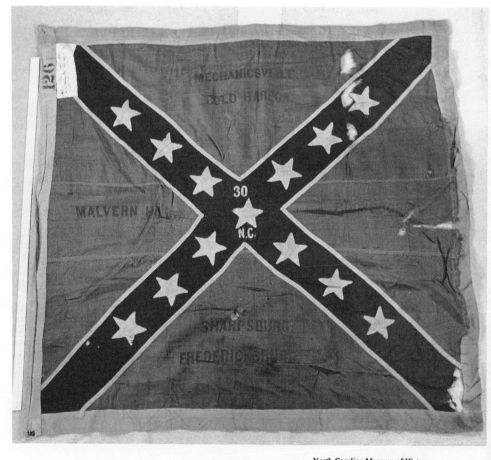

30th Regt. N.C.T. battle flag captured at Spotsylvania Court
House on May 12, 1864, by Pvt. Robert W. Ammerman,
Co. B, 148th Pennsylvannia Volunteers

finally got it over the crest of the ridge. The one who last got hold it I guess was made a hero of. being no braver doubtless than the ones who lost their lives in the effort. At no place during the whole war, did the enemies dead lie thicker.[30]

Pvt. Robert W. Ammerman of the 148th Pennsylvania received the Medal of Honor for the flag capture.[31]

To seek protection from the enfilading fire pouring down from the Bloody Angle, the Confederates took shelter behind a series of traverses behind the front line. These traverses had been built perpendicular to the main line by the previous Southern occupants, creating a series of log pens each of which served as a small fortress and became a miniature but extremely bloody battlefield.[32] Colonel Parker was disabled in the advance, being wounded slightly.[33] Colonel Bennett of the 14th became concerned about the precarious position of the 30th on the brigade's right flank and, according to William Ruffin Cox, the 2nd Regt.'s colonel, Bennett "offered to take his regiment from left to right, under a severe fire, and drive back the

30. Watkins, *Movement of the 14th North Carolina*, p. 24.
31. Returned battle flag with War Dept. No. 126 now in the North Carolina Museum of History, Raleigh, and the museum's file containing an historical analysis of the flag's probable captor by a process of deduction; *OR*, vol. 36, pt. 1, pp. 348 and 1020; and Richard Rollins, ed., *The Returned Battle Flags* (Redondo Beach, California: Rank and File Publications, 1995), p. 12 and in the North Carolina section of the 1905 Confederate Veterans Re-Union publication, "The Flags of the Confederate Armies" reprinted in the book. I am grateful to Curator Tom Belton of the North Carolina Museum of History for his help on the flags of the 30th Regiment.
32. Col. Risden Tyler Bennett of the 14th Regiment in Clark, *N.C. Regiments*, 1:724. John H. Worsham, *One of Jackson's Foot Cavalry* (New York: The Neale Publishing Company, 1912), p. 209; Varina Davis Brown, *A Confederate Colonel at Gettysburg and Spotsylvania* (Columbia, South Carolina: The State Company, 1935), p. 135. It is impossible to understand the fighting at the Bloody Angle at Spotsylvania without comprehending the traverses. I am grateful to Robert K. Krick for explaining the traverses to me and for allowing me to read his unpublished manuscript, "'An Insurmountable Barrier between the Army . . . and Ruin:' The Confederate Experience at Spotsylvania's Bloody Angle."
33. Clark, *N.C. Regiments*, 1:724; Ardrey Diary. Parker's May 12 wound is not mentioned in his compiled service record and was apparently not "officially" recorded.

growing masses of the enemy on our right."[34] Having extracted the reluctant permission of Ramseur to go to the 30th's aid,[35] Bennett led his regiment rightward across the traverses. At the time the 14th's movement began, the 30th was "engaged in a hand-to-hand counter in and over the works" with the Federals.[36] Colonel Bennett described the rightward advance:

> Communicating to the regiment about the odds about to be faced, we went down the line and drove into the traverses by a front of fours. Out of there we expelled the enemy, giving him cold steel and other reforms. I can see in my imagination at the head of the column, as it drove into one of these bloody pens, a conscript from Edgecombe county in the very forefront, without a gun, using an iron ramrod as his support and weapon, shouting to his comrades to strike home. The boys had petted the old man, who complained all the time of his rheumatic pains and told the boys neer to run away in a fight and leave him. I think he was tired of life; he perished gloriously. We beat the enemy, a re-inforcement coming to his aid being almost annihilated.[37]

There was little effective shelter against the hail of bullets, and movement beyond the traverses meant death. Five Delaware boys under 20 years of age surrendered to Thomas J. Watkins of the 14th while he was on the brigade's extreme right at the position of the 30th. Watkins ordered them to the rear. According to Watkins:

> They remarked I had as well shoot them where they were as it would be certain death to go out in the fusilade of shot and shell then flying over our heads. But the laws of war are inexorable and I told them my orders. They essayed to go but was killed every one of

---

34. Cox, "Ramseur," p. 240; Schaub, "Memoir," pp. 27-28, also tells of Colonel Bennett's offer to Ramseur as does Bennett himself in Clark, *N.C. Regiments*, 1:724.
35. William Ruffin Cox says, "This hazardous offer was accepted as a forlorn hope. . . ." Cox, "Ramseur," p. 241.
36. *Ibid.*
37. Clark, *N.C. Regiment*, 1:724.

them before they had gone ten paces. Such was war. I never regretted any incident of the whole war more than this one.[38]

To the right of Ramseur, Harris' Mississippi and then McGowan's South Carolina brigades tried to retake the Bloody Angle with charges as brave and reckless as that of Ramseur. The savage fighting at the Bloody Angle went on without pause for 22 hours until 3:00 a.m. on May 13. At that time the Confederates withdrew to a new line at the base of the salient. One soldier of Ramseur's brigade wrote home:

> You would hardly recognize any of us at present. Every one looks as if he had passed through a hard spell of sickness, black and muddy as hogs. There was no one too nice that day to drop himself behind the breast-works. Brigadiers and Colonels lay as low in the trench and water as the men. It rained all that day and night, and the water was from three to six inches deep all along.[39]

The 30th and its fellow regiments of Ramseur's brigade covered themselves with glory on May 12. At least three sources report that General Lee said in person, "Gen. Ramseur, you have saved the Army today," or words to that effect.[40] If Lee did in fact say those words, they were certainly merited. Ewell called the brigade's action, "a charge of unsurpassed gallantry."[41] As an observer of the charge in Daniel's brigade, Sgt. Cyrus Watson of Co. K, 45th Regt. N.C.T., put it, "The first men that came to our assistance was that brigade of North Carolin-

---

38. Watkins, *Movement of the 14th North Carolina*, p. 24.
39. Walter Raleigh Battle to "My dear Folks," May 14, 1864. Johnston, "Letters of George and Walter Battle," letter no. 28.
40. Cowper, *Letters of Major-General Bryan Grimes*, p. 52; letter of J. L. Schaub, Co. B, 14th Regt. N.C.T. to "Comrade" O. C. Whitaker, dated June 5, 1909, Julius L. Schaub Collection MS#93, Troup County Georgia Archives, LaGrange, Georgia; Watkins, *Movement of the 14th North Carolina*, p. 24. Douglas Southall Freeman's judgment was that Ramseur had deserved Lee's compliment: "Seldom in the war had one Brigade accomplished so much in fast, close fighting." Freeman, *Lee's Lieutenants*, 3:448.
41. *OR*, vol. 36, pt. 1, p. 1072.

ians commanded by the peerless Ramseur. This brigade always seemed to be in the right place at the right time."[42] The events of May 12, 1864, perfectly support Watson's comment. Ramseur had his men up early that morning, and they had kept their powder dry, unlike the men of Johnson's division holding the apex of the salient, where the breakthrough occurred.[43] Ramseur's brigade stemmed the Federal tide at the critical moment, and Ramseur had his brigade's gallantry, and well as his own leadership, to thank for his promotion to major general less than three weeks later on June 1, 1864.

The price of such glory, however, was heavy. The losses were appalling. The 30th Regiment lost 45 dead, including 31 killed outright and 14 who eventually succumbed to their wounds, 40 wounded who were not captured and 84 captured, including 4 wounded, a total loss of 169.[44] Many of the wounded must have had experiences similar to that of Pvt. John W. Bone of Company I who was severely wounded (by being shot through the right breast and lungs with the ball coming out beside his backbone and lodging in his clothes) in the May 12 morning charge of Ramseur's brigade. He then lay between the lines after the Confederate withdrawal on the morning of Friday, May 13, exposed to the weather and a crossfire, only managing to crawl back to the Southern lines on Sunday, May 15. Bone, though wounded himself, mourned the May 12 death of his company commander, Capt. James I. Harris, who had written a lengthy account of the Gettysburg Campaign in a letter home to Lt. Burton Williford the previous August.

After the Confederate withdrawal to the base of the salient, Grant pulled back also, leaving Lee with the need to determine the Union position. Believing Grant was moving to his right, Lee sent Ewell's corps on a reconnaissance which carried his men on a northwestward swing and then eastward on May 19. Ramseur's brigade led the way. Colliding with Union Second

---

42. Clark, *N.C. Regiments*, 3:51.
43. James A. Walker, "The Bloody Angle," in *The Southern Historical Society Papers* (reprint: Wilmington, North Carolina: Broadfoot, 1990), 21:235-6.
44. See the casualty roster appended to this book. The records do not make it absolutely clear, but some of the Spotsylvania casualties of the 30th regiment must have been incurred on days other than May 12, particularly May 19 when the regiment took part in the battle of Harris Farm.

Corps Heavy Artillery units—inexperienced in combat but superior in numbers to Ewell—Ramseur initiated the action, later known as the battle of Harris Farm, because he feared awaiting a Union assault could be disastrous. After a swift advance, Ramseur realized that both his flanks were about to be enveloped, so he pulled back, and the day closed with a fierce three or four hour standup fight at close range in a drenching rain until Ewell withdrew at nightfall. Ewell lost 900 men.[45] Among May 19th's most significant losses was the 30th's Col. Francis Marion Parker, shot through the abdomen on the right side.[46] The wound would disable him from service with the Army of Northern Virginia for the remainder of the war.

On May 20, Colonel Parker, in a very weak condition, started for Richmond in an ambulance with the wounded Lt. Col. E. A. Osborne of the 4th Regiment. Parker's brother-in-law, Fred Philips had charge of the wagon train. Osborne recalled:

> The day was hot and we were parched with fever and thirst; but he supplied us from time to time with refreshing draughts of buttermilk and ice which the good people of the country gave him. It was served in a horse-bucket; but never was sweeter or more refreshing draughts served, nor men more grateful than we were.[47]

The 30th moved to Hanover Junction on May 22 and entrenched until May 27 when the brigade took position at Pole Green Church on Topotomoy Creek, north of Mechanicsville, later moving to a place on the Mechanicsville Road about seven miles from Richmond on May 29. On May 30, the brigade, temporarily under the command of the 14th's Colonel Bennett, moved on the enemy's left flank and engaged them at Bethesda Church. During the night of May 30, the brigade withdrew and fortified a new line. The 30th discovered on June 2 at midnight that the enemy was retiring from the regimental front. The 30th captured a line of sharpshooters left to hold the abandoned works. Pursuing the retiring enemy for one and half miles, they

---

45. *OR*, vol. 36, pt. 1, pp. 1072 and 1082. Matter, *If It Takes All Summer*, pp. 316-325; Walter Raleigh Battle to Mother, May 25, 1864. Johnston, "Letters of George and Walter Battle," letter no. 29.
46. Compiled service record, Francis Marion Parker.
47. Clark, *N.C. Regiments*, 1:274.

Pvt. John T. Nichols
Co. D, 30th Regt. N.C.T.
Captured at Cold Harbor, June 3, 1864

were found drawn up in a strong line of battle across the Mechanicsville Road and a sharp engagement occurred. Here, on June 2, Captain Ardrey of Company K, the "Mecklenburg Beauregards," received his first wound of the war. That morning he fell asleep in the works and dreamed he was wounded in the head with a minié ball. In the engagement that evening his dream came true, except he was struck by a shell fragment. All thought Ardrey was killed, but the wound was not fatal. After receiving the ministrations of Dr. Briggs at the field hospital, who offered him a nice breakfast and a drink of whiskey, and being cared for at Moore's Hospital for officers in Richmond by Drs. Mason and Sherrod and Miss Cassie Gibbon of Charlotte, Ardrey was sufficiently recovered to rejoin the 30th in the Shenandoah Valley on July 21. The 30th and the other troops of Rodes' division held the Union right flank in place on June 3, and prevented it from giving assistance to Grant's other corps assaulting Lee's line during the battle of Cold Harbor.[48]

Major organizational changes were necessitated in the Army of Northern Virginia by the casualties of May, as well as certain failures in command. Upon Ramseur's June 1 promotion to major general, he was given command of Early's division while Early assumed command of Ewell's corps. William Ruffin Cox, colonel of the 2nd Regt. N.C.T., a native of Halifax County and Parker's junior in age by nearly five years and in rank by 18 months, was promoted to brigadier general on May 31 and placed in command of Ramseur's former brigade, including the 30th. The brigade's temporary commander, Colonel Bennett, was wounded in the action on June 2, 1864.[49] After attempted flank marches failed on June 6 and 7, the brigade was moved on June 11 to the vicinity of Gaines' Mill where it remained in reserve until the morning of June 13.[50]

48. Ardrey Diary; Record of Events, Companies A and C, 30th Regt. N.C.T.; Schaub, "Memoir," p. 29; R. Wayne Maney, *Marching to Cold Harbor: Victory & Failure, 1864* (Shippensburg, Pennsylvania: White Mane Publishing, 1995), pp. 123-124.
49. Warner, *Generals in Gray*, p. 65; Ardrey Diary; Bennett in Clark, *N.C. Regiments*, 1:727; Manarin and Jordan, *N.C. Troops*, 5:393.
50. Schaub, "Memoir," pp. 29-30. Captain Ardrey of Co. K of the 30th was wounded on June 2 with a head wound he had dreamed about the morning before and did not rejoin the regiment until July 21. (The actual event differed from his dream only in that the wound was by a shell

Capt. William M. B. Moore
Co. F, 30th Regt. N.C.T.
Killed at Cedar Creek, October 19, 1864

334

At 3 a.m. on June 13, Cox's brigade took up a line of march toward Louisa Court House, heading for Lynchburg and the Shenandoah Valley where Early's corps had been directed by Lee in order to stop Hunter's depredations. On the 16th the brigade arrived at the Rivanna River near Charlottesville, having marched over 80 miles in four days. Lynchburg was reached on June 18.[51]

Due to his wounds, the paths of Francis Marion Parker and the 30th now diverged permanently, but Parker's interest in and concern for his regiment remained. On June 18, 1864, Parker wrote from home to Brig. Gen. W. R. Cox about his concern for the vacancies in the lower field offices of the regiment, recommending the 30th's Capt. W. M. B. Moore of Co. F for lieutenant colonel and Capt. D. C. Allen of Co. C for major. Parker admitted that his action in making these recommendations was unofficial but added, "In fact, I do not see how this matter can well be attended to unless I do it, although not present with the command." Parker pointed out that the gentlemen he was recommending were well known to Cox and the entire brigade "as skillful and competent officers." Parker added a postscript, stating that if any scruples arose about promoting Moore and Allen over more senior captains of the regiment, "I can only say that I have good and sufficient reasons for so doing."[52]

Neither promotion was ever made and the 30th finished out the war under the command of a company grade officer, usually either Captains Allen, Ardrey or McMillan. Captain Moore was recovering from a wound received on May 8 at the time of Parker's letter to Cox and would later be killed at Cedar Creek in October.[53]

---

fragment and not a bullet.) Ardrey Diary, June 2 - July 21, 1864. Schaub was wounded in the leg on May 19, Schaub, "Memoir," p. 28, but does not seem to have fallen out. His itinerary continues during Ardrey's absence and is relied on for that time period.

51. *Ibid.*, p. 30.
52. William Ruffin Cox Papers #4286, Southern Historical Collection, University of North Carolina.
53. Clark, *N.C. Regiments*, 2:502-3; Manarin and Jordan, *N.C. Troops*, 8:372. The captaincy of David Charles Allen of Company C, the "Brunswick Double Quicks," dated from May 2, 1862, and that of William M. B. Moore from March 10, 1862. Manarin and Jordan, *N.C. Troops*, 8:342 and 372. Although the name is somewhat garbled, it appears from the Ardrey Diary, September 8, 1864, that Capt. John

At daylight on June 19, the brigade set off from Lynchburg in pursuit of Hunter, reaching Liberty, 25 miles away over rough roads. On the 20th the brigade followed Hunter into Buford's Gap and on the 21st it advanced to Big Lick and then to "Hanging Rock Pass," where Hunter finally escaped. The brigade had been without rations for two days, marching 20 and 25 miles per day. On June 22, the men rested.[54]

On June 23, the brigade marched for Staunton via Buchanan. On their way through Lexington on Saturday, June 25, 1864, Early's men solemnly marched past Stonewall Jackson's grave. It was a scene of Homeric resonance. Mecklenburg County's Sgt. Aaron Leonidas DeArmond of Company K, 30th Regt., recorded the memorial march in his diary:

> Came to Lexiton and Jacksons corps went through the graveyard whair Jenerall Jackson lay and hornerd his grave by coming to reverse armes and past out through the graveyard through the proses till we came out in the street. then to a rite sholder shift arms.[55]

Cornelius McMillan of Company E, the "Duplin Turpentine Boys," took command of the 30th Regiment upon his return to the regiment on September 8, 1864, following his recovery from a wound. Having been elected captain on August 28, 1861, it appears that he was the 30th's senior captain, outranking Moore and Allen. Parker's opposition to McMillan's command of the regiment probably arose from McMillan's court martial for conduct unbecoming an officer on or about October 28, 1862, and his public reprimand in front of the regiment with suspension from his command for one month. Manarin and Jordan, *N.C. Troops*, 8:362. The inspection report of Cox's brigade for September 30, 1864, discussed below, shows Captain McMillan to be in command of the 30th, as he was to be intermittently until the end of the war. In Clark, *N.C. Regiments*, 4:462, Brig. Gen. William Ruffin Cox commented with regard to Captain McMillan that "[h]is promotion was marred by the want of that one essential of a commanding officer, 'discipline,' yet he was otherwise faithful and diligent in the discharge of his duties." One of the few candid glimpses of Captain McMillan is that given by Capt. W. E. Ardrey in a diary entry dated Feb. 1, 1864: "I am tenting with Capt. McMillan and Dr. Lawson, having a lively time of it as they are full of fun." William Ruffin Cox refers to Moore as "Major Moore" and tells of his death at Cedar Creek, "before he received his promotion," indicating perhaps that he, Cox, had at least followed Colonel Parker's suggestion and recommended Moore for promotion to major.

54. Schaub, "Memoir," p. 30.
55. DeArmond Diary.

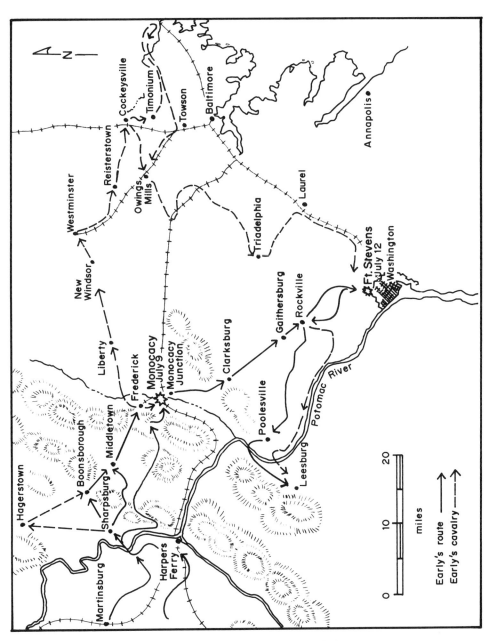

Early's raid into Maryland and the
District of Columbia, July 1864

The 30th arrived in Staunton on June 27 with half of the men barefoot. On June 28, less than two months after fighting with their backs against the wall for their very survival at Spotsylvania, Cox's men started northward down the Shenandoah Valley on a march which in the next two weeks would carry them to the very suburbs of Washington. "What a tramp!" recalled Chaplain Betts.[56] They reached Winchester on July 2 and marched 24 more miles on July 3 to Leetown. On July 4 they marched to Harper's Ferry which the enemy evacuated that night. After helping themselves to the provisions there, the brigade marched at night to Shepherdstown and crossed the Potomac early on July 6, the regiment's third crossing of that river in 22 months.[57]

On July 7, now in Maryland, Cox's brigade marched through Rohersville toward Cramptons Gap, skirmishing with the enemy. On July 8, the brigade marched through the gap to Jefferson and bivouacked, and July 9, they met the enemy at Monocacy Junction and took position on the left of Ramseur's division (Cox's brigade continued to be a part of Rodes' division while Ramseur, upon his promotion to major general, had taken command of a division composed of the North Carolina brigades of Brig. Gens. Robert D. Johnston and William G. Lewis and the Virginia brigade of Brig. Gen. Robert Lilley). General Gordon's division crossed the Monocacy River, outflanking the Union left and causing the Union forces to fall back. Cox's brigade joined in the pursuit, marching at daylight and travelling 20 miles before camping 4 miles from Rockville on the Georgetown Pike.[58] The 30th Regiment suffered only one casualty at Monocacy, Pvt. James M. Rackley of Company I who was captured.[59]

On July 11, the brigade again marched at daylight. It was a very hot day and the men were covered in clouds of dust, many falling out along the line. Around noon the column arrived in sight of Washington, in the vicinity of Fort Stevens and Fort DeRussy. Rodes' division, being in front, immediately formed line of battle and threw out skirmishers. Sgt. Aaron Leonidas

---

56. Betts, *Experiences*, p. 60.
57. Schaub, "Memoir," p. 30.
58. *Ibid.*, p. 31.
59. Casualty roster appended to this book.

DeArmond of Co. K, 30th Regt. N.C.T., recorded the events of July 11:

> ... landed at the District, District of Columbia, at 11 a clock and Sent out our Sharp Shooters and they open fiar uppon there fortificatn and the yankeys open there canon uppon our lines of battle and that knight our Regt. was Set out on pickett.[60]

Hesitancy about attacking such heavily fortified works caused the Confederates to pause long enough for Union reinforcements to arrive on the scene and force Jubal Early to refrain from launching an assault on July 11.[61] On July 12, the men were under arms at daybreak, being issued 40 rounds, but things were generally quiet along the line of Cox's brigade, except for the occasional firing of artillery, until the middle of the afternoon. Being "Set out on pickett" in front of the brigade, however, the soldiers of the 30th were probably engaged in skirmishing as the day wore on and very likely among the Confederates who fired on President Abraham Lincoln when he mounted the parapet of Fort Stevens to watch the fighting.[62] Late in the afternoon, the enemy advanced. The line of 30th Regiment skirmishers was driven in and the 14th Regiment drove back a heavy reconnoitering force.[63] Sgt. DeArmond described the events of July 12 in his diary:

> Still on picket and at 6 o clock the yankys advanced in a line of battle and droave our pickets back for 400 yards
> Then we rec'ied reanforsemints and drove them back to whare we had our first a stabbeshed line and hit them till a bout midknight then our Army commenced fauling back and march all knight[64]

60. DeArmond Diary.
61. Schaub, "Memoir," p. 32; B. F. Cooling, *Jubal Early's Raid on Washington 1864* (Baltimore, Maryland: The Nautical & Aviation Publishing Company of America, 1989), pp. 117-124.
62. *Ibid.*, pp. 141-143.
63. The diary of Major Joseph Harrison Lambeth, 14th Regt. N.C.T., (ViHMss5: 1L1765:1, Virginia Historical Society, Richmond, Virginia), hereinafter referred to as Lambeth Diary. See, report of action of July 12, 1864, by Jubal Early in *OR*, vol. 37, pt. 1, pp. 348-9.
64. DeArmond Diary.

The enemy suffered a loss of nearly 300 in killed and wounded.[65] The 30th Regiment suffered 9 casualties at Fort Stevens, including 2 killed, 1 mortally wounded, 1 mortally wounded and captured, 2 wounded and captured, and 3 captured.[66]

Cox's brigade began retreating from the Washington defenses about 11:00 p.m., on July 12. Major Lambeth of the 14th Regiment remarked that he "was never so sleepy in his life," during this all night march. The troops halted to rest for ten minutes each hour. Chaplain Betts of the 30th tried to sleep in a cemetery along the road, but tied the reins of the two horses under his charge to his arm through a fence to keep the horses from being stolen. He was soon awakened from his slumbers when one horse apparently bit the other. On July 13, the men of the 30th marched through Rockville and Poolesville toward the Potomac. On the morning of July 14, after passing through Poolesville, the brigade waited for the wagon train to get over the river and then crossed the Potomac at White's Ford, halting near Leesburg for the rest of that day and also the next.[67] On July 16, the brigade marched 4 miles to Leesburg and then took the Berryville Pike toward Snicker's Gap. The enemy caught the column about 4 miles from the Gap and took 20 wagons before being driven off. Passing through Snicker's Gap, the brigade encamped beyond.[68]

On July 17, the brigade crossed the Shenandoah River at Castleman's Ferry and camped near Rock Ford in the vicinity of Berryville.[69] On July 18, the enemy crossed the river at Parkers Ford. Gordon's and Echols' divisions moved up in the enemy's front while Rodes' division advanced on the left. About two hours before sunset, they had a "sharp and bloody engagement."[70] Beating the Northerners in a foot race for a stone wall lying half way between the opposing lines, the brigade poured a heavy fire into the enemy and repulsed them, capturing three

65. Schaub, "Memoir," p. 52; Cooling, *Early's Raid on Washington*, pp. 145-155.
66. Casualty roster appended to this book.
67. Schaub, "Memoir," p. 32; Lambeth Diary; Betts, *Experiences*, pp. 60 and 61.
68. Schaub, "Memoir," p. 32; Lambeth Diary.
69. Schaub, "Memoir," p. 32; Lambeth Diary.
70. Schaub, "Memoir," p. 32; Lambeth Diary; Clark, *N.C. Regiments*, 1:172.

Sgt. Maj. Francis Michael Fitts
30th Regt. N.C.T.
Wounded at Snicker's Gap, July 18, 1864

flags and driving them back across the river.[71] The 30th Regiment suffered 7 fatalities at Snicker's Gap on July 18 along with 14 wounded and 1 captured.[72] Sgt. Aaron Leonidas DeArmond was mortally wounded in the Snicker's Gap fight.

On the night of July 19, the brigade marched through Millwood to the Valley Pike at Newtown, moved to Middletown on July 21, crossed Cedar Creek toward Strasburg, and rested on July 23. On July 24, Rodes' division fought the battle of Kernstown against Union forces under Crook. When Ramseur's division fell upon the enemy's left flank, Rodes attacked and routed the Federals, pursuing them as far as Stephenson's Depot, 6 miles beyond Winchester. Besides taking part in the battle, Rodes' division marched 27 miles that day. On July 26, the brigade marched to Martinsburg, tearing up the railroad line in the vicinity on July 27 and 28.[73]

Election for Governor was held in the 30th Regiment on July 27, 1864. Vance received 77 votes and Holden 3.[74]

On July 29, the brigade advanced to Williamsport, then marched back to Martinsburg again on July 30. On July 31, the brigade travelled to Bunker Hill where it rested until August 4 when it marched to Williamsport, crossing the Potomac back into Maryland on August 5 and taking position near St. James College. On August 6, the brigade recrossed the Potomac at Williamsport and Marched back towards Martinsburg, reaching Bunker Hill on August 7.[75]

Sheridan was now in command of the Union forces in the area, and on August 10 he began a southerly movement from Halltown to Berryville intended to force Early to withdraw from the lower Valley. In response, Cox's brigade marched to just east of Winchester and formed line of battle, moving on August 11 toward Newtown. On the morning of August 12, the brigade moved to Hupp's and Fisher's hills near Strasburg in the afternoon. There it held position until August 17 when the enemy retreated upon the arrival of Kershaw's division, fresh from Richmond, which took position at Front Royal on Sheridan's left flank. The Confederates pursued, taking posi-

---

71. *Ibid.*, 1:260.
72. Casualty roster appended to this book.
73. Schaub, "Memoir," p. 33.
74. Ardrey Diary.
75. Schaub, "Memoir," p. 33.

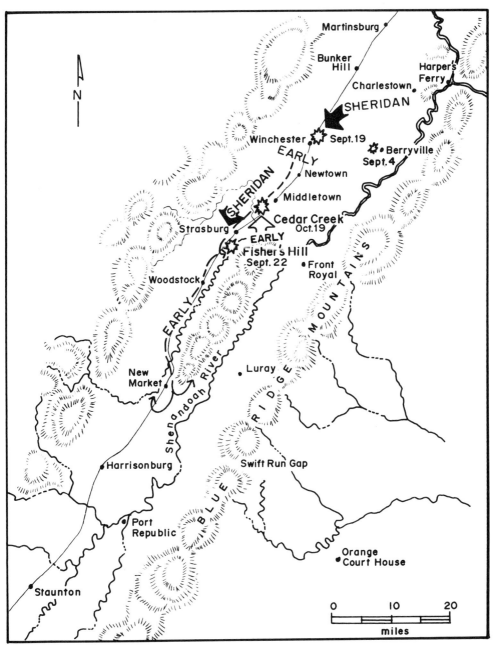

The Shenandoah Valley Campaign, 1864

tion beyond Winchester on August 18. On August 19, Cox's brigade marched to Bunker Hill and on August 21 toward Harper's Ferry, meeting Sheridan's force near Cameron's Depot and skirmishing for the rest of the day.[76] In this action, the 30th Regiment lost 5 killed and 9 wounded.[77]

On August 22, the enemy retreated and the brigade pursued them through Charles Town, bivouacking on August 24. On August 25, the brigade marched through Leetown, came upon a large force of enemy cavalry, and drove it back through Shepherdstown and across the Potomac. On August 27, the brigade marched to Bunker Hill and onto Smithfield on the 29th to drive back a force attacking the Confederate cavalry. On August 31, the brigade marched to Martinsburg and drove off a cavalry force, returning to Bunker Hill. On September 2, the brigade marched to Stephenson's Depot to protect the Confederate trains, but marched right back to reinforce Confederate cavalry which had been attacked.[78]

On September 3, the brigade marched to Bunker Hill where it drove back an enemy cavalry force. On September 4, the brigade moved to the vicinity of Berryville, and on September 5 back to Stephenson's Depot where it met another large force of cavalry and again drove it back toward Martinsburg. Sheridan at this time was moving his army southward from Charles Town and taking position in the vicinity of Berryville across Opequon Creek from Early.[79]

The two armies now settled into a two week waiting game opposite one another. Cox's brigade continued to fend off cavalry probes. After a quiet day on September 6, Cox's brigade moved out to meet a cavalry demonstration, and after quiet days on September 9 and 10, the brigade marched by Bunker Hill to Darksville and drove back a large body of cavalry on September 11. The situation was quiet on September 12, and the brigade marched towards Berryville and back to Stephenson's Depot on

---

76. *Ibid.*, p. 24. This phase of the 1864 Shenandoah Valley Campaign is discussed in Jeffrey D. Wert, *From Winchester to Cedar Creek, The Shenandoah Campaign of 1864* (Carlisle, Pennsylvania: South Mountain Press, Inc., 1987), pp. 29-35.
77. Casualty roster appended to this book.
78. Schaub, "Memoir," p. 34-35.
79. *Ibid*; Wert, *Winchester to Cedar Creek*, pp. 38-39.

September 13. On September 15 and 16, the brigade remained in camp, while on September 17 it marched to Bunker Hill and, on September 18, back again to Stephenson's Depot.[80]

In the meantime, on September 15, the Army of the Valley was seriously weakened by the departure for Richmond of Kershaw's First Corps Division and Cutshaw's artillery battalion.[81] On September 19, Sheridan crossed Opequon Creek and attacked Early in the battle of Winchester. Cox's brigade was pulled back from Stephenson's Depot, and, arriving before Winchester about 9 a.m. as a part of Rodes' division, held the center of the Confederate line between Ramseur's division on the right and Gordon's division on the left. Cox's brigade was in the thick of the fight, as usual. Early on in the fighting, Colonel Bennett of the 14th Regiment was captured and General Rodes was killed. J. L. Schaub of the 14th recalled:

> Rodes was a few paces behind us. His fine black horse, which he had ridden so long, got excited under the bursting shells, and the General held him with difficulty. But it was but a few minutes until a piece of shell struck General Rodes on the head, knocking him to the ground, where he died in a few minutes.[82]

After a fierce all day battle, the Confederates were eventually forced to retire due to Union pressure on their left flank, coming from the north.[83] The 30th Regiment lost 17 casualties at Winchester on September 19: 1 mortally wounded, 7 wounded without being captured and 9 captured, three of whom were wounded.[84] Early's army retreated to Fisher's Hill near Strasburg, marching all night. During the retreat from Winchester, the 30th's Chaplain Betts, already deeply saddened by the defeat and his viewing of General Rodes' body in a private home in town, came upon an affecting sight:

---

80. Schaub, "Memoir," p. 35.
81. "Official Diary of First Corps," in *The Southern Historical Society Papers* (reprint: Wilmington, North Carolina: Broadfoot, 1990), 7:510.
82. J. L. Schaub, "Gen. Robert E. Rodes," *Confederate Veteran*, vol. 16, no. 6 (June, 1908):269.
83. Schaub, "Memoirs," p. 35-36; Ardrey Diary; Wert, *Winchester to Cedar Creek*, pp. 94-97.
84. Casualty roster at end of this book.

Riding along and very sad, at midnight, I overtake one or two thousand Federal prisoners. They began to sing, "We are going home to die no more." My heart was touched. I shed tears as I thought many of them would die in Southern prisons.[85]

Jubal Early's army took up what appeared to be a strong position at Fisher's Hill. But on September 22, 1864, a series of blunders allowed Union flank maneuvers to succeed. A Federal force under Crook turned the Confederate left flank by climbing over Little North Mountain, routing the cavalry under Lomax which held the left of the Confederate line. About 3 p.m., Brig. Gen. Bryan Grimes spotted the flank maneuver as it was taking place and urged Ramseur, now in command of Rodes' division, to send assistance to the cavalry, but Ramseur, uncharacteristically, failed to act in time. When the Union attack came about 4:00 p.m., the cavalry broke immediately.[86] While Grimes resisted the onrushing Northerners with his brigade, Cox's brigade was hurried to the left and took position on a ridge facing east. However, the line to the right and rear of the brigade gave way in confusion just as the brigade was about to give Crook's men a "warm reception," and orders were received to retreat by the right flank, which was done in good order.[87] William Ruffin Cox recounted the closing actions of his brigade at Fisher's Hill:

> On moving to the left I had a brisk skirmish with a part of Crook's men, but did not encounter his main force. From the firing in the direction of our line it was soon apparent that our army was falling back. I now met General Lomax with a part of his men, and he kindly conducted me by the nearest route to the turnpike over which we were retreating. It was full dusk when we reached the road. Colonel A. S. ["Sandy"] Pendleton, an admirable officer and an accomplished gentleman of the corps staff, met me and requested that my brigade be thrown across the road to cover the retreat. The brigade was promptly formed, advanced rapidly to a

85. Betts, *Experiences*, p. 64.
86. Cowper, *Letters of Major-General Bryan Grimes*, p. 69.
87. Schaub, "Memoirs," p. 37.

fence, where it met the Federals in a hand-to-hand encounter, repulsed them and stopped the pursuit for the night. It was near me that Colonel Pendleton, whom I had intimately known when on Jackson's staff, fell mortally wounded.[88]

The 30th Regiment lost 15 casualties at Fisher's Hill: 2 wounded and 13 captured, of whom 1 was wounded.[89] Another Southern retreat up the Valley now took place through and beyond Woodstock. On September 23, the retreat continued to Mount Jackson and on to Rude's Hill. After making a stand on September 24 and retiring before the enemy for 9 miles in line of battle, Cox's brigade marched 5 miles on the Port Republic road and camped. On September 25 the brigade marched toward Port Republic, crossed the river, and took position near Brown's Gap. On September 26, sharp skirmishing with enemy cavalry occurred, and on September 27, the brigade drove off a force of enemy cavalry from Port Republic.[90]

Following the disaster at Fisher's Hill, General Lee sent Kershaw's division back to the Valley to bolster Early's forces. Kershaw came up from Swift Run Gap and joined Early about noon on September 26.[91] Perhaps cheered by the arrival of reinforcements, the Confederates were ready for some sight-seeing in spite of their recent military reverses. The brigade camped near Weyer's Cave, and Chaplain Betts explored the cave along with the band of the 4th Regiment. "Grand sight! Eternal night!" recorded Chaplain Betts. James Columbus Steele of the band recalled, "In the hall called the Ballroom, we played many pieces of music, among which was 'Sweet Home,' 'Vacant Chair,' and others, anything sounded solemn but especially these pieces alluded to. Rev. A. D. Betts, chaplain of the 2nd Regiment enjoyed the music, but tears were streaming down his cheeks. He was a grand man."[92] On September 28, the

---

88. Cox, "Ramseur," p. 251; Wert, *Winchester to Cedar Creek*, pp. 122-123 interprets Cox's account of Fisher's Hill to mean that Cox blundered by wandering too far south to be of any use in defending the Confederate left flank against Crook's onrushing troops.
89. Casualty roster appended to this book.
90. Schaub, "Memoir," p. 37.
91. *OR*, vol. 43, pt. 1, p. 576.
92. Betts, *Experiences*, p. 65; James Columbus Steele, *Sketches of the Civil*

brigade moved to Waynesboro, and on September 29 and 30, it rested.[93]

On September 30, 1864, Cox's brigade was inspected by Capt. W. C. Coughenour, the brigade assistant adjutant general and inspector general. The inspection report states that the 30th Regiment N.C.T., commanded by Capt. J. C. McMillan (of Company E), was in a much depleted state, having only 8 officers and 110 enlisted men present, only about one-sixth of the total of 726 present and absent and about ten per cent of full strength. Twenty-nine enlisted men were absent without leave, and two were under arrest or in confinement. Col. F. M. Parker, among those absent with leave was noted to be in the hospital at Tarboro. The regiment had four cooks. Of particular interest are the regiment's arms, a mixture of .58 caliber Enfields and Springfields and antiquated .69 caliber smoothbores. The 30th had 3,420 rounds of ammunition on hand. Deficiencies were greater in clothing than in accoutrements: 5 cartridge boxes, 3 cap boxes, 51 bayonet scabbards, 25 shoulder belts, 3 waist belts, 58 overcoats, 36 coats, 42 trousers, 35 shirts, 37 drawers, 57 pairs of shoes, 65 boots, 24 stockings, 5 haversacks, 50 knapsacks, and 6 canteens. The men, even after their recent vicissitudes, were noted to have "soldierly" military bearing, good military appearance, and good discipline.[94] It is extremely interesting to note that in this period, the inspection reports for Early's army found that of the 13 brigades in the Army of the Valley, only three, those of Cox, Grimes, and Robert D. Johnston (all from North Carolina), were rated as having good discipline, the other ten being rated as "lax," "bad," or "indifferent." North Carolina's policy of supplying clothing to its own troops probably had lot to do with this disparity.[95]

War especially of Companies A, C, and H from Iredell County, N.C. and the 4th Regimental Band (Statesville, North Carolina: Brady Printing Company, 1921), pp. 39-40.

93. Schaub, "Memoir," p. 37.

94. Inspection report for Cox's brigade, September 30, 1864, National Archives Record Group 109, Microcopy no. 935, roll 10, 33-P-24. I am grateful to Robert K. Krick for his guidance in gaining access to the inspection reports.

95. Theodore C. Mahr, The Battle of Cedar Creek: Showdown in the Shenandoah, October 1-30, 1864, 2nd edition (Lynchburg, Virginia: H. E. Howard, Inc., 1992), p. 15.

On October 1, Early marched to and beyond Mount Sidney, taking position on the Valley Pike. Here the army remained until October 6.[96] While in camp, apparently at Mount Sidney, Brig. Gen. Bryan Grimes penned the following candid and interesting letter to Col. F. M. Parker. Rarely is the historian able to find a document like this letter which pierces the veil of silence which usually falls upon the intrigues of command and really "tells all," at least as Bryan Grimes saw it.

_____ _____, Va.
Oct. 4, 1864

My Dear Col

I regret to learn that your wounds are longer in healing than you had supposed but hope that you might be enabled to return before long. ~~Yesterday~~ My object in writing is to inform you of a conversation held on yesterday with Maj. Genrl. Ramseur in which his purpose was to state that he had written a private communication to Genrl. Bragg requesting that you might be nominated for promotion to Brig. Genrl. with assignment to your old Brigade and to suggest that if you had any political friends, who could support your claims that there would be but little doubt of the appointment. He seemed to think that the Brigade had deteriorated under its present organization and that a change was absolutely necessary. I trust that you will not have to wait much longer for your just deserts.
Doubtless you have heard of our recent

[page 2]

failures in the Valley, and may consider yourself truly fortunate in your absence from the Command. The like of such stampede has never been witnessed in the Army of Virginia, and

96. Schaub, "Memoir," pp. 36-37; Cowper, *Letters of Major-General Bryan Grimes*, pp. 71-72; Jedediah Hotchkiss, *Make Me a Map of the Valley: The Civil War Journal of Stonewall Jackson's Topographer* (Dallas, Texas: Southern Methodist University Press, 1973), pp. 234-235.

if the routs(?) heretofore given the army(?) are to be judged by this of ours, it was only necessary to have pushed the victory to have annihilated the whole Army.

Our men as well as officers are losing confidence in Genrl. Early's ability to conduct a campaign on so large a scale as this has been, but our chief loss has been the death of Maj. Genrl. Rodes, who cannot be replaced. Ramseur is at present in command of the Division and the assignment may be made permanent. He is daring and brave, as you know, but deficient in some other qualifications, but decidedly preferable to any other in this army. If Rodes had lived this disorder would never have occurred. Wishing you speedy recovery, I am in great haste truly your friend,

Bryan Grimes[97]

This letter is a treasure trove of information. First of all, it shows that Grimes and Parker were close friends. This is clearly indicated by the candid nature of the letter. Secondly, it reveals that Ramseur preferred Parker to Cox as commander of his old brigade. Thirdly, it attests a mutual belief of Grimes and Cox, probably discussed by the two of them before, that Ramseur, although brave and daring, was deficient in other qualities, here unstated, but obviously considered important by the two of them in a commander. Fourthly, it testifies to Grimes' admiration for Rodes. And fifthly, it plainly evidences the low morale in the Army of the Valley and its lack of confidence in Lt. Gen. Jubal Early just over two weeks before the climactic battle of Cedar Creek. While it might be thought that such a candid and obviously hastily written communication would be kept confidential by the recipient, as will be seen it was utilized by Colonel Parker—or rather by his "political friends"—to attempt to accomplish the object suggested by Ramseur.

While these intrigues were going on, Sheridan launched a 10 day campaign of torching the farms and fields of the Shenan-

---

97. This remarkable letter from Bryan Grimes to Francis Marion Parker, dated Oct. 4, 1864, is contained within Parker's compiled service record.

doah Valley on September 29. Columns of smoke rose far and wide, infuriating the Confederates.[98]

On October 6, the Army of the Valley moved out from Mount Sidney and arrived at New Market on October 7. The "brave and daring" Ramseur probably spoke for many of the men of his division, including members of the 30th Regiment, when he said in a letter to his brother-in-law, David Schenck, on October 10, "This is a time of great trial. We are called on to show that we are made of the true metal. Let us be brave, cheerful and truthful. Remembering that Might is not Right."[99] On October 12, Robert E. Lee wrote Jubal Early almost imploring him to take the offensive:

> I have weakened myself very much to strengthen you. It was done with the expectation of enabling you to gain such success that you could return the troops if not rejoin me yourself. I know you have endeavored to gain that success, and believe that you have done all in your power to insure it. You must not be discouraged, but continue to try. I rely upon your judgment and ability, and the hearty cooperation of your officers and men still to secure it. With your united force it can be accomplished.[100]

As if anticipating Lee's letter—coincidentally leaving on the day he wrote it—Early led the Army of the Valley northward, with Fisher's Hill being reached on October 13. On the evening of October 18, the 30th moved out of the trenches on Fisher's Hill on a night-long flank march, crossing the North Fork of the Shenandoah River and then picking their way along the river's right bank on the northwestern slope of Massanutten Mountain. Pvt. J. W. Bone recalled, "The way was so narrow and rough that we had to get in one rank and use our guns against the ground to keep from going down the hill too fast." By about

---

98. *OR*, vol. 43, pt. 1, pp. 29 and 577-578; Wert, *Winchester to Cedar Creek*, pp. 143-5.
99. Letter dated October 10, 1864, from Stephen Dodson Ramseur to David Schenck, Ramseur Papers, Southern Historical Collection..
100. *OR*, vol. 43, pt. 2, p. 892. D. S. Freeman discussed Early's decision to advance northward which led to the battle of Cedar Creek in Freeman, *Lee's Lieutenants*, 3:595-596.

4:30 a.m. on October 19, the Confederates were ready to wade the North Fork again and fall upon the left flank of Sheridan's Army. The attack struck like a sledgehammer upon the Northerners. Captain Ardrey recorded, "Pickets waded the Shenandoah and attacked the enemy before they were formed. Some found in their tents and on the sinks."[101]

The battle of Cedar Creek which was fought on October 19, 1864, began as a great Confederate success with the Union army reeling backwards from the dawn flank assault. Jubal Early's failure to press his gains and the afternoon assaults of the Union troops rallied into action by Sheridan ultimately resulted in the collapse the Confederate line. Cox's brigade stoutly held their position, only to be outflanked when Evans' brigade gave way to their left. The cry then became "Flanked, we are flanked!" Some of the brigade then fell back to a stone fence and there fought for an hour until General Ramseur fell mortally wounded. Then all seemed lost and a general stampede began with Cox's brigade being one of the last to leave the field.[102] Pvt. J. W. Bone said, "Every man was looking out for himself. I ran until I was very warm and had to stop and walk. The balls and shells were striking all around me."[103]

The 30th Regt. N.C.T. lost 19 casualties at Cedar Creek, about 16% of its September 30, 1864, strength. These included 2 killed, 1 mortally wounded, 7 wounded and 9 captured, of which 1 was wounded.[104] While fairly small in comparison to losses earlier in the war (77 at Sharpsburg and 115 at Chancellorsville), these were staggering losses in proportion to the 30th's greatly reduced strength in the fall of 1864. Coming on top of the 17 casualties at Winchester and 15 at Fisher's Hill, casualties of these dimensions could not be long sustained.

The disorganized body of soldiers retreated up the Valley, reaching New Market on October 20. Here they remained in camp until November 10. By October 22, Brig. Gen. Bryan Grimes had been placed in command of Rodes' old division following the death of Ramseur.[105] On Oct. 30, 1864, at New Market, Capt. W. C. Coughenour again inspected Cox's bri-

---

101. Bone, "Service," p. 36; Ardrey Diary.
102. Schaub, "Memoir," p. 38. The closing scenes of the battle are described in Mahr, *The Battle of Cedar Creek*, pp. 301-303.
103. Bone, "Service," p. 36.
104. Casualty roster appended to this book.
105. Cowper, *Letters of Major-General Bryan Grimes*, p. 76.

gade. The inspection report shows that the 30th's strength had only been slightly reduced in the intervening month in which the battle of Cedar Creek had occurred, with 5 officers and 100 men present for duty. The military bearing of Cox's whole brigade was noted to be soldierly and their discipline good. The only negative comment made about the 30th Regiment was that its morning reports were made irregularly. The .69 caliber smoothbores had disappeared, and only .58 caliber Enfields were now carried by the regiment. Capt. W. E. Ardrey commanded the regiment which had 3,500 rounds of ammunition on hand, about 35 per soldier. Deficiencies in most areas had been reduced since the September 30 inspection except that the men appear to have had no overcoats or blankets.[106]

The 30th Regiment, along with the rest of Cox's brigade, remained in the vicinity of New Market in the Shenandoah Valley until mid-December, 1864. The day of November 1, 1864, was set aside to commemorate the fallen Rodes and Ramseur. Chaplain Betts preached and noted in his diary that Cox's brigade had lost 305 men killed or died of wounds since departing winter quarters, leaving 300 widows and 105 children.[107] Chaplain Betts ventured to prepare seats for worship on November 9, but the next day, November 10, the whole army marched down the Valley to Woodstock. "So we will never use our seats! God grant we may find seats in heaven," Betts wrote in his diary that night.[108] The army passed Middletown on November 11 and was between Middletown and Winchester on November 12, but the enemy retired, not disposed to fight. Early then retired and the army was back in its camps near New Market by November 14.[109] On November 22, the brigade marched to Rude's Hill and drove back some enemy cavalry.[110]

---

106. Inspection report for Cox's brigade, October 30, 1864, National Archives Record Group 109, Microcopy 935, Roll 11, 10-P-31. Deficiencies of 109 overcoats and 100 blankets are noted. With only 105 present for duty in the 30th Regiment, it is apparent that these items were lacking for almost all personnel. Since the regiment was only deficient 58 overcoats on September 30, it is likely that the increased deficiency was due to heavier items being thrown away in the flight from the battlefield of Cedar Creek.
107. Betts, *Experiences*, p. 68.
108. *Ibid.*, pp. 68-69.
109. Cowper, *Letters of Major-General Bryan Grimes*, pp. 85-86; Schaub, "Memoir," p. 39; Betts, *Experiences*, p. 69.
110. Ardrey Diary; Schaub, "Memoir," p. 39; Cowper, *Letters of Major-General Bryan Grimes*, pp. 86-87.

Cox's brigade was again inspected by W. C. Coughenour on November 30, 1864. Col. F. M. Parker was noted to be still absent in Halifax County, North County, recovering from his wounds. Capt. W. E. Ardrey commanded the 30th Regiment which had augmented its strength by fifty per cent in the past month with six officers and 152 men present for duty. Armed with .58 caliber Enfields, the command was deficient 30 rifles, 67 cartridge boxes and 67 cap boxes. While still, at the onset of winter, deficient 107 overcoats, the number of men lacking blankets had been reduced to 45. Other deficiencies of the 30th Regiment included 48 coats, 91 shirts, 45 pairs of shoes, 41 drawers, 71 boots, 36 stockings, 55 haversacks, 31 knapsacks, and 35 canteens. The entire brigade was noted to have a soldierly military bearing, good military appearance, and good discipline. With respect to personal cleanliness, this notation was made: "Not very neat. It is impossible for the men to get soap to wash themselves or their clothes." It was also noted that damages had not been committed by the men "beyond the destruction of timber for fuel." J. W. Bone wrote about this period in the Shenandoah Valley, "We had but few tents . . . and most of the men's clothes were getting very thin from exposure. We had but little protection from the cold mountain winds that were blowing down upon us."[111]

On December 15, 1864, the 30th and the balance of Grimes' division marched up the Valley through ten inches of snow the men found on the ground in the morning. As the men marched, the snow became a wet mush, soaking their feet. It is not difficult to imagine that the 30th Regiment's 45 shoeless men must have had suffered greatly. That night, trees were cut down log heaps were made, and fires started, around which the men spread their blankets and fell down to sleep. Arriving at Staunton late on December 15, the train cars were not yet ready, so the men had to stand around in the street without a fire until they could be loaded into box cars. Travelling all night on the train, they arrived in Petersburg late on December 16. Marching a mile from the town, the 30th encamped.[112]

Orders were now received to build winter quarters. On December 29, 1864, Capt. W. C. Coughenour again inspected

111. Bone, "Service," p. 37.
112. *Ibid.*, p. 38; Schaub, "Memoir," p. 39; Cowper, *Letters of Major-*

Cox's brigade at "Camp Rodes near Dunlop's Station." The inspector noted, "The men are now building their cabins." The 30th Regt. N.C.T. was under the command of Captain McMillan and its numbers had increased to 10 officers and 179 men present for duty with 184 present at the inspection. The regiment was armed with .58 caliber Enfields and Springfields, being deficient only 6 rifles and having 4,150 rounds of ammunition on hand. Deficiencies in accoutrements included 52 cartridge boxes and 46 cap boxes, and clothing was extremely lacking: 139 overcoats, 120 coats, 174 stockings, and 80 blankets. The brigade continued to be noted for its soldierly military bearing and good military appearance and discipline. It was noted that the men were not very neat due to a want of soap. The inspector also recorded that damages included about 450 rails near New Market. "Impossible to tell who did it. Not settled."[113] This was an interesting concern indeed, given the massive destruction wreaked in the Valley by Sheridan.

As the year of 1864 drew to a close, back in North Carolina, Col. F. M. Parker's "political friends," as Grimes had termed them, set to work to obtain a brigadier generalship for Parker. On December 1, 1864, the following letter was sent to Secretary of War Seddon and signed by the member of "the Administration's party," (presumably those of Gov. Zeb Vance's party) in the North Carolina General Assembly:[114]

———————————— •♦• ————————————

Raleigh, N.C.
December 1st 1864

Hon. Sec. of War:

We would respectfully recommend for promotion Col Francis M. Parker of the 30th N C Troops on the following grounds:
Previous to the war he was a Colonel of Militia was among the first to volunteer in his section, and entered the service as

General Bryan Grimes, pp. 89-90.
113. Inspection report for Cox's brigade, December 29, 1864, National Archives Record Group 109, Microcopy No. 935, Roll 13, 24-P.32.
114. This letter dated Dec. 1, 1864 to the Secretary of War from the members of "the Administration's party" in the North Carolina General Assembly

2nd Lt in the 1st N.C. Regiment but was soon chosen Captain under very flattering circumstances. For his conspicuous gallantry in command at the battle of Big Bethel he was chosen Colonel of the 30th N.C.T. and has continued to command in all the various campaigns to this day, when it finds him the oldest Colonel on active duty in the whole N. Carolina line. He has been three times seriously and dangerously wounded , first at Sharpsburg—then at Gettysburg—then at Spotsylvania C.H.—each of which compelled his absence some months and during those intervals the promotions were made and conferred on others, present to render immediate service, to the exclusion of Col. Parker who was in a tedious and precarious confinement and unable to respond to any call his gallantry had so often entitled. During the long service in command of his Regiment he has been in every situation calculated to test a soldiers worth and merit. For a long time before going to Virginia he was in a separate command in charge of the important District of Cape Fear. He has frequently been left in command of his Brigade, and during the tedious winter encampments he has ever been found vigilant and attentive and on the Battlefield he was always at the post of duty. A christian by profession and practice, strictly sober and reliable and of an untiring will and energy, he bears on his person the enduring memorials of fearless and faithful discharge of duty. It is therefore eminently due to merit that he should receive that reward and promotion which his long service and his gallantry entitle him to.

House of Commons:
H. Joyner (Halifax)
A. H. Davis (Halifax)
Daniel Fowle (Wake)
Eugene Grissom (Granville)
T. Henry (Bertie)
S. F. Phillips (Orange)
M. Carter (Beaufort)

---

and the documents with its submission to the authorities in Richmond are contained within Parker's compiled service record. The counties set forth are those given for the members of the Assembly of 1864-65, Regular Session, Raleigh, November 21-December 23, 1864, in *North Carolina Government, 1585 - 1979* (Raleigh: North Carolina Department of the Secretary of State, 1981), pp. 330-332.

J. G. Shepherd (Cumberland)
S. S. Harrison (Caswell)
McGehee (Caswell)
Thos. J. Morrisey (Robeson)
Saml L. Love (Haywood)
McCormick (Cumberland)
R. F. Johnston (Davie)
W. A. Smith (Johnston)
W. G. Banks (Johnston)
J. M. Lyle (Macon)
W. N. Patterson (Orange)
C. F. Lowe (Davidson)
P. P. Peace (Granville)
L. C. Benbury (Chowan)
Dan L. Russell, Jr. (Brunswick)
Lewis Hanes (Davidson)
L. Q. Sharpe (Iredell)
David Cobb (Edgecombe)
F. A. McMillan (Ashe)
B. F. Little (Richmond)
H. H. Best (Greene)
E. J. Harrington (Moore)
Richd H. L. Bond (Gates)
Wm. A. Duke (Camden)
J. H. Riddick (Perquimans)
W. H. Wheeler (Forsyth)
A. J. Murrell (Onslow)
L. C. Lathan (Washington)
S. T. Stancell (Northhampton)
Geo N. Lewis (Nash)
L. D. Farmer (Edgecombe)
J. J. Baxter (Currituck)
A. D. McLean (Cumberland)
E. C. Grier (Mecklenburg)
A. J. Boyd (Rockingham)
F. George (Columbus)
M. K. Crawford (Wayne)
Wm. T. Alston (Warren)
J. M. Caho (Wayne)
P. Murphy (Sampson)
J. L. Brown (Mecklenburg)

Wm K. Davis (Franklin)
W. B. Lane (Craven)
Thos J. Judkins (Warren)
J. S. Amis (Granville)
C. F. Faucette (Alamance)
R. McAden (Alamance)
F. E. Shober (Rowan)
A. C. Cowles (Yadkin)
Jas. L. Carson (Rutherford)
G. H. Alford (Wake)
Calvin Rogers (Wake)
C. Perkins (Pitt)
Wm. J. Headen (Chatham)

Senate:

John B. Odom (Northumberland)
M. L. Wiggins (Halifax)
Jonathan Horton (Watauga)
Jas E. Matthews (Stokes)
Jesse H. Powell (Edgecombe)
Thos J. Pitchford (Warren)
J. W. Ellis (Columbus)
Nathan Whitford (Craven)
E. W. Hall (New Hanover)
J. P. Speight (Greene)
A. G. Taylor (Nash)
Wm Kirby (Sampson)
Benj Aycock (Wayne)
W. R. Ward (Duplin)
W. M. Grier (Mecklenburg)
W. Harris (Warren)
Saml C. Bryan Lt. Col 25th Regt NCT (Cherokee)
B. Wright (Cumberland)
G. M. Mebane (Alamance)
D. W. Courts (Rockingham)

This letter was forwarded to Senator William Theophilus Dortch the very next day, December 2, 1864. It went under cover of a letter from Senator Jesse H. Powell of Edgecombe County which stated, "Convinced that the long and continued service of Col. Parker merit consideration and reward from the authorities at Richmond my party has seen fit to get up this memorial. With the hope that you may add your support to our action I am yours very truly Jess H. Powell, Senator"

Coincidentally, Parker's cousin, former Governor Henry T. Clark, on December 3, 1864, forwarded to a Captain Philips—doubtless Parker's relative—Bryan Grimes' October 4, 1864, letter to Parker. Governor Clark wrote a cover letter pointing out that Grimes' letter, "contains the direct testimony of Genl Ramseurs recommendation with the additional fact that his old Brigade needed Col. Parkers superintendence." Brig. Gen. Grimes' letter and Governor Clark's cover letter found their way into Parker's compiled service record and must have been reviewed by the authorities in Richmond as they considered the request of the members of the N.C. General Assembly for Parker's promotion.

The December 1 letter from members of the General Assembly received the swift endorsements of Lieutenant General Holmes and of Senator Dortch, and Congressmen Robert Rufus Bridgers and Burgess Sidney Gaither. Once in Richmond, however, the matter was referred to Gen. Robert E. Lee who signed the following endorsement on January 7, 1865:

> To be returned to His Exc'y the President. Col. Parker has been several times wounded; has been pronounced permanently disabled for service in the field and upon his own application it has been recommended that he be placed in the Invalid Corps and assigned to light duty. The papers in his case were on yesterday forwarded through the Surg General as required by existing orders.
>
> E. Lee
Genl

It can well be imagined that, if Lee saw the October 4, 1864, letter from Grimes to Parker, Lee did not like it.

Parker was transferred to the Invalid Corps on January 17, 1865.[115] Lt. Col. Edward A. Palfrey, assistant adjutant general, on Jan. 26, 1865, wrote an endorsement referring the matter to Lt. Gen. Holmes who in an endorsement dated in Raleigh, February 25, 1865, wrote the following:

> Col. Parker is at present by my assignment in command of this post. I respectfully recommend that an order be issued confirming the appointment. Col. W. H. Clark 24th N.C.T. heretofore in command was captured by the Enemy some days ago at Dinwiddie Court House.

In the meantime, perhaps aware of Lee's handling of the question of Parker's promotion, Senator Dortch on January 17, 1865, had written the Secretary of War requesting that Parker be assigned to the command of Salisbury or some other post in North Carolina. Parker firmly declined:

H. Q. Post
Raleigh, N.C. Feb. 24th 1865

Maj. C. S. Stringfellow
A.A.G.
Major
Relative to the application of Senator Dortch for my assignment to command of the Post at Salisbury, I beg leave to state that I do not at this time desire that position. My experience as Commandant of this Post warns me that I have not yet sufficiently recovered from the effects of a wound received on the 19th of May last.
    I therefore do not wish to undertake any duty which I feel unable to perform.
    I am Major
    very respectfully
    your obdt servt
    F M Parker
    Col comdg

---

115. Manarin and Jordan, *N.C. Troops*, 8:321.

Private Bone recalled that Colonel Parker came to the regiment in Petersburg to resign as colonel on account of his summer wound, but no other source mentions such a visit.[116]

During the winter of 1864-1865, the late fall augmentation in regimental strength ceased and the number of men absent without leave increased. An inspection of Cox's brigade conducted at Dunlop's Station on January 29, 1865, found the 30th, commanded by Captain McMillan, with 10 officers and 167 men present and 3 officers and 42 men absent without leave, a decrease in regimental strength of 6.3% and an increase in AWOLs of 25%.[117] On February 25, 1865, Capt. John B. Brown conducted an inspection of Cox's brigade at Camp Rodes and found the 30th, still commanded by Capt. John Cornelius McMillan, to have 5 officers and 176 men present for duty, a 2.2% increase in strength since January, 1865, but a 4.2% decrease from December, 1864. Significantly, the number of men absent without leave had again increased substantially to 3 officers and 49 men, a 15.5% increase since January, 1865, and a 44% increase since December, 1864, with a total only slightly less than one third of the regimental strength. The brigade was noted to have soldierly military bearing and good military discipline and appearance and the 30th was armed with Enfields and Springfields. The inspector noted that 30th Regiment suffered from grave clothing deficiencies, particularly pants and underclothing. Bayonets, scabbards and cartridge boxes were also much needed. Deficiencies included 67 overcoats, 275 coats, 200 trousers, 205 shirts, 120 pairs of shoes, 125 stockings, 46 blankets, 200 knapsacks, 160 canteens, and 50 tents. The inspector noted that the brigade was camped three miles from Petersburg, Virginia, and comfortably quartered in 6-10 man cabins.[118]

116. Bone, "Service," p. 39.
117. Inspection report for Cox's brigade, January 29, 1865, National Archives Record, Group 109, Microcopy 935, Roll 14, 26-P.51.
118. Inspection report for Cox's brigade, February 25, 1865, National Archives Record, Group 109, Microcopy 935, Roll 15, 6-P.62.

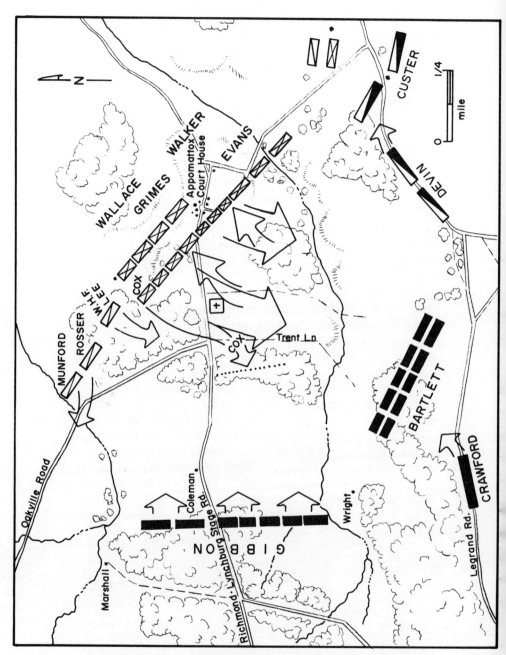

Cox's brigade at Appomattox Court House, April 9, 1865

PART NINE
March - April, 1865
Petersburg & Appomattox,
Close of the war in North Carolina

As February, 1865, turned into March, the drama now rapidly drew to a close for both Colonel Parker, back in North Carolina, and for the 30th Regiment at Petersburg, Virginia. Sherman entered North Carolina, heading for Goldsboro and then for Raleigh. Parker was the commander of the garrison of Raleigh at the end of February,[1] and as such was ordered on March 7 by General Braxton Bragg, commander of the Department of North Carolina, to hurry troops through Raleigh on their way to Kinston to resist Sherman's advance.[2] By March 25, Gen. P. G. T. Beauregard was advising Col. Delaware Kemper, commander of the post at Hillsborough, 30 miles northwest of Raleigh, that he should comply with a request that Colonel Parker might have made to guard bridges, but that Parker could not order Kemper to do so.[3] With the fall of Richmond the Confederate situation in North Carolina rapidly deteriorated. On the day Lee suffered the destruction of a large part of his army on the retreat to Appomattox and Sherman received word at Goldsboro of the fall of Richmond and made ready to issue orders for an immediate advance toward Raleigh,[4] the following plaintive message was issued:

HEADQUARTERS DEPARTMENT OF NORTH CAROLINA
Raleigh, April 6, 1865.

Col. S. D. Thruston,
Commanding Post, Raleigh:

---

1. *OR*, vol. 47, pt. 2, p. 1293.
2. *Ibid.*, p. 1343.
3. *OR*, vol. 47, pt. 3, pp. 683 and 689.
4. *Ibid.*, pp. 112 and 118-119.

Colonel: From the newspapers it appears you are now commanding the post of Raleigh, lately commanded by Colonel Parker. No order changing the command having emanated from or been made known to these headquarters, the general commanding desires to learn for his information by whose order the change was made. You will please send an official copy of the order.

Very respectfully, your obedient servant,

JOHN B. SALE,
Assistant Adjutant General.[5]

Clearly, confusion and disorganization was settling upon the Department of North Carolina and the post of Raleigh. No response to Sale's inquiry is found in the *Official Records.* Other sources do not mention any lapse in Parker's command of the post. It is evident that Parker withdrew westward along with the rest of Gen. Johnston's Confederate forces when Raleigh was taken by Sherman on April 13, 1865. Thirteen days later, on April 26, in accordance with the terms of surrender agreed upon by Sherman and Johnston, Col. Francis Marion Parker surrendered at Greensboro as senior officer of the Invalid Corps.[6]

———————————— ◆●◆ ————————————

Back in Virginia, on March 25, 1865, the 30th Regiment and Cox's brigade were ordered out to support the Confederate assault on Fort Steadman. As the brigade moved, the 30th's Chaplain A. D. Betts departed to go home on leave. He later commented:

I had no idea that I was to see the soldiers and Chaplains no more. How tender would have been the leave-taking, if I had known it was my last sight of those with whom I had been so long associated.[7]

The orderly sent to lead the brigade to the front got lost and arrived late. Consequently, Cox's brigade arrived at the trenches

---

5. *Ibid.*, p. 763.
6. Hill, *Confederate Military History*, 7:683-685; document in Francis Marion Parker Papers, North Carolina Division of Archives and History.
7. Betts, *Experiences*, p. 76.

only in time to help cover the Confederate withdrawal from Fort Steadman.[8] Following the failed assault on the fort, Cox's brigade was placed in the trenches south of Petersburg on the right of Grimes' division near Battery 45.[9] Cox's men successfully held these trenches against Grant's general assault on the Confederate line throughout the day of Sunday, April 2, 1865. This success was due in part to an extension of the brigade line made possible by stationing members of a black engineer corps in unoccupied trenches on the brigade's right—the only use, according to Cox, of blacks in combat by the Confederates in the war.[10] On the evening of April 2, Grimes' division was ordered to abandon the works and withdraw to the north side of the Appomattox River. Following the Hickory Road, the division recrossed the Appomattox at Goode's bridge and reached Amelia Court House on the morning of April 5.[11]

During the retreat from Richmond, the 30th and Cox's brigade suffered large numbers of stragglers like the rest of Lee's army. During this retreat to Appomattox the 30th Regiment lost 3 wounded and 62 captured, of whom 5 were wounded. However, it is clear from all of the sources that the 30th and Cox's brigade maintained organization and discipline until the surrender.

On April 6, 1865, Cox's brigade made a fighting retreat westward under intense enemy pressure, most likely as a part of the northernmost of the three major parts of the Confederate army attempting to cross Sailor's Creek and Little Sailor's Creek. They joined Gordon's corps as it withdrew along the

---

8. Bone, "Service," pp. 39-41; Cox in Clark, *N.C. Regiments*, 4:450-451.
9. *Ibid*; Cowper, *Letters of Major-General Bryan Grimes*, p. 104.
10. Cox in Clark, *N.C. Regiments*, 4:453. According to Schaub, "Memoir," p. 41, on April 2, after the advancing enemy was driven back the volunteer sharpshooters then pursued, driving a line of skirmishers back through fields for half a mile. "Our whole brigade was then deployed as skirmishers, moved to the left towards front of Petersburg and fare in front of our entrenched lines and engaged enemys skirmishers all day." The dominance of Cox's brigade in their sector of the line before Petersburg apparently coincided with the capture of Fort Steadman by 60 men under Capt. Plato Durham of the 12th Regt. N.C.T., of Brig. Gen. Robert Johnston's North Carolina Brigade (formerly Iverson's) of Grimes' division. Cowper, *Letters of Major-General Bryan Grimes*, pp. 107-108.
11. *Ibid.*, p. 109.

Jamestown Road past the Lockett House to Sailor's Creek.[12] The bridge across Sailor's Creek was found to be blocked by wagons. Grimes' division made a last stand on the ridge just east of Sailor's Creek before breaking and running upon being outflanked. Grimes himself had to scramble down Sailor Creek's steep bank on his horse, Warren, and, cross the creek with enemy bullets whistling around him, galloping to safety on the western side.[13] As the enemy approached, Cox, with Lewis' brigade in his rear as the last organized command in front of Sailor's Creek, marched his brigade through the protection of the woods rather than retreat down the road under enemy artillery fire. Emerging from the woods Cox marched his brigade in column to the scene of the disaster. It became a famous story in later years, told by Cox and recounted by Gov. Zeb Vance, that Robert E. Lee, observing the scene on horseback from a knoll, inquired of an aide, "What troops are those?" "Cox's North Carolina Brigade," was the reply. Then it is reported that, taking off his hat and bowing his head with goodly courtesy and kindly feeling, he said, "God bless gallant old North Carolina!"[14]

That night, Grimes' division crossed the Appomattox River at the High Bridge. On April 7, the retreating Confederates continued to be hard pressed by the Federals. Gordon's corps

---

12. Christopher M. Calkins, "Confederates on the Jamestown Road" in *Thirty-Six Hours Before Appomattox* (n.p.: C. M. Calkins, 1980), no page numbers; Christopher M. Calkins, *From Petersburg to Appomattox* (n.p.: The Farmville Herald, n.d.), p. 31.
13. Cowper, *Letters of Major-General Bryan Grimes*, pp. 110-111.
14. W. R. Cox quoting Governor Vance in Clark, *N.C. Regiments*, 4:455-456. This accolade would have had to be given by Lee at about the same time he was asking Maj. Gen. William Mahone to "keep those people back." William Mahone, "On the Road to Appomattox" William C. Davis, ed., *Civil War Times Illustrated*, vol. 9, no. 9 (Jan., 1971):9. According to Calkins, "Furl That Banner," in *Thirty Six Hours before Appomattox* and Calkins, *From Petersburg to Appomattox*, pp. 31-32, Lee at this time was on Big Sailor's Creek Overlook observing the rout of Anderson's corps. The road from the crossing of Sailor's Creek west of the Lockett House upon which Cox's brigade would have marched passes beyond Big Sailor's Creek Overlook. It remains something of a mystery as to when Lee saw Cox's brigade at Sailor's Creek, as Cox claims. Colonel Parker stated that Lee gave a similar accolade on the morning of April 9, 1865, at Appomattox as Cox's brigade swept by him to the charge: "God bless old North Carolina." Parker in Clark, *N.C. Regiments*, 2:504.

followed the South Side Railroad west to Farmville, north of which Gordon's rearguard fought a fierce action in which Union Brig. Gen. Thomas Smythe was mortally wounded—the last Union general officer to be killed in the war.[15] Upon Mahone's call for assistance in repelling an attack on his division at Cumberland Church, Grimes ordered three brigades, including Cox's, to double quick to Mahone's position. Charging the enemy, they recaptured some of Poague's artillery and took a large number of prisoners.[16] It was at Cumberland Church on the night of April 7 that Grant's first note seeking Lee's surrender was delivered.

The following day, Saturday April 8, Cox's brigade marched unmolested toward Appomattox Court House via New Store. Forty years later, Sgt. A. D. McGill of Company H, 30th Regt. N.C.T. vividly recalled that evening's bivouac:

> On Saturday night, April the 8th, 1865, after many wearisome marches and continuous fighting since leaving the trenches at Petersburg, Grimes's Division went into camp about five miles from Appomattox. About sunset and before halting for the night, we heard the thunder of artillery in our front. The sound of artillery was familiar to our ears. We heard it unceasingly on the left of our line of march and as incessantly in our rear, but to hear the sound of guns in our front plainly indicated that we were being surrounded, and that we should soon be called upon to crown a glorious career by a glorious death.
>
> We were informed, however, that we might sleep that night—which was welcome news to men who had scarcely closed their eyes in sleep for eight or nine days and nights.
>
> We did not take long to prepare supper, for we had nothing to prepare. A few of the boys had a handful of

---

15. Calkins, "General Smythe Mortally Wounded," in *Thirty-Six Hours before Appomattox*; Warner, *Generals in Blue*, pp. 465-466.
16. Cowper, *Letters of Major-General Bryan Grimes*, pp. 112-113; Mahone, "On the Road to Appomattox," pp. 42-43; Monroe F. Cockrell, ed., *Gunner with Stonewall: Reminiscences of William Thomas Poague* (Jackson, Tennessee: McCowat-Mercer Press, 1957; reprint: Wilmington, North Carolina: Broadfoot Publishing Company, 1987), pp. 117-118.

corn, which they parched and ate, but by far the greater number lay down on the bare ground weary and supperless, but faithful and brave.

I was fortunate in having a tea cup full of corn meal and about an inch square of fat meat, which I had carried through all the toilsome marches and dreadful scenes of that retreat without an opportunity of cooking it. In camp that night, I could not find in our brigade a frying-pan, oven, spider or any other kind of cooking utensil; so I thought for a while that I should be constrained to carry my handful of meal and my square inch of fat bacon for a while longer. But at last I found a long handled shovel, in which I made up my dough and baked a little cake of bread about the size of a biscuit, though not nearly so thick. I then fried the bacon, which turned out to be all grease and which I ate out of the shovel. This was my last cooking experience in Lee's army.

We did not sleep long. About twelve o'clock, I received orders from regimental headquarters to get my men ready to move at once. Weary, hungry and footsore, the gallant boys were harder to arouse than usual, but we were soon on the march again—whither we did not know. At daybreak we reached Appomattox and when it was light enough for us to see we saw dead men and horses, a sure indication that we had reached the scene of the conflict.[17]

The 14th Regiment reached the village of Appomattox Court House about 3:00 a.m., about four hours before the 30th. Upon their arrival, these men of Cox's brigade lay down in the principal street of the village to rest. They could go further. The enemy was now across the road in their front.[18]

---

17. A. D. McGill, *Daily News and Observer*, Raleigh, North Carolina, April 11, 1865, p. 5; Bone, "Service," p. 46, contradicts McGill by stating that the 30th was issued rations on the evening of April 8. All the evidence about Lee's army on the evening of April 8 indicates that McGill, and not Bone, had the correct memory of the 30th's commissary.

18. Schaub, "Memoir," p. 42; Bone, "Service," p. 46, agreeing with McGill's time table, says that the 30th halted at Appomattox Court House "about light." That is four hours or so after Schaub says he arrived there. Perhaps the regiments were separated.

As day dawned on the fateful morning of April 9, 1865, the 30th Regiment and the rest of Cox's brigade formed in line of battle west of the village of Appomattox Court House intent on driving the enemy from his blocking position astride the road to Lynchburg. Major General Grimes, their divisional commander, held a council of war with Major Generals Gordon and Fitzhugh Lee. Grimes, impatient with Gordon saying the cavalry should attack and Fitz. Lee wanting the infantry to do it, finally declared that it was somebody's duty to attack and that should be done immediately. He felt satisfied that the enemy could be driven from the cross-roads, and decided that he would undertake it himself, whereupon Gordon said, "Well, drive them off."[19] Grimes obtained permission to take other troops with him, including the divisions of James A. Walker (formerly Early's) and Bushrod Johnson (commanded by Brig. Gen. William Wallace) as well as that of Brig. Gen. Clement A. Evans (formerly Gordon's).[20]

Line of battle was formed and at about sunrise the Confederates went forward.[21] Maj. Thomas G. Jones, Gordon's aide de camp recalled, "Spring was just budding forth, and the morning sun glistening from every budding leaf and tree, shed a halo on the red battle flags with the starry crosses, as if nature would smile on the nation dying there."[22] The rebel yell went up, and the Confederate line advanced en echelon by brigade at intervals of 100 paces.[23] "[W]e had no idea we were so near the end," remembered Pvt. J. W. Bone.[24]

19. Cowper, *Letters of Major-General Bryan Grimes*, pp. 114-115.
20. *Ibid*; William Kaigler, "Concerning Last Charge at Appomattox," *Confederate Veteran*, vol. 6, no. 11 (Nov., 1898):524; Christopher M. Calkins, *The Battles of Appomattox Station and Appomattox Court House, April 8-9, 1865* (Lynchburg, Virginia: H. E. Howard, Inc., 1987), pp. 58 and 277-278, n. 92, where Calkins states that there is reason to believe that Grimes' division was formed on the right on the Confederate front line. Calkins shows the position of Cox's brigade on the right of Grimes' division on a map on p. 61.
21. McGill, Raleigh *Daily News and Observer*.
22. Thomas G. Jones, "Last Days of the Army of Northern Virginia," in *The Southern Historical Society Papers* (reprint: Wilmington, North Carolina: Broadfoot, 1990), 21:57-103 at p. 85. Jones later became Governor of Alabama.
23. W. R. Cox in Clark, *N.C. Regiments*, 4:457; Walter A. Montgomery, 2nd Lt., Co. F, 12th Regt. N.C.T., "Appomattox and the Return Home" in Clark, *N.C. Regiments*, 5:260.
24. Bone, "Service," p. 46.

Early in the advance, a Federal battery to the Confederate left opened fire. Sergeant McGill of the 30th recalled, "On reaching the crest of the first rising ground, the Federal artillery opened upon our advancing line."[25] The first shell burst in the line of the 14th Regt. N.C.T., killing Stanly County's Sgt. Ivey Ritchie of Company H, the "Stanly Marksmen." Sergeant Ritchie was the last fatality of the war in Cox's brigade and perhaps the last Confederate infantryman to die in the Army of Northern Virginia.[26] Sergeant McGill recalled, "We drove the enemy steadily back, capturing at least part of the artillery in our front. One of the guns was turned half over in a ditch, as I remember seeing it, when I passed."[27] This was undoubtedly a gun of Bvt. Maj. Egbert W. Olcott's Battery M, 1st U.S. Artillery.[28]

The Federal cavalry was rapidly driven from its blocking position across the Lynchburg Road. The Confederate line of battle then swung to the left, changing its axis from generally north-south to generally east-west. Grimes sent an officer to Gordon announcing their success, and that the Lynchburg Road was now open.[29] The moment of triumph was brief. As the

25. McGill, Raleigh *Daily News and Observer*.
26. See the list of casualties at Appomattox in Calkins, *The Battles of Appomattox Station and Appomattox Court House*, p. 233. Accounts of Ivey Ritchie's death are found in Smith, *The Anson Guards*, p. 297 and in a letter from Major N. E. Jenkins to his daughter, April 9, 1906, North Carolina Division of Archives and History, Raleigh, North Carolina. Also see the touching account of the visit to Ivey Ritchie's grave after the surrender by his brother, Sgt. Marvel Ritchie, of the "Stanly Yankee Hunters," Company D of the 28th Regt. N.C.T. in a letter written in the 1920s in the Marvel Ritchie Papers, Private Collections #883, North Carolina Division of Archives and History, Raleigh, North Carolina. Whether Ivey Ritchie was the last Confederate infantryman to fall at Appomattox is, of course, a much disputed question. For example, E. V. Turner and H. C. Wall, 23rd Regt. N.C.T. in Clark, *N.C. Regiments*, 2:266-267, claimed that a member of the 1st Bn. N.C. Sharpshooters was the last to fall. I am grateful to David Deese, editor of the Stanly *News and Press*, Albemarle, North Carolina, and Robert Mabry, also of Albemarle, Commandant of the Ivey Ritchie Camp of the Sons of Confederate Veterans, for providing me with information about Sgt. Ivey Ritchie, 14th Regt. N.C.T..
27. McGill, Raleigh *Daily News and Observer*.
28. Calkins, *The Battles of Appomattox Station and Appomattox Court House*, pp. 66 and 70-71; *OR*, vol. 46, pt. 1, p. 1246.
29. Schaub, "Memoir," pp. 42-43; Cowper, *Letters of Major-General Bryan Grimes*, pp. 116-117; W. R. Cox in Clark, *N.C. Regiments*, 4:457-8;

Confederates continued to move forward, a large force of
enemy infantry sprang up and the Confederates' flanks were

Major N. E. Jenkins to daughter, April 9, 1906, North Carolina Division
of Archives and History. In placing Cox on the right flank of Grimes'
division, I follow the map in *Five Points in the Record of North Carolina
in the Great War of 1861-5* (Goldsboro, North Carolina: Nash Brothers,
1904), p. 57 and the interpretation of Christopher Calkins, both in his
The Battles of Appomattox Station and Appomattox Court House cited
above, and in *The Appomattox Campaign, March 29 - April 9, 1865*
(Conshohocken, Pennsylvania: Combined Books, Inc., 1997), map on p.
160. In describing Grimes' division as wheeling by the left flank, I
follow Calkins and Douglas Southall Freeman, *Lee's Lieutenants*, 3:728.
Grimes' description of the advance in Cowper, *Letters of Major-General
Bryan Grimes*, pp. 116-118, admits of no other interpretation.
However, there is contradictory evidence. Our faithful witness, Sgt.
Julius L. Schaub of the 14th Regt. N.C.T., stated in Julius L. Schwab
(sic), "Some Closing Events at Appomattox," *Confederate Veteran*, vol.
8, no. 2 (Feb., 1900):71 that Cox's brigade formed on Grimes' left rather
than right flank: "[W]e . . . formed a line on the left of the road, the other
troops having formed on the left of the road. We soon advanced . . . with
Cox's Brigade on the extreme left of the division, and I saw no other
troops on our left. . . . Continuing to advance, we seemed to swing more
and more to the left, and had left the road a long way to our right when
ordered to halt. . . . At this time we could see no Yankees, but a dense
woods about a hundred yards in our front was 'full of them.' When the
order came to retire, and the brigade started in execution of the movement, a Federal line of battle charged out of the woods toward us, hoping
to stampede or capture us. The it was the Gen. Cox gave the command
to right-about face and charge. We stopped at an old rail fence and
poured a volley into the enemy; then quickly retired on the division over
a ridge." T. R. Lackie, a soldier of the 16th Michigan Infantry, Bartlett's
Third Brigade, First Division, Fifth Corps, a brigade which stood in line
on April 9 with Joshua Chamberlain's First Brigade, First Division,
Fifth Corps on its left and Turner's division of Ord's Twenty-Fourth
Corps on its right, also indicates that Cox's brigade may have been on
Grimes' right. After describing a conversation following the surrender
with members of the 1st North Carolina (a regiment of Cox's brigade),
Lackie states: "Another notable incident connected with this episode of
Appomattox was the firing of a volley into the Union lines as the flag of
truce was fluttering. It came from that part of Gen. Gordon's line which
was refused to the left and faced south. Gen. Griffin, commander of the
Fifth Corps, with his staff was standing southeast of Chamberlain's
right flank, and the bullets flew past their heads. Gen. Griffin, according
to one writer, said: 'Do they mean to murder us after they had surrendered?' Who can say that volley was not fired but the First North
Carolina of Grimes's Command?" T. R. Lackie, "Reminiscences of
Appomattox," *Confederate Veteran*, vol. 8, no. 3 (March, 1900):124.
On balance, however, the interpretation given by Calkins and Freeman,
based on Grimes' description of the attack in Cowper, *Letters of Major-
General Bryan Grimes*, pp. 116-118, makes the most sense.

soon overlapped. A captured Federal officer was brought to Cox and acquainted him with the fact that, although the Federal cavalry had been cleared from the Lynchburg Road, the way westward was now blocked by the 10,000 infantry of Ord's Twenty-Fourth Corps.[30] Upon reaching a commanding position, Cox could see many columns of enemy infantry advancing with the apparent intent of capturing the North Carolinians. At this point, firing resumed, when Capt. Henry A. London of Grimes' staff rode up and told Cox, "Gen. Grimes directs you to retire."[31] It was evident that an armistice had been agreed upon. Grimes ordered that his division withdraw by the left flank. He directed Cox to refuse the division's right flank by facing westward, and to maintain his position in line of battle and not show himself until the rear of the division's other brigades were 100 yards distant and then to fall back in line of battle in order to protect the division's rear and right flank from assault.[32] In retiring slowly, Cox discovered that there was danger of his command being surrounded and captured. In the emergency, Cox, through his aide, James S. Battle, ordered the regimental commanders of his brigade to meet at the brigade center as they retired. Pointing out a gradually rising hill between his troops and the enemy, Cox directed that the regimental commanders face their troops about, double quick to the crest of the hill, and before the enemy should recover from their surprise, halt, fire by brigade, and then with like rapid movement face about and rejoin the division. Cox's orders were obeyed with alacrity, as described in his oft-quoted account of the maneuver:

> Raising the "rebel yell," the brigade with celerity and precision, promptly and faultlessly executed the order, and having gained the brow of the hill, the enemy, anticipating a determined struggle, commenced to deploy and prolong their line as if on parade. But before the movement was fully executed, the command

30. W. R. Cox quoted in James I. Metts, "Last Shots Fired at Appomattox," *Confederate Veteran*, vol. 7, no. 2 (Feb., 1899):52 and in Clark, *N.C. Regiments*, 4:458.
31. *Ibid.*; H. A. London, "The Last Volley at Appomattox," *Confederate Veteran*, vol. 7, no. 12 (Dec., 1899):557-8.
32. Cowper, *Letters of Major-General Bryan Grimes*, p. 117.

rang out along the Confederate line clear and distinct above the din of battle, "Halt, ready, aim, fire!" And while the encircling troops were surprised and stunned by the audacity of the charge and the unusual character of the fire, the brigade safely withdrew and regained the division, which in the meantime had been skirmishing as it withdrew. General Gordon, superbly mounted, as we passed by exclaimed, "Grandly and gloriously done!"

This was the last charge of the Army of Northern Virginia.[33]

There were, of course, many who disputed Cox's claim. And as the years passed, there came to be much hairsplitting with claims to the last charge, the last volley, the last shot, the last infantryman or cavalryman killed. However, it is very likely that Cox's men did in fact fire the last volley discharged by infantrymen of the Army of Northern Virginia in line of battle.[34]

---

33. W. R. Cox in Clark, *N.C. Regiments*, 4:458. William Rand Kenan, adjutant of the 43rd Regt. N.C.T. of Grimes' old brigade commanded by Col. D. G. Cowand, recalled, "[M]y recollection is, on retiring in column of fours from the field, our brigade (Grimes) passed about sixty feet in rear of Cox's Brigade, which was in line of battle. Gen. Cox, mounted on his horse, gave the command, in clear, distinct, tones, 'Ready, aim, fire!' and the order was so well executed that it sounded like the report of one gun. This was the last." quoted in Metts, "Last Shots Fired at Appomattox," p. 52. The account of Walter A. Montgomery, 2nd Lt., Co. F, 12th Regt. N.C.T. seems reliable: "[W]hen the men of Johnston's [Lea's] Brigade [of Walker's division] were ordered back I heard thereafter no continuous firing of small arms. The advance was supported by a battery of five pieces in position on the western slope of the hill, and that battery kept up its fire some minutes after the infantry had ceased to be engaged. . . . The battle was severer on our right and we understood at the time that General Cox, with his brigade, had the brunt of it, and that they claimed the honor firing the last round." Clark, *N.C. Regiments*, 5:260.
34. See, for example, Capt. William Kaigler, commanding the sharpshooters of Evans' division, and Clement Evans, in Kaigler, "Concerning Last Charge at Appomattox," p. 524. This article quotes a letter from Brig. Gen. Clement Evans and William Kaigler, "Last Charge at Appomattox," *Confederate Veteran*, vol. 7, no. 8 (August, 1899):357, which claimed the honor of firing the last shots for Evans' sharpshooters. Capt. B. M. Collins, 12th Regt. N.C.T., of Johnston's brigade fired the last musket. It is clear that there continued to be considerable firing at will by individuals as Grimes retreated and the Federals advanced into the

Even among members of the 30th Regiment there were conflicting claims. Sgt. A. D. McGill claimed on the 50th anniversary of the surrender to have covered the withdrawal of Cox's brigade from the field as a part of a line of skirmishers:

> The enemy, seeing us moving to the rear, again advanced; their advance was checked by Cox's brigade. Cox's brigade again took up the movement to the rear, toward the Court House, the withdrawal being

---

western edge of the village of Appomattox Court House. E. R. Harris of Company G, 14th Regt. N.C.T., Cox's brigade, recalled firing the last shots from behind an old barn while protecting a piece of field artillery at the end. "First—and Last," *Confederate Veteran*, vol. 31, no. 11 (Nov., 1923):438. This incident is also described by Capt. W. T. Jenkins, Co. A, 14th Regt. N.C.T. in the Raleigh, *Daily News and Observer*, April 11, 1905, p. 3, and in a letter from Major N. C. Jenkins, 14th Regt. N.C.T., April 9, 1906, North Carolina Division of Archives and History. Henry Kyd Douglas claimed the honor of firing the last shots at Appomattox for his brigade of Walker's division in *I Rode with Stonewall* (Chapel Hill: University of North Carolina Press, 1940), p. 317. There were numerous claims by cavalrymen to firing the last shot or making the last charge, such as N. B. Bowyer (of the 10th Virginia Cavalry, Beale's brigade, W. H. F. Lee's division), "Reminiscences of Appomattox," *Confederate Veteran*, vol. 10, no. 2 (Feb., 1902):77-78; E. E. Bouldin (14th Virginia Cavalry, Beale's Brigade), "The Last Charge at Appomattox," in *The Southern Historical Society Papers* (reprint: Wilmington, North Carolina: Broadfoot, 1990), 33:250-254; W. L. Moffett (14th Virginia Cavalry), "The Last Charge," in *The Southern Historical Society Papers* (reprint: Wilmington, North Carolina: Broadfoot, 1990), 36:13-16; John E. Bouldin (14th Virginia Cavalry), "Our Last Charge," *Confederate Veteran*, vol. 22, no. 12 (Dec., 1914):557; M. J. Billmyer (1st Virginia Cavalry, Munford's Brigade), "The Last Charge at Appomattox," in *The Southern Historical Society Papers* (reprint: Wilmington, North Carolina: Broadfoot, 1990), 33:191-2. Union General Sheridan witnessed a fierce last minute fight between his cavalry and Martin Gary's brigade of South Carolina cavalry. Phillip H. Sheridan, "The Last Days of the Rebellion," Illinois M.O.L.L.U.S. vol. 1 (1891), pp. 427-439 at pp. 435-436. There was a desperate last minute struggle for the guns of Starke's artillery battalion, as described in Percy G. Hawes, "Last Days of the Army of Northern Virginia," *Confederate Veteran*, vol. 27, no. 9 (Sept., 1919):341-342. Also see, A. L. Long, "Letter from General A. L. Long," in *The Southern Historical Society Papers* (reprint: Wilmington, North Carolina: Broadfoot, 1990), 9:423-4, where Long told of the fight at Starke's guns, but also recalled a later "last shot" fired by "Colonel Duke Johnston's batteries or Colonel Pogues's." However, none of the claimants describe a volley fired by infantry in line of battle.

covered by a line of sharpshooters. I had the honor to be one of this last line of skirmishers, in charge of the sharpshooters of the 30th Regiment.[35]

Capt. D. C. Allen, commanding the 30th Regt. N.C.T. at Appomattox claimed that the last shots were fired by the 30th and in particular by his own company, the "Neuse River Guards," of Wake and Granville Counties. Allen stated:

> [U]nder Cox's order to take my regiment and support a battery then firing, General Cox took the rest of the brigade from the field of action while I remained and fired on the enemy advanced on my flank; they halted and lay down, and immediately another line advanced on my flank, when I changed front and fired another round, the enemy halting and laying down flat.
> Neither line returned my fire. Then I received order to join my command. I think the Federals were informed of the surrender, or they would have wiped us from the earth.[36]

The exact location of the encounter described by Captain Allen is difficult to determine, but it probably took place at the

---

35. McGill, Raleigh *Daily News and Observer*. This account doesn't mention shots being fired during the withdrawal, but it is most likely that there were. Cox recalled that the skirmish line during his brigade's withdrawal toward the village of Appomattox Court House was made up of the 2nd Regt. N.C.T. and parts of the 1st and 3rd Regts. N.C.T.. Capt. W. T. Jenkins, in the Raleigh, *Daily News and Observer*, said that Cox threw out the 4th and 14th Regiments under Jenkins' command to cover the brigade's withdrawal. The presence of a contingent from the 30th in that last skirmish line was to be expected because the brigade sharpshooters were drawn from all of the brigade's regiment. The brigade sharpshooters often served as the brigade's skirmishers, for example, in the attack upon the Union position on the Mummasburg Road at Gettysburg on July 1, 1863.
36. D. C. Allen in a letter to Colonel Parker quoted by Parker in his history of the 30th Regt. in Clark, *N.C. Regiments*, p. 505. A final action on the edge of the village of Appomattox Court House shortly before 10:00 a.m. on April 9, 1865, is described by Bvt. Col. Joseph B. Pattee, 190th Pennsylvania, commanding 150th, 190th and 191st Pennsylvania Infantry Regts., Third Brigade, Second (Ayres') Division, Fifth Corps, in *OR*, vol. 46, pt. 1, pp. 877-878.

Confederate artillery position at the western edge of the village of Appomattox Court House.

After the withdrawal of Cox's brigade, the men of the 30th stacked arms and began piling up fence rails for protection, expecting to be attacked at any time. It was at this point that someone passed by and said "That Lee had surrendered."[37] This was probably about 10 a.m., Sunday, April 9, 1865. A cessation of hostilities had been agreed upon so that Lee could meet with Grant to discuss surrender. Following that afternoon's meeting between Lee and Grant at the McLean House and the formal agreement as to the terms of surrender, the 30th went into bivouac east of Appomattox Court House.

It was about this time that Major General Grimes rode up to his old regiment, the 4th Regt. N.C.T.—the 30th's comrades in arms on so many hard fought battlefields from the Seven Days to Appomattox—for the purpose of shaking the hand of each member of his old command who had followed him through four years of suffering, toil and privation. A cadaverous, ragged, bare-footed man grasped Grimes by the hand, and, choking with sobs, said: "Good-bye, General; God bless you; we will go home, make three more crops, and try them again."[38]

Sergeant McGill of the 30th recalled:

> In a short wile after the surrender took place; we had more Yankees than rebels in our midst. There was the utmost consideration and good will. We had nothing to eat; General Grant sent us coffee and crackers in abundance. There was no demonstration of rejoicing; no firing of salutes; no cheering. It was a beautiful Sabbath day, and, after the surrender, as quiet and peaceful as a Sabbath in Scotland.[39]

---

37. Bone, "Service," p. 46.
38. Cowper, *Letters of Major-General Bryan Grimes*, p. 120.
39. McGill, Raleigh *Daily News and Observer*. A. D. McGill was born in Scotland. He was a 19-year-old resident of Cumberland County when he enlisted as a private in Company H, 30th Regiment N.C.T. on January 16, 1862, at Camp Wyatt. He was promoted to corporal in 1863. McGill's rank at Appomattox is shown as corporal in Manarin and Jordan, *N.C. Troops*, 8:397, but he is listed as a sergeant in the "Appomattox Paroles," in *The Southern Historical Society Papers* (reprint: Wilmington, North Carolina: Broadfoot, 1990), 15:259.

30th Regt. N.C.T. battle flag surrendered at
Appomattox Court House on April 9, 1865

That evening, General Gordon had the Second Corps form in a hollow square or column on a hill and addressed them, stating the terms of surrender. After complimenting the men for their bravery, endurance and constancy, Gordon advised all to go home, follow the laws and make as good citizens as they had soldiers and history would hand down their fame to the coming ages.[40]

The 30th surrendered at Appomattox Court House, Virginia, under the command of Capt. D. C. Allen with 6 officers and 147 enlisted men.[41] During the Appomattox Campaign and prior to the surrender, the 30th suffered 3 wounded, 5 wounded and captured, and 59 other captured, including those captured in the hospitals.[42] Clearly, since the number present for duty in the 30th at the end of February, 1865, was only 177 and the number surrendered at Appomattox plus those captured during the campaign equals 213, a number of men detailed for duty elsewhere in February must have joined the regiment for the retreat from Richmond. Pvt. J. W. Bone noted the presence of such men with his company at Appomattox.[43]

The "detail" men present aside, the 30th Regt. N.C.T. at Appomattox was a stalwart body of veteran soldiers. Out of the 153 surrendered, 66 or 43% had been previously wounded. Of those, 16 (more than one in ten) had been wounded twice. Five brave soldiers, all noncoms, shared the honor with Colonel Parker of having survived the war after having been wounded three or more times each, with 1st Sgt. R. M. Crumpler of Company A taking the crown of a dolorous sort, with four previous war wounds, the most of any of the 30th at the surrender. These five bore on their bodies (in the words of the North Carolina General Assembly) the marks of the 30th Regiment's arduous service:

---

40. Schaub, "Memoir," p. 44; War Diary of R. M. Crumpler, Company A, 30th Regt. N.C.T., organization records, United Daughters of the Confederacy, Box 4, Papers of Miss Georgia Hicks, Historian, UDC, North Carolina Division of Archives and History, Raleigh, North Carolina. John B. Gordon places this speech at the conclusion of the stacking of arms by the Confederates on April 12, 1865. Gordon, *Reminiscences*, pp. 448-450.
41. "Paroles of the Army of Northern Virginia," in *The Southern Historical Society Papers* (reprint: Wilmington, North Carolina: Broadfoot, 1990), 15:253-260.
42. See casualty roster appended to this book.
43. Bone, "Service," p. 47.

1st Sgt. Robert M. Crumpler of Company A, wounded at Gaines' Mill, Chancellorsville, Kelly's Ford, and Fort Stevens.[44]

1st Sgt. John Gilliam Newsom of Company B, wounded at Malvern Hill, Chancellorsville, and Kelly's Ford.[45]

Sgt. Arthur Forbes of Company F, wounded in the Seven Days and at Chancellorsville and Kelly's Ford.[46]

Corp. John W. Lawrence of Company H, wounded at Gaines' Mill, Gettysburg, and Cold Harbor.[47]

Corp. William L. Hood of Company K, wounded at Gettysburg; in the May, 1864, campaign; and at Cedar Creek.[48]

Sgt. R. M. Crumpler of Sampson County was barefoot at Appomattox, having marched in this state for two days before the surrender. A friend gave him a pair of shoes on the evening of April 8, but his feet were too sore for him to wear them.[49]

On Wednesday, April 12, 1865, in accordance with the terms of surrender, the 30th Regt. N.C.T. stacked arms and passed into history. Sgt. A. D. McGill of Company H recalled the event:

[O]ur troops were marched to Appomattox Court House where we found the "boys in blue" drawn up in line. For the last time the men in gray formed line in front of them. They saluted us with their arms and flags; we then stacked arms, broke ranks and turned our faces southward toward home. I left Appomattox with my little company of twelve men—all that were left of one hundred and sixty-six![50]

44. Manarin and Jordan, *N.C. Troops*, 8:326.
45. *Ibid.*, p. 338.
46. *Ibid.*, p. 375.
47. *Ibid.*, p. 396.
48. *Ibid.*, p. 417.
49. Crumpler Diary.
50. McGill erroneously places the surrender parade on Tuesday, April 11,

379

Photo courtesy of Fred Prouty, Jr.

1st Sgt. John Gilliam Newsom
Co. B, 30th Regt. N.C.T.
Surrendered at Appomattox, April 9, 1865

The soldiers of the 30th presented an awe-inspiring sight at Appomattox Court House at that last parade. These were the men described by Federal Brig. Gen. Joshua L. Chamberlain, designated by Grant to receive the Confederate surrender at Appomattox on April 12, 1865:

> Before us in proud humiliation stood the embodiment of manhood: men whom neither toils and sufferings, nor the fact of death, nor disaster, nor hopelessness could bend from their resolve; standing before us now, thin, worn, and famished, but erect, and with eyes looking level into ours, waking memories that bound us together as no other bond. . . .[51]

The men of the 30th received their paroles and started on their long way home. Sgt. Robert M. Crumpler recalled:

> On the 12th, we broke camp early in the morning and marched up to Gen. Grant's headquarters, where we surrendered our arms, and there were ordered back to our original camp; but before we reached it, we were turned back, received our paroles, and started for home, all greatly relieved that the war was over and we were alive.[52]

Private Bone, of Company I, noted that only three other of the 110 original members of his company remained and remembered: "We were turned out into the world most of us without any money, with one weather-beaten suit of clothes, and nothing to eat, entirely on the mercy of somebody else." Bone arrived home in Nash County on Tuesday, April 18, the same day Capt. W. E. Ardrey reached Charlotte, riding on the train the last part of the journey from China Grove.[53] It wasn't until April 21 that Sergeant Crumpler, of Company A, reached his home in Sampson County.[54]

rather than Wednesday, April 12.

51. Joshua Lawrence Chamberlain, *The Passing of the Armies* (New York: G. P. Putnam's Sons, 1915; reprint: New York: Bantam Books, 1993), p. 195.
52. Crumpler Diary.
53. Bone, "Service," p. 48-53; Ardrey Diary.
54. Crumpler Diary.

The years passed. The recollections of the scenes of defeat at Appomattox were transformed by a miracle of time and memory from bitterness into pride and triumph in the face of adversity. It was truly as Walt Whitman had said:

RECONCILIATION

Word over all, beautiful as the sky,
Beautiful that war and all its deeds of carnage must in time
    be utterly lost,
That the hands of the sisters Death and Night incessantly
    softly wash again, and ever again, this soil'd world;
For my enemy is dead, a man divine as myself is dead,
I look where he lies white-faced and still in the coffin - I draw
    near,
Bend down and touch lightly with my lips the white face in
    the coffin.

Forty years after the event, Sergeant McGill could look back, not in anger, but with powerful nostalgia for his comrades of the 30th Regiment North Carolina Troops and of Army of Northern Virginia:

> Forty years have passed since that 9th of April. Time has blotted out many things from the memory of us all; scenes have changed and the Appomattox of today is unlike the battlefield of forty years ago, where that heroic eight thousand received permission to go to their homes and "there remain undisturbed."
>
> The great leaders on both sides, the principal actors in the sad close of that drama, have passed away; the remaining participants in the closing scenes at Appomattox—the boys of '65—are rapidly crossing over the river to rest, we trust, under the shade of the trees. Very soon the last of that splendid army shall have passed from earth to join their comrades on the eternal shore.[55]

---

55. McGill, Raleigh *Daily News and Observer*.

"There was no such army as that which followed Lee."
— William Ruffin Cox

EPILOGUE

Francis Marion Parker survived the Civil War by nearly forty years. Unlike many of his class and rank, Parker did not seek public office or enter business, but returned to his beloved plantation in Halifax County to live out his days as a farmer with his beloved wife, Sally, and their growing family. In all, they had nine children:

Children of Col. Francis M. Parker (Sept. 21, 1827-January 18, 1905) and wife, Sarah Tartt Philips (November 22, 1835-September 22, 1906)[1]

1.) Mary Parker (1853-1935), married John Battle in 1886.
2.) James Philips Parker (1855-1942), married Mary McPherson of California in 1887. Appointed to the U.S. Naval Academy as midshipman in 1873, and attaining the rank of lieutenant commander by 1900,[2] James P. Parker eventually became a commodore in the United States Navy.
3.) Theophilus Parker (1857-1920), unmarried.
4.) Harriet Burt Parker (1860-1926), married Peter Spruill in 1880.
5.) Haywood Parker (1864-1945), married Josephine Patton of Asheville, N.C. in 1889 and practiced law in Asheville.
6.) Francis M. Parker, Jr. (1867-1914), unmarried.
7.) Sally Philips Parker (1870-1964), unmarried.
8.) Katherine Drane Parker (1873-1962), unmarried.
9.) Frederick Marshall Parker (1875-1939), married Aimee Wheeler Vibber of Montville, Connecticut.

---

1. I am grateful to Frank M. Parker, Jr., for providing me with this information regarding Parker's children.
2. Edward W. Callahan, ed., *List of Officers of the Navy of the United States and of the Marine Corps from 1775 to 1900* (no place of publica-

In 1870, the Parkers' neighbors included a mulatto carpenter named Hilliard Parker, evidently the same man to whom Parker had instructed Sally to entrust the overseeing of the plantation during his absence.[3]

Parker maintained an extremely cordial correspondence with his two most greatly admired comrades in arms, D. H. Hill and Bryan Grimes. In 1872 Parker responded to a request from Grimes, apparently for a photograph for the library at Grimesland. Parker apologized that he had none to send but a "small size photograph" taken just at the close of the war.[4]

———————◆◆◆———————

Parker's thoughts returned to Big Bethel, Virginia, on the 16th anniversary of the battle when he wrote this note to D. H. Hill:

Halifax Co. N.C.
June 10, 1877

Gen. D. H. Hill
My Dear General
Do you ever think of your old Regiment on this their maiden day? I will warrant that <u>you</u> have a share of their thoughts, as it occurs, and by no one of them with kinder feelings than by your friend

F. M. Parker[5]

---

tion or publisher given, 1901; reprint: New York: Haskell House Publishers, Ltd., 1969), p. 421.
3. 1870 U.S. Census for Halifax County, North Carolina.
4. Letter from Francis M. Parker to Bryan Grimes, March 4, 1872, Bryan Grimes Papers, North Carolina Division of Archives and History, Raleigh, North Carolina. Parker went on to say in this letter, "Should I meet with a favorable opportunity, and you still desire it, I will have a larger one taken for your library." It seems likely that the photograph of Parker in Clark, *N.C. Regiments*, 2:495 is a copy of the one sent to Grimes. In 1865, Parker turned 38, about the age that he appears in the photograph in Clark.
5. Letter from Francis M. Parker to D. H. Hill, June 10, 1877, D. H. Hill Papers, North Carolina Division of Archives and History, Raleigh, North Carolina.

In 1879, Parker wrote Grimes asking him to use his influence with Gov. Thomas J. Jarvis, Grimes' fellow Pitt countian, so that Parker might receive Governor Jarvis' recommendation for appointment by the president to take the 1880 United States Census. There is a plaintive quality to the opening line of Parker's letter to Grimes, as his aristocratic code must have made the very making of the request distasteful: "It is very unpleasant to me to trouble my friends, but necessity drives us to many things unpleasant."[6]

Parker received the appointment as Federal census taker in Halifax County in 1880. He enumerated himself as a farmer, age 53, in Brinkleyville Township along with his wife, Sally, age 44, and nine children: Mary, 27, teacher; James P., 25, naval officer; Theophilus, 22, laborer; Hattie, 20, without occupation; Haywood, 15, at school; F. M., 12, at school; Sally, 9, at school; Kate, 7, at school; and Fred M., 4. Parker's farm consisted of 35 acres tilled, 4 acres meadow, and 610 acres woodland with the farm valued at $6,000, farm implements valued at $150, and livestock valued at $200. Buildings and repairs in 1879 had cost $20 and fertilizer in 1879 had cost $30. Parker had hired labor in 1879 for 7 weeks at a cost of $18. In November, 1879, Parker had on hand 3 horses, 1 mule, 2 working oxen, 3 milk and 5 other cows, 7 sheep (from which was clipped 16 lb. of wool), 16 swine, and 22 chickens. In 1879, Parker's farm produced three bales of cotton along with 1 bushel of pulse, 20 bushels of Irish potatoes, 40 bushels of sweet potatoes, 67 bushels of wheat, 230 bushels of Indian corn, and 350 bushels of oats.[7]

In 1883, Parker wrote to Pulaski Cowper thanking him profusely for sending a copy of his "pamphlet," *Extracts of Letters of Major-General Bryan Grimes to His Wife.* "What he has written, is true to the letter. I was there. Then to think that after such a gallant, useful, and honourable career, he should have fallen by the bullet of a cowardly dastardly assassin: too bad, too bad."[8]

---

6. Parker to Grimes, March 18, 1879, Bryan Grimes Papers.
7. 1880 U.S. Census, Halifax County, N.C.
8. Letter from Francis M. Parker to "Mr. Cowper," May 7, 1883, Bryan Grimes Papers.

In 1885, Parker was a deputy collector of Internal Revenue, a "red legged grasshopper" as Parker joked in a letter to D. H. Hill.[9]

As the years passed, Parker remained extremely proud of his command, the 30th Regiment. He wrote the regiment's history in Walter Clark's massive compendium, *Histories of the Several Regiments and Battalions from North Carolina in the Great War 1861-'65*, referring to himself in the Caesarian third person. Parker seems to have been especially proud of his regiment's service at Chancellorsville on the morning of May 3, 1863, taking special note of the thanks given his regiment on that occasion by Brig. Gen. Ramseur and vehemently denying (in two letters in the 1890s) that the Stonewall Brigade had been anywhere near his regiment in its final advance to Fairview and the Chancellor House.[10]

Parker was heavily involved in Confederate veteran activities in the later years of his life. On May 29, 1894, he took part in one of the greatest Confederate memorial events of the age. In a huge procession numbering 10,000 that marched through the streets of Richmond before 100,000 spectators on the occasion of the dedication of Soldiers' and Sailors' Monument on Libby Hill, Colonel Parker rode next to H. Kyd Douglass in a large cavalcade of horsemen of Confederate distinction, headed by Gen. John B. Gordon, acting as aides to the parade's chief marshal, Gen. Fitzhugh Lee. Ahead marched 13 little girls representing the 13 Confederate states followed by 2,000 boys and girls in Confederate colors and 180 VMI cadets. Behind came the governor of Virginia, the Virginia Militia, numerous military units from other Southern states, and a large contingent of Confederate veterans led by white-haired Gen. Wade Hampton.[11] By 1898, Parker was commander of the Third Brigade,

---

9. Parker to Hill, August 18, 1885, D. H. Hill Papers.
10. Typewritten copy of letter from A. [certainly mistaken transcription of F.] M. Parker, apparently to Fred Philips, May 29, 1891, Stephen D. Ramseur Papers (PC.138.1), North Carolina Division of Archives and History, Raleigh, North Carolina; Letter from Parker to James I. Metts, January 15, 1899, in James I. Metts, *Longstreet's Charge at Gettysburg, PA* (Wilmington, North Carolina: Morningstar Press, 1899), pp. 37-38; the same letter is published in Metts, "The Thirteenth (sic) North Carolina at Chancellorsville," *The Sunny South*, August 17, 1901.
11. "Unveiling of the Soldiers' and Sailors' Monument," in *The Southern*

North Carolina Brigade, United Confederate Veterans.[12] He attended the May 20, 1898, reunion of the North Carolina Division in Charlotte.[13] Parker resigned from his post as Third Brigade Commander due to ill health in 1902.[14]

As the new century dawned, the Federal census taker in 1900 found a 73-year-old F. M. Parker still farming his plantation in Brinkleyville Township, Halifax County. His household consisted of himself, his 65-year-old wife, Sally, and three unmarried children, Theophilus, 43; Sally P., 30; and Kate D., 27.[15] Francis Marion Parker died at the age of 77 at his home in Enfield on the morning of January 18, 1905. Word of Parker's death reached the North Carolina General Assembly just in time for its annual commemoration of Robert E. Lee's birthday on January 19, and the Legislature adjourned after adopting a resolution in memory of Robert E. Lee and Colonel Parker.

The January 19, 1905, resolution of adjournment honoring Lee and Parker was adopted by a unanimous rising vote by the House of Representatives upon the motion of Representative A. D. McGill of Cumberland County, the former Sergeant of the 30th Regiment who the night before Appomattox had cooked his last meal with Lee's army on a long handled shovel:

> *Resolved by the House of Representatives,* That, in obedience to the sentiment of the people of North Carolina, who reverence the memory and valor of those patriots who sacrificed their lives and fortunes to the sacred cause of Southern independence and to commemorate the birthday of the immortal leader of the Confederate armies, this, the anniversary of the birthday of Robert E. Lee, has been made a legal holiday in North Carolina; therefore, be it

Historical Society Papers (reprint: Wilmington, North Carolina: Broadfoot, 1990), 22:342.

12. "United Veterans in North Carolina," *Confederate Veteran*, vol. 6, no. 5 (May, 1898):221.
13. "North Carolina Reunion Proceedings," *Confederate Veteran*, vol. 6, no. 6 (June, 1898):246.
14. "Gen. Francis M. Parker," *Confederate Veteran*, vol. 10, no. 10 (Oct., 1902):439.
15. 1900 U.S. Census for Halifax County, North Carolina.

Resolved, That, in memory of General Robert E. Lee and also in honor of that gallant North Carolina hero, Colonel F. M. Parker who died yesterday (January 18th), that the House of Representatives do now adjourn until Friday, January 20th, at 11 o'clock.[16]

Francis Marion Parker was buried in the churchyard of the Calvary Episcopal Church at Tarboro. "[H]is funeral was largely attended, there being present a considerable number of his old comrades in arms."[17]

Other members of the 30th Regt. N.C.T. provided significant post-war service to their state in the North Carolina General Assembly. The faithful diarist and sometime regimental commander Capt. William Erskine Ardrey represented Mecklenburg County in the North Carolina House of Representatives in the 1877, 1879, 1885 and 1901 sessions and in the North Carolina Senate in the 1891 session.[18] Capt. D. C. Allen, who also commanded the regiment at times, represented Columbus County in the North Carolina House of Representatives in 1899 and 1902.[19] Sgt. Archibald D. McGill, the Scotsman, represented Cumberland County in the North Carolina House of Representatives in the 1889, 1891, 1905, and 1911 sessions, serving on the commission that erected the North Carolina Commission at Appomattox on the 40th anniversary of the surrender in 1905.[20] A high point of A. D. McGill's service in the 1905 session of the General Assembly was moving the adoption of the January 19, 1905, resolution of adjournment in honor of Robert E. Lee and McGill's former commanding officer in Lee's army, Colonel

---

16. House Resolution 324, *House Journal*, January 19, 1905, p. 142. See also, *Senate Journal*, January 19, 1905, p. 104.
17. Ashe and Weeks, *Biographical History of North Carolina*, 7:360-361.
18. J. B. Alexander, *The History of Mecklenburg County from 1840 to 1910* (Charlotte, North Carolina: Observer Printing House, 1902), pp. 59-60; *North Carolina Government 1585-1979* (Raleigh, North Carolina: North Carolina Department of the Secretary of State, 1981), pp. 457, 459, 465, 469, and 479.
19. *Ibid.*, pp. 477 and 479.
20. *Ibid.*, pp. 468, 469, 483, and 488; "North Carolina Monument at Appomattox," *Confederate Veteran*, vol. 13, no. 3 (March, 1905):112.

Parker.[21] Brave 1st Sgt. Robert M. Crumpler, the 30th's most frequently wounded soldier surviving to surrender at Appomattox (with four wounds, received at Gaines' Mill, Chancellorsville, and Kelly's Ford, Virginia, and Fort Stevens, District of Columbia), represented Sampson County in the North Carolina House of Representatives in the 1895, 1897, and 1899-1900 sessions.[22]

Colonel Parker's brother-in-law, Frederick Philips, the 30th's adjutant and assistant quartermaster, who had fallen wounded at the Bloody Lane at Sharpsburg and Kelly's Ford, became a prominent lawyer and was elected Superior Court Judge from Edgecombe County in the Second Judicial District, serving an eight year term from 1882 to 1890.[23]

Chaplain A. D. Betts continued his long career as a Methodist minister in the post-war period and was active in Confederate veteran affairs. In letters to the editor of the *Confederate Veteran* magazine, he spoke out against holding dances at Confederate veteran reunions[24] (for which he was roundly criticized).[25] Betts also urged that the railroads make ticket arrangements so that Confederate veterans did not have to travel on Sunday to the 1902 reunion in Dallas, Texas.[26] As difficult as it may be for some in this secular age to understand Betts' objections to dancing and travelling on Sunday, it is clear that Betts acted out of deep concern for his former spiritual charges of the 30th Regiment, their Confederate veteran comrades, and their offspring. In 1901 Chaplain Betts said:

> The reunions would be much more helpful to old and young, socially, intellectually, and spiritually, if the foolish dance were left out. What man or woman of any

---

21. House Resolution 324, *House Journal*, January 19, 1905, p. 143.
22. *North Carolina Government 1585-1979*, pp. 474, 476, and 478.
23. *Ibid.*, p. 578.
24. A. D. Betts, "Dance on My Father's Grave," *Confederate Veteran*, vol. 9, no. 8 (August, 1901):344; A. D. Betts, "Confederate Reunion Balls," *Confederate Veteran*, vol. 19, no. 11 (Nov., 1911):517.
25. John W. Tucker, "Confederate Reunion Balls," *Confederate Veteran*, vol. 20, no. 4 (April, 1912):149.
26. A. D. Betts, "Suggestions Concerning Reunions," *Confederate Veteran*, vol. 10, no. 2 (Feb., 1902):52.

sense can propose a dance just after hearing the battle described in which their father lost his life?[27]

By November, 1911, his concern was focused on the souls of those old veterans who were not yet saved:

> I love the old soldiers. I preached to thousands of them in Lee's army. Many have gone to heaven. Among the living there are many faithful, fervent Christians. But some have never given their hearts to God, and will soon be lost forever if they are not saved promptly. I go to Reunions to pray with them and help them to think about their souls, but a worldly crowd comes along to dance and help them forget their souls.[28]

Betts' campaign against dancing at Confederate veteran reunions resulted in a statement opposing such dances being signed in 1912 by three North Carolina bishops, 21 presiding elders, and nine editors of religious papers.[29]

A. D. Betts passed on to his eternal reward on December 18, 1918, "having lived a beautiful Christian life and blessed many souls during his long ministry."[30]

And the veterans of the 30th Regiment went marching on, some into extreme old age. Incredibly, of North Carolina's last ten surviving old Confederate soldiers, two—one black, one white—were veterans of the 30th Regiment. On Sept. 16, 1946, Frank McGhee, born in about 1835, died near Oxford, North Carolina at the age of 110. He served from Sept. 7, 1861, to January, 1865, as the servant of Capt. Richard P. Taylor, Company G, 30th Regt. N.C.T.. McGhee was pensioned as a Confederate veteran in 1928 and received a stipend which had increased to $26.25 per month by 1946 as a Class B soldier, still significantly less than the $72 per month paid to Class A soldiers by the State of North Carolina.[31]

---

27. Betts, "Dance on My Father's Grave," p. 344.
28. Betts, "Confederate Reunion Balls," p. 517.
29. A. D. Betts, "Don't Favor Confederate Balls," *Confederate Veteran*, vol. 20, no. 7 (July, 1912):346.
30. "Rev. A. D. Betts," *Confederate Veteran*, vol. 27, no. 5 (May, 1919):188.
31. Jay S. Hoar, *The South's Last Boys in Gray* (Bowling Green, Ohio: Bowling Green State University Popular Press, 1986), pp. 218-223 and 461.

The last surviving veteran of the 30th Regt. N.C.T. was Cpl. Charles Skinner Riggan of Vaughn in Warren County, North Carolina. He was born Oct. 27, 1842, and died at the age of 104 on March 26, 1947—only two months before the birth of the author of this book. Charlie Riggan enlisted August 16, 1861, at Littleton, survived wounds received at Spotsylvania Court House and Cedar Creek in 1864, and went on to surrender at Appomattox.[32] In 1983, Florence N. (Mrs. Henry C. Sr.) Thompson shared her thoughts about her great uncle Charlie Riggan with Jay Hoar:

> I knew "Uncle Charlie" during 1930-1947. He was a jolly, good-natured retired farmer and visited our home in 1934. He picked a lively banjo and traveled through county and country to parties, which he loved. He'd dance all night amid 'pretty music, pretty flowers, and pretty women.' He surely was to touch a lady on her bosom at dances if possible. (It usually was accidental!) He read his Bible faithfully, was very knowledgeable with it, and often discussed it with friends. Roy Riggan, a grandson, of Castalia, agrees that people knew Uncle Charlie as happy, constantly walking about, hands behind his back or in front snapping his fingers, whistling softly "Dixie," "Aura Lee" and songs of the Old South; and that he walked with both feet on the ground—sort of a skipping step, sliding his feet along almost as a dance step. He ate little. One meal a day. A cup or so of coffee. Milk was his favorite food. He enjoyed his little toddy. He belonged to the Vaughn Baptist Church and is buried in its cemetery just east of town off Hwy 158. His philosophy was "Live and let live."[33]

What manner of men were these, Francis Marion Parker and his men of the 30th? As for F. M. Parker, one is led from a study of his life to the inescapable conclusion that his role models

32. *Ibid.*, pp. 255-257.
33. *Ibid.*, p. 256.

must have been the heroes of the American Revolution—one of whose famous names he bore—and beyond those American heroes to their idols, the Roman heroes, particularly Cincinnatus. The assessment of his fellow regimental commander, William Ruffin Cox, gives evidence of this:

> F. M. Parker, the courteous and refined Colonel of the Thirtieth Regiment, was a brave, cool, and excellent officer and ever observant of his duties to the cause and to his command.[34]

Modest in the extreme, lacking any political ambition, devoted to his family and farm, Parker emulated the virtues of Washington and the Roman hero Cincinnatus, answering the call to duty in war where he provided heroic service, only to return home to his agricultural pursuits. One scholar has pointed out:

> It has been said that Washington was the last of the classical heroes, as Napoleon was the first of the romantic heroes. . . . The contrast is not so much between eras as between two conceptions of the morality of power. And it was, after all, a romantic poet, Lord Byron, who ended his *Ode to Napoleon* this way:
>
> Where may the wearied eye repose
> When gazing on the Great;
> Where neither guilty glory glows,
> Nor despicable state?
> Yes - one - the first - the last - the best;
> The Cincinnatus of the West
> Whom envy dared not hate,
> Bequeath'd the name of Washington
> To make men blush there was but one.[35]

---

34. W. R. Cox in Clark, *N.C. Regiments,* 4:461.
35. Gary Wills, *Cincinnatus, George Washington and the Enlightenment* (Garden City, New York: Doubleday & Company, Inc., 1984), pp. 240-241.

The model of the American founders would certainly have been held up before a young man bearing the name of a Revolutionary War hero. Certainly, Washington was the pre-eminent example. Parker would have had the opportunity to see the 1857 copy by William J. Hubbard of the Houdon statue of Washington with its Cincinnatian symbols of plow, sword and fasces standing on the south grounds of the State Capitol in Raleigh.

In truth, however, Francis Marion Parker offers little more than a marble visage to the reader of his letters. Devoutly religious in his own measured way, this man of duty and honor reveals very little of his own inner feelings, even in these intimate communications to his beloved wife, Sally. Parker's letters reveal him to have been a cool and capable Southerner of the planter and slave owning class. Even though his ante-bellum wealth and property were by no means great as compared with many of his contemporaries, Parker was firmly ensconced in the bosom of North Carolina's upper class through a web of connections of his family and friends—from his cousin, wartime Gov. Henry T. Clark, to his brother-in-law, the Rev. Dr. Robert Brent Drane of Wilmington, to his boyhood acquaintance, Robert F. Hoke of Lincolnton. His political philosophy, beyond devotion to his State and the South, is not expressed. Not a whisper of doubt about the South's "Peculiar Institution" anywhere appears. Instead, the sentiment that most completely pervades Parker's letters is one of certainty and confidence in the triumph of what Parker believed as a righteous cause. Even as late as March, 1864, Parker writes home, gently urging his wife to be cheerful and refrain from writing discouraging letters to him:

> You must not write such gloomy letters to me; you will cause me to have the same feelings and views. We must leave every thing in the hands of that Good Being who is able to take care of us.
>
> Our prospects were never brighter, than at present. The army is in the best spirits; surely the people at home should not be despondent.[36]

---

36. Colonel Parker's letter home of March 12, 1864 (p. 317).

It was the men of Parker's class who led the South into the war, and their hold on power was broken for a time by the Southern defeat. While they gradually regained power in North Carolina between 1865 and 1900, their world had changed forever as undreamed of and unwanted—by his class—changes came on the scene.

As for Parker's men who served under his command in the 30th Regiment, perhaps no finer tribute was written than that by their brigade commander in the last year of the war, William Ruffin Cox, speaking generally of the men of Lee's army:

> There was no such army as that which followed Lee. In its ranks were men from all orders of society, of property and of education. They were accustomed to the use of firearms and to riding horseback. There was a comradeship and individuality among them. Ever cheerful in camp or on the march, they discussed around the camp fire the conduct of the officers and the merits of the battles they had fought; and so resourceful were they in battle, that the commands of the officers were often unnecessary to enable them to seize strategic advantages, or even when dispersed, to rally in squads, and continue the struggle, inflicting severe punishment upon the enemy.[37]

As Douglas Southall Freeman has said, "'Consciousness of duty faithfully performed'—that was the consolation which became their reward, their pride, their bequest."[38]

---

37. Clark, *N.C. Regiments*, 4:456.
38. Freeman, *Lee's Lieutenants*, 3:752.

APPENDIX A

Capt. James I. Harris' Account of
Ramseur's Brigade in the Gettysburg Campaign

James I. Harris, a native of Georgia, was a 27-year-old resident of Nash County, North Carolina, serving as the "Public Register," when on September 10, 1861, he was elected 2nd lieutenant of the "Ladies' Guards." This became Company I of the 30th Regiment North Carolina Troops when that regiment was organized at Camp Mangum near Raleigh on September 28, 1861. Harris owned one slave who was a fugitive in 1860. He refers in the letter to North Carolina as his adopted state.

Harris was elected 1st lieutenant on April 1, 1862, and was promoted to captain on July 1, 1862, when Company I's Capt. William T. Arrington was killed in the battle of Malvern Hill, Virginia. Harris missed the First Maryland (Sharpsburg) Campaign, being reported in Richmond's General Hospital No. 24 with intermittent fever on August 19, 1862, the day the 30th Regiment marched north from the vicinity of Richmond. After being present at the battles of Chancellorsville and Gettysburg, Captain Harris was killed at the battle of Spotsylvania Court House on May 12, 1864.

Entering the Gettysburg Campaign, the 30th Regiment N.C.T. formed a part of Brig. Gen. Stephen Dodson Ramseur's brigade of Maj. Gen. Robert E. Rodes' division of Lt. Gen. Richard S. Ewell's Second Corps of Gen. Robert E. Lee's Army of Northern Virginia. Along with the 30th Regiment commanded by Col. Francis M. Parker, Ramseur's brigade was composed of the 2nd Regt. N.C.T. commanded by Maj. Daniel W. Hurtt, the 4th Regt. N.C.T. commanded by Col. Bryan Grimes, and the 14th Regt. N.C.T. commanded by Col. Risden Tyler Bennett.

Captain Harris set down this newly discovered account of the Gettysburg Campaign, less than two months after the battle when he finally had time to recover from the rigors of the campaign and found occasion to write. The account is in the form of a letter to his friend and comrade, 1st Lt. Burton B.

Williford, who was at home recovering from wounds suffered on May 3, 1863, in the battle of Chancellorsville two months before the battle of Gettysburg.

Lieutenant Williford was an 18-year-old resident of Nash County when he enlisted in Company I on September 10, 1861, the same day as Harris. Williford mustered in as a private and was promoted to sergeant on November 1, 1861. He was elected 2nd lieutenant on March 27, 1862, and was promoted to 1st lieutenant on July 2, 1862. Just like Harris, his rapid promotions came due to the company's officer casualties at Malvern Hill. Harris' letter mentions that Williford commanded the company during the First Maryland Campaign.

Williford was wounded in the groin and right thigh at Chancellorsville on May 3, 1863. He resigned on December 11, 1863, by reason of "lameness" and his resignation was accepted December 13, 1863.

Capt. James I. Harris' account of the Gettysburg Campaign written to his young friend Lieutenant Williford is fluid and highly literate. It attempts to mask the horrors of the fighting with a brisk sense of humor and an emphasis on the ladies encountered along the way. The reader carries away from the document a feeling of sadness that a mind and a pen as sharp as those of Captain Harris did not survive the war for more useful employment in the fields of peace.[1]

---

1. The information on James I. Harris is taken from the 1860 U. S. Census of Nash County, North Carolina; Manarin and Jordan, *N.C. Troops*, 8:401; and his compiled service record. The information on Burton B. Williford is taken from Manarin and Jordan, *N.C. Troops*, 8:401. That Williford was the addressee of the letter is deduced from the contents of the letter indicating he was an officer of the company and from fragmentary documents of Williford's relating to his resignation which have remained with the letter to the present time. The letter is remarkably well preserved on 20 sheets of lined white (now slightly brownish) writing paper. Each sheet is approximately 7 1/2" X 12" and is formed by the folding in two of a 15" X 12" sheet, written on front and back. Captain Harris' letter came years ago by forgotten means into the papers of Superior Court Judge Walter Bone of Nash County, North Carolina. Since Judge Bone passed away, it has been preserved by his daughters, Peggy B. Tousignant, Barbara B. Biggs, and Shirley B. Beal, who kindly gave their permission to publish it.

Orange County C.H. Va.
August 24, 1863

Dear Friend Burton,

You who have so long been in Camp and understand so well its duties can imagine and make some allowance for what might be taken by a misconstruction of others as neglect. I shall not attempt to screen myself fully from censure, for if our positions were changed and you did not write to me oftener than I have to you I must confess that I should be down on you like a thousand o' brick. I would certainly have written oftener, had Kearney[2] not been with me. He wrote nearly every week and I concluded gave all the news and perhaps more than I could, since I scarcely can leave my quarters except to go on duty. In addition I have been quite busy in making out Pay Rolls, Descriptive Lists, etc., etc., of late. You know that I despise excuses, and I only render these to prevent a total misapprehension on your part of my "posish."

Well, Burton, I suppose that you would like to read a little something about our trip in making the grand invasion. Really, I don't know, now that you have seen so many accounts, that I can add anything that will interest you, and I must confess that I scarcely know how or where to commence.

Previous to our leaving Hamilton's Xing there was a grand review of the army by General Lee. Our division was drawn up on the large open flat below Dickerson's House, east of our encampments. Our brigade was on picket duty and we were only notified of it in time to get on the field. The division was drawn up in three columns, Daniel's Brigade[3] being in our front line

---

2. Kearney W. Arrington was an 18-year-old Nash County resident when he enlisted in Wilson County on June 4, 1861, as sergeant in Company E, 19th Regt. N.C.T. (2nd Regt. N.C. Cavalry). He was present or accounted for until transferred to Company I, 30th Regt. N.C.T., upon appointment as 2nd lieutenant to rank from February 22, 1863. He was promoted to 1st lieutenant on or about December 14, 1863. Arrington was wounded in the left leg and captured at Spotsylvania Court House on May 12, 1864, and was held a prisoner in Washington, at the Old Capitol Prison, at Point Lookout, and at Fort Delaware until transferred to City Point, Virginia, for exchange on February 27, 1865. Manarin and Jordan, *N.C. Troops*, 2:136 and 8:401.
3. The brigade of Brig. Gen. Junius Daniel consisted of the 32nd, 43rd, 45th, and 53rd Regts. N.C.T. and the 2nd N.C. Battalion Infantry.

and occupying a space equal to the front of two of our old brigades. Everything was in nice trim and to older eyes than ours in the Service it would have proved a scene of much interest. Many ladies graced the occasion with their presence, who with long feathers in their caps and long skirts reaching almost to the ground sat their spirited chargers as if they too knew "something of War." The men, "with shoulders square, with pieces resting in the hollow of the right shoulder, eyes to the front resting about fifteen paces distant on the ground" marched steady to the cadenced step, wheeling at the turning point, with as much grace and firmness of step as Napoleon's men could have done.

I held myself proudly erect neither looking to the right or left until I got opposite the Ladies, when an irresistible attraction drew my head round at right angles from the direction in which I was marching and my eyes resting on su-per-la-tive beauty. Egad, Burton I was wounded—no smitten I mean and I don't know what took place that day afterward—you know that I am a very susceptible young man any day. But Goodness Gracious, I started to write to you about my trip to Md. & Pa. and here I am writing about everything else in general and nothing in particular, even about fickle woman, no, angels on earth I mean—well it makes no difference any way for even as they occupy a permanent place in my af-fections so shall they have it in my letter.

In a day or two came the order to "Comdg. offrs. of Cos. to reduce their baggage to a mere change of clothing and without excitement to prepare leisurely but surely for a long march." The next day this order was practically carried into effect and long before day on the morning of the 4th of June we were on the march in the direction of Guiney's Depot. Various were the conjectures among the men as to our probable destination a great many affirming that our trip would end at Richmond— others knowing that Drewerys Bluff, Petersburg and even No. Carolina was the point we were aiming for. The day had advanced not far however when all such illusions were dispelled by our making a sudden change of direction there near the depot—almost equal to a countermarch, and striking off in the direction of Culpepper C.H.

I need say but little of our march or the little incidents that daily occurred—of the beauty of the mountain scenery, of the

398

mountain lassies, of the innumerable bouquets showered on us on all sides—of the waving of Handkerchiefs, and the loud shouts of the soldiery—of the long marches per day or the wading of rivers. Suffice it to say that our march was a pleasant one more like a triumphal procession than otherwise.

Berryville[4] was the first point that seemed to give anything like a promise for fight. When we passed through Millwood distant only 8 or 9 miles, the enemies cavalry was but about 3/4 of an hour in advance of us. We pushed on and soon saw indications of a fight that had but recently been going on between our cavalry, and that of the enemy; at about 11 or 12 o'clock we had arrived within one mile of town. Our advance had been in sight and our first salutation recd was a loud boom from a Cannon and the buzzing of a shell which exploded about 200 or 300 yards, in our front not far from some medical wagons and some ambulances. This created a general squandering among them quite to our amusement.

John, James & Jim began to find business back with the wagons and I had [to] take my baggage myself. The attack was now planned and our brigade selected to flank the town and approach it by way of the Pike leading toward Charlestown. It was excessively warm and we marched in quick time about 5 miles before we halted our men on the above named Pike and within about 600 yards of the town. I don't believe that I ever was so near exhausted before. Soon we moved forward and came in sight of their fortifications on the verge of town on the right side of the road and now deserted. The cowards had deserted the place and given leg bail, leaving over 100 of their sick as prisoners. We passed on through town and there stood their tents just as they had left them a few minutes before— sutlers tents filled with everything that luxurious living could call for, and officers and privates tents filled with everything that convenience could demand. Here we rested for a short time and then pushed on after the retreating enemy. Some said that they had gone to reinforce Millroy at Winchester, others said

---

4. The fight at Berryville, Virginia, occurred on June 13, 1863, and is described by Maj. Gen. Robert E. Rodes, Harris' division commander, in *OR*, vol. 27, pt. 2, pp. 547-548. 1st Lt. (later Capt.) William Erskine Ardrey, of Company K, "Mecklenburg Beauregards," 30th Regt. N.C.T. recorded, "Great rejoicing by the citizens to be relieved from the ridicule and insults of the enemy." Ardrey Diary.

that they had gone in the direction of Bunker Hill. The latter was correct. We turned off and passed the place we camped or rather bivouacked at the same place we did last fall when we paid Berryville a visit. We had not proceeded far when indications of a retreat in good earnest became plainly visible. Overcoats, blankets, etc. were cut to pieces and thrown away completely lining the roadside for many hundred yards. Now came on a rain the best description of which I can give you is to say—it was a rain "what was a rain." Our boys hallooed—whooped and huzzaed, slipped, slided forward backward zigzag, up, down, well every way that the most fertile imagination could picture or pen describe. On—on we went never failing to be greeted at every house by the wayside by any number of the fair sex who seemed much delighted to see us and who seemed as if they would lose their arms in waving their handkerchiefs.

That night we slept 6 or 7 miles from Berryville, and as had become usual a perfect hurricane came along.

By daybreak next morning we were on the march—struck through by Smithfield and by 12 or 1 o'clock was at Bunker Hill—rested a short time and then marched off toward Martinsburg[5] at which place or rather in sight of which place we arrived just before sunset.

Soon dispositions for the attack were made. From all the information we could gain the lowest estimate we could place on the enemy's strength was 5,000. As had been the case at Berryville, our plan was to attack at two or three different points at once. Our brigade, when within one mile of the town, moved off to the left of the turnpike while Iverson's moved to the right and occupied the heights fronting those on which the town was built. Considerable shelling now commenced, the enemies batteries being planted on the opposite side of the town. By sunset our line of battle was formed and we advanced into town rapidly. Before we had got half way the black rows of Yankees were plainly seen on the heights beyond the town. It was their backs however which we saw, for they were getting away as fast as their legs could carry them. Our cavalry now charged through town like a streak of lightning and on after the flying wretches. A huge column of smoke now was high in the air & I thought

5. The June 14, 1863, attack on Martinsburg is described by Maj. Gen. Rodes in *OR*, vol. 27, pt. 2, pp. 548-549.

that the rascals had fired the town. It proved to be the long platform at the station on which was piled long rows of corn & hay. Our reception was all that we could have desired. The ladies seemed wild with joy. They showered bouquets on us and running out in the street met us, shaking hands, howd'ye, howd'ye, howd'ye. It was said that Iverson's brigade[6] had about fifteen minutes the start of ours, but so rapid was our movement that we got in town full fifteen before he did. We stopped in the street, a few minutes and then moved rapidly forward again on the road toward Williamsport. We did not go more than a mile however before we were ordered back & by 9 o'clock p.m. were lying on the ground just on the edge of town, that would rival that about Seven Pines for roughness. Long before this the point of our cavalry charge began to manifest itself, and prisoners came in by the score. Five pieces of field artillery together with some of the finest artillery horse I ever saw also were brought in amid the shouts of our men.

Well to cut the matter short, I had a tolerable time of it. Went in town next morning and had just about as much fun in the way of an argument with a Union lady as I could have wished.

Left about 11 or 12 o'clock and slept on the southeast edge of Williamsport in "my Maryland." Went in town next day—done a little trading—went out a piece and had some fun with the ladies near camp. A lady in town though Union in sentiment gathered and offered me some very nice cherries which I of course gladly accepted—altogether rather dull. Our brigade in our division was the first to cross the Potomac and I will add was the first to be sent forward to Hagerstown. This created some jealousy in the other brigades and it was not uncommon to hear the sneering remark "be bound if there is any advantage given, Ramseur's Brigade will get it."[7] We rested at Williamsport two days, at Hagerstown two. I went into the last named place trading—fell in with a very nice gentleman who would have me go with him to see some ladies. I begged to be excused, but it

---

6. Brig. Gen. Alfred Iverson commanded another of the brigades of Rodes' division. Iverson's brigade consisted of the 5th, 12th, 20th, and 23rd Regts. N.C.T..

7. Captain Ardrey recorded that the 30th, "[c]rossed the Potomac, though very reluctantly. Ramseur's brigade was the vanguard of Lee's army into Maryland, the wish of all was they would be spared to recross the river . . . ." Ardrey Diary.

was "no go." I had to go. Well off we went and I tell you I had a nice time of it. I left Crowell[8] at the store—soon he came out and as he passed he spoke to me. The ladies asked him in. I introduced him around, and we cornered off staid until after dinner—had plenty of splendid music, only plague take it—I forgot every <u>new piece</u> I ever had, seen, heard or thought of & had to call for her favorite. It did not make much difference anyway for she pitched in and played everything I ever heard and quite a variety that I never had, the names of which—some I pretended to be familiar with and others to know nothing of & don't know yet. About 3 1/2 o'Clock p.m. we exchanged cards all around and Crowell and myself took leave of Miss Mollie V. Hurley and Miss Mollie Smith, a friend and visitor of Miss Hurley's.[9]

I must now hasten on to scenes of a different character and which has draped every state in our beloved Confederacy in mourning—stopping, however at some of the most important places to give some little incident that transpired. You will recollect that for every 4 or 5 miles in this country there is a village of more or less note, at every one of which I could take up a page in describing or giving something of what took place. After leaving Hagerstown the most of the inhabitants seemed excited only by idle curiosity—but when we arrived at Chambersburg, Pa. men, women and children looked as sullen as an opossum and as sour as a crab apple.[10] About midway of the town we halted and rested. The curious lookers-on were assembled about us as usual. "What is the population of your place," I asked of a very nice looking youth.

"I don't know," was his reply.

"Were you born and raised here?" I asked.

8. Jonas W. Crowell transferred from Company D, 5th Alabama Infantry, to Co. I, 30th Regt. N.C.T. on April 5, 1863, and was promoted to 1st sergeant on May 1, 1863. He was hospitalized at Richmond, Virginia, with a gunshot wound of the left thigh on June 3, 1864. Crowell surrendered at Appomattox Court House, Virginia, on April 9, 1865. Manarin and Jordan, *N.C. Troops*, 8:404.

9. Captain Ardrey recorded, "We found there [in Hagerstown] many sympathizers with the South. White handkerchiefs floating from every window; Hagerstown is noted for the pretty ladies." Ardrey Diary.

10. Captain Ardrey recorded that in Chambersburg, "[a]ll the citizens looked upon us with scorn and contempt, it is strictly a Union hole." Ardrey Diary.

"Yes sir," said he.

"Then," says I, "I don't give you credit for as much knowledge as I thought your looks indicated."

"I have never taken the pains to inquire," said he.

I felt rather piqued that the fellow should so coolly refuse to tell what I felt satisfied that he knew. When we started on the march a few minutes after, I saw a good looking, but rather corpulent, old gent sitting on the steps of some of the closed stores. "What is the population of your place, Sir?" said I.

"It seems to be quite numerous at present," said he.

Sold again, thought I, and bit my lip and went on. A day or two more and we had reached Carlisle without opposition. Went into barracks—had plenty of ice and fared finely. Sunday evening I went over in the City. Sitting near a pump some ladies came down the street with a goblet and stopping at the pump one of them commenced pumping water. I immediately stepped up and offered my services. "Shall I have the pleasure of waiting on you ladies?" said I.

"You can if you desire" they replied.

This "kinder" cut me. "I have no particular desire to wait on anyone," I replied, "but courtesy always demands my services when ladies are to be made the recipients. I presume that our presence here is rather 'sour grapes' though," I remarked.

"I hope that that will not cause us to make ourselves so contemptible as some of your southern ladies," they remarked.

I felt the blood tingling in my ears and rushing in my face like a whirlpool and I feared almost to trust myself to speak. "Our ladies are not contemptible," I replied, "they have to act in self defense, it is your soldiery that is both cowardly and contemptible," I remarked with much vehemence. They suddenly changed their manner and seemed to talk and act more courteously afterward. Capt. Morris, who was with me, and myself now started on our return to barracks and having "run the block," stopped on the way and got a good supper. The old lady professed herself very favorable to our cause—knew Genl. Iverson, Major Miller, Genl. Stewart (Brig Genl),[11] Col. Sol. Williams,[12] and many other Southern officers. She was all talk.

---

11. Brig. Gen. George Hume "Maryland" Steuart, then commanding a brigade in Edward Johnson's division of Ewell's Second Corps.
12. Col. Solomon Williams of the 2nd Regt. N.C. Cavalry was killed at the commencement of the Gettysburg Campaign at Brandy Station, Vir-

If I had such a wife, I should divide the day into several parts and prohibit her coming in my presence oftener than once or twice per day at farthest. It would take me two thirds of my time to digest what I would have to swallow in the other third. While professing the utmost friendship for us, she said, "Oh! me how I wish this <u>wretched rebellion</u> could be put down," and went on chattering as if unaware that we were Southerners. Morris looked at me and smiled but said nothing. She had a beautiful young sister to whom she introduced me. She appeared to be of quite a different material from her elder sister, but by gracious I would not marry her for the world for fear that she might become suddenly afflicted with the same disease.

At an early hour on Tuesday morning the 30th of June we left Carlisle bearing to the left and crossing the Cumberland Mountains at Mount Holly Gap, issuing from the mountains at a little place called Paper Town. I think that there are more rocks at this place than in all of No. Carolina. The whole side of the mountain seems completely covered for 2 or 3 ft. deep altogether with small stones. In crossing this mountain our whole division could be plainly seen at once. The road was as straight as you ever saw a stretch on a R.R., the ascents and descents being gradual. As usual, I saw considerable fun on the march having during this whole time enjoyed splendid health.

I tell you Burton if you wish to go to see a show of babies, just go to Pennsylvania. I am glad I have them to fight this generation for I should be afraid to risk it the next. I suggested that they should change the name of the little village through which we passed to Babytown. It seemed to please a lady standing in her yard, with a chuckle headed little fellow in her arms and about 1/2 dozen swinging around the skirt of her dress all nearly the same size—very much. We camped that night about 14 miles from Gettysburg. For the first time when any work or fighting was to be done our brigade was the rearmost in our division and consequently we were rather late in getting off next morning. When about 6 miles from Gettysburg the boom of the cannon began to burst upon the ear & our march hitherto pretty rapid was increased in speed and we never halted until we got almost on the edge of the battlefield. Some of the brigades

ginia, on June 9, 1863. Williams was a native of Nash County, North Carolina. See Krick, *Lee's Colonels*, p. 400; Manarin and Jordan, *N.C. Troops*, 2:104.

in our division had already been engaged when we arrived and as we were entering the field the 3rd Alabama Regt. joined our brigade. I understand that Rodes' old brigade did not come up to the scratch—as they ought—that day, and this Regt. by some means was cut off.

Our line of battle was formed about 2 1/2 o'clock p.m. in about 600 yards of that of the enemy. When within about 300 yards of them we came in full view. They occupied a position behind a Rock Wall which ran in a diagonal direction from our lines, the left being much the nearest point. After perfecting our arrangements, which required only a few seconds, we were ordered to charge the wall in question. Genl. Ramseur led the charge in person.[13] As I have before said, the left or rather the enemy's right and our left was much the nearest together. Consequently, our men all seemed disposed to make for that point. The enemy fled at the approach of our skirmishers but owing to the fact of our men massing themselves at one point, created momentary confusion and our men dropped down in a deep cut in the road. Just before we got to the road Bob Winstead's leg was shattered by a minié ball; he fell at my side saying "Ah! Lord my leg is broken all to pieces," and fell over on his side.[14] I got about half way down in the road when finding that we were getting mixed up, I called to my company to come out. I left and ran down the stone fence about 60 yards. For a minute whole regiments seemed mixed up without any regularity or order among any of them. It was not a panic—for no one appeared excited—the enemy was running, but it was created simply because the line was not preserved but a general massing at one point.

---

13. For a complete discussion of Ramseur's assault, see footnote #131 on p. 292.
14. Theophilus T. Winstead was an 18-year-old Nash County resident when he enlisted in Company I, 30th Regt. N.C.T., on March 4, 1862. He was captured at Frederick, Maryland, September 12, 1862, and paroled and transferred to Aiken's Landing, Virginia, where he was received on October 6, 1862, and declared exchanged on November 10, 1862. He was wounded in the right leg and captured at Gettysburg, the leg later being amputated below the knee. He was paroled at Baltimore on November 12, 1863, and transferred to City Point, Virginia, where he was received for exchange on November 17, 1863. Winstead retired to the Invalid Corps on July 8, 1864. Manarin and Jordan, *N.C. Troops*, 8:412.

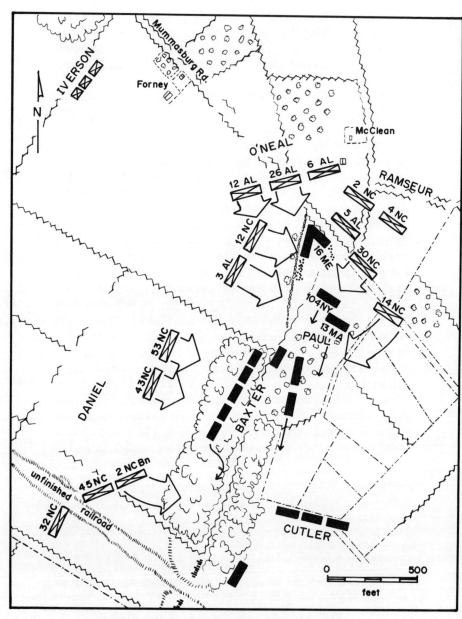

Gettysburg, Pennsylvania, July 1, 1863
Ramseur rolls up the Union
First Corps flank (approx. 4:15 p.m.)

Soon a new line was formed along the edge of the stone wall. Just at this time Col. Parker was wounded by a shell—he passed on telling us that he was wounded but to move forward.[15] We did so, but changed direction by flank, found that we were in advance of those cooperating on our right and left and halted for a few minutes for them to come up. We were now on a plain and in 6 or 800 yards of Gettysburg. The enemy was still retreating before the steady advance of our skirmishers. Those acting on our flanks now coming up, we again commenced advancing— during all this time a warm engagement had been going on just to our right between the enemy, who held position in a thickety woods, and the 12th N.C. Troops; still farther to the right Daniel's brigade was hotly engaged and further still was Pettigrew's brigade. I saw the place where P's brigade fought a day or two afterward and the field was black with slain Yankees.[16] The 43rd N.C. also charged the enemy in a deep cut in the R.Road—the Yanks threw up caps, hdkfs, etc., in token of surrender but it is said that they did not understand what they meant and fired into them killing and wounding any number of them.

Nearly parallel with our lines and running into Gettysburg from a southwesterly direction was a R.Road graded but not laid. We had got to within about 400 yards of this road when a long black line of Yankees came streaming out of the deep cut of the R.Road and marching in retreat by the flank into Gettysburg. We could not fire into them, although our rifles would have cut them up, for our skirmishers [were] then far in advance of us. Fifteen minutes before a rapid movement by the left flank by file right would have cut off their retreat, but our men were too much jaded to effect it. We took a great many prisoners, but halted when we got into Gettysburg. This was fatal to our interests. The enemy had gained his point. Behind Gettysburg rose high hills, which by a little art could be made impregnable.

---

15. For another account of Colonel Parker's wounding, see p. 293.
16. Brig. Gen. James Johnston Pettigrew commanded a brigade in Maj. Gen. Henry Heth's Third Corps Division, composed of the 11th, 26th, 47th, and 52nd Regts. N.C.T.. In the murderous toe-to-toe fight against the Iron Brigade on McPherson's Ridge west of the town of Gettysburg on July 1, 1863, Pettigrew's brigade lost 1,000 to 1,100 in killed and wounded, the 26th Regt. N.C.T. alone losing 549 out of 800. Clark, *N.C. Regiments*, 5:120.

It was the policy of the Yankees, having only two corps to hold us in check until the remainder of their force could come up and occupy the heights above named.

Alas! alas that our Generals should have ever decided on attempting to wrest that stronghold from them. Before that hill lie thousands of the bravest youths that our Confederacy had to boast of. They were glorious boys, but now "They sleep, the sleep of death and hear of wars no more." I should say that we invaded Pennsylvania with full 80,000 men. If placed on the defensive, I think that we might have defied the combined armies of the U. States, in fact I honestly believe that it was the finest army ever carried on the field. During the night and early part of the next day (the 2nd) the other divisions of our army came up and got into position. Every thing was a dead calm save an occasional shot from a picket; it was only that which precedes a terrible storm. Running parallel with and about half a mile distant from the range on which the Yanks had taken position was another range but considerably of less elevation. On this range was planted our batteries. At precisely 20 minutes past 4 o'clock p.m. more than 100 field pieces opened their thunder and sent forth hissing and screaming through the air their missiles of destruction. Quick as thought, Booom, boom, boom, rang along the whole Yankee line. And for 3 hours and 10 minutes this terrible cannonading continued, not once even slackening in the least, now and then a caisson exploding as if to add grandeur to the scene. We were lying in the streets of Gettysburg and were completely out of danger. Consequently were as it were mere spectators. It was the grandest scene that I ever witnessed or ever expect to. I don't suppose that history records a case of anything like its equal.

All at once it ceased and stillness reigned supreme. The awful storm with all its attendant thunders had passed and now nothing disturbed the deep calm save the stray shot of a picket or the deep rumbling of the distant thunder of a cannon far away to our right as it echoed and re-echoed among the surrounding hills.

Cheering news reached us from the right, to the effect that Longstreet had steadily driven the Yanks before him for about 5 miles, and was gradually working around their flank. How much was true I cannot say—doubtless he gained a very decided success. By this time, dusk had set in and "attention" rang along our lines. The "fancy work," as Genl. Rodes expressed it, of storming the enemy's batteries on their stronghold was the order of the night.[17] Before sketching our movements on that memorable night—memorable not for that which transpired but from the deep emotions it called up in every man's bosom composing our brigade—I will briefly, for the second time allude to our position. As before stated our lines on the right ran along a range of hills running parallel with those on which the enemy was posted and 5 or 6 miles in length. This ground was occupied by the Corps of Longstreet and A. P. Hill. Suddenly, our lines made an acute angle to the right down the turnpike road leading through Gettysburg on to—I don't know where. Down this road our Corps was posted, our brigade occupying a position on the verge of the town nearest the angle. When we marched off in the night in question, we struck in a diagonal direction as if to intersect with A. P. Hill at a point farther down his lines than at the aforesaid turnpike. After going about 500 yards however we changed direction, formed line of battle and advanced from the direction of Hill's position. The enemy as if aware of our intention commenced bombing us, but fortunately throwing their shells too high.

It was cloudy and the moon had not yet risen, consequently it was quite dark. In our front was a gentle rise of some eminence, just beyond a ravine down which ran a road leading out of town and now about parallel with our lines. On either side of this road was a stone wall behind which was posted Yankee infantry. Still after this another small hill was to cross and yet another narrow ravine before the hill—on which was planted the enemies batteries—could be reached. Thus you will perceive some of the difficulties we had to encounter even before reaching the point at which the final struggle would be made. Our skirmishers about 20 yards in our front have reached the summit of the first eminence and have drawn the fire of those of the enemy. Our orders are to charge them at the point of the bayonet without firing a gun and the word is "North Carolina to the rescue." You can just discern our skirmishers in our front.

---

17. The movements of Ramseur's brigade on the evening of July 2, 1863, are described by Rodes in *OR*, vol. 27, pt. 2, p. 556, and by Ramseur in *OR*, vol. 27, pt. 2, pp. 587-588. This incident of the battle of Gettysburg is recounted in Harry W. Pfanz, *Gettysburg: Culp's Hill & Cemetery Hill* (Chapel Hill: University of North Carolina Press, 1993), pp. 276-282.

They have commenced firing on them—away to our left the ball has opened. You can now better imagine our feelings than describe.

Daniel was in our rear to support us. To tell the truth, I dreaded his men equally as much or more than I did the Yankees, for the day before was the first engagement they had ever been in, and you know how much men become excited under fire in the day, much less in the night. I cautioned my men to stick together and to pay attention to orders, not to fire, but to make for the enemy with all possible haste as soon as so ordered. We had now reached the top of the hill and our skirmishers are descending just in advance of us. "Cease firing," was sung out by the Yankee Commander of skirmishers, on the opposite hill. I was glad to hear that command, for the bullets had already for some time been coming uncomfortably near.

"Halt, lie down," is whispered along down our lines—this was another comforter. Our pickets could now hear the enemy speaking a low tone and officers telling their men to "cover their files," "let them come" etc, etc.

Suddenly "attention, about face, and forward march" is whispered. Whew! What a relief. It was far better than Mrs. Winfield Scott's "third relief." Many a heart was made glad. A careful reconnaissance had sufficed to demonstrate the impracticability of a successful issue to our contemplated charge. Hence the order for the retrograde movement. We dropped back about 150 yards to a small or narrow road running parallel with our lines. Here we halted, lay down on our arms, and rested for the remainder of the night.[18]

The next day—the third of the struggle—dawned beautifully—every thing was as quiet as if no enemy were in miles of us. Not even the fire of a picket disturbed the tranquil that reigned Supreme. Ah! Heaven grant that it could have held its

---

18. Adjt. Fred Philips of the 30th Regt. N.C.T., in a letter to Hon. David Schenck dated October 27, 1891, in typescript in the Ramseur Papers, North Carolina Division of Archives and History, recalled that Ramseur's brigade was left in an extremely exposed position between the lines of the two armies following the brigade's refraining from joining in the night assault on Cemetery Hill:

"The morning light revealed the perilous position in which the brigade was left during the night. . . . We were much nearer the enemy than our friends. . . ."

sway during that day, that the after events could be effaced and the brave spirits that melted away before that dreadful height could be recalled and added to the army that they once ornamented.

The day wore gradually on. By 9 o'clock the skirmishing had become pretty heavy. The Yankees, anxious to regain the ground that they had lost the night before, now charged our picket line—our pickets gave way—the Yankees advance to the top of the hill and have a commanding view of our position. Our brave Capt. Allen[19] is in our front rallying his skirmishers for the charge—Ruffin and Walker belonging to the first corps volunteer to assist—"Forward" is the word, and, at a double quick with loud yells our men drive the enemy in confusion back down the hill, capturing several prisoners. This caused the enemy to open on us with their batteries, throwing ball, shell, canister and grape in rapid succession.

Now a Bombshell explodes just on my left mortally wounding Lt. Conner Co. G[20] and shattering Baldy Wester's leg just below the knee,[21] while he is giving Genl. Ramseur a drink of water. It is a narrow escape for all parties.

---

19. Capt. David Charles Allen, aged about 27, commanded Company C, the "Brunswick Double Quicks," of the 30th. Called by Colonel Parker, "as gallant a man as ever drew a blade." Captain Allen survived to surrender at Appomattox after firing some of the last shots of the Army of Northern Virginia. Manarin and Jordan, *N.C. Troops*, 8:342; Clark, *N.C. Regiments*, 2:504-505.

20. Ira T. Connell was a 17-year-old Granville County resident when he enlisted as private on September 7, 1861, in the "Granville Rangers," which became Company G, 30th Regt. N.C.T.. Connell was promoted to sergeant on May 1, 1862 and to 1st sergeant in May-June, 1863, and was elected 3rd lieutenant on June 26, 1863. He was killed at Gettysburg, on July 3, 1863. Manarin and Jordan, *N.C. Troops*, 8:382.

21. Archibald H. Westray was a 23-year-old Franklin County resident when he enlisted as private in Company I, 30th Regt. N.C.T. on March 1, 1862. He was wounded in the right leg and captured at Gettysburg on July 3, 1863. He was paroled in Baltimore on September 25, 1863, and transferred for exchange, being retired to the Invalid Corps on July 12, 1864. Manarin and Jordan, *N.C. Troops*, 8:411. Adjt. Fred Philips of the 30th remembered in his October 27, 1891, letter in the Ramseur Papers, North Carolina Division of Archives and History that, "We were too close to the enemy for them to use shell." It appears that Philips' memory failed him on that point nearly 30 years after the event in light of Harris' testimony about the wounding of Ira T. Connell and "Baldy" Westray.

411

Well, Burton, if I can make anything intelligible for I think that I have laid this letter down four hundred and ninety nine times and am fretted 3/4 out of my life. I have just been on Inspection and although the guns are in <u>very</u> good condition, yet here comes an order from Major Sillers,[22] calling the attention of Co. Commanders to the remarks of Capt. Halsey, Inspector[23] which I presume are not what was to be desired, since Co. F is only excepted; I have not seen them yet.

Where did I leave off my narrative? Oh! we are in the road where Wester was wounded. Well the enemy continued to shell us like thunder; soon here comes Blount Walker[24] with the whole covering of his shoulder on the back of it torn off and the bone so badly shivered as to show the marrow. It is a bad looking sight, but he bears it like a true soldier and goes on unsupported to the Hospital. Our batteries have now opened and the duel of yesterday is fought over with all its fury. We are now about midway between them and occasionally receive a shot from each.

About one o'clock p.m. our batteries cease, and as far as the eye can reach on the right long rows of infantry clear the woods and enter the field and move down towards the line occupied by us but to the right of us. It was a grand sight, never did men move in better lines—never did a flag wave over a braver set of men. The Yankees saw them as plainly as we did, and all the way

22. William W. Sillers, of Harvard's Scientific School's class of 1859, was a 22-year-old resident of Sampson County on April 20, 1861 when he enlisted as private in the "Sampson Rangers," which became Company A, 30th Regt. N.C.T.. He was elected 1st lieutenant on August 3, 1861, and transferred to the 30th Regiment's Field and Staff when he was elected major of the regiment on May 1, 1862. Sillers was wounded at Malvern Hill, Virginia, on July 1, 1862. Promoted to lieutenant colonel on September 3, 1863, Sillers commanded the 30th after Colonel Parker's wounding at Gettysburg until Sillers was mortally wounded at Kelly's Ford, Virginia, on November 7, 1863, dying on November 9, 1863, at Gordonsville, Virginia. *Harvard Magazine*, vol. 95, no. 5 (1993):122; Manarin and Jordan, *N.C. Troops*, 8:321 and 324.
23. This was most likely Capt. Don P. Halsey, assistant adjutant general of Iverson's brigade. *OR*, vol. 27, pt. 2, p. 563; Crute, *Confederate Staff Officers*, pp. 67, 94, and 103.
24. John Blount Walker was a 24-year-old resident of Nash County when he enlisted in Company I, 30th Regt. N.C.T. on April 25, 1862. He was wounded in the right shoulder while "in the skirmish line" at Gettysburg. Walker was hospitalized at Gettysburg where he died of his wounds on or about August 13, 1863. Manarin and Jordan, *N.C. Troops*, 8:410.

down the inclined plane they throw shell into their lines with as much precision as if in 100 yards. But still undaunted, they move steadily forward. I expected when they got on the line with us that we would move forward with them, but I was mistaken; on they went, and we retained our position. I presume it was well enough—scarcely had they passed our lines an hundred yards when they commenced falling back by the hundred—wounded I suppose.

Alas! the newspapers have furnished you with the results of that fatal—I will not say unfortunate—charge. The prize for which we contended was a rich one, but in contending for it we lost the flower of chivalry—the pride of our Country, I will not dwell on this any longer. That night at 12 o'clock we were waked up and marched back to the hill and on the turnpike road before alluded to, taking position just to the right of it and just against a Yankee Hospital. A little after daybreak we had thrown up a pretty good breastwork and now stood prepared to receive the shock if the enemy felt prepared to give it. It was ascertained however that the Yankees had commenced to "change base" before we did. No signs of an advance this day—raining all day. About midnight commenced falling back toward Hagerstown—marched very slowly, marching only about six miles the first day. Arrived at Hagerstown on the third day about 1 o'clock. Camped there three days just on picket part of the time. Fared first-rate—changed position and formed line of battle reaching from a point near the outskirts of town to a point on the Potomac below Falling Waters, which is 5 or 6 miles below Williamsport. Remained in line of battle until late next day when it became very evident that no general engagement was going to be had here and we moved down to Williamsport. Arrived there after dark remained until nearly (12) midnight. Commenced crossing—had to wade mud knee deep 3 or 4 hundred yards before we got to the river. This was rough & tough; waded the river striking us to our armpits; crossed without accident. Marched about 3 miles through the rain—lay down perfectly drenched and slept about two hours. Waked up as wet and mangy as a huntsman's dog. Left here about 11 o'clock— halted & camped to the right of and near Martinsburg. Left there early next morning and marched to Darksville. Remained here several days—was taken quite sick. Dr. advised me to go to the Hospital; refused to go. Ordered back to

Martinsburg—went in an ambulance. Learned that we were ordered then to tear up R. Road. Went to private house, did not remain more than two hours before I was sent after: the work was done & our services not needed. Fell back to Darksville— quite sick yet. Next morning started towards Winchester; passed it about 2 o'clock—weather extremely hot. Next morning continued the march toward Front Royal. Capt. Holmes[25] and myself left behind to hire conveyance; happen to [have] the good luck to get on an empty ambulance just as we are about paying 25 Dols. to be carried 18 miles. Our men marched all the way that day—as hot as ever was—& 4 miles beyond to assist Genl. Wright's brigade who had been attacked early that day by the Yanks. Early that night, fell back about 5 miles up the river in the direction of Luray. Next day marched about half the day—rested about a half day. Fell back towards Madison— plenty of rain on the way—remained there a day or two fell back to Orange C.H. and are here awaiting further orders to fall back or fight Yankees or do anything else which will be conducive to our Country's welfare. Our camp is in a pretty place and we fare very well. Have brigade drill two or three times a week and invariably drill twice per day, Saturdays and Sundays excepted. Furloughs have come in vogue again, and Capts. Moore[26] and Allen and Lt. McNeil[27] have left for "dear old home in the good

---

25. James C. Holmes was a 35-year-old farmer residing in Sampson County on April 20, 1861, when he was elected 2nd lieutenant of the "Sampson Rangers," which became Company A, 30th Regt. N.C.T.. He was elected captain on August 3, 1861, and was appointed major and transferred to the regiment's Field and Staff on September 3, 1863. Medical records dated April 24, 1864 indicate he was medically unfit for duty. Holmes was transferred to the Invalid Corps on August 19, 1864. Manarin and Jordan, *N.C. Troops*, 8:321 and 323.
26. William M. B. Moore was a 25-year-old Edgecombe County resident when he was elected on August 31, 1861, as 1st lieutenant of the "Sparta Band," Company F, 30th Regt. N.C.T.. He was promoted to captain on March 10, 1862. Moore was wounded in the left breast at Spotsylvania Court House, Virginia, on May 8, 1864, and was killed at Cedar Creek, Virginia, on October 19, 1864. Manarin and Jordan, *N.C. Troops*, 8:372. Colonel Parker stated, "When Moore fell, there was not a more gallant soldier left in the Army of Northern Virginia." Clark, *N.C. Regiments*, 2:503.
27. Henry J. McNeil was a 22-year-old Moore County resident when he enlisted on August 15, 1861, as corporal in Company H, the "Moore County Rifles," of the 30th Regt. N.C.T. He was elected 1st lieutenant

old North State." Allen wrote you a day or two before he left. I insisted that he should call to see you either in going or returning—he half promised that he would. Lt. Forte has also written you.

Really, you <u>must excuse me</u> for not writing. I have not written to Mother but twice since I left Maryland. By the bye, I will take occasion to ask you at this point which you like best: letters oftener and shorter or seldom and of the length of the present. I have had 5 conscripts added to my Company since I have returned to Va. I was opposed to it, but they preferred my Co. to any other & I hated to refuse them. One has since departed—James Burrows[28] from near Battleboro. He is a rare specimen of human depravity. I understand that the Messrs. Pitt & Price have at last fallen into the hands of those who I hope will take care of them until they can attain that justice so long withheld by their own neglect in trying to obtain it. This is the way the thing moves. I think the day may soon come when the woods will become too hot for the comfort of those degraded beings who have perjured themselves and forsaken their Country's cause and given her up to be ravaged and laid waste by a fiendish and cowardly foe. Thrice cursed is he who deserts his country's cause in the hour of her greatest need. I understand that the deserters give a variety of excuses for their cowardly act, among others that I treated them so bad they couldn't stand it. While Capt. Arrington[29] was yet alive—and all concede that he was a model of a Capt.—he had his defamers. When you commanded in the first Maryland Campaign <u>you</u> were found fault of and even a petition sent up, and I am so bad that men can't stay with me? I wonder <u>who could</u> please?

I am sorry to see that my old adopted state has so far yielded to an ambitious traitor's influence, as to give thought, much less

---

on May 1, 1862, and was wounded at Gettysburg. McNeil was wounded in the right leg at Spotsylvania Court House, Virginia, on May 19, 1864. He resigned on March 27, 1865. Manarin and Jordan, *N.C. Troops*, 8:391.

28. James Borrows enlisted, conscripted according to Harris, as private in Company I, 30th Regt. N.C.T., on July 30, 1863, and deserted on August 7, 1863. Manarin and Jordan, *N.C. Troops*, 8:403.

29. Capt. William T. Arrington, Harris' predecessor as captain of Company I, was killed at Malvern Hill, Virginia, on July 1, 1862. Arrington had been appointed captain upon enlistment at age 40 on September 10, 1861. Manarin and Jordan, *N.C. Troops*, 8:401.

expression, to sentiments so conflicting with our principles and so destructive to our interests. Holden ought to be hung and every rascal who utters disloyal sentiments to the South ought to be shot.[30] I had forgotten to tell you that I had quite a political discussion with a "Northern Democrat" in Carlisle and being in pretty good "plight," I tell you I gave it to him just right. There were over one hundred, two-thirds of whom were soldiers, standing around.

Not one of the deserters from my company have returned under the Presidents Proclamation. Some said they just wanted to go home—now they have a fair opportunity of returning & refuse. How flimsy their excuses and how palpably they have lied.[31]

Well, Burton, I have not given you "everything in detail," but I should say have written quite enough to weary your patience in reading unless it was more interesting. How are the young ladies? I wish that I could get an opportunity to come home, but I think of giving way for Kearney. I quarrelled with him for not being in time this time. Present my respects to all. Tell Miss Lucy that I am the one she ought to have sent her love to. Since I think that I am the greatest appreciator of female beauty and intelligence living—however I am very much obliged for the "small morsel" sent. All send their kindest wishes. Write soon.

Believe me as ever your friend,
J. I. Harris

P.S. Kearney furnishes the envelope. Excuse this short letter. I will do better next time. J.I.H.

---

30. For more details on William W. Holden and his peace movement, see footnote #142 on p. 297.
31. The question of desertion among North Carolina troops is discussed in Richard Reid, "A Test Case of the 'Crying Evil': Desertion among North Carolina Troops during the Civil War," *North Carolina Historical Review*, vol. 58 (1981):234-262. Reid concludes that "desertion among North Carolina's troops was not the massive 'crying evil' once believed," and attributes North Carolina's bad reputation in this regard to distrust of North Carolina by Virginians.

APPENDIX B
Casualties of the 30th Regt. N.C.T.

The following is a list of the casualties suffered by the 30th Regiment North Carolina Troops during the war, extracted from the roster in Louis H. Manarin and W. T. Jordan, Jr., *North Carolina Troops 1861-1865, A Roster*, 13 vols. (Raleigh, North Carolina: North Carolina Division of Archives and History, 1966-93), 8:321-423. An astcrisk indicates that the casualty is deduced to have occurred in that particular action—due, for example, to the proximity in time that the soldier was reported wounded in the hospital.

Service in the 30th Regt. N.C.T. was most definitely hazardous to one's health. Of the 1,608 men (98 officers and 1510 soldiers) who are recorded as having served with the 30th Regiment during the war in the roster in Manarin and Jordan's book, a total of 517 died while assigned with the regiment—a devastating death rate of 32.1% or nearly one out of three.

A total of 305 men died of disease while serving with the 30th, about 50% more than the regiment's 212 battle deaths. Of those dying of disease, one fifth or 61, died in prison, the largest number at Elmira. Only 21 men of the 30th died of disease in 1861, the smallest number in one year. The largest number of deaths by disease in one year, 105, occurred in 1862, and none of those were in prison. Of the 98 who died of disease in 1863, 6 were in captivity. By 1864, one half of the deaths by disease (25 of 51) occurred in a prison camp. All of the 30 deaths by disease suffered by the 30th in 1865 occurred in prison. Most sickness-related deaths were caused by typhoid, diarrhea, and small pox. Death by disease was overwhelmingly the province of the enlisted men. Only one officer, Company F's 19-year-old 2nd Lt. James W. Pitt of Edgecombe County, died on August 3, 1862, in a hospital in Richmond, Virginia, of "feb[ris] typh[oid]."[1]

---

1. Manarin and Jordan, *N.C. Troops*, 8:372.

The notation (G) after a name indicates that the man galvanized, or joined the Union Army in order to be released from captivity. Generally, galvanized Union soldiers were sent out west so that they did not have to fight their own people. Dee Brown, *The Galvanized Yankees* (Urbana, Illinois: University of Illinois Press, 1963) is an excellent study of the subject. It is interesting to note that 392 men of the 30th Regt. were captured during the war from the battles of Gaines' Mill through Cedar Creek (October 18, 1864), but only 16 (4% or 1/25th) galvanized in spite of many long dreary months of captivity.

Private James T. Rivenbark of Company E, the "Duplin Turpentine Boys," presents one of the most interesting case studies of a galvanizer—one which may offer some insight into why this particular soldier, at least, chose to join the Union army. James T. Rivenbark was part of one of two pairs of Rivenbark brothers who were first cousins. All four men were mustered into Company E in Duplin County on the same day, August 28, 1861, the day the company was organized. James T. Rivenbark, age 18, and his brother, Joseph Rivenbark, age 17, mustered in and served as privates. Among the cousins and neighbors enlisting with them were the brothers Teachey Rivenbark, age 18, and William Rivenbark, age 19. James' brother, Joseph Rivenbark was mortally wounded at Gaines' Mill, later dying of his wounds in Richmond. James' cousin, William Rivenbark, who mustered in as a corporal, was killed at Malvern Hill. Cousin Teachey Rivenbark was promoted to sergeant in the fall of 1862 after being wounded at Gaines' Mill. Teachey was then promoted to 1st Sergeant in August 21, 1864, after returning to duty from being wounded at Kelly's Ford. James T. Rivenbark was promoted to corporal in the fall of 1861 soon after enlistment, but he was reduced to ranks on July 20, 1863. He was captured near Front Royal, Virginia, on July 23-24, 1863, during the retreat from Gettysburg. No other soldiers were captured or otherwise became casualties that day. Private Rivenbark was confined at Point Lookout, Maryland, until taking the Oath of Allegiance and joining Company F, 1st U.S. Volunteers, U.S. Army, on February 23, 1864. It may be surmised that James T. Rivenbark joined the Union Army in part because he was angry over being reduced to ranks and in part because of his bitterness over the deaths of his younger brother and cousin. However, it should be noted that he galvanized only after seven months in captivity—so the real truth is uncertain and will never be known.[2]

Many sad tales can be gleaned from the roster of the 30th Regiment. Company I's 52-year-old Pvt. William Bass of Nash County died of pneumonia in March, 1863, three months after enlisting as a substitute, leaving five small children in the care of the man in whose place he entered the army.[3] Two brothers from Moore County, 2nd Lt. Archibald A. Jackson and Pvt. Burgess C. Jackson were both killed in the fierce fighting at the Bloody Angle of Spotsylvania on May 12, 1864.[4]

The briefest recorded service with the regiment was that of 46-year-old Pvt. Daniel O'Neal of Company H who deserted the day he enlisted, August 18, 1862, as the 30th was preparing to set off on the First Maryland campaign.[5] The roster also lists one soldier who was apparently allowed out of the army on the basis of being a conscientious objector, Company C's Pvt. Daniel Hinshaw of Chatham County, who enlisted July 15, 1863, and was discharged November 24, 1863, by reason of being a member of the Society of Friends.[6]

2. *Ibid.*, p. 369; 1850 U.S. Census of Duplin County, North Carolina. Certain assumptions as to family relationships are made from the 1850 Census in which James T. Rivenbark, age 8, and Joseph Rivenbark, age 6, are enumerated in the household of William Rivenbark, a 35-year-old farmer. William is listed as living near a household headed by David Rivenbark, a 40-year-old farmer, who numbers among his four sons, William Rivenbark, age 9, and Teachey Rivenbark, age 6. The assumption that these two household heads, William and David Rivenbark, were brothers is reinforced by the location between their homes of a household headed by William Rivenbark, a 66-year-old farmer, perhaps the grandfather of the 30th Regiment soldiers.
3. Manarin and Jordan, *N.C. Troops*, 8:402.
4. *Ibid.*, pp. 391 and 395.
5. *Ibid.*, p. 398.
6. *Ibid.*, p. 356.

Gaines' Mill, June 27, 1862

Killed 13
Mortally wounded 11
Wounded 50
Captured 1

<u>Field and Staff</u>
Killed Lt. Col. Kell, James T.

<u>Company A</u>
Wounded Sgt. Royal, Hardy S.
Pvt. Goodrich, James T.
Tew, Blackman
Royal, Nevil
Williamson, James

<u>Company B</u>
Wounded Pvt. Bell, William S.
Bobbitt, Burwell B.

<u>Company C</u>
Killed Pvt. McCall, John W.
Wounded 3rd Lt. Cain, Lorenzo Dow
Cpl. Howard, George W.
Pvt. Danford, Abram
Russ, Stewart
Stanly, Stewart
Swain, Benjamin F.

<u>Company D</u>
Mortally wounded Pvt. Mason, Joseph
Wounded Sgt. Ray, Zeddock D.
Pvt. Davis, James T.
Peed, William C.
Pollard, William H. H.
Wilkins, James A.

<u>Company E</u>
Killed Pvt. Blanton, Morris
Boney, James T.
Strickland, William W.
Mortally wounded Pvt. Bowen, John R.
Rivenbark, Joseph
Rouse, Barnet
Wounded Cpl. Wells, John H.
Pvt. Dickson, Harrell
Evans, Adin*
Dickson, James
Johnson, James C.
Malpass, Carleton
Mobley, M. V.

420

Norriss, William W.
Rivenbark, Teachey
Wallace, William Thomas

Company F
Killed Pvt. Bryant, John
Everett, William
Robison, William
Mortally wounded Pvt. Dew, William
Wounded 3rd Lt. Eagles, Lorenzo Dow
Pvt. Edwards, Montgomery
Forbes, Arthur
Forbes, James
Moore, Thomas J.
Pittman, Reddin E.
Wiggins, Martin W.

Company G
Killed Pvt. Parrish, Matthew
Mortally wounded Cpl. Hunt, James A.
Pvt. Hunt, Isaac B.
Wounded Cpl. Hunt, John O.
Pvt. Badgett, John D.
Frazier, Pumfred B.
Sizemore, William P.

Company H
Killed Pvt. Wicker, William M.
Mortally wounded Cpl. Buie, Daniel
Wounded Sgt. Deaton, James P.
Pvt. Baker, Alfred
Brafford, Eli
Brown, James
Carr, Dennis
Cox, William O.
Graham, Jarratt B.
Knight, Benjamin
Lawrence, John
Captured Pvt. Buchanan, William May

Company K
Killed Sgt. Tedder, Sidney
Pvt. Davis, George W.
Hood, Abner B.
Mortally wounded Sgt. Steel, Andrew F.
Pvt. McMullen, James H.
Thomason, John L.
Wounded Pvt. Massingill, R. S.
Wolfe, John N.

Malvern Hill, July 1, 1862
Killed 21
Mortally wounded 16
Mortally wounded and captured 1
Wounded 86
Captured 3
Wounded and captured 3

Field and Staff
Wounded Maj. Sillers, William W.

Company A
Killed Cpl. Pipkin, Lewis H.
Pvt. Baggot, James W.
Mortally wounded Cpl. Royal, Sherman
Wounded Cpl. Johnson, William H.
Pvt. Brown, George E.
Cox, Robert Gaston
Godwin, Nathan H.
Howard, Thomas M.
Pope, Wiley
Register, Edward M.
Captured Pvt. Pope, Alexander
Wounded and captured Pvt. Boon, Stephen

Company B
Killed Pvt. Shearin, Nicholas L.
Shearin, Richard R.
Mortally wounded Pvt. Duke, Robert W.
Thompson, John A.
White, James J.
Wounded Sgt. Harriss, John Amos
Pvt. Bishop, Alfred
Davis, Burwell P.
Duke, George J.
Gill, Philip D.
Loughlin, John
Neal, Dudley H.
Newsom, John Gilliam
Captured Sgt. Loughlin, James J.

Company C
Mortally wounded 1st Lt. Greer, Ephraim J.
Pvt. Harris, George W.
Pvt. Hewett, Uriah
Mortally wounded and captured Pvt. Hickman, Robert
Wounded Sgt. Butler, Benjamin I.
Tharp, John L.
Cpl. Leonard, Samuel B.
Pvt. Dew, David C.

422

Flynn, James Washington
Lambeth, William
Larkins, Robert S.
McCall, Paul S.
Milliken, Isaac
Mott, John
Potter, Henry G.
Tharp, William H.
Wescott, Samuel W.

Company D
Killed Cpl. Allen, James P.
Pvt. Davis, Arrington J.
Davis, J. A.
Jones, Isham F.
Wheelons, James
White, Almon W.
Wounded Cpl. Ferrell, James E.
Pvt. Garner, John T.
Mangum, Calvin T.
O'Neal, Hardy
Pierce, George W.
Pierce, James T.
Piper, Wesley Y.
White, James
Wilkins, Elijah
Williams, Samuel S. D.

Company E
Killed Cpl. Rivenbark, William
Pvt. Cavenaugh, Obed E.
Wounded Cpl. Fussell, Andrew Grayham
Pvt. Cavenaugh, Jacob W.
Cavenaugh, James David
Henderson, Jesse R.
Pickett, William D.
Wounded and captured Pvt. Bland, John J.

Company F
Killed Sgt. Williford, S. T.
Pvt. O'Neal, John
Phillips, David J.
Walston, James
Webb, Hardy
Mortally wounded Pvt. Crisp, Eason
Wounded Sgt. Cherry, Spencer
Cpl. Felton, Richard
Pvt. Boyce, William
Denton, Levi
Harrell, David

Hathaway, Henry
Moore, John J.
Morgan, James B.
Vick, William

Company G
Killed Pvt. Chalkley, Benjamin T.
Mortally wounded Pvt. Blackwell, John
Frazier, A. S.
Traylor, A. M.
Wounded 2nd Lt. Cliborne, Robert F.
Pvt. Barnett, George P.
Cheatham, William A.
Hammie Richard F.
Hobgood, James M.
Kittrell, William H.
Reames, George W.

Company H
Killed Pvt. Cole, George C.
Mortally wounded Pvt. Mashburn, J. D.
McCulloch, William
Wicker, K. W.
Wounded 2nd Lt. McLeod, Louis H.
Cpl. Morrison, Horace
Pvt. Cox, John Louis
Hunter, Charles A.
Hunter, John Reaves, Jr.
McNeill, Laughlin
Riddle, George W.
Yancy, Thomas A.
Captured Pvt. McFatter, Alexander
Wounded and captured Pvt. McAulay, William

Company I
Killed Capt. Arrington, William T.
Mortally wounded Pvt. Langley, Singleton
Winbourne, Ruffin F.
Wounded Cpl. Bryan, James H.
Pvt. Bass, John S.
Batchelor, Henry H.
Bone, John Wesley
Brantley, J. Redmond
Lewis, Arnold L.
Price, Joel L.
Sherwood, George A.
Vick, Exum R.
Williams, Henry H.
Williams, Micajah Thomas
Winstead, George T.
Woodard, John E.

Company K
Killed Pvt. Robinson, James R.
Wounded 3rd Lt. Downs, John T.
Pvt. Bently, Moses W. H.
Black, James H.
Jennings, George W.
Younts, John A.

South Mountain, September 14, 1862
Mortally wounded 1
Wounded 3
Captured 10

Company D
Captured Pvt. Pierce, James T.
Tilley, John R.
Musician Joyner, John L.

Company E
Wounded Pvt. Edwards, Elsberry B.
Morgan, William Gray
Captured Pvt. Madra, Andrew J.
Morton, Isaac
Walston, William Franklin

Company H
Mortally wounded Cpl. Baker, Henry C.
Wounded Capt. Wicker, Jesse Johnson
Captured Sgt. Buie, John
Pvt. McDougald, Duncan

Company I
Captured Pvt. Bissett, Payton
Williams, Joseph J.

Sharpsburg, September 17, 1862
Killed 9
Mortally wounded 6
Mortally wounded and captured 1
Wounded 40
Captured 20
Wounded and captured 1

Field and Staff
Wounded Col. Parker, Francis Marion
Adjt. Philips, Frederick

Company A
Killed Pvt. Brown, George E.
Wounded Pvt. Hobbs, Abraham
Holland, John R.
Howard, Fleet Hiram
Musician Clarkson, Thomas M.
Captured Pvt. McLamore, William S.

Company B
Wounded Cpl. Robertson, Peter E.
Pvt. Kimball, Nathaniel
Myrick, William W.
Shearin, Thomas G.

Company C
Killed Sgt. Edwards, William H.
Mortally wounded Pvt. Harvell, John V.
Wounded Doshier, Henry Dow
Captured Sgt. Wescott, John W.
Pvt. Coleman, George W.
Howard, John J.

Company D
Killed 2nd Lt. Rogers, Charles M.
Mortally wounded 3rd Lt. Gill, William J.
Wounded Pvt. Cooper, William W.
Penny, Solomon W.
Captured Pvt. Allen, Marion Francis

Company E
Mortally wounded Pvt. Butler, Ben Age
Wounded Sgt. Wells, James W.
Pvt. Best, John B.
Dickson, Riol
Hanchey, John William

Company F
Killed Pvt. Harrell, David
Vick, Lorenzo
Wounded 1st Lt. Harrell, George K.
Cpl. Walston, Franklin
Pvt. Dickens, Ephraim
Hathaway, Augustus
Little, Jesse C.
Pittman, George W.
Warren, Lemuel
Musician Webb, Newett
Captured Cpl. Brown, W. H.
Pvt. Bryant, Charles
Jones, Levi
Lawrence, John J.

426

Company G
Wounded Pvt. Frazier, James H.
Captured Sgt. Brooks, James L.
Pvt. Brooks, Henry R.
Daniel, William H.
Wounded and captured 3rd Lt. Crews, Alexander

Company H
Killed Pvt. Brown, James
Mortally wounded and captured Pvt. Lawrence, Bennett
Wounded Pvt. Matthews, John B.
McDonald, Neill
McFarland, Andrew
Monroe, James A.
Sloan, David H.
Wicker, Thomas
Wicker, William Fordham
Captured Pvt. McDonald, James S.
McFarland, John A.
Shaw, D.C.

Company I
Killed Pvt. Lewis, Edward W.
Mortally wounded Cpl. Manning, Moses V. B.
Wounded Sgt. Renfrow, Perry V.
Pvt. Griffin, James D.
Whitley, Jolley B.
Captured Sgt. Batchelor, Van Buren
Pvt. Winstead, Hilliard H.

Company K
Killed Pvt. Black, James H.
Dunn, Andrew Jackson
Mortally wounded Pvt. Baker, Jeptha
Stephenson, James R.
Wounded Cpl. Ezzell, Moses F.
Pvt. Culp, Aley A.
Johnston, David E.
Weeks, Rufus B.
Captured Pvt. DeArmond, Aaron Leonidas
Howey, John Hoyle
Williamson, William E.

Fredericksburg, December 13, 1862
Mortally wounded 1
Wounded 14
Captured 1

Company A
Wounded Pvt. Taylor, T. J.
Williamson, James

Company C
Wounded Pvt. Butler, John C.
Captured Pvt. Pilgrim, McGilbert

Company D
Wounded Pvt. Allen, Elias G.
Lumbley, William L.
Wilkins, Elijah

Company E
Wounded Pvt. Hanchey, John William
Pickett, John L.

Company F
Wounded Pvt. Little, Jesse
Mayo, James

Company G
Wounded Pvt. Holbrook, Paterson B.

Company H
Mortally wounded Pvt. McDougald, Duncan

Company I
Wounded Pvt. Jones, Alsey M.

Company K
Wounded Pvt. DeArmond, Aaron Leonidas
Russell, William D.

Chancellorsville, May 3, 1863
Killed 22
Mortally wounded 15
Wounded 75
Captured 1
Wounded and captured 2

Company A
Killed Pvt. Holland, John R.
Naylor, Ransom
Underwood, Daniel R.
Mortally wounded Pvt. Bradshaw, William K.
Duncan, Charles W.
Weeks, John A.
Wounded Sgt. Royal, Hardy S.
Williamson, Henry

428

Cpl. Crumpler, James M.
Pvt. Butler, Edward N.
Kelly, James M.
Parker, James M.
Rackley, George W.
Taylor, T. J.
Taylor, William J.
Walker, James C.

Company B
Killed Pvt. Bishop, Samuel D.
Brack, B. Baker
Brack, George W.
Mortally wounded Pvt. Patterson, Green R.
Wounded Cpl. Hundley, George W.
Pvt. Arrington, James L.
Bobbitt, Burwell B.
Buff, Peter
Duke, George J.
Hardy, Francis M.
Kimball, Nathaniel
Pegram, Robert S.
Shearin, Thomas G.
Captured Cpl. Newsom, John Gilliam

Company C
Killed Pvt. Gore, John
Greer, Lewis T.
Simmons, John B.
Mortally wounded Pvt. Shew, Joel
Stanly, Peter
Wounded 1st Lt. Bennett, Solomon W.
2nd Lt. Swain, John R., Jr.
Pvt. Inscore, James
Shew, Jacob W.
Staley, Enoch
Vines, William T.

Company D
Killed Pvt. Wheelons, John Wesley
Mortally wounded Pvt. Bowlin, Willis N.
Wounded 2nd Lt. Ferrell, James E.
Sgt. Allen, Henry C.
Cpl. Ferrell, John C.
Pvt. Branton, Charles E.
Ferrell, Francis M.
Forsyth, James R.
Peed, William C.
Peed, William H.
Wadford, Alexander
Wilkins, Elijah

Company E
Killed Pvt. Wallace, William Thomas
Wounded Capt. McMillan, John Cornelius
3rd Lt. Ellis, John W.
Pvt. Jones, James W.
Manellis, John
McNellis, John

Company F
Killed Pvt. Moseley, Allen
Mortally wounded Sgt. Wiggins, Martin W.
Pvt. Johnson, Ellis
Wounded Pvt. Forbes, Arthur
Harrell, Peter
Madra, Andrew J.
Phillips, Richard
Roberson, James
Walston, William Franklin
Wounded and captured Pvt. Mercer, Jacob J.

Company G
Killed Pvt. Blevins, John
O'Briant, William G.
Mortally wounded Pvt. Blevins, Andrew
Hobgood, William P.
Wounded 1st Lt. Badgett, James W.*
Sgt. Badgett, William J.
Pvt. Brooks, Henry R.
Brooks, Richard D.
Church, Calton
Harris, William H.
Hobgood, James M.
Loftice, William A.

Company H
Mortally wounded Pvt. McIver, K. H.
Wounded Sgt. Cole, Green B.
Pvt. Hunter, Charles A.
Sloan, David H.

Company I
Killed Pvt. Griffin, John B.
Odom, Jacob E.
Smith, Albert
Stallings, Franklin
Winstead, George T.
Mortally wounded Pvt. Bass, John S.
Wood, William
Wounded 1st Lt. Williford, Burton B.
3rd Lt. Perry, Sidney R.
Cpl. Gay, George W.

Pvt. Batchelor, Andrew J.
Batchelor, Henry H.
Batchelor, Redmun W.
Crickman, Josiah Gordon
Culpepper, John
Joyner, George Washington
Sherwood, George A.
Winters, George
Wounded and captured Pvt. Jones, John R.

Company K
Killed Cpl. Hartis, Wilson L.
Pvt. Barnett, Robert C.
Rea, James Milton
Mortally wounded Pvt. Witherspoon, M. J.
Wounded Pvt. Bales, James Parks
Barefoot, Noah Gideon
Glover, Benjamin C.
Johnston, James Henry
Johnston, S. A.
Thompson, Lewis
Younts, John A.

Gettysburg, July 1-3, 1863
Killed 5
Mortally wounded 6
Mortally wounded and captured 1
Wounded 28
Captured 21
Wounded and captured 9
Deserted 1

Field and Staff
Wounded Col. Parker, Francis Marion

Company A
Wounded and captured Sgt. Merritt, Isaac W.
Cpl. Brewer, Abraham H.

Company B
Wounded Pvt. Loughlin, John
Captured Sgt. Williams, Robert D.
Pvt. Myrick, William W.
Pvt. Shearin, Landon T.

Company C
Killed Pvt. Hewett, Samuel M.
Mortally wounded Pvt. Swain, George T.
Captured Pvt. Mott, John
Robinson, Alexander S.

Wounded Cpl. Smith, Benjamin
Pvt. Williams, Joseph

Company D
Killed Pvt. Goodin, John C.
Mortally wounded Pvt. Mason, Israel H.
Wounded Capt. Allen, Charles N.
Sgt. Cousins, John A.
Pvt. Barker, John W.
Pollard, Willie G.
Reavis, Joseph H.
Captured Pvt. Allen, Marion Francis
Brassfield, James W.
Brown, John W.
Lawrence, William H.
Wounded and captured Pvt. Long, Alexander V.

Company E
Mortally wounded Pvt. Henderson, James W.
Wounded Pvt. Best, John B.
Lanier Jacob W.
Southerland, James
Captured Pvt. Savage, John

Company F
Mortally wounded and captured Pvt. Hathaway, Henry
Wounded Pvt. Crisp, Levi
Madra, Andrew J.
Captured Pvt. Corbitt, William W.
Dew, Lewis
Pittman, George W.

Company G
Killed 3rd Lt. Connell, Ira T.
Wounded Cpl. Cheatham, David T.
Captured Pvt. Hammie, Richard F.
Wounded and captured Pvt. Cheatham, James T.

Company H
Killed Pvt. Wicker, Louis M.
Wounded 1st Lt. McNeil, Henry J.
2nd Lt. Jackson, Archibald A.
3rd Lt. Brown, Alexander H.
Cpl. Hight, Joseph J.
Pvt. Jackson, B. C.
Lawrence, John
McAulay, William
Phillips, John H.
Wicker, Thomas
Captured Pvt. Campbell, A. T.
Campbell, George W.

432

Matthews, Nathan
Utley, John William (G)
Wounded and captured Morris, David P.
Deserted Cpl. Brown, Andrew S.

Company I
Killed Pvt. Whitley, Jolley B.
Mortally wounded Pvt. Walker, Benjamin F.
Walker, John Blount
Wounded Pvt. Joyner, Nelson V.
Winstead, G. J.
Captured Pvt. Joyner, George Washington (left behind as nurse)
Joyner, Ira E.
Rackley, Parson N.
Wounded and captured Pvt. Vick, Willie R.
Westray, Archibald H.
Winstead, Theophilus T.

Company K
Mortally wounded Pvt. Griffith, Aaron E.
Wounded Cpl. Bales, Elijah
Pvt. Hood, William L.
Wounded and captured Cpl. Russell, William D.

Bristoe Station, October 12-14, 1863
Killed 1
Mortally wounded 2
Wounded 5
Captured 1

Company D
Wounded Pvt. Lloyd, George E.

Company E
Mortally wounded Pvt. Grady, John W.
Wounded Pvt. Bradshaw, James B.
Captured Pvt. Cavenaugh, George W.

Company F
Mortally wounded Pvt. Webb, Morrison
Wounded Pvt. Forbes, Randolph

Company G
Wounded Pvt. Harris, Richard P.

Company H
Wounded Pvt. Starnes, Thomas

Company I
Killed Pvt. Ruffin, Charles H.

433

Kelly's Ford, November 7, 1863
Killed 5
Mortally wounded 5
Wounded 20
Captured 140
Wounded and captured 10
Deserted 1

Field and Staff
Mortally wounded Lt. Col. Sillers, William W.
Wounded Adjt. Philips, Frederick

Company A
Killed Pvt. Boswell, William H.
Wounded Pvt. Cobb, Obed
Dove, Monroe
Frizeland, Jacob
Warrick, T. J.
Williamson, James
Captured Sgt. Draughon, Miles S.
Pvt. Alsbrook, S.C.
Butler, Hartwell
Duncan, James D.
Godwin, Nathan H.
Hall, William G.
Holshouser, Ambrose N.
Ivy, W. L.
Parting, Henry A.
Rogister, James
Steele, James H.
Williamson, David
Winscoff, George W.

Company B
Killed Pvt. Aycock, Samuel
Mortally wounded 2nd Lt. Davis, Weldon Edwards
Wounded Sgt. Williams, Robert D.
Captured 1st Lt. Nicholson, John Hiram
Sgt. Harriss, John Amos
Cpl. Hundley, George W.
Paschall, Samuel A.
Pvt. Askew, John
Borgus, Reuben
Carter, William J. (G)
Collins, David
Darnell, James R.
Haithcock, Alfred Loftin
Harris, John N.
Inscoe, William
Kimball, Nathaniel
Kirkland, Stephen H.

434

Pegram, John J.
Shearin, Gardiner E.
Shearin, John L.
Williams, William A.
Wounded and captured Sgt. Newsom, John Gilliam

Company C
Wounded Pvt. Patterson, John J.
Captured Sgt. Russ, Stewart
Pvt. Blackwelder, W.
Costner, Jacob B. (G)
Danford, John William
Dew, David C.
Gallimore, Ransom
Harvell, James M.
Hewett, Lorenzo D.
McCall, Paul S.
Pendergrass, J. R.
Riddling, William A. (G)
Vuncannon, J. P.
White, Eli M.
Deserted Pvt. Ballenton, J. N.

Company D
Captured 1st Lt. Abernathy, Sidney S. (Immortal 600)
2nd Lt. Ferrell, James E.
Sgt. Cousins, John A.
Ray, Zeddock D.
Cpl. Ware, William J.
Pvt. Barker, John W.
Branton, Charles E.
Champion, Jerry M.
Mangum, Calvin T.
Marcom, William A.
O'Neal, Hardy
O'Neal Loftin
Peed, William H.
Pierce, George W.
Pollard, Joshua H. (G)
Pollard, Samuel R. (G)
Pollard, Willie G.
Ray, David A.
Ray, Henry C.
Ray, William B.
Smith, Thomas G.
Tilley, John R.
Tilly, William H. L.
Ward, William
Wilkins, William
Wounded and captured Sgt. Ellen, James B.
Cpl. Allen, Elias G.

435

Company E
Killed Pvt. Thompson, Andrew J.
Wounded 2nd Lt. Johnson, Ira J.
Sgt. Rivenbark, Teachey
Pvt. Turner, David W.
Captured Pvt. Cavenaugh, James David
Laney, Lewis C.
Pickett, John L.
Register, Samuel C.
Rich, Christopher C.
Southerland, James (G)

Company F
Wounded Sgt. House, James W. J.
Pvt. Barnes, Spencer
Forbes, Arthur
Leigh, Theophilus.
Lewis, John I.
Redick, Epinetus
Captured Cpl. Brown, W. H.
Walston, Franklin
Pvt. Fountain, Almon L.
Morgan, James B.
Pitt, Theophilus
Roberson, James
Walston, Rufus
Wounded and captured Pvt. Dixon, Henry O.

Company G
Captured Sgt. O'Brien, Alfred D.
Cpl. Knott, Lawson
O'Brian, Alexander P.
Pvt. Daniel, Robert M.
Greenway, Samuel
Hester, George W.
Holbrook, Paterson B.
Howard, Joseph M.
King, James D.
Ottaway, John
Parker, Archibald D.
Sollice, D. Vaughn
Wilkerson, James W.
Wounded and captured Pvt. Daniel, William H.

Company H
Mortally wounded Cpl. McFatter, Alexander
Captured 3rd Lt. Brown, Alexander H. (Immortal 600)
Sgt. Buie, John
Pvt. Hunter, John Reaves, Jr.
Kelly, William A.
McDonald, James S.

436

Monroe, J. P.
Monroe, James A.
Phillips, John H.
Riddle, George W.
Womack, James Rufus
Yancy, Thomas A.
Wounded and captured Pvt. Shaw, D.C.
Sloan, David H.

Company I
Killed Cpl. Batchelor, William D.
Wounded Pvt. Pridgen, Drewry
Captured Sgt. Batchelor, Van Buren
Renfrow, Perry V.
Cpl. Barkley, James H.
Culpepper, William J.
Pvt. Batchelor, Neverson A.
Davis, Miles
Deans, William
Denson, Alexander
Edwards, James
Griffin, Archibald Calhoun
Griffin, Jesse R.
Hunt, James A. F. (G)
Johnston, Henry
Joyner, Jonas A.
Lewis, Arnold L.
Lindsey, Richard
Pridgen, Henry H. (G)
Pridgen, Josiah J.
Sherwood, George A.
Vick, James F. (G)
Walker, Richmond D. (G)
Walker, Worrell P.
Whitfield, John W.
Williams, Henry H. (G)
Williams, Nathan C.
Woodard, John E.
Wounded and captured Sgt. Bryan, James H.
Pvt. Brantley, J. Redmond
Pender, John

Company K
Killed Capt. Witherspoon, John G.
Mortally wounded Sgt. Boyce, Samuel J.
Pvt. Rayner, Lovet
Wounded Pvt. Alexander, Samuel D.
McLane, Thomas
Captured Sgt. DeArmond, Aaron Leonidas
Cpl. Culp, Aley A.
Pvt. Adkins, William H.

437

Alexander, J. L.
Bailey, James A.
Graham, John W.
Myers, James
Wolfe, Robert B.

Mine Run, November 27-December 1, 1863
Captured 2

Company A
Captured Pvt. Pope, William Bright

Company B
Captured Pvt. Shearin, Richard E.

Wilderness, May 5-6, 1864
Killed 1
Wounded 4
Captured 2

Company D
Captured Cpl. Thomas, Robert H. B.

Company E
Wounded Pvt. Bostick, Bryant W.

Company G
Killed Cpl. Sizemore, William P.

Company H
Wounded Pvt. Cole, George W.
Lloyd, Manley
Taylor, Jackson

Company K
Captured Pvt. Sample, William

Spotsylvania Court House, May 8-23, 1864
Killed 31
Mortally wounded 14
Wounded 40
Captured 80
Wounded and captured 4

Field and Staff
Wounded Col. Parker, Francis Marion
Captured Adjt. Arrington, Peter W.

Company A
Killed 1st Lt. White, Lallister M.
Sgt. Howard, Thomas M.
Rackley, George W.
Pvt. Jackson, Martin G. B.
Johnson, L. W.
Page, Jacob S.
Reynolds, John R.
Tindell, Miles S.
Mortally wounded Pvt. Butler, Joseph
McLamore, William S.
Wounded Pvt. Frizeland, Jacob
Taylor, T. J.
Captured Capt. Williams, Gary F.
Sgt. Johnson, William H.
Cpl. Herring, Timothy J.
Pvt. Allman, Gideon
Bass, William E.
Bell, Robert
Boon, Stephen
Boone, Nicholas
Butler, Raidford D.
Howard, Fleet Hiram
Hutchinson, Andrew Jackson
McKenzie, Reddin
Pope, Wiley
Taylor, William J.
Williamson, James

Company B
Wounded Sgt. Newsom, John Gilliam
Cpl. Shearin, Thomas W.
Pvt. Arrington, James L.
Neal, Dudley H.
Pegram, Mitchell S.
Riggan, Charles S.
Saintsing, John A.
Captured Sgt. Shearin, John D.
Pvt. Riggan, Isham S.
Pvt. Riggan, Sugar A.

Company C
Killed Pvt. Pilgrim, William H. H.
Wanett, William A.
Williamson, John
Mortally wounded Pvt. Klutts, Tobias
Skipper, Wesley W.
Wounded Pvt. Criss, Wiley
Dickens, Andrew J.
Lunsford, James R.
Moore, Theophilus

Captured 2nd Lt. Swain, John R., Jr.
Sgt. Milliken, Isaac
Pvt. Butler, John C.
Coleman, James
Hickman, Robert
Johnson, A. L.
Johnson, A. Marion
Miller, Alexander B.
Smith, Reuben
Wounded and captured Pvt. Hendron, Solomon R.

Company D
Killed Pvt. Bailey, Young F.
Wounded Sgt. Ferrell, John C.
Pvt. Davis, Jesse A.
Moore, William Henry H.
Captured Pvt. Edwards, Walter
King, Allen F.
King, Caswell
Lumbley, William L.
Rogers, John Henry

Company E
Killed Sgt. Henderson, Brantly B.
Wells, James W.
Mortally wounded Pvt. Brown, John
Wounded Pvt. Hunter, Martin
Mallard, William W.
Malpass, Carleton
Captured Cpl. Pierce, Nixon
Pvt. Edwards, Isaac N.
Hamilton, W. S.
Mallard, John W.
Parker, Jacob W.
Piner, James J.
Strickland, David R.
Tucker, William

Company F
Killed 1st Lt. Harrell, George K.
Sgt. Cherry, Spencer
Whitehurst, W. Thomas
Pvt. Dickens, Ephraim
Price, Thomas
Mortally wounded 2nd Lt. Eagles, Lorenzo Dow
Pvt. Chrisp, William G.
Harrell, E. T.
Wamack, William D.
Wounded Capt. Moore, William M. B.
Pvt. Burgess, Hardy
Corbett, Dempsey

440

Keele, William
Summerlin, George
Captured Pvt. Chrisp, W. S.
Corbitt, William W.
Hathaway, James J.
Madra, Andrew J.

Company G
Killed Pvt. Crawford, James S.
Harris, William H.
Wilson, Samuel R.
Wounded Sgt. Badgett, William J.
Pvt. Collins, Samuel A.
Captured Sgt. Simpson, Dean
Pvt. Church Calton
Dickerson, Martin
Franklin, Thomas F.
Hammie, Richard F.
Harris, Richard P.
Hobgood, James M.*
Merritt, Benjamin H.
Slaughter, William P.
Stanton, James R.
Wounded and captured Pvt. Connell, Wyatt G.

Company H
Killed Sgt. Morrison, Horace
Pvt. Jackson, Burgess C.
Mortally wounded 2nd Lt. Jackson, Archibald A.
Wounded 1st Lt. McNeil, Henry J.
Pvt. Dudley, Laban
Matthews, Hardie
McIver, D. N.
Underwood, John A.
Captured Capt. Wicker, Jesse Johnson
Sgt. McIntosh, David G.
Pvt. Burgess, W. H.
Campbell, A. T.
Center, Charles H.
Cox, William O.
Green, James L.
Hornaday, Louis D.
Horne, Pleasant
King, W. H.
McFarland, Andrew
Rogers, James (G)
Rose, Henry B.
Starnes, Ephraim
Thomas, Murphy J.
Wounded and captured Pvt. Baker, Alfred

441

Company I
Killed Capt. Harris, James J.
Pvt. Dortridge, Richard J.
Jones, Alsey M.
Mortally wounded Pvt. Rigsbee, William C.
Wounded Pvt. Bone, John Wesley
Jones, Calvin F.
Pitt, James W.
Captured Pvt. Crickman, Josiah Gordon
Griffin, William B.
Winter, George
Wounded and captured 1st Lt. Arrington, Kearney W.

Company K
Killed Sgt. Lee, James T.
Weeks, Rufus B.
Pvt. Alexander, James M.
Squires, James W.
Mortally wounded Pvt. Johnston, S. A.
Duckworth, Thomas P.
Ross, J. N.
Wounded Cpl. Nichols, Burges G.
Russell, William D.
Pvt. Dixon, S. L.
Hall, John G.
Nelson, John H.
Captured Pvt. Adams, William
Adkins, William H.
Dunn, George
Nichols, J.
Pierce, James M.
Simpson, Marcus L.
Smith, J. S.

Cold Harbor, Virginia, June 1-3, 1864
Killed 1
Mortally wounded 1
Wounded 11
Captured 1

Company A
Wounded Pvt. King, Stephen J.

Company D
Wounded Pvt. Pierce, James T.
Captured Sgt. Nichols, John T.

Company E
Killed Pvt. Butler, H. G.
Mortally wounded Pvt. Lanier, Jacob W.

442

Company F
Wounded Pvt. Chrisp, S. E.*
Webb, Bennett

Company G
Wounded Pvt. Blevins, Shadrach
Daniel, Jesse

Company H
Wounded Pvt. Lawrence, John

Company I
Wounded Sgt. Crowell, Jonaw W.
Pvt. Fryer, Lawrence D.
Sykes, William Jordan

Company K
Wounded Capt. Ardrey, William Erskine

Fort Stevens, District of Columbia, July 12, 1864
Killed 2
Mortally wounded 1
Mortally wounded and captured 1
Captured 3
Wounded and captured 2

Company B
Killed Sgt. Shearin, Thomas G.
Mortally wounded Pvt. Hardy, Francis M.

Company D
Killed Pvt. Penny, Solomon W.

Company F
Wounded and captured Pvt. Redick, Epinetus

Company G
Captured Pvt. Bobbitt, Isham C.
Cheatham, James T.
Wounded and captured Pvt. Dement, Henry F.

Company H
Mortally wounded and captured Pvt. Hagler, Hiram

Company K
Captured Pvt. Robinson, William H.

Snicker's Gap, Virginia, July 18, 1864
Killed 5
Mortally wounded 2
Wounded 14
Captured 1

Field and Staff
Wounded Sgt. Major Fitts, Francis Michael

Company A
Wounded Pvt. King, Lewis D.

Company D
Wounded 3rd Lt. Rogers, Martin L.
Pvt. Harris, Henry

Company E
Killed Pvt. Teachey, James W.
Wounded Pvt. Teachey, Jacob T.
Captured Capt. Johnson, Ira J.

Company F
Killed Cpl. Felton, Richard
Mortally wounded Pvt. Wells, Louis Redmon
Wounded Pvt. Forbes, James
Johnson, A. C. J.
Morgan, Thomas

Company H
Killed Pvt. Crotts, Elijah
Wounded Pvt. McIntosh, Francis M.
Starnes, D. A.

Company I
Killed Pvt. Gupton, Thomas
Wounded 3rd Lt. Perry, Sidney R.
Pvt. Batchelor, Ruffin L.

Company K
Killed Sgt. Black, John N.
Mortally wounded Sgt. DeArmond, Aaron Leonidas
Wounded Pvt. Bailey, William
Saville, John Crockett

Near Charles Town, West Virginia, August 21, 1864
Killed 5
Wounded 9

Company A
Killed Pvt. Pennington, John

444

Company B
Killed Pvt. Williams, William A.

Company C
Wounded Cpl. McDowell, William J.

Company D
Killed Cpl. Forsyth, James R.
Pvt. Wilkins, Elijah

Company E
Killed Sgt. Newkirk, George B.
Wounded Pvt. Bland, John J.
Cavenaugh, Jacob W.
Turner, David W.

Company F
Wounded Pvt. Walston, William Franklin
Warren, Lemuel

Company G
Wounded Sgt. Fuller, James N.
Pvt. Frazier, James H.
Hunt, David Z.

Winchester, Virginia, September 19, 1864
Mortally wounded 1
Wounded 7
Captured 6
Wounded and captured 3

Company A
Wounded and captured Pvt. Cox, Robert Gaston
Howard, William S.

Company B
Wounded Pvt. Shearin, John L.

Company C
Wounded Capt. Allen, David Charles
Captured Sgt. Wescott, John W.
Pvt. Sprinkle, Hugh

Company D
Wounded Pvt. Cooper, William W.
Ferrell, A. L.
Captured Pvt. Peed, William C.

Mortally wounded Pvt. Dickson, Riol
Captured Pvt. Mobley, M. V.

Company G
Captured Pvt. Critcher, William H.

Company H
Captured Pvt. Hendricks, E.
Wounded and captured Matthews, Hardie

Company K
Wounded 1st Lt. Downs, John T.
Pvt. Howey, John Hoyle
Johnston, James Henry

Fisher's Hill, Virginia, September 22, 1864
Wounded 2
Captured 12
Wounded and captured 1

Company A
Captured Pvt. Honeycutt, Miles C.
Pennington, Henry

Company C
Wounded Pvt. Robbins, Jonathan
Captured Sgt. Smith, Benjamin

Company D
Wounded Pvt. King, John
Captured Pvt. Canady, Francis R.
Pvt. Davis, James T.

Company E
Captured Sgt. Dempsey, Kinchen H.
Pvt. Boney, Hiram S.
Pvt. Bradshaw, James B.

Company G
Captured Cpl. Cawthorn, John W.
Pvt. Cheatham, William A.

Company K
Captured Pvt. Pierce, Orren L.
West, William M.
Wounded and captured Sgt. Culp, Aley A.

446

Cedar Creek, Virginia, October 19, 1864

Killed 2
Mortally wounded 1
Wounded 7
Captured 8
Wounded and captured 1

Field and Staff
Wounded Sgt. Major Fitts, Francis Michael

Company A
Captured Sgt. Hobbs, Judson

Company B
Wounded Pvt. Riggan, Charles S.
Captured Pvt. Cloyd, J. M.

Company C
Captured Pvt. Simmons, Lewis

Company D
Mortally wounded Pvt. Bailey, Jeremiah
Captured Pvt. Davis, William E.

Company E
Wounded Pvt. Pickett, William D.*
Captured Cpl. Teachey, W. B.
Pvt. Lanier, Brantly
Shute, Henry Blakney

Company F
Killed Capt. Moore, William M. B.
Wounded Pvt. Bell, Bennett
Little, Jesse

Company G
Killed Pvt. Elliott, Green B.

Company I
Captured Pvt. Culpepper, John

Company K
Wounded Pvt. Barefoot, Noah Gideon
Hall, John G.
Wounded and captured Pvt. Hood, William L.

447

Appomattox Campaign, April 2-9, 1865
(Does not include the Surrender on April 9, 1865)
Wounded 3
Captured 59
Wounded and captured 5

Company A
Captured Cpl. Crumpler, James M.
Pvt. Cox, Robert Gaston
Frizeland, Jacob
Howard, Joseph C.
Ogburn, N. S.
Rogers, William
Wammack, Levi T.

Company B
Captured Pvt. Miles, James
Wounded and captured Pvt. Aycock, George G.
Carroll, William Henry
Shearin, John L.

Company C
Captured Pvt. Armfield, John J.
Haywood, Richard
Kimel, Daniel A.

Company D
Captured Sgt. Cousins, John A.
Cpl. Ware, William J.
Pvt. Cooper, William W
Jones, William H.
King, John
Vaughan, John G.
Ward, Isaac B.

Company E
Wounded Capt. McMillan, John Cornelius
Pvt. Beasley, Edward
Captured 2nd Lt. Newton, Samuel B.
Cpl. Benton, Ellis A.
Pvt. Carr, John James
Cavenaugh, Jacob W.
Helms, Archey
Knight, Thomas H.
Manellis, John
Murray, Thomas M.
Sholar, James H.
Tadlock, S. D.
Wounded and captured Sgt. Best, John B.

<u>Company F</u>
Wounded Pvt. Felton, Eli
Captured Pvt. Leigh, Theophilus
Mathews, Roderick
Walston, Levi
Warren, Lemuel
Wounded and captured 2nd Lt. House, James W. J.
<u>Company G</u>
Captured Pvt. Barnes, Hillmond
Blevins, Harvey

<u>Company H</u>
Captured Pvt. Morris, David P.
Wicker, Charles B.
Yancy, Thomas A.

<u>Company I</u>
Captured Pvt. Anderson, Thomas J.
Armstrong, Gray
Batchelor, Redmun W.
Batchelor, Ruffin L.
Capps, William Henry
Griffin, James D.
Grimmer, Elias G.
Pitt, William M.
Walker, Worrell P.

<u>Company K</u>
Captured Sgt. Russell, William D.
Pvt. Bently, Moses W. H.
Fields, Absalom F.
Graham, John W.
Hall, Joseph F.
Harvey, John F.
McQuay, Joseph F.
Miller, David M.
Nelson, John H.
Rayl, John F.
Richardson, William W.
Simmons, Elisha
Thomas, Lewis R.

Miscellaneous Actions

<u>Company A</u>
Wounded Pvt. Lewis, Archibald A., June 22, 1862
Captured Pvt. Autry, William, September 29, 1862

<u>Company B</u>
Wounded Pvt. Pegram, Robert B., June 26, 1862
Captured Pvt. Hardy, Francis M., September 12-13, 1862
Captured Pvt. Pegram, John J., September 12-13, 1862
Captured Pvt. Buff, Peter, November 4, 1862
Wounded Pvt. Thomas, William H., April 30, 1863
Captured 3rd Lt. Loughlin, James J., July 21, 1863
Captured Pvt. Jackson, Marion J., October 22, 1863
Captured Pvt. Harriss, William L., August 9-10, 1864
Captured Pvt. Finch, Ira J., August 10, 1864
Wounded Pvt. Pegram, John J., January, 1865

<u>Company C</u>
Captured Pvt. Everhart, Jacob (G), July 22-24, 1863
Wounded and captured Pvt. Miller, John L., July 23, 1863
Wounded Pvt. Bicknell, Benjamin E., November 1, 1863

<u>Company D</u>
Wounded Capt. Grissom, Eugene, June 22, 1862
Captured Pvt. Manus, Francis, July 7, 1863
Wounded Pvt. Tilly, William Bedford, unspec. date after 1863

<u>Company E</u>
Wounded Sgt. Henderson, Brantly B., September 21, 1862
Captured Pvt. Sholar, James H., September 29, 1862
Captured Pvt. Strickland, David R., September 29, 1862
Captured Pvt. Rivenbark, James T., July 23-24, 1863 (G)
Captured Pvt. Brigman, John, May 31, 1864
Captured Pvt. Brown, Felix, May 31, 1864
Captured Pvt. Rogers, Jobe B., May 31, 1864
Captured Pvt. Steel, Robert, May 31, 1864
Mortally wounded Pvt. Carter, Linton, August 26, 1864
Captured Pvt. Carr, John James, unspec. date

<u>Company F</u>
Captured 3rd Lt. Moore, Samuel Rufus, July 26, 1863
Killed Pvt. Langley, Morrison, May 31, 1864

<u>Company G</u>
Wounded and captured Pvt. Dement, Henry F., September 30, 1862
Mortally wounded Cpl. Burroughs, William A., May 30, 1864
Captured Pvt. Roberson, Z. R., September 25, 1864

Company H
Wounded Pvt. Phillips, John H., June, 1863
Captured Pvt. Kelly, David W., July 5, 1863
Captured Pvt. Eason, James Scarborough, June 10, 1864

Company I
Captured Cpl. Cobb, Jefferson, September 12, 1862
Captured Pvt. Winstead, Theophilus T., September 12, 1862
Captured Pvt. Williams, Jospeh J., May 22, 1864
Captured Pvt. Rackley, James M., June 9, 1864
Captured Pvt. Vick, Joseph J. (G), September 25, 1864

Company K
Wounded Pvt. Thompson, Lee, August 12, 1862
Captured Pvt. Hall, John G., September 12, 1862
Captured Pvt. Squires, John Brown, September 12, 1862
Captured Pvt. Hartis, John H., September 17, 1862
Mortally wounded Pvt. Lee, Samuel B., May 24-25, 1864
Wounded Pvt. Hood, William L., May 27, 1864
Captured Pvt. Massingill, R.S., May 30, 1864
Wounded Pvt. McLure, J. A., May 30, 1864
Captured Pvt. Bailey, Elias D., July 8, 1864
Wounded Pvt. Bently, Moses W. H., August 22, 1864
Captured Pvt. Pierce, Orren L., September 13, 1864

BIBLIOGRAPHY

BOOKS AND ESSAYS

Alexander, Edward Porter. *Military Memoirs of a Confederate*. New York: Charles Scribner's Sons, 1907; reprint: New York: Da Capo Press, 1993.

Alexander, J. B. *The History of Mecklenburg County from 1840 to 1910*. Charlotte, North Carolina: Observer Printing House, 1902.

Ashe, Samuel A. "Francis Marion Parker," in Samuel A. Ashe and Stephen B. Weeks. *Biographical History of North Carolina from Colonial Times to the Present*. 8 vol. Greensboro, North Carolina: Charles L. Van Noppen Publisher, 1898.

Barrett, John G. *The Civil War in North Carolina*. Chapel Hill: University of North Carolina Press, 1963.

Bates, Samuel P. *History of the Pennsylvania Volunteers, 1861-5*. 10 vol. Harrisburg, Pennsylvania: Singerly, 1869-1871; reprint Wilmington, North Carolina: Broadfoot, 1993.

Bauer, K. Jack, ed. *Soldiering: The Civil War Diary of Rice C. Bull*. Novato, California: Presidio Press, 1977.

Bergeron, Arthur W., Jr. *Guide to Louisiana Confederate Military Units 1861-1865*. Baton Rouge: Louisiana State University Press, 1989.

Betts, Alexander Davis. *Experiences of a Confederate Chaplain*. W. A. Betts, ed. Greenville, South Carolina: n.p., 1907.

Bigelow, John, Jr. *The Campaign of Chancellorsville*. New Haven: Yale University Press, 1910; reprint: Dayton, Ohio: Morningside House, Inc., 1991.

Blair, William Alan. *Encyclopedia of the Confederacy*. 4 vol. New York: Simon & Schuster, 1993.

Boatner, Mark M., III. *The Civil War Dictionary*. New York: David McKay & Company, 1959.

453

Boddie, John Bennett. *Southside Virginia Families*, 2 vol. Redwood City, California: John Bennett Boddie, 1956; reprint: Baltimore: Clearfield Company, Inc., 1991.

Branch, Paul, Jr. *The Siege of Fort Macon*. Morehead City, North Carolina: Paul Branch, Jr., 1982.

Bridges, Hal. *Lee's Maverick General*. New York: McGraw Hill Book Co., 1961.

Brown, Dee. *The Galvanized Yankees*. Urbana, Illinois: University of Illinois Press, 1963.

Brown, Edmund Randolph. *The Twenty-Seventh Indiana Volunteer Infantry*. Monticello: E. R. Brown, 1899.

Brown, Varina Davis. *A Confederate Colonel at Gettysburg and Spotsylvania*. Columbia, South Carolina: The State Company, 1935.

Busey, John W., and David G. Martin. *Regimental Strengths and Losses at Gettysburg*. Hightstown, New Jersey: Longstreet House, 1986.

Caldwell, J. F. J. *The History of a Brigade of South Carolinians First Known as "Gregg's" and Subsequently as "McGowan's Brigade."* Philadelphia: King & Baird, 1866; reprint: Morningside Bookshop: Dayton, Ohio, 1984.

Calkins, Christopher M. *From Petersburg to Appomattox*. n.p.: The Farmville Herald, n.d.

——. "Confederates on the Jamestown Road" in *Thirty-Six Hours Before Appomattox*. n.p.: C. M. Calkins, 1980.

——. *The Battles of Appomattox Station and Appomattox Court House, April 8-9, 1865*. Lynchburg, Virginia: H. E. Howard, Inc., 1987.

——. *The Appomattox Campaign, March 29-April 9, 1865*. Conshohocken, Pennsylvania: Combined Books, Inc., 1997.

Callahan, Edward W., ed. *List of Officers of the Navy of the United States and of the Marine Corps from 1775 to 1900*. no place of publication or publisher given, 1901; reprint: New York: Haskell House Publishers, Ltd., 1969.

Chamberlain, Joshua Lawrence. *The Passing of the Armies*. New York: G. P. Putnam's Sons, 1915; reprint: New York: Bantam Books, 1993.

Clark, Walter, ed. *Histories of the Several Regiments and Battalions from North Carolina in the Great War 1861-1865*. 5 vols. Raleigh, North Carolina: E. M. Uzzell, 1901.

Cockrell, Monroe F., ed. *Gunner with Stonewall: Reminiscences of William Thomas Poague*. Jackson, Tennessee: McCowat-Mercer Press, 1957; reprint: Wilmington, North Carolina: Broadfoot Publishing Company, 1987.

Cooling, B. F. *Jubal Early's Raid on Washington 1864*. Baltimore, Maryland: The Nautical & Aviation Publishing Company of America, 1989.

Cowper, Pulaski. *Extracts of Letters of Major-General Bryan Grimes to His Wife Written While in Active Service with the Army of Northern Virginia*. Raleigh: Alfred Williams & Co., 1884. reprint edited by and with new material by Gary Gallagher. Wilmington: Broadfoot Publishing Company, 1986.

Craft, David. *History of One Hundred Forty-First Regiment, Pennsylvania Volunteers, 1862-1865*. Towanda, Pennsylvania: Reporter-Journal Print Co., 1885.

Crute, Joseph H. *Confederate Staff Officers*. Powahatan, Virginia: Dewent Books, 1982.

Delpino, Irene Roach. *A Broad River Digest*. Philadelphia, Pennsylvania: Omega Press Inc., 1990.

Donald, David Herbert, ed. *Gone for a Soldier: The Civil War Memoirs of Private Alfred Bellard*. Boston: Little, Brown and Company, 1975.

Douglas, Henry Kyd. *I Rode with Stonewall*. Chapel Hill: University of North Carolina Press, 1940.

Dowdey, Clifford and Louis H. Manarin. *The Wartime Papers of Robert E. Lee*. New York: Da Capo, 1987.

Five Points in the Record of North Carolina in the Great War of 1861-5. Goldsboro, North Carolina: Nash Brothers, 1904.

Folk, Edgar E. and Byrum Shaw. *W. W. Holden, A Political Biography*. Winston-Salem: John F. Blair, 1982.

Fox, William F., ed. *New York at Gettysburg*. 3 vol. Albany: J. B. Lyon Company, 1900-1902.

Freeman, Douglas Southall. *Lee's Lieutenants: A Study in Command*. 3 vol. New York: Charles Scribner's Sons, 1942.

Furguson, Ernest B. *Chancellorsville 1863: The Souls of the Brave*. New York: Alfred A. Knopf, 1902.

Gallagher, Gary W. *Stephen Dodson Ramseur: Lee's Gallant General*. Chapel Hill: University of North Carolina Press, 1985.

———., ed. *Fighting for the Confederacy: The Personal Recollections of General Edward Porter Alexander*. Chapel Hill: University of North Carolina Press, 1989.

Gordon, John B. *Reminiscences of the Civil War*. New York: Charles Scribner's Sons, 1903.

Hallock, Judith Lee. *Braxton Bragg and Confederate Defeat*. Tuscaloosa, Alabama: University of Alabama Press, 1991.

Hamilton, J. G. de Roulhac. *Reconstruction in North Carolina*. New York: Columbia University Press, 1914; reprint: Gloucester, Massachusetts: Peter Smith, 1964.

Hamlin, Augustus Choate. *The Battle of Chancellorsville*. Bangor, Maine: Hamlin, 1896.

Harris, William C. *William Woods Holden: Firebrand of North Carolina Politics*. Baton Rouge: Louisiana State University Press, 1987.

Hassler, Warren W., Jr. *Crisis at the Crossroads: The First Day at Gettysburg*. University, Alabama: University of Alabama Press, 1970.

Hewett, Janet B., et al., eds. *Supplement to the Official Records of the Union and Confederate Armies*. 100 volumes projected. Wilmington, North Carolina: Broadfoot, 1994-1998.

Hill, Daniel Harvey. *Bethel to Sharpsburg*. Raleigh: Edwards & Broughton, 1926.

———. *Confederate Military History: North Carolina*. Clement A. Evans, ed. 12 vol. Atlanta: Confederate Publishing Company, 1899; reprint: Wilmington, North Carolina: Broadfoot Publishing Company, 1987.

Hoar, Jay S. *The South's Last Boys in Gray*. Bowling Green, Ohio: Bowling Green State University Popular Press, 1986.

Holzer, Harold and Mark E. Neely, Jr. *Mine Eyes Have Seen the Glory: The Civil War in Art*. New York: Orion Books, 1993.

Hotchkiss, Jedediah. *Make Me a Map of the Valley: The Civil War Journal of Stonewall Jackson's Topographer*. Dallas, Texas: Southern Methodist University Press, 1973.

Johnson, Allen, et al., eds. *Dictionary of American Biography*. 20 vol. New York: Charles Scribner's Sons, 1932.

Jones, J. William. *Christ in the Camp or Religion in the Confederate Army*. Atlanta: The Martin & Hoyt Co., 1904.

Ketchum, Richard M. *The American Heritage Picture History of the Civil War*. New York: American Heritage Publishing Co., Inc., 1960.

Krick, Robert K., *Lee's Colonels*. 3rd edition rev. Dayton, Ohio: Morningside Publishing, 1991.

Mahr, Theodore C. *The Battle of Cedar Creek: Showdown in the Shenandoah, October 1-30, 1864*. 2nd edition. Lynchburg, Virginia: H. E. Howard, Inc., 1992.

Manarin, Louis H. and W. T. Jordan, Jr., eds. *North Carolina Troops 1861-1865, A Roster*. 13 vols. Raleigh, North Carolina: North Carolina Division of Archives and History, 1966-93.

Maney, R. Wayne. *Marching to Cold Harbor: Victory & Failure, 1864*. Shippensburg, Pennsylvania: White Mane Publishing, 1995.

Martin, David G. *Gettysburg July 1*. Conshohocken, Pennsylvania: Combined Books, Inc., 1995.

Matter, William D. *If It Takes All Summer, The Battle of Spotsylvania*. Chapel Hill: University of North Carolina Press, 1988.

McPherson, James M., ed. *The American Heritage New History of the Civil War*. New York: Viking Penguin, 1996.

Metts, James I. *Longstreet's Charge at Gettysburg, PA*. Wilmington, North Carolina: Morningstar Press, 1899.

Mobley, Joe, ed. *The Papers of Zebulon Baird Vance*. 2 vol. Raleigh: North Carolina Division of Archives and History, 1995.

Norman, William M. *A Portion of My Life*. Winston-Salem: John F. Blair, 1959.

North Carolina Government, 1585-1979. Raleigh: North Carolina Department of the Secretary of State, 1981.

Pfanz, Harry W. *Gettysburg: Culp's Hill & Cemetery Hill*. Chapel Hill: University of North Carolina Press, 1993.

Pierson, William Whatley, Jr., ed. *Whipt 'Em Every Time: The Diary of Bartlett Yancey Malone*. Jackson, Tennessee: McCowat-Mercer Press, 1960; reprint: Wilmington, North Carolina: Broadfoot Publishing Company, 1987.

Powell, William S. *The North Carolina Gazetteer*. Chapel Hill: University of North Carolina Press, 1968.

——., ed. *Dictionary of North Carolina Biography*. 6 vol. Chapel Hill, North Carolina: University of North Carolina Press, 1979.

——. *North Carolina through Four Centuries*. Chapel Hill: University of North Carolina Press, 1989.

Priest, John Michael. *Before Antietam*. Shippensburg, Pennsylvania: White Mane Publishing Company, Inc., 1992.

Rhea, Gordon C. *The Battle of the Wilderness, May 5-6, 1864*. Baton Rouge: Louisiana State University Press, 1994.

Riddick, Kate. "The Enfield Blues," *Prize Essays Presented to the North Carolina Division*. n.p.:United Daughters of the Confederacy, 1937-38.

Robertson, James I. *The Stonewall Brigade*. Baton Rouge: Louisiana State University Press, 1963.

Robinson, Blackwell P. "The Episcopate of Levi Stillman Ives," in Lawrence Foushee London and Sarah McCulloch Lemmon, eds. *The Episcopal Church in North Carolina, 1701-1959*. Raleigh: Episcopal Diocese of North Carolina, 1987.

Robinson, William Morrison, Jr. *The Confederate Privateers*. New Haven: Yale University Press, 1928; reprint: Columbia, South Carolina: University of South Carolina Press, 1994.

Rollins, Richard, ed. *The Returned Battle Flags*. Redondo Beach, California: Rank and File Publications, 1995.

Rowland, Dunbar. *Military History of Mississippi 1803-1898*. Jackson, Mississippi: Dept. of Archives and History, 1908; reprint: Spartanburg, South Carolina: The Reprint Company, 1978.

Sears, Stephen W. *Landscape Turned Red: The Battle of Antietam*. New Haven, Connecticut: Ticknor & Fields, 1983.

——. *To the Gates of Richmond*. New York: Ticknor and Fields, 1992.

Shakleford, George Green. *George Wythe Randolph and the Confederate Elite*. Chapel Hill, North Carolina: University of North Carolina Press, 1988.

Silverstone, Paul H. *Warships of the Civil War Navies*. Annapolis: Naval Institute Press, 1989.

Smith, W. A. *The Anson Guards*. Charlotte, North Carolina: Stone Publishing Co., 1914.

Steele, James Columbus. *Sketches of the Civil War especially of Companies A, C, and H from Iredell County, N.C. and the 4th Regimental Band*. Statesville, North Carolina: Brady Printing Company, 1921.

Tatum, Georgia Lee. *Disloyalty in the Confederacy*. Chapel Hill: University of North Carolina Press, 1934.

United States Naval War Records Office. *Official Records of The Union and Confederate Navies in the War of the Rebellion.* 30 vol. Washington: Government Printing Office, 1894-1927.

United States War Department. *The War of the Rebellion: A Compilation of the Official Records of the Union and Confederate Armies.* 70 volumes in 128 parts. Washington: Government Printing Office, 1880-1901.

Warner, Ezra J. *Generals in Gray.* Baton Rouge, Louisiana: Louisiana State University Press, 1959.

——. *Generals in Blue.* Baton Rouge: Louisiana State University Press: 1964.

Watkins, Thomas J. *Notes on the Movement of the 14th North Carolina Regiment.* Wadesboro, North Carolina: Anson County Historical Society, 1991.

Wellman, Manly Wade. *Rebel Boast.* New York: Henry Holt and Company, 1956.

Wert, Jeffrey D. *From Winchester to Cedar Creek, The Shenandoah Campaign of 1864.* Carlisle, Pennsylvania: South Mountain Press, Inc., 1987.

Wills, Gary. *Cincinnatus, George Washington and the Enlightenment.* Garden City, New York: Doubleday & Company, Inc., 1984.

Wise, Stephen R. *Lifeline of the Confederacy.* Columbia, South Carolina: University of South Carolina Press, 1988.

Worsham, John H. *One of Jackson's Foot Cavalry.* New York: The Neale Publishing Company, 1912.

PERIODICALS

Allen, Columbus H. "About the Death of Col. C. D. Dreux." *Confederate Veteran*. vol. 15, no. 7 (July, 1907):307.

Andrews, C. H. "General Wright at Sharpsburg." *Atlanta Journal*. Nov. 2, 1901.

"Appomattox Paroles." *The Southern Historical Society Papers*. reprint: Wilmington, North Carolina: Broadfoot, 1990. 15:259.

Beall, T. D. "Reminiscences about Sharpsburg." *Confederate Veteran*. vol. 1 (1893):246.

Betts, A. D. "Dance on My Father's Grave." *Confederate Veteran*. vol. 9, no. 8 (August, 1901):344.

———. "Suggestions Concerning Reunions." *Confederate Veteran*. vol. 10, no. 2 (Feb., 1902):52.

———. "Confederate Reunion Balls." *Confederate Veteran*. vol. 19, no. 11 (Nov., 1911):517.

———. "Don't Favor Confederate Balls." *Confederate Veteran*. vol. 20, no. 7 (July, 1912):346.

Billmyer, M. J. "The Last Charge at Appomattox." *The Southern Historical Society Papers*. reprint: Wilmington, North Carolina: Broadfoot, 1990. 33:191.

Bouldin, E. E. "The Last Charge at Appomattox." *The Southern Historical Society Papers*. reprint: Wilmington, North Carolina: Broadfoot, 1990. 33:250.

Bouldin, John E. "Our Last Charge." *Confederate Veteran*. vol. 22, no. 12 (Dec., 1914):557.

Bowyer, N. B. "Reminiscences of Appomattox." *Confederate Veteran*. vol. 10, no. 2 (Feb., 1902):77.

Cox, Jacob D. "Forcing Fox's Gap and Turner's Gap." Robert U. Johnson and Clarence C. Buel, eds. *Battles and Leaders of the Civil War*. 4 vol. New York: The Century Company, 1884-89. 2:583-590.

Cox, William R. "Major-General Stephen D. Ramseur: His Life and Character." *The Southern Historical Society Papers*. reprint:Wilmington, North Carolina: Broadfoot, 1990. 18:254.

Curtis, Finley Paul, Jr. "Chancellorsville." *Confederate Veteran*. vol. 25, no. 7 (July, 1917):303-5.

"Dedication of Henry Wyatt Monument." *Confederate Veteran*. vol. 20, no. 11 (Nov., 1912):506.

"First—and Last." *Confederate Veteran*. vol. 31, no. 11 (Nov., 1923):438.

"Gen. F. M. Parker, Commanding Third Brigade." *Confederate Veteran*. vol. 6, no. 5 (May, 1898):221.

"Gen. Francis M. Parker." *Confederate Veteran*. vol. 10, no. 10 (Oct., 1902):439.

Gorman, George, ed. "Memoirs of a Rebel, Being the Narratives of John Calvin Gorman, Captain, Company B, 2nd North Carolina Regiment, 1861-1865, Part I, South Mountain and Sharpsburg." *Military Images*. vol. 3, no. 3 (Nov-Dec., 1981):4.

——. "Memoirs of a Rebel being the Narratives of John Calvin Gorman, Captain, Company B, 2nd North Carolina Regiment, 1861-1865. Part II: Chancellorsville and Gettysburg." *Military Images*. vol. 3, no. 6 (May-June, 1982):24.

Grattan, George D. "The Battle of Boonsboro Gap or South Mountain." *The Southern Historical Society Papers*. reprint: Wilmington, North Carolina: Broadfoot, 1990. 39:31-44.

Hawes, Percy G. "Last Days of the Army of Northern Virginia." *Confederate Veteran*. vol. 27, no. 9 (Sept., 1919):341.

Hill, Daniel H. "Lee's Attacks North of the Chickahominy." Robert U. Johnson and Clarence C. Buel, eds. *Battles and Leaders of the Civil War*. 4 vol. New York: The Century Company, 1884-89. 2:352.

——. "The Battle of South Mountain, or Boonsboro." Robert U. Johnson and Clarence C. Buel, eds. *Battles and Leaders of the Civil War*. 4 vol. New York: The Century Company, 1884-89. 2:559-581.

Jenkins, W. T. *Daily News and Observer*. Raliegh, North Carolina. April 11, 1905.

Jones, Thomas G. "Last Days of the Army of Northern Virginia." *The Southern Historical Society Papers*. reprint: Wilmington, North Carolina: Broadfoot, 1990. 21:57.

Kaigler, William. "Concerning Last Charge at Appomattox," *Confederate Veteran*. vol. 6, no. 11 (Nov., 1898):524.

——. "Last Charge at Appomattox." *Confederate Veteran*. vol. 7, no. 8 (August, 1899):357.

Lackie, T. R. "Reminiscences of Appomattox." *Confederate Veteran*. vol. 8, no. 3 (March, 1900):124.

"Letter from Wright's Brigade." *Augusta Daily Constitutionalist.* October 18, 1862.

London, H. A. "The Last Volley at Appomattox." *Confederate Veteran.* vol. 7, no. 12 (Dec., 1899):557.

Long, A. L. "Letter from General A. L. Long." *The Southern Historical Society Papers.* reprint: Wilmington, North Carolina: Broadfoot, 1990. 9:423.

Longley, F. M. "Commander J. L. Schaub." *Confederate Veteran.* vol. 20, no. 4 (April, 1912):179.

Mahone, William. "On the Road to Appomattox." William C. Davis, ed. *Civil War Times Illustrated.* vol. 9, no. 9 (Jan., 1971):9.

Mast, Greg. "North Carolina Troops in Confederate Service: An Order of Battle." *Company Front.* (November/December 1990):9.

McGill, A. D. *Daily News and Observer.* Raleigh, North Carolina. April 11, 1865. p. 5.

McIntosh, David Gregg. "The Campaign of Chancellorsville." *The Southern Historical Society Papers.* reprint: Wilmington, North Carolina: Broadfoot, 1990. 40:88.

Metts, James I. "Last Shots Fired at Appomattox." *Confederate Veteran.* vol. 7, no. 2 (Feb., 1899):52.

———. "The Thirteenth (sic) North Carolina at Chancellorsville." *The Sunny South.* August 17, 1901.

Moffett, W. L. "The Last Charge." *The Southern Historical Society Papers.* reprint: Wilmington, North Carolina: Broadfoot, 1990. 36:13.

"North Carolina Monument at Appomattox." *Confederate Veteran.* vol. 13, no. 3 (March, 1905):112.

"North Carolina Reunion Proceedings." *Confederate Veteran.* vol. 6, no. 6 (June, 1898):246.

"Official Diary of First Corps." *The Southern Historical Society Papers.* reprint: Wilmington, North Carolina: Broadfoot, 1990. 7:510.

"Paroles of the Army of Northern Virginia." *The Southern Historical Society Papers.* reprint: Wilmington, North Carolina: Broadfoot, 1990. 15:253.

Patterson, Gerard A. "The Death of Iverson's Brigade." *Gettysburg Magazine.* no. 5 (July, 1991):13-18.

Raleigh North Carolina *Standard* October 1, 1862.

Raper, Horace W. "William W. Holden and the Peace Movement in North Carolina." *North Carolina Historical Review*. vol. 31 (1954):493-516.

Reid, Richard. "A Test Case of the 'Crying Evil': Desertion among North Carolina Troops during the Civil War." *North Carolina Historical Review*. vol. 58 (1981):234-262.

"Rev. A. D. Betts." *Confederate Veteran*. vol. 27, no. 5 (May, 1919):188.

Schaub, J. L. "Gen. Robert E. Rodes." *Confederate Veteran*. vol. 16, no. 6 (June, 1908):269.

Schwab (sic), Julius L. "Some Closing Events at Appomattox." *Confederate Veteran*. vol. 8, no. 2 (Feb., 1900):71.

Terry, William. "The 'Stonewall Brigade' at Chancellorsville." *The Southern Historical Society Papers*. reprint: Wilmington, North Carolina: Broadfoot, 1990. 14:364-370.

Tucker, John W. "Confederate Reunion Balls." *Confederate Veteran*. vol. 20, no. 4 (April, 1912):149.

"United Veterans in North Carolina." *Confederate Veteran*. vol. 6, no. 5 (May, 1898):221.

"Unveiling of the Soldiers' and Sailors' Monument." *The Southern Historical Society Papers*. reprint: Wilmington, North Carolina: Broadfoot, 1990. 22:342.

Waddell, A. M. "General George Burgwyn Anderson—The Memorial Address." *The Southern Historical Society Papers*. reprint: Wilmington, North Carolina: Broadfoot, 1990. 14:392.

Walker, James A. "The Bloody Angle." *The Southern Historical Society Papers*. reprint: Wilmington, North Carolina: Broadfoot, 1990. 21:235-6.

UNPUBLISHED SOURCES

Ardrey, William Erskine. Diary. Davidson College.

Bone, J. W. "Record of J.W. Bone's Service in the Civil War. Co. I 30th Reg. N.C." typewritten manuscript. Stanly County Public Library. Stanley, North Carolina.

Calder, William. Papers. Southern Historical Collection. University of North Carolina.

Cox, William Ruffin. Papers. Southern Historical Collection. University of North Carolina.

Crumpler, R. M. Diary. Papers of Miss Georgia Hicks. United Daughters of the Confederacy. North Carolina Division of Archives and History. Raleigh, North Carolina.

DeArmond, Aaron Leonidas. "To Hold Sweet Communion: Letters and Diaries from a Confederate Sergeant Aaron Leonidas DeArmond." private collection of Martha R. Brown. Winston-Salem, North Carolina.

Gibson, William. Report. Charles H. Andrews Papers. Southern Historical Collection. University of North Carolina.

Gould, John M. Papers. Dartmouth College Library. Hanover, New Hampshire.

Grimes, Bryan. Papers. North Carolina Division of Archives and History. Raleigh, North Carolina.

Hill, D. H. Papers. North Carolina Division of Archives and History. Raleigh, North Carolina.

Hopkins, Samuel. Diary and Journal ("The Battle") manuscript. Alexander Library Special Collections and Manuscripts Department. Rutgers University. New Brunswick, New Jersey.

Jackson, A. A. Letter to Dear Sister. Chapel Hill Rare Books. Chapel Hill, North Carolina.

Johnston, Hugh Buckner, ed. "The Civil War Letters of George Boardman Battle and of Walter Raleigh Battle of Wilson, North Carolina." typescript. Wilson County Public Library. Wilson, North Carolina.

Krick, Robert K. "'An Insurmountable Barrier between the Army . . . and Ruin:' The Confederate Experience at Spotsylvania's Bloody Angle." unpublished manuscript.

Lambeth, Joseph Harrison. Diary. Virginia Historical Society. Richmond, Virginia.

Pfanz, Donald C. "History through Eyes of Stone: The Story of the Monuments in Fredericksburg National Military Park." Visitors Center at Chancellorsville, Virginia.

Ramseur, Stephen Dodson. Papers. North Carolina Division of Archives and History. Raleigh, North Carolina.

Ritchie, Marvel. Papers. North Carolina Division of Archives and Records. Raleigh, North Carolina.

Schaub, Julius L. Memoir. Julius L. Schaub Collection. Troup County Archives. LaGrange, Georgia.

Shinn, James W. "Notes written during the war." Osborne Papers. Southern Historical Collection. University of North Carolina.

Wills, George W. Letters. Southern Historical Collection. University of North Carolina.

REFERENCE

1830 U.S. Census of Edgecombe County, North Carolina.

1850 U.S. Census of Duplin County, North Carolina.

1850 The Edgecombe County Agricultural Schedule.

1860 U.S. Census of Edgecombe County, North Carolina.

1860 U.S. Census of Halifax County, North Carolina.

1860 U.S. Census of Sampson County, North Carolina.

1870 U.S. Census for Halifax County, North Carolina.

1880 U.S. Census, Halifax County, North Carolina.

1900 U.S. Census for Halifax County, North Carolina.

Chancellorsville Battlefield Map. Orleans, New York: McElfresh Map Co., 1996.

Inspection report for Cox's brigade, September 30, 1864, National Archives Record Group 109, Microcopy no. 935, roll 10, 33-P-24.

Inspection report for Cox's brigade, October 30, 1864, National Archives Record Group 109, Microcopy 935, Roll 11, 10-P-31.

Inspection report for Cox's brigade, December 29, 1864, National Archives Record Group 109, Microcopy No. 935, Roll 13, 24-P.32.

Inspection report for Cox's brigade, January 29, 1865, National Archives Record, Group 109, Microcopy 935, Roll 14, 26-P.51.

Inspection report for Cox's brigade, February 25, 1865, National Archives Record, Group 109, Microcopy 935, Roll 15, 6-P.62.

INDEX

470

471

473

478

479